Sport Tourism

The study of sport tourism is on the cusp of moving from a descriptive phase of research into an analytical phase. Consequently, many academics and graduate students are searching for theories upon which to ground their work. This book draws upon theories and concepts from sociology and anthropology (the socio-cultural perspective), sport and tourism studies, and business studies. One of the dangers of a new area of study is that the body of knowledge is built on a range of seemingly unrelated studies. By grounding work in a theoretical perspective, future work can be linked to, and contribute to building a cohesive understanding of various aspects of sport tourism.

This book is an edited collection, written by some of the top scholars in the field, providing a compendium of theories and concepts that can be used to frame research on various aspects of sport tourism.

This volume was previously published as a special issue of the journal *Sport in the Global Society*.

Dr Heather Gibson is an Assistant Professor in the Department of Recreation, Parks and Tourism at the University of Florida.

Sport in the Global Society
General Editors: J.A. Mangan and Boria Majumdar

Special issue: Sport Tourism: Concepts and Theories

Sport in the global society
General Editors: J.A. Mangan and Boria Majumdar

The interest in sports studies around the world is growing and will continue to do so. This unique series combines aspects of the expanding study of *sport in the global society*, providing comprehensiveness and comparison under one editorial umbrella. It is particularly timely, with studies in the aesthetic elements of sport proliferating in institutions of higher education.

Eric Hobsbawm once called sport one of the most significant practices of the late nineteenth century. Its significance was even more marked in the late twentieth century and will continue to grow in importance into the new millennium as the world develops into a 'global village' sharing the English language, technology and sport.

Other Titles in the Series

Disreputable Pleasures
Less Virtuous Victorians at Play
Edited by Mike Huggins and J.A. Mangan

Italian Fascism and the Female Body
Sport, Submissive Women and Strong Mothers
Gigliola Gori

Rugby's Great Split
Class, Culture and the Origins of Rugby
League Football
Tony Collins

Terrace Heroes
The Life and Times of the 1930s Professional
Footballer
Graham Kelly

Soccer and Disaster
International Perspectives
Paul Darby, Martin Johnes and Gavin Mellor

Barbarians, Gentlemen and Players
A Sociological Study of the Development of
Rugby Football
Second Edition
Eric Dunning and Kenneth Sheard

Capoeira
The History of an Afro-Brazilian Martial Art
Matthias Röhrig Assunção

British Football and Social Exclusion
Edited by Stephen Wagg

The First Black Footballer
Arthur Wharton 1865–1930: An Absence of
Memory
Phil Vasili

Sport, Civil Liberties and Human Rights
David McArdle and Richard Giulianotti

Sport Tourism

Concepts and Theories

Edited by
Heather Gibson

Routledge
Taylor & Francis Group

LONDON AND NEW YORK

First published 2006 by Routledge
2 Park Square, Milton Park, Abingdon, Oxon, OX14 4RN

Simultaneously published in the USA and Canada
by Routledge
270 Madison Ave, New York NY 10016

Routledge is an imprint of the Taylor & Francis Group

Transferred to Digital Printing 2008

© 2006 Taylor and Francis Group Ltd.

Typeset in Minion 10.5/13pt by the Alden Group Oxford

British Library Cataloguing in Publication Data
A catalogue record for this book is available from the British Library

Library of Congress Cataloging in Publication Data
A catalog record for this book has been requested

ISBN10: 0-415-34809-9 (hbk)
ISBN10: 0-415-46418-8 (pbk)

ISBN13: 978-0-415-34809-6 (hbk)
ISBN13: 978-0-415-46418-5 (pbk)

CONTENTS

Editor: HEATHER GIBSON

Series Editors' Foreword   ix

Notes on Contributors   xi

Acknowledgements   xv

Sport Tourism: Concepts and Theories. An Introduction
HEATHER GIBSON   1

Part One
Understanding Sport Tourism: Socio-cultural Perspectives

1   **Leisure Constraint Theory and Sport Tourism**
TOM HINCH, EDGAR L. JACKSON, SIMON HUDSON AND
GORDON WALKER   10

2   **Serious Leisure, Social Identity and Sport Tourism**
IAN JONES AND B. CHRISTINE GREEN   32

3   **Something Lived, Something Learned: Nostalgia's Expanding
Role in Sport Tourism**
SHERANNE FAIRLEY AND SEAN GAMMON   50

Part Two
Sport and Tourist Studies: Theories and Paradigms

4   **Towards an Understanding of 'Why Sport Tourists Do What They Do'**
HEATHER GIBSON   66

5   **Building Sport Event Tourism into the Destination Brand: Foundations
for a General Theory**
LAURENCE CHALIP AND CARLA COSTA   86

6   **Sport Tourism as an Attraction for Managing Seasonality**
JAMES HIGHAM   106

7   **Host and Guest Relations and Sport Tourism**
ELIZABETH FREDLINE   131

8   **Sport Tourism, Cityscapes and Cultural Politics**
    MICHAEL SILK AND JOHN AMIS   148

    Part Three
    Business Studies: Concepts and Paradigms
9   **Marketing Sport Tourism: Creating Synergy between Sport**
    and Destination
    TRACEY HARRISON-HILL AND LAURENCE CHALIP   170

10 **Service Quality Perspectives in Sport Tourism**
    DES THWAITES AND SIMON CHADWICK   189

11 **Public Sector Support for Sport Tourism Events: The Role**
    of Cost-benefit Analysis
    TREVOR MULES AND LARRY DWYER   206

12 **A Grounded Theory of the Policy Process for Sport and Tourism**
    MIKE WEED   224

13 **The Management of Sport Tourism**
    MARGARET DEERY AND LEO JAGO   246

    Conclusion   258

    Index   265

Series Editors' Foreword

Only a day before the final announcement for the host city of the 2012 Olympic Games was made, the frenzy had reached such heights that lip-reading experts were consulted by delegates from aspiring cities to get a split-second advantage over others in trying to know whether their dream had come true. As Francois Grojean, a professor of psycholinguistics at the University of Neuchatel in Switzerland noted, 'should Rogge close his lips after the phrase 'And the host city is,' Paris will party. If the mouth stays open, it's London's lucky day.'i[1]

This almost surreal scenario was not altogether new. The International Cricket Council meeting that decided the rights to host the 1996 world cup is thus described in the records of the Indian Board of Control:

'The meeting on 2 February was a grueling one lasting nearly thirteen and a half hours. It was a battle of wits with the ICC solicitors being dragged into the meeting. The ICC solicitors argued in favour of a 'special majority' to decide on the venue of the world cup, but the representatives of the subcontinent countered such arguments effectively...Members of all countries present in the meeting appreciated the logic and rationality of the arguments of the joint bidders. The joint bidders found support from full members of the ICC had no other option but to allot the 1996 world cup to India, Pakistan and Sri Lanka.'ii[2]

The 1996 world cup, as is well known, marked the start of what we have called elsewhere the 'shift', the move of cricket's nerve center to the sub-continent.iii[3]

As to why countries, let alone cities, go to such lengths to host international sporting engagements, why Prime Ministers and other state leaders campaign for such rights, what are the economics of purse behind such bids and what are the long term social and political consequences of hosting modern sports spectacles are questions that have continued to exercise the social scientists for years. *Sport Tourism* not only answers these questions but does much more; it provides models for the analysis of such concerns.

Modern sporting spectacles, it wouldn't be a far cry to assert, are often more political than events of real politik. Prior to the cricket world cup in South Africa (2003), Ali Bacher, the man behind the show, insisted that the first World Cup in the African continent would 'go beyond cricket'. This tournament, he had suggested, was South Africa's big effort at 'unification through sport'. 'Clearly, racial integration and political unification will be highlighted at Cup 2003. The Rugby World Cup in 1995–96 had united the nation, but this unity could not be sustained.'iv[4]

In trying to achieve these aims, the organizing committee had come up with novel policies to promote cricket in South Africa and other African countries. They had identified 41 leading sports figures around the world as cricket ambassadors—including legendary Kenyan Olympic middle-distance runner Kip Keino, a trio of golf champions in Gary Player, Retief Goosen and Ernie Els, rugby captain Francois Pienaar, cricketers Graeme Pollock and Basil D Oliviera, South African soccer heroes Lucas Radebe and Doctor Khumalo, former Formula One world champ Jody Scheckter, Olympic marathon gold medallist Josiah Thugwane, swimming champion Penny Heyns, and South Africa's 'Mr Paralympics' Fanie Lombaard. Then there was the spectacle involving the toss—54 gold medallions, each weighing an ounce, were crafter to commemorate each game. These coins had the face of President Thabo Mbeki engraved on one side and the venue and date of the game on the other. Six official stamps were released before the event—the first one had the Dazzler, the tournament mascot, on it. Even the choice of the zebra, with black-and-white stripes, was a conscious anti-apartheid symbol.v[5]

Was South Africa in any way unique in what it was trying to achieve through sport? Is there a pattern followed by governments across the world to promote sports tourism? Do sports tourists succumb to such image building strategies or are they humans who exercise rational choice? Is there a global model for destination branding or is such branding dependent on expediency? *Sport Tourism* answers these questions and seeks to expose the frameworks behind destination branding across the globe.

The collection, as the Editor states, by no means covers all possible theories, but invaluably 'provides an overview of some of the most commonly used theoretical perspectives in sport, tourism and leisure studies.'vi[6]

Boria Majumdar

J.A. Mangan
Series Editors
Sport in the Global Society

Notes

i[1]   www.dw-world.de/dw/article/0,1564,1640175,00.html
ii[2]   Minutes of the Board of Control for Cricket in India, 1993.
iii[3]   Majumdar, Mangan, 'Epilogue', *Cricketing Cultures in Conflict: World Cup 2003*.
iv[4]   Outlook, 28 October 2002.
v[5]   Ibid.
vi[6]   Gibson, 'Introduction', 134.

Notes on Contributors

John Amis is an Associate Professor at the University of Memphis where he holds joint appointments in the Department of Health & Sport Sciences and the Department of Management. Amis' research interests have predominantly centered on organizational change and the identification, utilization and management of intangible resources. He has had over 35 articles and book chapters published in journals such as *Academy of Management Journal, Journal of Applied Behavioral Science, European Marketing Journal,* and *Journal of Sport Management. Global Sport Sponsorship*, co-edited with Professor T. Bettina Cornwell, was published in July 2005. Amis has delivered over 30 papers at international conferences and has been invited to provide key note addresses at seminars and conferences in Europe and North America.

Simon Chadwick works at Birkbeck College, the University of London, where he is Programme Director for the MSc in Sport Management and the Football Industry. He is Editor of the International Journal of Sports Marketing and Sponsorship and also founder and leader of the Academy of Marketing's Sport Marketing Special Interest Group. Simon has researched and published extensively in the area of sport marketing (particularly the sponsorship of professional football) and is co-editor of 'The Business of Sport Management' and 'The Business of Tourism Management', and 'The Marketing of Sport' (all published by FT Prentice Hall).

Laurence Chalip is Professor and Coordinator of the Sport Management Program at the University of Texas at Austin. He has published three books, three monographs, and over 60 articles and book chapters. He is a Research Fellow and Zeigler Award Winner of the North American Society for Sport Management, and has won two service awards from the Sport Management Association of Australia and New Zealand. In 2000, Dr. Chalip was named to the International Chair of Olympism.

Carla A. Costa is an Assistant Professor in the Department of Kinesiology and Health Education at the University of Texas at Austin. Her research has appeared in such journals as the Journal of Sport Management, European Sport Management Quarterly, International Journal of Sports Marketing and Sponsorship, and Sport Culture and Society.

Margaret Deery has a PhD in tourism management from La Trobe University, Melbourne. She is currently Principal Research Fellow with Sustainable Tourism Co-operative Research Centre (STCRC) having been the Director for the Centre for Hospitality and Tourism Research at Victoria University. Associate Professor Deery's research interests cover a number of tourism areas including sport tourism, visitor information centres, business events, volunteers in heritage attractions and the social impacts of tourism on communities. She has more than 40 journal, book chapters and conference publications and book on the *National Business Events Study: An Evaluation of the Australian Business Events Sector.*

Larry Dwyer PhD is Qantas Professor of Travel and Tourism Economics at the University of New South Wales. He publishes widely in the areas of tourism economics, tourism management and event management, with over 150 publications in international journals, government reports, chapters in books, and monographs. Larry maintains strong links with the tourism industry at international, national, state and local levels. He has undertaken an extensive number of consultancies for public and private sector tourism organisations within Australia as well as consulting work overseas for international agencies, including the World Tourism Organisation. Larry is Head of the Sustainable Destinations Research Program of the Sustainable Tourism Cooperative Research Centre in Australia. He is on the Editorial Board of nine international tourism journals.

Sheranne Fairley is an Assistant Professor in the Department of Sport Management at the University of Massachusetts Amherst where her primary research interests focus on the consumer behavior of sport fans, sport tourism, volunteerism, event management, and destination promotion. She has published her research in the Journal of Sport Management, Event Management, Sport in Society, and has coauthored three research monologues.

Liz Fredline is a Senior Research Fellow with the Sustainable Tourism CRC and Senior Lecturer at Griffith University. Her primary research interest is in the area of Social Impact assessment particularly with regard to tourism events, but also with regard to more generalised forms of tourism. This has led to an interest in holistic impact evaluation, aimed at integrating economic, social and environmental impact assessment techniques to gain a fuller understanding of the impacts of tourism and events. Liz has strong quantitative research design and analysis skills.

Sean Gammon is a senior lecturer at the University of Luton in the Department of Tourism and Leisure. He teaches on both the under and post graduate programmes, and is currently responsible for co-editing a special issue of the journal of sport tourism, focussing on heritage. Sean has written extensively in sport tourism; particularly in areas associated with motivation, heritage and nostalgia. He is presently undertaking research exploring the popularity and design of stadia tours.

Heather Gibson is an Associate Professor in the Department of Tourism, Recreation and Sport Management at the University of Florida. She is also an Associate Director for the Center for Tourism Research and Development. Dr Gibson teaches and researches in leisure and tourism behavior working primarily from a sociological perspective. In particular much of her work focuses on gender, age and the contribution of leisure, sport and tourism to the quality of life.

B. Christine Green is an Assistant Professor in the Department of Kinesiology and Health Education at The University of Texas at Austin. She holds the Judy Spence Tate Fellowship for Excellence, and serves as the Director of the University of Texas Sport Development Lab. Her research focuses on sport development and the marketing of sport events. It has appeared in leading tourism, leisure, and sport journals, and has been funded in four countries. She is a member of the editorial board of three journals in the field, and currently serves as Editor of *Sport Management Review*. Green was elected a Research Fellow of the North American Society of Sport Management in 2005.

Tracey Harrison-Hill lectures within the department of Tourism, Leisure, Hotel and Sport Management at Griffith University. Wanting to better understand consumers' consumption decisions and behaviour within the service sector industries of tourism, sports and leisure drives her research, which is grounded within the marketing discipline. Her recent work has involved sport tourists' use of the Internet to search and share information and to establish and communicate their identities.

James Higham holds the position of Associate Professor at the University of Otago, Dunedin, New Zealand. His empirical research serving the field of sport tourism has been published in journals such as *Tourism Management, European Sport Management Quarterly, International Journal of Tourism and Hospitality Research* and *Journal of Sport Management*, among others. In 2004 he co-authored (with Prof. Tom Hinch, University of Alberta) a research-based book titled *'Sport Tourism Development'* (Channel View Publications, UK) and, in the same year, published an edited book titled *'Sport Tourism Destinations: Issues, Opportunities and Analysis'* with Elsevier Butterworth Heinemann (Oxford, UK).

Tom Hinch is a Professor with the Faculty of Physical Education and Recreation at the University of Alberta. He recently co-authored *Sport Tourism Development* with James Higham and has an active research program in sport tourism. A re-occurring theme in his research is the way that people relate to place and the implications that this relationship has on sustainable development in tourist destinations.

Simon Hudson is an Associate Professor in the Haskayne School of Business at the University of Calgary. He has a marketing degree from Brighton, England, an MBA from California, and a PhD from Surrey, England. Prior to working in academia, he spent several years working in the tourism industry in Europe, and six years running his own business. He moved to Canada from the UK six years ago. Dr Hudson has published numerous journal articles and book chapters from his work, and has three books to his name: 'Snow Business'; 'Sport & Adventure Tourism' and 'Tourism & Hospitality Marketing'. He is known worldwide for his work on the ski industry, and has been invited as a keynote speaker to many international conferences.

Edgar L. Jackson is Professor in the Department of Earth and Atmospheric Sciences, University of Alberta. A native of Great Britain and a graduate of the London School of Economics and Political Science, Dr. Jackson emigrated to Canada in 1968, where he completed a master's degree at the University of Calgary (1970) and a Ph.D. at the University of Toronto (1974). He began his teaching career at the University of Toronto in 1974 and moved to the University of Alberta in 1975, where he is now Professor in the Department of Earth and Atmospheric Sciences.

He was an Associate Editor of the *Journal of Leisure Research* from 1988 to 1995, Secretary of the Canadian Association for Leisure Studies (CALS) for two three-year terms (1987–1993), and President of CALS for 1996 to 1999. He received both the Allen V. Sapora Research Award and NRPA's Roosevelt Research Award in 1995. He was elected to the Academy of Leisure Sciences in 1989 and served as its President in 1995–1996. Dr. Jackson maintains the websites for the Academy of Leisure Sciences and the Canadian Association for Leisure Studies.

Leo Jago is Deputy CEO and Director of Research for Australia's national Sustainable Tourism Cooperative Research Centre. He is seconded from Victoria University where he is a Professor in Tourism and was formerly the Director of the Centre for Hospitality and Tourism Research. Leo's research interests cover tourism marketing, events and sport.

Ian Jones is a Principal Lecturer in Sport and Leisure Studies/Management at the University of Luton. His main teaching and research interests are in the areas of Sports Fandom and Spectatorship, Serious Leisure and Research Methods. He is co-author of *Research Methods for Sport Studies*

(Routledge, 2004) and the *Dictionary of Tourism and Leisure* (Routledge, forthcoming). Ian is also Head of Undergraduate Programmes at Luton Business School.

Trevor Mules is a senior lecturer in tourism economics at the Australian International Hotel School in Canberra. He has published widely in the area of special and sporting events and their economic impacts, and has consulted on the topic to Australian State and Federal Government agencies.

Michael L. Silk (Ph.D. University of Otago) is an Assistant Professor who contributes to the Graduate Physical Cultural Studies Program and the Undergraduate Sport Commerce and Culture Minor at the University of Maryland. His research is committed to the critical, multidisciplinary and multi-method interrogation of sporting practices, experiences, and, structures, focusing on the production and consumption of space, the governance of bodies, and, the performative politics of identity within the context of neo-liberalism. Dr. Silk is particularly interested in the reconfigurations of physical and imagined space and place within the machinations and operations of late capitalism, and, through teaching and research, attempts to create a critical and political space that engages crucial questions of social justice. He has recently published papers in *Cultural Studies* ↔ *Critical Methodologies, Media, Culture & Society*, the *International Journal of Media and Cultural Politics*, the *Journal of Sport and Social Issues*, the *Sociology of Sport Journal*, the *Journal of Sport Management*, and *Sport in Society*. He is editor of two books: *Sport & Corporate Nationalisms* and *Qualitative Methods in Sports Studies*.

Des Thwaites is Senior Lecturer in Marketing at the Leeds University Business School. His research interests focus on the sport and leisure sectors with specific reference to marketing, management and tourism issues. Publications have appeared in a broad range of mainstream and sector specific journals including International Journal of Advertising, Journal of Marketing Management, Journal of General Management, Journal of Services Marketing and Journal of Sport Management.

Gordon Walker is an Associate Professor in the Faculty of Physical Education and Recreation at the University of Alberta. Gordon was a recreation programmer with the City of Moose Jaw for five years before obtaining his Masters degree at Arizona State University and his Doctorate degree at Virginia Tech. His research focuses on leisure motivations, constraints, experiences, and benefits, using a cross-cultural social psychological approach.

Mike Weed is with the Institute of Sport and Leisure Policy in the School of Sport and Exercise Sciences at Loughborough University. His research interests relate to all areas of the relationship between sport and tourism, but particularly to the motivations and behaviours of sports tourists and sports spectators. He is also interested in 'meso-level' and innovative qualitative approaches to research and in methods of research synthesis. He is author (with Chris Bull, Canterbury) of *Sports Tourism: Participants, Policy and Providers* (Elsevier).

Acknowledgements

I would like to say thank you to all of the authors who took the time of contribute to this book. I know what a scarce thing an academic's time is and for many of you writing chapters is a thankless task, often with little reward. Hopefully when you see your work amongst all of the other papers in this collection you will agree 'it was worth it.' I think collectively, we have made a good contribution to the next phase of sport tourism scholarship and practice.

I would also like to thank Laurence Chalip who worked with me on the initial planning stages of this book. Laurence thanks for helping me brainstorm ideas for chapters and for identifying potential authors who could write about particular topics.

Sport Tourism: Concepts and Theories. An Introduction

Heather Gibson

Since the mid-1990s attention has been increasingly given to sport tourism from both the sport and tourism industries and from academics. Travel to take part in or watch sport is nothing new per se, although the use of the term sport tourism to describe this type of travel has become more pervasive over the last ten years. In fact, around the world various governments have initiated sport tourism strategies that have had varying degrees of success. In the realm of academe, the range of scholarly work on sport tourism has increased since the late 1990s. Seven specialist books have been published[1] and several editions of tourism and sport journals have been devoted to sport tourism: *Tourism Recreation Research*, 22, 1 (1997); *Journal of Vacation Marketing*, 4, 1 (1998); *Visions in Leisure and Business*, 18 (spring 1999); *Current Issues in Tourism*, 5, 1 (2002); *Journal of Sport Management*, 17, 3 (2003); and the *European Journal of Sport Management*, 5, 3 (2005). As befitting a relatively new area of scholarly

Heather J. Gibson, Department of Tourism, Recreation and Sport Management, University of Florida, PO Box 118208, Gainesville, FL 32608-8208, USA. Correspondence to: hgibson@hhp.ufl.edu enquiry, some of the early writings were devoted to discussions over 'what is sport tourism?' In general, there is agreement that sport tourism constitutes two types, an active type and a passive form[2]. However, Redmond[3] suggested that in line with a trend in tourism in general there appears to be a third form of sport tourism, that concerned with nostalgia. Thus, I suggested that sport tourism could be defined as 'leisure-based travel that takes individuals temporarily outside of their home communities to participate in physical activities [Active Sport Tourism], to watch physical activities [Event Sport Tourism], or to venerate attractions associated with physical activities [Nostalgia Sport Tourism]'[4].

As sport tourism scholarship moves beyond the initial definitional stages, there is also agreement that the purpose of our work should move beyond description towards explanation. Scholars, both from the wider sport and tourism fields as well as those from within the new sub-field of sport tourism, have critiqued much of the existing body of knowledge as being atheoretical or constituting nothing more than a series of unrelated case studies. As with the sister disciplines of sport, tourism and leisure studies, these critiques and concerns are symptomatic of the stage of development of this area. For example, concerns over the lack of theoretically grounded work and the development of 'our own' theories have been raised in tourism[5] and in leisure studies[6]. The consensus in these fields seems to be that while theory generation is a possibility, that linking their work to theories in the well-established parent disciplines such as sociology, social psychology, geography and anthropology might be more beneficial right now, as these fields continue to strive towards a higher degree of academic credibility[7]. Moreover, connecting work in these newer fields to that in the more established disciplines may provide a more solid grounding for this work that not only increases an author's ability to explain, but also links such work to a wider body of knowledge that has used similar theoretical perspectives.

Kelly suggests theory is a word that is commonly used but is largely misunderstood[8]. He explains that on the one hand, to some scientists theory is regarded as a model of explanation that has a degree of permanence and is derived from empirical observations. To others, theories may not be characterized by such a degree of permanence, but are systematic explanations of phenomena based on observations that suffice at a particular point in time, but are open to reinterpretation at a later point. Whether, one thinks of theory in 'law like terms' or whether a more fluid definition is adopted, Kelly suggests that all theoretical models share the same ideas:

1. Theory is an act of explanation that is communicated to others.
2. Theory is systematic and discloses its presuppositions and evidence.
3. Theory is always subject to question and criticism.
4. Theory development is something we do whenever we attempt to explain to others the antecedents and conditions of occurrences.

Moreover, as Weber explains, all theories are incomplete [9]. They do not explain absolutely everything about a phenomenon. There are always some explanatory tenets left out and, as such, the decisions as to what was included should also be considered when using a theory as this will be indicative of the subjectivity of the theory developer as to what he or she considered important or what Gouldner[10] called 'domain assumptions'. Thus, in contrast to the esoteric, hard to understand law like rhetoric that many students think of when they hear the word 'theory', theory refers to an explanation, a model that can help us understand phenomena, in our case various aspects of sport tourism. Moreover, if we ground our studies in appropriate theories, this will not only increase the explanatory power for a particular study, but it will help link our study to similar work thereby creating a line of research on a particular topic, which again increases the explanatory power associated with that work. So instead of unconnected case studies on various aspects of sport tourism, by grounding work in a particular theoretical perspective, a set of studies increases our knowledge about a particular topic.

Thus, the purpose of this collection is to provide sport tourism scholars with a compendium of theories that might be used to understand and explain various aspects of sport tourism that they might be interested in studying. The content of the collection is by no means exhaustive of all possible theories, but it provides an overview of some of the most commonly used theoretical perspectives in sport, tourism and leisure studies.

The collection is divided into three parts. Part one draws upon three theoretical frameworks embedded in a socio-cultural approach. Ed Jackson was one of the first researchers to extensively use the constraints framework in leisure studies. In this essay Tom Hinch, Simon Hudson and Gordon Walker join Jackson. Hinch et al., provide an overview as to how the constraints framework has been used in existing sport tourism work. The authors then adopt a historical approach to examine the various stages of development of the constraints framework in North American leisure studies. Hinch et al., provide definitions of the three types of constraints: intrapersonal, interpersonal and structural, and explain how our assumptions about how these constraints interact with behavioural choices have changed over the past ten years from the conceptualization of constraints as insurmountable barriers to participation to the idea of constraint negotiation. They conclude by suggesting how Walker and Virden's[11] model of constraints originally developed in relation to outdoor recreation might be applied to sport tourism. Indeed, a case study of how a constraints model has been applied to downhill skiing is presented and five areas for future research are suggested. As part of their suggestions for future research, the authors suggest that the large body of literature that now exists within leisure studies on constraints needs to be integrated with the growing body of tourism, and now sport tourism research, that is using this perspective. This recommendation is certainly consistent with the overall purpose of this collection.

Another framework developed within leisure studies that has been applied to sport tourism work is the concept of serious leisure[12]. Chris Green and Ian Jones describe the six characteristics of serious leisure and discuss how various forms of sport tourism participation might be analysed and explained using what they call serious sport tourism. They pay particular attention to two of the characteristics, social and personal identity formation and subcultures. Drawing upon social identity theory they suggest that patterns of involvement in sport tourism should be examined in terms of the degree to which an individual identifies with an activity. For example, the more involved will exhibit different behaviours than the less involved. Likewise, the concept of identity is also linked to the idea of subcultures. Groups of individuals who share the same interest in an activity such as surfing or snow boarding often develop their own values, attitudes and norms. Thus, understanding the characteristics of a subculture is imperative in gaining a true understanding of the meanings and the behaviours particular sport tourists exhibit. Taking some of these ideas further, Sheranne Fairley and Sean Gammon discuss the role that nostalgia can play in these sport tourism subcultures.

Social researchers have increasingly addressed the quest for nostalgia over the past ten years. Dann explains how nostalgia has been integrated into tourism both in terms of marketing materials and also in the way destinations around the world have been renovated[13]. For example, he points to the Raffles Hotel in Singapore as an example whereby the renovation of this famous hotel adopted a décor that recreated its glorious past during the height of the British Empire. Fairley and Gammon analyse various aspects of nostalgia sport tourism including fantasy camps and sports halls of fame. They also point to another form of nostalgia, that of social nostalgia. They suggest that as well as the nostalgia that is evoked by visiting tangible sites of former sporting glory such as sports stadia or museums, nostalgia can also be evoked by a group of sport tourists who have a history of participating together in a particular experience, such as an annual bus trip to watch their football team play. The theoretical perspectives discussed by Fairley and Gammon's and Green and Jones can be used independently or in combination as they share some common concepts that could contribute to a more in-depth understanding of sport tourism participation, particularly of the highly specialized and long-term variety such as sports fans who have a long history of travelling to support their team.

The second part of the collection outlines five theoretical perspectives that have been used extensively in tourism and sport studies. I explore the application of role theory from sociology to the development of tourist role typologies as a way of classifying and understanding different types of tourist. I suggest that applying some of the typologies used in mainstream tourism studies[14] might help the debates over the different types of sport tourist. While recognizing Weber's[15] warning that such typologies should only be regarded as ideal types and not every type of tourism will fit into their classification systems, I suggest that in the quest to better identify and explain different types of sport tourism behaviour, lessons from tourism studies might be worth pursuing. Indeed, Green and Jones' discussion on the supposition that individuals may view their participation in serious sport tourism as a compensation or alternative to unsatisfying roles in their every day lives is a guiding premise for this essay, as Zurcher's[16] concept of ephemeral roles is evoked to suggest why participation in sport tourist roles might provide a liminoid space apart from the everyday.

Another area that has received much attention in tourism studies is the issue of destination image or destination branding. Much of the attention from governments around the world has been on event sport tourism and the notion that if a city and or country hosts one of the mega sports events such as the Olympic Games or the FIFA World cup, the attention the destination will receive will translate into increased tourism and economic investment following the event. Laurence Chalip and Carla Costa suggest that previous work on destination image and destination branding has been approached from two different research paradigms that have traditionally been viewed as not being inherently complimentary. On the contrary, Chalip and Costa suggest that such thinking has hampered the development of a coherent theory of destination branding. In their essay they propose a theoretical framework that outlines a comprehensive approach to both developing a destination brand through sport tourism and understanding the behaviours of the sport tourists who interact with that destination. This essay is inherently linked to many of the others in this collection, both those in part one which draw more heavily on sociology, social psychology and anthropology, and those in part three which address more readily the management and marketing of sport tourism.

Another key idea in tourism research that has both academic and applied implications is the issue of seasonality. It has long been recognized that destinations are seasonal in their ability to attract tourists. Seasonality is largely linked to climate changes throughout the year. Thus, for example, a northern hemisphere destination known for winter sports will peak in its popularity in December, January and February with shoulder seasons in November, March and April. Whereas, a beach destination in the northern US may only be fully operational between the 4 July weekend and Labour Day Weekend (first Monday in September), about a ten week period. Thus, one of the issues in destinations where the economy is based on tourism, is how can they extend the tourist season? Higham suggests that one way of doing this is through sport, particularly by having regularly scheduled league games that attract a reasonably-sized fan base throughout the non-peak tourism months. He explores the way Rugby Super 12 has worked with this in the New Zealand context drawing upon Leiper's[17] tourist attraction system. Higham examines the various strategies used by sport and tourism agencies to combat seasonality, as well as the ways in which rugby union has been changed to promote its attractiveness beyond the traditional fan base.

From the early days of tourism however, it has been recognized particularly by residents of tourist communities that the benefits of tourism might be outweighed by the negative effects of having a large numbers of visitors in your hometown or city. Elizabeth Fredline explores some of the models that have been used in tourism studies to understand the social impacts of tourism on host communities. The quest in any tourism endeavour is to decrease the potentially negative impacts on the host community and to increase the positive impacts. Fredline provides an historical overview of strengths and weaknesses of the extrinsic and intrinsic models of community impact that have been widely used. She then outlines four event sport tourism case studies from Australia and discusses the strategies that have been used by these host communities to maximize the benefits and minimize the negatives. She suggests that there is still much work to be done to refine the conceptual models and the instruments used to gather the data, but one way forward is for future researchers to ground their work in these models and then to suggest ways in which the models can be adapted, thereby creating a consistent body of research within which a line of progress is identifiable.

While, work on host and guests has been evident in tourism studies since the early days, a newer concern has been the regeneration of the urban landscape to attract tourists. While some of the most famous tourist attractions around the world are located in cities, with the decline of traditional industrial and commercial interests in many cities around the world there has been a concern over how to revitalize these urban centres. Mike Silk and John Amis provide a perspective grounded in cultural studies to suggest an approach to examine the spatial transformation occurring in many of these cities and how it is inextricably linked to both local and global politics and capitalist interests. The authors apply this theoretical perspective to examine the redevelopment of two US cities, Baltimore and Memphis. They point out that a major component of the urban redevelopment in these cities is building new sporting stadia to anchor the new face of these cities. Thus, for example, the Oriole Park at Camden Yards is a central part of the gentrification of the Inner Harbor as a place for shopping and eating out in restaurants. The authors provide a critical framework that asks the question 'who benefits from these revitalization projects'?

Part three of the collection examines various concepts and paradigms pertinent to the business of sport tourism. Tracey Harrison-Hill and Laurence Chalip discuss the concept of the marketing mix in the context of sport tourism. They argue, in contrast to common ways of thinking, that the marketing process involves much more than advertising. In so doing, they illustrate the application of some of the concepts discussed in the first two parts of this collection such as subcultures, constraints and urban regeneration and their relevance to the marketing mix as both a conceptual framework and developing a marketing plan for a sport tourism project. Throughout their discussion they illustrate each component of the marketing mix with examples from various sport tourism events, pointing out both the positives and the mistakes that were made in each instance. As part of this discussion, Harrison-Hill and Chalip refer to the issue of service quality, a topic that is developed further in this section by Des Thwaites and Simon Chadwick.

Thwaites and Chadwick use Club La Santa in Lanzarote (Canary Islands) as a case study against which to examine the use of service quality in sport tourism work. They discuss the various dimensions of service quality and then examine one model, the gap analysis model[18], in detail. The authors address the unique issues related to service quality in marketing an experience such as a sport-related holiday as opposed to more tangible products in the traditional retail environment. They apply a theatrical analogy to the sports environment to show how the two entertainment contexts share many of the same characteristics. Thwaites and Chadwick conclude their essay by discussing ways in which to measure service quality in sport tourism situations.

Another key component of sport tourism, especially for governments and host communities, is the economic impact of sport tourism, particularly event-based sport tourism. There is intense competition among towns and cities around the world to host sports events from the big mega events, such as the Olympic Games and World Cup Soccer, to the smaller annual championship games of various sports including golf, tennis, basketball and so forth. Trevor Mules and Larry Dwyer discuss the primary concepts associated with assessing economic impact in sport tourism and sport studies. They review the estimation techniques used to measure economic impact and assess the advantages and disadvantages of each technique. Mules and Dwyer introduce the concept of cost-benefit analysis which takes into account the public sector support that is often used to fund sports events, but which is often left out of any economic impact analysis figures, but without which the mega events could not be staged; however, the long terms detrimental effects to the host communities are often ignored until they become evident after the event has finished.

Mike Weed presents a grounded theory analysis of the government policy towards sport tourism in the UK. This model is the result of a longitudinal study of sport tourism policy and addresses how the decisions are made in government agencies to support (or not support) the development and promotion of various forms of sport tourism in the UK. Weed identifies the various levels at which decisions are made in local and national government and how the ideology of staff in key agencies can contribute to the success or failure of any initiatives, including the use of public sector monies to underpin sport tourism events. The author identifies the territoriality of staff in sport and tourism agencies and the barriers this has for cross-sectoral policy, which is needed if sport tourism is to become a viable developmental strategy in the UK. Weed concludes by suggesting that sport tourism development is likely to have more success at the local and regional levels than as a national sport and tourism strategy. This appears to be the case in most countries around the world at present.

Marg Deery and Leo Jago draw upon the Australian sport tourism strategy to discuss the issue of collaboration and strategic planning, both essential components, if national sport tourism strategies are to have a chance of success. Like Weed, the authors point to the unique aspect of sport tourism that requires the collaboration of what in many countries has often been two separate agencies/departments and fields of study, sport and tourism. They suggest that most governments, both local and national, that have invested in a sport tourism strategy have focused on event sport tourism. Thus, the authors discuss the various components and models of management that relate to event sport tourism at the operational level. They identify some of the unique aspects of sport tourism event management, one of the key ones being the relative impermanence of the event planning team. Management teams are often formed to organize one event and once that event is completed then the team often disperses. This contrasts to more traditional organizations that have a greater sense of permanence. Thus, greater flexibility and strategies of dealing with volunteer labour force are more central to sport tourism event management than in other situations. The authors suggest that recognition of the different management requirements of sport tourism events is key to the long-term development and sustainability of sport tourism in countries around the world.

The essays in this collection address a wide spectrum of theories and applications, ranging from the higher level theorizing of behaviour that tends to be thought of as the exclusive realm of the academic, to frameworks that seem to have more ready applications. Throughout the essays that follow, the reader's attention is drawn to the interrelationships between the concepts discussed by each of the authors. Recognizing the interrelationships between concepts is not only the hallmark of good scholarship, but it is also essential to the future development of sport tourism scholarship as we need to generate a cohesive body of knowledge that explains a diverse phenomenon that involves among others, behavioural, policy, economic, social and management aspects and impacts. The reader is also urged to view all theories both as a tool to advance scholarship and to enhance practice. As Yiannakis argues in his discussion on the need for academic researchers to breach the divide between them and practitioners, 'if applied sociology of sport is to speak to the needs of society and the concerns of the various constituencies that stand to benefit from such research and involvement, sport sociologists must be encouraged to pursue with vigour and commitment the roles of applied researcher, consultant, knowledge broker, and change agent'[19]. Yiannakis is not suggesting anything that contradicts the aim of this collection. On the contrary, he suggests that there are four phases in the application process: explanatory research (the goal of this collection of essays), operational research (another goal of this collection), knowledge transfer and implementation.

Thus, it is hoped that the theoretical perspectives discussed in this collection will be integrated into the next phase of sport tourism research as we move forward in building a knowledge base underpinned by explanatory research as well as aiding in the development of sport tourism ventures informed by such research.

Notes

[1] J. Standevan and P. De Knop, *Sport Tourism* (Champaign, IL: Human Kinetics, 1999). J. Higham, *Sport Tourism Destinations* (Kidlington, UK: Butterworth-Heinemann, 2005). T. Hinch and J. Higham, *Sport Tourism Development.* (Clevedon, UK: Channel View Publications, 2003). S. Hudson, *Sport and Adventure Tourism* (Binghamton, NY: Haworth Hospitality Press, 2003). B. Ritchie and D. Adair, *Sport Tourism: Interrelationships, Impacts and Issues* (Clevedon, UK: Channel View Publications, 2004). M. Weed and C. Bull, *Sports Tourism: Participants, Policy and Providers* (Oxford, UK: Elsevier Butterworth-Heinemann, 2004). D. Turco, R. Riley and K. Swart, *Sport Tourism* (Morgantown, VA: Fitness Information Technology, Inc., 2003).

[2] Standevan and De Knop, *Sport Tourism.* T. Hinch and J. Higham , 'Sport Tourism: A Framework for Research', *International Journal of Tourism Research*, 3, 1 (2001), 45–58. C. Hall, 'Adventure, Sport and Health Tourism', in B. Weiler and C.M. Hall (eds), *Special Interest*

Tourism (London: Bellhaven Press, 1992), pp.141–58. Weed and Bull, *Sports Tourism: Participants, Policy and Providers*.

[3] G. Redmond, 'Changing Styles of Sports Tourism: Industry/Consumer Interactions in Canada, the USA and Europe', in M. Sinclair and M. Stabler (eds), *The Tourism Industry: An International Analysis* (Wallingford: CAB International, 1991), pp.107–20.

[4] H. Gibson, 'Sport Tourism: A Critical Analysis of Research', *Sport Management Review*, 1, 1 (1998), 45–76, p.49.

[5] G. Dann and E. Cohen, 'Sociology and Tourism', *Annals of Tourism Research*, 18, 1 (1991), 155–69.

[6] F. Coalter, 'Leisure Sciences and Leisure Studies: The Challenge of Meaning', in E. Jackson and T. Burton (eds), *Leisure Studies; Prospects for the twenty-first century* (State College, PA: Venture Publishing, 1999), pp.507–18.

[7] C. Aitchison, 'Poststructural Feminist Theories of Representing Others: A Response to the "Crisis" in Leisure Studies' Discourse', *Leisure Studies*, 19, 3 (2000), 127–44.

[8] J. Kelly, *Freedom To Be: A New Sociology of Leisure* (New York: Macmillan, 1987), p.2.

[9] M. Weber, *The Methodology of the Social Sciences*, trans. E. Shils and H. Finch (New York: Free Press, 1949).

[10] A. Gouldner, *The Coming Crisis in Western Sociology* (New York: Basic Books, 1970). Cited in Kelly, *Freedom To Be*, p.2.

[11] G. Walker and R. Virden, 'Constraints on Outdoor Recreation', in E. Jackson (ed.), *Constraints to Leisure* (State College, PA: Venture Publishing, 2005).

[12] R. Stebbins, 'Serious Leisure: A Conceptual Statement', *Pacific Sociological Review*, 25, 2 (1982), 251–72. R. Stebbins, *Amateurs, Professionals, and Serious Leisure* (Montreal: McGill Queen's University Press, 1992).

[13] G. Dann, 'Tourism: The Nostalgia Industry of the Future', in W. Theobold (ed.), *Global Tourism: The Next Decade* (Oxford, UK: Butterworth-Heinemann, 1994), pp.56–67.

[14] E. Cohen, 'Toward a Sociology of International Tourism', *Social Research*, 39, 1 (1972), 164–82. P. Pearce, *The Social Psychology of Tourist Behaviour* (Oxford, UK: Pergamon, 1982). C. Mo, D. Howard and M. Havitz , 'Testing an International Tourist Role Typology', *Annals of Tourism Research*, 20, 2 (1993), 319–35. A. Yiannakis and H. Gibson , 'Roles Tourists Play', *Annals of Tourism Research*, 19, 2 (1992), 287–303.

[15] Weber, The Methodology of the Social Sciences.

[16] L. Zurcher, 'Role Selection: The Influence of Internalised Vocabularies of Motive', *Symbolic Interaction*, 2, 2 (1979), 45–62.

[17] N. Leiper, 'Tourist Attraction Systems', *Annals of Tourism Research*, 17, 3 (1990), 371–2.

[18] A. Parasuraman, V. Zeithmaml and L. Berry, 'A Conceptual Model of Service Quality and its Implications for Future Research. *Journal of Marketing*, 49, 1(1985), 41–50.

[19] A. Yiannakis, 'Toward an Applied Sociology of Sport: The Next Generation', in A. Yiannakis and S. Greendorfer (eds), *Applied Sociology of Sport* (Champaign, IL: Human Kinetics, 1992), p.16.

Leisure Constraint Theory and Sport Tourism

Tom Hinch, Edgar L. Jackson, Simon Hudson
& Gordon Walker

Introduction

Despite a flurry of recent publications, sport tourism is still in its infancy as an area of academic investigation. As such, it is characterized by ideographic studies which have merit in terms of specific situations but which have had limited success in advancing the field in a systematic manner. This fact leaves the area open to academic criticism based on the prevalence of descriptive rather than explanatory or predictive research. The broader field of leisure research has faced similar censure but has countered it by adapting theories used in other realms to help drive leisure research agendas. Leisure studies researchers have also introduced unique theoretical approaches that have advanced the field. One such theoretical approach focuses on leisure constraints.

Leisure constraints have been defined as 'factors that are assumed by researchers and/or perceived or experienced by individuals to limit the formation of leisure

T.D. Hinch, Faculty of Physical Education and Recreation, Edmonton, Alberta, Canada. Correspondence to: tom.hinch@ualberta.ca preferences and/or to inhibit or prohibit participation and enjoyment in leisure' [1]. Researchers would be well served by using constraints-based approaches to drive research questions related to sport tourism. In doing so, insight could be gained as to why sport tourists behave in certain ways and, by extension, why the sport tourism industry is characterized by its own unique idiosyncrasies.

Areas of Constraint in Sport Tourism

Leisure, sport and tourism are closely related concepts (Figure 1). For the purposes of this discussion, leisure is considered in a broad sense as:

> that portion of an individual's time that is not directly devoted to work or work-connected responsibilities or to other obligated forms of maintenance or self-care. Leisure implies freedom and choice and is customarily used in a variety of ways, but chiefly to meet one's personal needs for reflection, self-enrichment, relaxation, or pleasure. While it usually involves some form of participation in a voluntarily chosen activity, it may also be regarded as a holistic state of being or even a spiritual experience [2].

In defining sport as 'a structured, goal-oriented, competitive, contest-based, ludic physical activity' [3], it is clearly situated as a subset of leisure. One possible exception is professional sport, although the spectator consumption of this activity clearly falls within the parameters of leisure. Tourism, in turn, can be defined as 'the travel of non-residents to destination areas as long as their sojourn does not become a permanent residence' [4]. While business travel falls outside of the leisure concept, pleasure-based travel is clearly a form of leisure and in this paper, tourism refers to leisure-based travel [5]. The spheres of sport and tourism also converge within the realm of leisure and it is this shaded area in Figure 1 that provides the context for this discussion on constraints.

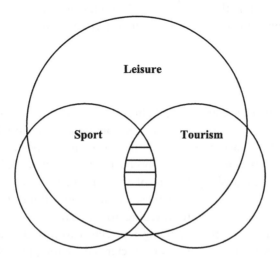

Figure 1 The Relationship between Leisure, Sport and Tourism.

Although sport tourism is a relatively new concept in terms of contemporary academic vernacular, its scope of activity is far from a recent phenomenon. The notion of people travelling to participate and watch sport dates back to the ancient Olympic Games and, in modern times, the practice of stimulating tourism through sport has existed for over a century. Within the last few decades, however, the tourism industry has more fully realized the significant potential of sport tourism and is aggressively pursuing this market niche. Broadly defined, sport tourism includes travel away from one's primary residence to participate in a sport activity for recreation or competition, travel to observe sport at the grassroots or elite level, and travel to visit a sport attraction such as a sports hall of fame or water park [6]. From an attraction perspective, sport tourism has been defined as 'sport based travel away from the home environment for a limited time where sport is characterized by unique rule sets, competition related to physical prowess and a playful nature' [7]. In both cases, it is clear that there are constraining forces that can limit an individual's travel behaviour associated with attending sport events, actively engaging in sporting activities away from the home environment or visiting distant sport heritage sites.

From a constraints perspective, the fundamental question is why do some people not participate in sport tourism activities or not participate to the extent that they may desire? One of the obvious answers to this question includes geographic factors. By definition, tourism requires travel between home communities and the tourist destination. The more isolated the destination or the longer the distance to a destination, the greater the constraint [8]. While not specifically couched in the terminology of constraints, geographers have articulated this idea through the development of distance decay theory which highlights the inverse relationship between increasing distance and the number of travellers visiting a destination [9]. Beyond this fundamental constraint of tourism, there exists a broad range of other constraints. Initial insight into the nature of these constraints can be gained by considering them within the context of: (1) typologies of sport tourism activity; (2) sport attraction frameworks; and (3) the interface of the sport and the tourism delivery systems.

Activity Typologies

A typology developed by Gibson highlights three distinct realms of sport tourism activities: event-based activities, active participation, and nostalgia-based sport travel [10]. Event-based activities are epitomized by major sporting festivals such as the Olympic Games but also include a broad range of large-, medium- and small-scale events. The distinguishing feature of this category in terms of constraints is that the focus is on the spectators at these events. Those things that discourage or prevent potential spectators from travelling to the event need to be considered. Perceptions of crowding or price-gouging represent two possible constraints. Active sport tourism refers to sport activities characterized by the physical involvement of the tourist directly in the sport. Golfers and downhill skiers are two examples of sport tourists falling into this category. In contrast to more sedentary spectators at sporting events, active sport tourists may face a broader range of physical constraints associated with fitness and health. Nostalgia sport tourists include those who travel to venerate sporting facilities and museums, along with the growing number of tourists visiting fantasy sport camps where they can be transported back to their youth or mingle with their sporting heroes. While nostalgia sport tourists may share a variety of constraints with their event and active counterparts, they are more likely to be constrained by lower levels of supply and perhaps by lack of awareness about existing opportunities.

Attraction Systems

Leiper's attraction system can also be used to suggest the nature of constraints in sport tourism [11]. While the idea of sport as a tourist attraction is not new [12], the theoretical basis of sport as a tourist attraction is just beginning to be addressed in a systematic fashion [13]. Leiper defines a tourist attraction as 'a system comprising three elements: a tourist or human element, a nucleus or central element, and a marker or informative element. A tourist attraction comes into existence when the three elements are connected' [14]. Leisure constraints may be found within each of these components. Given the interdependent nature of the attraction system, a constraint in any one of its components is likely to compromise the empirical relationship, thereby diminishing the attraction's capacity.

The first component of Leiper's attraction system is the human element [15]. The tourist or human element consists of persons who are travelling away from home to the extent that their behaviour is motivated by leisure-related factors. Five assertions are made about the nature of this behaviour:

> First, the essence of touristic behaviour involves a search for satisfying leisure away from home. Second, touristic leisure means a search for suitable attractions or, to be more precise, a search for personal (*in situ*) experience of attraction systems' nuclear elements. Third, the process depends ultimately on each individual's mental and non-mental attributes such as needs and ability to travel. Fourth, the markers or informative elements have a key role in the links between each tourist and the nuclear elements being sought for personal experience. Fifth, the process is not automatically productive, because tourists' needs are not always satisfied (these systems may be functional or dysfunctional, to varying degrees) [i.e., constraints] [16].

Examples of sport tourists include athletes, spectators, coaches, officials, media and an assortment of other groups for whom sport is an important part of their travel experience. Each of these groups faces their own unique set of constraints. Competitive athletes, for example, often have to qualify for competition based on performance measures.

The second major element of the tourist attraction system is the nucleus, which refers to the site where the tourist experience is produced and consumed. More specifically, in the context of sporting attractions, the attributes of the sporting activity make up the nucleus of the attraction [17]. In the case of sport tourism, this nucleus is determined by unique rule sets, competition related to physical prowess, and the ludic nature of a featured sport. Constraints may be embedded explicitly in the rules, in the competitive nature of the sport, and the type of physical prowess required. These constraints may also be imbedded in the ludic nature of the sport related to whether it is played at an elite or recreational level. Constraints related to the nucleus may also vary according to attraction hierarchies as perceived by the tourist. Some sport nuclei may serve as the primary attraction for the trip, while others are secondary attractions and still others are incidental or tertiary attractions [18]. Even when faced with a similar constraint (for example, cost of event admission), differing perceptions of the attraction within this hierarchy may mean that the power of the constraint varies substantially among potential visitors.

The third element of the attraction system consists of markers, or items of information about any phenomenon that is a potential nucleus element in a tourist attraction [19]. These markers may be positioned consciously or unconsciously to function as part of the attraction system. Examples of conscious attraction markers featuring sport are common. Typically, they take the form of advertisements showing visitors involved in destination-specific sport activities and events. An even more pervasive form of marker includes televised broadcasts of elite sport competitions and advertisements of non-travel products featuring sports in recognizable destinations. Broadcast listeners and viewers have the location marked for them as a tourist attraction, which may influence future travel decisions. These markers may serve as constraints where they are absent or where, in the case of media coverage, negative destination images are projected.

Interface between Sport and Tourism

Traditionally, the sport system and the tourism system have operated quite separately from each other. Tourism can be described in terms of an integrated system featuring tourists, transportation linkages, destinations (inclusive of attractions, accommodation, hospitality and services), and a marketing component. Fragmentation within these systems can introduce an assortment of supply-based constraints. The sport delivery system is characterized by a variety of public and private stakeholders. While profit-driven professional sports franchises receive much media attention, the vast majority of sport falls under the administration of the not-for-profit volunteer sector. This delivery system tends to suffer budget crises in times of economic restraint and must deal with the limitations as well as the benefits of a large voluntary sector. Limitations include the transitory nature of volunteers, a general lack of formal management training, and the tendency to focus on the performance aspect of the sport at the expense of important supporting functions. Despite the fact that the outputs of the sport delivery system serve as the product or attraction in the tourism delivery system, the lack of systematic cooperation between these two sectors has been a significant constraint to sport tourism [20].

Clearly, participation in sport tourism activities is influenced by constraints. The potential for modifying these constraints requires a fuller understanding of the process and conditions under which these constraints influence sport tourism behaviour. Despite the very recent initiation of research in this area, sport tourism researchers can effectively build on the more advanced state of research related to leisure constraints in general.

What Do We Know about Constraints To Leisure?

Systematic research on leisure constraints has existed as a distinct sub-field of investigation within leisure studies for about two and a half decades. It began with some key papers that were published in the early 1980s [21]. As Goodale and Witt have pointed out, however, the origins of the field of interest can be traced back over a much longer time-period: at least to the Outdoor Recreation Resources Review Commission studies of the early 1960s, and even to the origins of the North American parks and recreation movement in the nineteenth century [22].

Most of the research conducted in the 1980s was empirical, being based on theory at only the deepest and most implicit level [23]. Consequently, researchers tended to make assumptions about constraints which were not uncovered as limiting the development of the field until much later. There were two early assumptions that were particularly important. The first was the belief that the most significant effect of constraints on leisure is to block or limit participation; that is the absence or presence of constraints would explain why a person does or does not participate in an activity. To use subsequent language, structural constraints (those that intervene between preferences and participation, such as lack of time, the costs of participating, or inadequate facilities) were thought to be the only significant type of constraint. As a corollary, the emphasis was on activities and participation as outcomes of constraints, which, like the constraints items, were the most easily quantifiable and measurable aspects of leisure to investigate. The second major assumption was that constraints are immovable, static obstacles to participation.

Also in the early stages of leisure constraints research, a narrow range of methods was employed to collect data for the statistical analysis of relationships among leisure, constraints and other variables thought to be important (for example, socio-economic and demographic factors, the most influential of which were found to be age, gender and income). The dominant orientation was quantitative, usually consisting of a questionnaire in which lists of constraints thought to be important by researchers were rated by respondents in terms of their effects on participation.

The picture changed considerably in several distinct, but in hindsight interconnected, ways in the late 1980s and on into the 1990s. First, the field began to be characterized by more explicit and increasingly sophisticated theorizing, as researchers began to uncover previous false assumptions and explore new concepts. This occurred in two ways: innovative empirical research, and the emergence of a series of theoretical, model-based articles that challenged previous assumptions and set the stage for the more sophisticated empirical research that was to follow. New research directions and conceptual models are discussed in some detail below. Second – as was also happening more widely in leisure studies and indeed in the social sciences as a whole – the array of methods was widened, in particular with the incorporation of qualitative methods and the declining domination of the questionnaire. To a considerable extent, this shift occurred as a result of the influence of work published by feminist researchers, such as Bialeschki, Henderson and Shaw [24]. Third, criticisms began to be aired about constraints research and concepts, which generated a vigorous debate about the value of the insights to be gained from research conducted using a constraints-based perspective [25].

Theories and Models

Three specific developments occurred between about 1987 and 1991 that challenged the naïve thinking of early constraints research and changed its course. First, stimulated in part by an integrative review [26], there was not only a flurry of new empirical research activity but a growing awareness among leisure scholars of the pervasive importance of constraints, both in people's leisure lives and in diverse areas of leisure studies in which constraints had not previously been investigated.

Second, some very innovative research appeared. Scott, in a qualitative study of contract bridge, showed that people often take innovative steps to negotiate the constraints they face (this, in fact, was the first time the term 'negotiation' appeared in the constraints literature) [27]. Kay and Jackson demonstrated how many people manage to participate in their chosen leisure activities 'despite constraint' [28]. Shaw, Bonen and McCabe, having identified the counter-intuitive finding that it is often the more constrained people who participate more frequently than the less constrained, questioned the assumption that 'more constraints mean less leisure' [29]. Moreover, this last article pointed to the greater influence of social structure as a constraint on leisure behaviour than had previously been recognized in agency-based research conducted on the perceptions and responses of individuals. The third development was the publication of an increasingly sophisticated set of models of leisure and constraints. While constraints models had been published earlier in the 1980s [30], in retrospect the single most important conceptual development was the publication in *Leisure Sciences* of a seminal 1987 paper by Crawford and Godbey, 'Reconceptualizing Barriers to Family Leisure' [31]. Crawford and Godbey made two main contributions, which have not only been accepted as axiomatic by subsequent leisure constraints researchers, but which are fundamental to applying knowledge of leisure constraints to the understanding of constraints and sport tourism. First, Crawford and Godbey argued that it was not only participation and non-participation that were affected by constraints, but also preferences – in other words, lack of desire for an activity or lack of awareness could also be explained in part by constraints. Second, Crawford and Godbey broadened the range of constraints that could be recognized as affecting leisure behaviour. Thus, not only do constraints intervene between preferences and participation (Crawford and Godbey referred to this type of constraints as 'structural'), but they also affect preferences in several significant ways, most notably through the operation of two other types of constraints, which Crawford and Godbey referred to as 'intrapersonal' and 'interpersonal'. Intrapersonal constraints were defined by Crawford and Godbey as individual psychological states and attributes which interact with leisure preferences rather than intervening between preferences and participation. Intrapersonal constraints exist when, as a result of abilities, personal needs, prior socialization, and perceived reference group attitudes; individuals fail to develop leisure preferences. According to Scott [32] intrapersonal constraints predispose people to define leisure objects (activities, locales or services) as appropriate or inappropriate, interesting or uninteresting, available or not available, and so on. Interpersonal constraints are those that arise out of social interaction with friends, family and others. In a family context, for example, interpersonal constraints may occur when spouses differ in terms of their respective leisure preferences. As noted by Crawford and Godbey, these differences may impact both spouses' leisure preferences and leisure participation.

The next step in the modelling process occurred in the form of a 1991 'hierarchical model' in which Crawford, Jackson and Godbey recast the thinking that had gone into the earlier paper in terms of a sequential hierarchy of constraints [33]. They argued that, although most research attention had been paid to structural constraints, these were in fact the most distal and therefore probably the least important in shaping leisure behaviour, whereas intra- and interpersonal constraints, being more proximal, were likely to be more important influences on leisure. The notion that people might negotiate through these sequentially arranged constraints was only implicit in the hierarchical model, but became more explicit as the focus of attention in a subsequent 1983 article by Jackson, Crawford and Godbey [34]. The 'negotiation thesis', as it came to be known, was based on the idea that, despite experiencing constraints, people do find ways to participate in and enjoy leisure, even if such participation and enjoyment differ from what they would have been in the absence of constraints. The negotiation thesis was summarized in a flow-diagram model (Figure 2), and six specific propositions were presented, namely:

- Participation is dependent not on the absence of constraints (although this may be true for some people) but on negotiation through them. Such negotiation may modify rather than foreclose participation.
- Variations in the reporting of constraints can be viewed not only as variations in the experience of constraints but also as variations in success in negotiating them.
- Absence of the desire to change current leisure behaviour may be partly explained by prior successful negotiation of structural constraints.
- Anticipation of one or more insurmountable interpersonal or structural constraints may suppress the desire for participation.
- Anticipation consists not simply of the anticipation of the presence or intensity of a constraint but also of anticipation of the ability to negotiate it; and

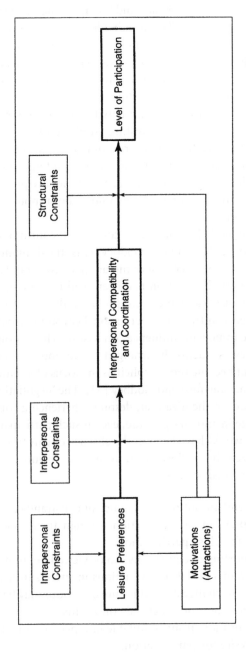

Figure 2 The Hierarchical/Negotiation Model /Source: E.L. Jackson, D.W. Crawford and G. Godbey, 'Negotiation of Leisure Constraints', *Leisure Sciences*, 15, 1(1993), 1–11.

- Both the initiation and outcome of the negotiation process are dependent on the relative strength of, and interactions between, constraints on participating in an activity and motivations for such participation.

Empirically-Based Knowledge about Constraints

Although the situation is changing, the bulk of published empirical research on constraints to leisure has focused on what Crawford and Godbey called 'structural constraints' [35]. Moreover, in the early stages of research much of the analysis was conducted on an item-by-item basis, consisting of cross-sectional correlations between scores on constraints items and two other sets of variables: measures of participation and non-participation, and socio-economic and demographic variables. Following the lead of McGuire in 1984, however, methods to reduce the complexity of item-by-item analysis were introduced into the field, such as factor analysis, cluster analysis, and multidimensional scaling [36]. Results from the use of these methods allowed patterns describing the impact of constraints to emerge that would likely have been obscured at the finer level of analysis previously employed, as well as to pinpoint more robust and generalizable relationships with associated variables. For the purposes of this essay, the following are the key findings from the analysis of structural constraints [37]:

- There is a stable and effectively universal range of categories of constraints to leisure, typically consisting of: (1) the costs of participating; (2) time and other commitments; (3) problems with facilities; (4) isolation (sometimes broken down into social isolation and geographical isolation); and (5) lack of skills and abilities.
- No type of constraint is experienced with equal intensity by everyone, although time- and cost-related constraints rank among the most widely and intensely experienced inhibitors of the achievement of leisure goals.
- The experience of constraints varies among individuals and groups: no sub-group of the population, and probably no individual, is entirely free from constraints to leisure.
- Relationships between categories of constraints and personal characteristics such as age and income also tend to be stable. The idealized composite graph shown in Figure 3a is a good example of the kinds of analysis and graphic presentation of quantitative data that typically emerge from questionnaire surveys, in which respondents are asked to rate the importance of varying numbers of constraints items (such as being too busy with their family, the costs of participating) in relation to aspects of constrained leisure. As the graph shows, when analysed and presented at a highly aggregate and general level, some interesting – and quite robust – patterns emerge about apparent changes in constraints across the life cycle. Thus, a lack of skills and abilities, although consistently rated as least important among every age group when averaged across a survey sample, gradually increases in importance as the life cycle progresses. In contrast – both in terms of the relative

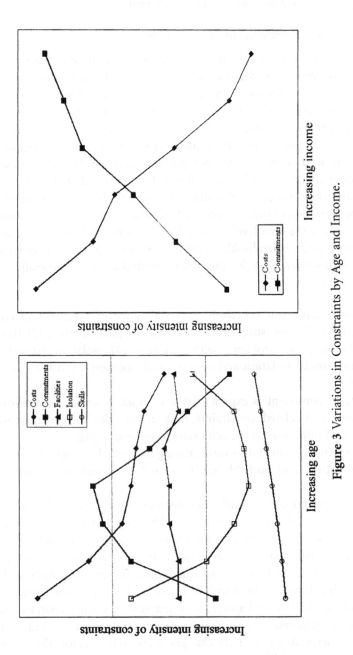

Figure 3 Variations in Constraints by Age and Income.

importance of the constraint and the direction of the relationship – costs as a negative influence on participation decline with advancing age. Most studies have shown that the number and quality of facilities as a constraint to leisure do not vary with age. As far as the remaining two categories are concerned, isolation (both *social* isolation, such as lack of companions, and *geographical* isolation, such as problems associated with distance, travel and accessibility) is typically characterized by a U-shaped relationship with age, meaning that it is most important in the early stages of the life cycle, declining until early middle age, and increasing once again in the later stages of life. In dramatic contrast, commitments and time constraints are usually characterized by a very strong inverted-U-shaped relationship, with the 30s, 40s and 50s being particularly time constrained.

- A similar picture emerges when variations in the reporting of constraints are analysed by income. The graph in Figure 3b demonstrates that – as one would expect – the costs of participation decline as a constraint with increasing income. However, time commitments increase, a trend that can be interpreted to suggest not only that increasing income is achieved at the cost of giving up free time, but also that individuals may make conscious choices about tradeoffs between free time and disposable income.

- Allowing for the limitations of drawing developmental-like inferences about individuals from cross-sectional aggregate data, what appears to emerge from the kinds of findings displayed in Figures 3a and 3b is that not only is there change in the individual constraints and combinations of constraints that people experience as they move through the life-cycle or through income categories, but also a process of *exchange* – of one combination of constraints for another.

As noted above, there has been less research on intrapersonal and interpersonal constraints. However, although there have been exceptions [38], quantitative empirical evidence to date supports the validity of distinguishing among intrapersonal, interpersonal and structural constraints, and that these are arranged in a sequential hierarchy [39]. Research has also shown that people adopt strategies to negotiate through the various levels in order to fulfil their leisure. For example Scott [40], in his 1991 study of participants in contract bridge, identified three main options: acquisition of information about limited opportunities for play; altered scheduling of games to adjust to reduced group membership and individuals' time commitments; and skill development to permit participation in advanced play. Strategies to adjust to time and financial constraints on leisure in general identified by Kay and Jackson [41] included reducing (but not entirely foregoing) participation, saving money in order to participate, trying to find the cheapest opportunity, making other (non-leisure-related) economies, reducing the amount of time spent on household tasks, and reducing work time. Similarly, Samdahl and Jekubovich [42] described how people change work schedules, alter their routines, and select activities that can meet their leisure goals. At a more general level, Jackson and Rucks [43] distinguished between cognitive and behavioural strategies, the latter being subdivided into modifications of leisure and of non-leisure, and further categorized into modifying the use of time, acquiring skills, changing interpersonal relations, improving finances, physical therapy and changing leisure aspirations.

One of the most innovative, and potentially fruitful, recent directions in this aspect of leisure constraints research has been conducted by Mannell and his colleagues [44]. Using structural equation modelling to empirically test alternative models of the process of leisure constraints negotiation, these researchers have vastly improved our understanding of how constraints operate in people's lives, and how they interact with other key variables, such as preferences and motivations. For example, Hubbard and Mannell tested for alternative constraint-negotiation models that specified different links between motivation, constraint, negotiation and participation [45]. They found the strongest support for the constraints-effects-mitigation model, which showed that, while there was no *direct* relationship between motivation and perceived constraint, motivation appeared to be strongly related to participation through its strong positive influence on efforts to negotiate constraints.

A Model for Sport Tourism Constraint Research

Walker and Virden [46], in a chapter in Jackson's [47] new book, describe a leisure constraints model that, although originally designed for outdoor recreation, could potentially also be applicable to the area of sport tourism (Figure 4). As the authors state, the left-hand side of their model is based in part on Jackson and Scott's 1999 contention that leisure preferences are affected by three factors: motivations, intrapersonal constraints and interpersonal constraints [48]. Because some individually-oriented factors (for example, personality traits, attitudes and beliefs, experience use history) affect leisure preferences either directly, or indirectly through motivations and intrapersonal and interpersonal constraints, or both, an antecedent micro-level construct is included. Similarly, because some socio-structural factors (for example, ethnicity, gender, socio-economic forces) affect leisure preferences either directly, or indirectly through motivations and intrapersonal and interpersonal constraints, or both, an antecedent macro-level construct is also included. Furthermore, the micro-level and macro-level constructs affect each other, as well as affecting the 'social and physical environmental conditions that are conducive to leisure behaviour' (that is, setting affordances [49]). Finally, underlying the entire model is the belief that leisure − including sport tourism − involves interaction with the social and physical environment. Thus, a sport tourist's perception of what constrains and what is afforded is affected by his or her previous experience.

According to Walker and Virden [50], the right-hand side of their model is based in part on Jackson and Scott's [51] contention that both interpersonal and structural constraints intervene between leisure preferences and actual participation; noting, however, that because the decision to participate is a distinct act, it must be included between these two variables. As a consequence, constraint negotiation

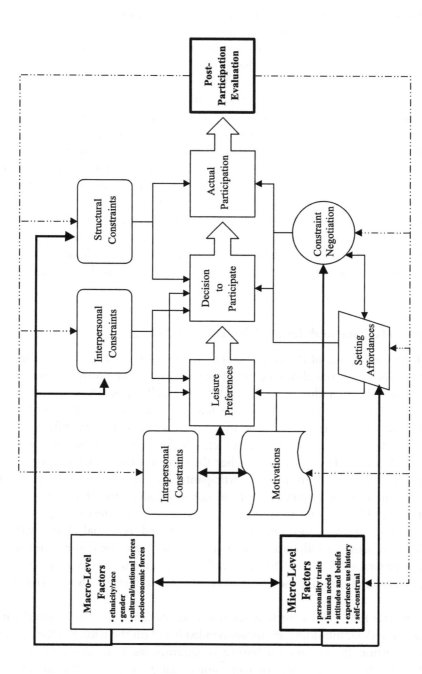

Figure 4 Leisure Constraints Model. Source: G.J. Walker and R.J. Virden, 'Constraints on Outdoor Recreation,' in E.L. Jackson (ed.), *Constraints to Leisure*, (State College, PA; Venture Publishing Inc, in press 2005).

(that is, how people try to ameliorate or alleviate the effects of constraints) is seen as a two-stage process which initially occurs as part of the decision-making process (thus mitigating intrapersonal and interpersonal constraints), and then occurs once again after structural constraints come into play (thus mitigating interpersonal and structural constraints). Additionally, constraint negotiation is affected by micro-level factors and, in a reciprocal fashion, setting affordances. Furthermore, setting affordances affect not only the sport tourist's preferences but also his or her decision process and, most directly, his or her actual participation. Finally, after actual participation does, does not, or does to a lesser degree or in a different way, occur, the sport tourist evaluates his or her experience and this feedback, in turn, affects: (1) his or her perceptions of the intrapersonal, interpersonal and structural constraints he or she has just encountered; (2) the success or failure of the constraint negotiation strategies he or she has just employed; and (3) what the setting may afford the next time he or she participates. In addition, this feedback also affects the sport tourist's original motivations for participating, as well as some of the micro-level factors (for example, his or her experience use history) that precede all of the above. To illustrate how Walker and Virden's leisure constraints model could be applied to sport tourism, downhill skiing is used as an exemplar in the following section.

A Constraints Framework for Studying Downhill Skiing

Downhill skiing is one of the classic sport tourism activities and is responsible for major international and domestic travel flows throughout much of Europe and North America. This industry is, however, facing challenging times. Not only have participation rates declined over the past few years but the Canadian Ski Council predicts that the market will decrease by 22 per cent over the next fifteen years – mainly because of changing demographics. The industry in Western Canada in particular has recently experienced higher than average dropout rates, lower than average conversion rates from new participants, and lower than average take-up from new immigrant populations. It is not surprising, therefore, that the ski industry in Western Canada is very interested in developing a better understanding of the constraints facing existing and potential skiers with the ultimate goal being to influence participation rates. A proposed constraints-based research programme related to downhill skiing therefore serves as a useful example for demonstrating the utility of constraints frameworks for sport tourism research.

Five general focal points for research questions designed to provide insight into constraints in downhill skiing are recommended based on the nature of the industry and the existing foundation for leisure constraints research. These focal points include: (1) the identification of constraints that may be specific to downhill skiing; (2) clarification of hierarchical relationships; (3) a re-examination of negotiation processes; (4) the study of specific sub-groups of participants; and

(5) the investigation of constraints related to the unique spatial characteristics of this industry.

- **Downhill skiing-specific constraints:** The existing body of research on leisure constraints provides useful insights into general patterns of participation associated with costs, discretionary time and a variety of other independent variables. However, there are emerging constraints that bear further investigation, such as the way culture influences participation. For example, Canada's ethnic face is changing, with the ratio of foreign-born residents in the 2001 Census reaching its highest level in seventy years. Initial observations suggest that there is a lower than average take-up of skiing as a leisure activity among members of these growing minority ethnic populations. The role of culture in constraining leisure has received little direct attention in sport tourism, and the disregard for culture as an independent variable is itself highly constraining [52]. More generally, research related to downhill skiing constraints needs to actively consider other new types of constraints. It is therefore crucial that relatively inexpensive and efficient quantitative methods of data collection and analysis be complemented by qualitative research based on personal interviews and group discussions. The reason for this is that qualitative research frequently uncovers constraints that are difficult or impossible to identify in pre-determined lists of items in quantitative surveys. Moreover, these constraints are frequently more powerful influences on leisure (and, by implication, sport tourism) than are the constraints items usually included in generic, general-population quantitative surveys.
- **Hierarchical relationships:** Previous research has shown that intra- and inter-personal constraints are more powerful influences on individuals' leisure decisions than structural constraints. Thus, while some effort should be directed towards identifying structural constraints and assessing their relationships with antecedent variables (for example, socio-economic and demographic characteristics; motivations), most attention should be placed on intra- and inter-personal constraints such as safety fears, self-consciousness and family commitments.

    Further analysis of the hierarchical relationships that underlie the various types of constraints to downhill skiing also needs to be conducted. This is especially important given that there are some conflicting findings in terms of hierarchical relationships. For example, in their 2000 study of constraints to skiers, Gilbert and Hudson did not find support for the hierarchical model of constraints, suggesting that people do not necessarily confront interpersonal constraints, as they move from intrapersonal to structural constraints [53]. This finding may suggest that in the case of skiing, interpersonal constraints often do not exist. The authors proposed a new model of leisure constraints pertaining to skiing suggesting that individuals need to overcome intrapersonal constraints in order to embark upon a leisure preference prior to confronting structural constraints. In the model, interpersonal constraints in relation to skiing are not confronted prior to structural constraints, or do not exist at all. Clearly, the hierarchical model requires further empirical testing, an observation made by previous researchers [54]. More generally, as Walker and Virden's [55] leisure constraints model suggests, development of a person's preference for downhill skiing occurs as a result of macro- and micro-level factors, intra- and inter-personal constraints, and individual motivations. Thus, in order to better understand this process, research on the relationships between and among these variables is needed, and the use of more sophisticated analytical techniques (for example, structural equation modelling) is necessary.

- **Negotiation:** Given the skiing industry's higher than average dropout rates and lower than average take-up rates, a more in depth understanding of how skiers in particular negotiate constraints is required. No studies related to skiing have investigated the strategies employed by individuals in adapting to, or alleviating, constraints. Although previous research has shown that skiers participate despite constraints [56], it is not clear how they negotiate these constraints. Beyond the negotiation of constraints for skiing alone, it is increasingly apparent that the way people negotiate constraints may be more complicated than previously thought. Gollwitzer contends that intending to behave in a certain manner is distinct from planning to behave in a certain manner as the latter involves deciding exactly when and where one will do so [57]. Thus, it may be important to differentiate between sport tourists who intend to go downhill skiing and those who plan to go downhill skiing (and, have selected a specific time and place to do so).

- **Sub-groups of skiers:** Specific sub-groups should be targeted in both quantitative and qualitative research. These would include those who have never participated, former participants and current participants. While a common core of items and questions can be developed for administration to all groups, specific types of constraints more relevant to each group also need to be developed (for example, reasons for lack of interest; reasons for ceasing participation; constraints on enjoyment; constraints on increasing the frequency of participation). In reality very little research has been conducted in understanding why skiers/boarders cease participation despite the fact that the Canadian ski industry is experiencing very high dropout rates – particularly amongst females – and low conversion rates amongst beginners. Related to this, it would be interesting to determine the effect of negative word-of-mouth communication on potential participants from people who no longer participate in the sport [58]. Iso-Ahola and his colleagues recognized that an area that requires further research is the 'interruption' of leisure activities [59]. They found that the tendency to seek novelty through new leisure activities declines with advancing life stages, whereas the tendency to maintain stability, though old and familiar leisure activities, increases with life stages.

- **Spatial constraints:** A characteristic that distinguishes many sport tourism activities (especially skiing) from most, if not all, leisure activities, is the spatial separation of origin and destination, resulting in the need to travel. Thus, more emphasis than in general leisure constraints research needs to be placed on 'geographical' and 'external' constraints concerned with relative location, destination attractivity, distance and travel, and on how these are 'internalized' into constraints associated with costs, disposable income, time availability, work and family commitments, and so on. While these types of spatial variables have been addressed by geographers in a variety of contexts, they have seldom been studied in the context of leisure constraints theory and certainly not in terms of downhill skiing in particular.

In addition to these five focal points for research questions that can be used to drive constraints-based research related to downhill skiing, a more systematic review of the literature in this area is required. Given the large amount of research that has been conducted on leisure and tourism constraints in the past two decades, coupled with its often fugitive nature in a wide variety of academic journals and other publications, some initial but serious and painstaking effort needs to be directed toward the compilation of a comprehensive electronic bibliography and data base. This should be followed by a synthesizing review of existing knowledge in more depth than we have been able to present here. A crucial part of the literature search would be to expand it beyond the leisure, recreation and tourism literatures, and canvass disciplinary (for example, geography, economics, sociology, psychology, et cetera) and interdisciplinary (for example, business, marketing) sources. Equally important is that the literature search not be confined to North American outlets, given that much of the existing research exists elsewhere, most notably in the UK, Western Europe and Australia, and is frequently conducted from alternative and innovative perspectives.

Conclusions

Considerable progress has been made in the understanding of constraints to leisure over the last two to three decades. Atheoretical empirical research no longer dominates the field, nor are the empirical and theoretical 'branches' as isolated from each other as they used to be. Indeed, as exemplified by Hubbard and Mannell's contribution [60], the most recent developments in leisure constraints research reflect an intertwining of theoretical thinking and empirical analysis, with the field moving ahead as new findings stimulate new interpretations, which in turn power the next stage of research. 'Leisure constraints research' is now well established as a recognizable and distinct sub-field within leisure studies, and thinking about constraints has also been assimilated into leisure research that is not overtly directed towards the specific goal of understanding leisure constraints. These developments provide significant and exciting opportunities for knowledge transfer between leisure studies and sport tourism research. Scholars in the latter field do not need to 're-invent the conceptual wheel' but are in the enviable position of being able to capitalize on an existing body of knowledge and, with care, apply it to the kinds of phenomena and behaviours in which they are interested. While it is true that leisure among the general population and sport tourism are not identical, there is no doubt that theoretical speculation and empirical research about sport tourism may be greatly enhanced by adopting a constraints-based approach.

Currently, there is little cohesiveness between the literature relating to leisure constraints, tourism and sport tourism but there does appear to be a movement towards interlinking these separate areas of research. Likewise, the research that does exist in sport tourism constraints is increasingly drawing on the lessons found in the general constraints literature. For example, it was mentioned at the beginning of the essay that in the early days of constraints literature, the dominant orientation was quantitative with an emphasis on uncovering structural constraints. More attention is currently being given to the antecedent constraints. Gilbert and Hudson's study is perhaps an example of the maturing of constraints research, whereby qualitative research was used to uncover 'hidden' constraints that had not yet been revealed through a quantitative approach [61].

However, the application of constraints research to sport tourism is clearly limited, and to better explore sport tourism, academics and professionals alike must understand and appreciate the constraints facing potential sport tourism participants. The study of sport tourist consumer behaviour should not only seek to understand the choice processes of tourists, but should endeavour to comprehend the range of constraints preventing non-sport tourists from becoming sport tourists. Most of the models of consumer behaviour in tourism assume that purchase is the outcome, and there is little reference to the negotiation of constraints [62]. This lack of research into the non-user and the associated constraints represents an important gap in consumer behaviour research applied to tourism. For many sport tourism products, such as skiing, demand has matured, and although growth via acquisition may satisfy the ever-demanding expectations of stakeholders in the short-term, success for many sport tourism organizations in the long-term could depend on converting non-users to users.

Notes

[1] E.L. Jackson, 'Will Research on Leisure Constraints Still be Relevant in the Twenty-first Century?', *Journal of Leisure Research*, 32, 1 (2000), 62.

[2] R. Kraus, *Recreation and Leisure in Modern Society* (6th ed.) (Toronto: Jones and Barlett Publishers, 2001), p.38.

[3] B.C. McPherson, J.E. Curtis and J.W. Loy, *The Social Significance of Sport: An Introduction to the Sociology of Sport* (Champaign: Human Kinetics Books, 1989), p.15.

[4] P.E. Murphy, *Tourism: A Community Approach* (New York: Methuen, 1985), p.9.

[5] V.L. Smith, *Hosts and Guests: The Anthropology of Tourism* (2nd Ed.) (Philadelphia: University of Pennsylvania Press, 1989).

[6] H.J. Gibson, S. Attle and A. Yiannkis, 'Segmenting the Active Sport Tourist Market: A Life Span Perspective', *Journal of Vacation Marketing*, 4, 1 (1997), 52–64.

[7] T.D. Hinch and J.E.S. Higham, 'Sport Tourism: A Framework for Research', *The International Journal of Tourism Research*, 3, 1 (2001), 45–58.

[8] T.D. Hinch and E.L. Jackson, 'Leisure Constraints Research: Its Value as a Framework for Understanding Tourism Seasonality', *Current Issues in Tourism*, 3, 2 (2000), 87–106.

[9] B. McKercher and A. Lew, 'Distance Decay and the Impact of Effective Tourism Exclusion Zones on International Travel', *Journal of Travel Research*, 42, 2 (2003), 159–65.

[10] H.J. Gibson, 'Sport Tourism. A Critical Analysis of Research', *Sport Management Review*, 1, 1 (1998a), 45–76.

[11] N. Leiper, 'Tourist Attraction Systems', *Annals of Tourism Research*, 17, 3 (1990), 367–84.

[12] J.F. Rooney, 'Mega Sports Events as Tourism Attractions: A Geographical Analysis', Paper Presented at *Tourism Research: Expanding the Boundaries*, Travel and Tourism Research Association, Nineteenth Annual Conference, (Montreal, Quebec, 1988).

[13] T.D. Hinch and J.E.S. Higham, *Sport Tourism Development* (Toronto: Channel View Publications, 2003).

[14] Leiper, 'Tourist Attraction Systems', 371.

[15] Ibid.

[16] Ibid., 371–2.

[17] A. Lew, 'A Framework of Tourist Attraction Research', *Annals of Tourism Research*, 14, 3 (1987), 553–75.

[18] J. Standeven and P. DeKnop, *Sport Tourism* (Champaign, IL: Human Kinetics, 1999); S. Gammon and T. Robinson, 'Sport and Tourism: A Conceptual Framework', *Journal of Sport Tourism*, 4, 3 (1997), 8–24.

[19] Leiper, 'Tourist Attraction Systems'.

[20] S.A. Glyptis, 'Sport and Tourism', in C.P. Cooper (ed.), *Progress in Tourism, Recreation and Hospitality Management* (London: Belhaven Press, 1991), pp.165–87; M. Weed and C. Bull, *Sports Tourism: Participants, Policy and Providers* (Oxford: Butterworth-Heinemann, 2004).

[21] J. Boothby, M.F. Tungatt and A.R. Townsend, 'Ceasing Participation in Sport Activity: Reported Reasons and Their Implications', *Journal of Leisure Research*, 13, 1 (1981), 1–14; D.A. Francken and M.F. Van Raiij, 'Satisfaction with Leisure Time Activities', *Journal of Leisure Research*, 13, 4 (1981), 337–352; G. Romsa and W. Hoffman, 'An Application of Non-Participation Data in Recreation Research: Testing the Opportunity Theory', *Journal of Leisure Research*, 12, 4 (1980), 321–328; P.A. Witt and T.L. Goodale, 'The Relationship Between Barriers to Leisure Enjoyment and Family Stages', *Leisure Sciences*, 4, 1 (1981), 29–49.

[22] T.L. Goodale and P.A. Witt, 'Recreation Non-Participation and Barriers to Leisure', in E.L. Jackson and T.L. Burton (eds), *Understanding Leisure and Recreation: Mapping the Past, Charting the Future*, (State College, PA: Venture Publishing, Inc., 1989), pp.421–49; A.L. Ferris, *National Recreation Survey, Outdoor Recreation Resources Review Commission, Study Report No. 19* (Washington, DC: US Government Printing Office, 1962); E. Mueller, G. Gurin, and M. Wood, *Participation in Outdoor Recreation: Factors Affecting Demand Among American Adults. Outdoor Recreation Resources Review Commission, Study Report No. 20.* (Washington, DC: US Government Printing Office, 1962).

[23] J.E. Stockdale, 'Concepts and Measures of Leisure Participation and Preference', in E.L. Jackson and T.L. Burton (eds), *Understanding Leisure and Recreation: Mapping the Past, Charting the Future* (State College, PA: Venture Publishing, Inc., 1989), pp. 113–150.

[24] A number of feminist researchers have used qualitative methods to examine constraints to leisure. Key contributions include: M.D. Bialeschki and S. Michener, 'Re-entering Leisure: Transition within the Role of Motherhood,' *Journal of Leisure Research*, 26 (1994), 57–74; C.J. Frederick and S.M. Shaw, 'Body Image as a Leisure Constraint: Examining the Experience of Aerobic Exercise Classes for Young Adults', *Leisure Sciences*, 17, 1 (1995), 57–89; K.A. Henderson, 'The Contribution of Feminism to an Understanding of Leisure Constraints', *Journal of Leisure Research*, 23, 4 (1991), 363-77; K.A. Henderson, K.A. and K. Allen, 'The Ethic of Care: Leisure Possibilities and Constraints for Women', *Loisir et Société*, 14, 1 (1991), 97–113; K.A. Henderson and M.D. Bialeschki, 'A Sense of Entitlement to Leisure as Constraint and Empowerment for Women', *Leisure Sciences*, 13, 1 (1991), 51–65; C.B. Rublee and S.M. Shaw,

'Constraints on the Leisure and Community Participation of Immigrant Women: Implications for Social Integration', *Loisir et Société*, 14, 1 (1990), 133–50; S.M. Shaw, 'Gender, Leisure, and Constraint: Towards a Framework for the Analysis of Women's Leisure', *Journal of Leisure Research*, 26, 1 (1994), 8–22.

[25]   D. Samdahl and N. Jekubovich, 'A Critique of Constraints Theory: Comparative Analyses and Understandings', *Journal of Leisure Research*, 29, 4 (1997a), 469–71; K.A. Henderson, 'A Critique of Constraints Theory: A Response', *Journal of Leisure Research*, 29, 4 (1997), 453–7; E.L. Jackson, 'In the Eye of the Beholder: A Comment on Samdahl and Jekubovich 1997, "A Critique of Leisure Constraints: Comparative Analyses and Understandings"', *Journal of Leisure Research*, 29, 4 (1997), 458–68; D. Samdahl and N. Jekubovich, 'A Rejoinder to Henderson's and Jackson's Commentaries on "A Critique of Leisure Constraints"', *Journal of Leisure Research*, 29, 4 (1997b), 469–71.

[26]   E.L. Jackson, 'Leisure Constraints: A Survey of Past Research', *Leisure Sciences*, 10, 3 (1988), 203–15.

[27]   D. Scott, 'The Problematic Nature of Participation in Contract Bridge: A Qualitative Study of Group-Related Constraints', *Leisure Sciences*, 13, 4 (1991), 321–36.

[28]   T. Kay and G. Jackson, 'Leisure Despite Constraint: The Impact of Leisure Constraints on Leisure Participation', *Journal of Leisure Research*, 23, 4 (1991), 301–13.

[29]   S.M. Shaw, A. Bonen and J.F. McCabe, 'Do More Constraints Mean Less Leisure? Examining the Relationships Between Constraints and Participation', *Journal of Leisure Research*, 23, 4 (1991), 286–300.

[30]   G. Godbey, 'Non-Participation in Leisure Services: A Model', *Journal of Park and Recreation Administration*, 3, 1 (1985), 1–13; E.L. Jackson and M.S. Searle, 'Recreation Non-Participation and Barriers to Participation: Concepts and Models', *Loisir et Société*, 8, 2 (1985), 693–707.

[31]   D.W. Crawford and G. Godbey, 'Reconceptualizing Barriers to Family Leisure', *Leisure Sciences*, 9, 2 (1987), 119–27.

[32]   Scott, 'The Problematic Nature of Participation in Contract Bridge'.

[33]   D.W. Crawford, E.L. Jackson and G. Godbey, 'A Hierarchical Model of Leisure Constraints', *Leisure Sciences*, 13, 4 (1991), 309–20.

[34]   E.L. Jackson, D.W. Crawford and G. Godbey, 'Negotiation of Leisure Constraints', *Leisure Sciences*, 15, 1 (1993), 1–11. It should be acknowledged that this linear, quantitatively-oriented model was not the only one to appear in the 1990s. For example, a non-linear model was proposed by K.A. Henderson and M.D. Bialeschki, 'Exploring an Expanded Model of Women's Leisure Constraints', *Journal of Applied Recreation Research*, 18, 4 (1993), 229–52.

[35]   Crawford and Godbey, 'Reconceptualizing Barriers to Family Leisure'.

[36]   F.A. McGuire, 'A Factor Analytic Study of Leisure Constraints in Advanced Adulthood', *Leisure Sciences*, 6, 4 (1984), 313–26.

[37]   Jackson, 'Will Research on Leisure Constraints Still be Relevant in the Twenty-first Century?'.

[38]   B.A. Hawkins, J. Peng, C.M. Hsieh and S.J. Eklund, 'Leisure Constraints: A Replication and Extension of Construct Development', *Leisure Sciences*, 21, 3 (1999), 179–92.

[39]   L.A. Raymore, G.C. Godbey and D.W. Crawford, 'Self-Esteem, Gender, and Socioeconomic Status: Their Relation to Perceptions of Constraint on Leisure Among Adolescents', *Journal of Leisure Research*, 26, 2 (1994), 99–118; L.A. Raymore, G.C. Godbey, D.W. Crawford and A. von Eye, 'Nature and Process of Leisure Constraints: An Empirical Test', *Leisure Sciences*, 15, 2 (1993), 99–113.

[40]   Scott, 'The Problematic Nature of Participation in Contract Bridge'.

[41]   Kay and Jackson, 'Leisure Despite Constraint'.

[42]   D. Samdahl and N. Jekubovich, 'A Critique of Constraints Theory: Comparative Analyses and Understandings', *Journal of Leisure Research*, 29, 4 (1997), 469–71.

[43] E.L. Jackson and V.C. Rucks, 'Negotiation of Leisure Constraints by Junior-High and High-School Students: An Exploratory Study', *Journal of Leisure Research*, 27, 1 (1995), 85–105.

[44] J. Hubbard and R. Mannell, 'Testing Competing Models of the Leisure Constraint Negotiation Process in a Corporate Employee Recreation Setting', *Leisure Sciences*, 23, 3 (2001), 145–63; R.C. Mannell and A. Loucks-Atkinson, 'Why Don't People Do What's "Good" For Them? Cross Fertilization Among the Psychologies of Non-Participation in Leisure, Health and Exercise Behaviors', in E.L. Jackson (ed.), *Constraints to Leisure* (State College, PA: Venture Publishing Inc., in press 2005).

[45] Hubbard and Mannell, 'Testing Competing Models of the Leisure Constraint Negotiation Process in a Corporate Employee Recreation Setting'.

[46] G.J. Walker and R.J. Virden, 'Constraints on Outdoor Recreation', in E. Jackson (ed.), *Constraints to Leisure* (State College, PA: Venture Publishing Inc., in press 2005).

[47] Jackson (ed.), *Constraints to Leisure*.

[48] E.L. Jackson and D. Scott, 'Constraints on Leisure and Recreation', in E. Jackson and T.L. Burton (eds), *Leisure Studies: Prospects for the Twenty-First Century* (State College, PA: Venture Publishing, 1999), pp. 299–321.

[49] R. Mannell and D. Kleiber, *A Social Psychology of Leisure* (State College, PA: Venture Publishing, Inc., 1997), p.345.

[50] Walker and Virden, 'Constraints on Outdoor Recreation'.

[51] Jackson and Scott, 'Constraints on Leisure and Recreation'.

[52] G. Chick and E. Dong, 'Cultural Constraints on Leisure', in E.L. Jackson (ed.), *Constraints to Leisure* (State College, PA: Venture Publishing, Inc., in press 2005).

[53] D. Gilbert and S. Hudson, 'Tourism Demand Constraints: A Skiing Participation', *Annals of Tourism Research,* 27, 4 (2000), 906–25.

[54] S.M. Shaw and L.B. Whyte, 'An Analysis of the Hierarchical Model of Leisure Constraints: Using Fear of Violence as a Case Study', Paper Presented at the *Eighth Canadian Congress on Leisure Research*, University of Ottawa, Ottawa, Ontario 1996. Samdahl and Jekubovich, 'A Critique of Constraints Theory: Comparative Analyses and Understandings'.

[55] Walker and Virden, 'Constraints on Outdoor Recreation'.

[56] Gilbert and Hudson, 'Tourism Demand Constraints: A Skiing Participation'.

[57] P. Gollwitzer, 'Goal Achievement: The Role of Intentions', in P. Gollwitzer and J. Bargh (eds), *The Psychology of Action: Linking Cognition and Motivation to Behaviour* (New York: Guildford Press, 1993), pp.287–312.

[58] S.J. Backman and J.L. Crompton, 'Differentiating Between Active and Passive Discontinuers of Two Leisure Activities', *Journal of Leisure Research*, 22, 3 (1990), 197–212.

[59] S.E. Iso-Ahola, E. Jackson and E. Dunn, 'Starting, Ceasing and Replacing Leisure Activities Over the Life-Span', *Journal of Leisure Research*, 26, 3 (1994), 227–49.

[60] Hubbard and Mannell, 'Testing Competing Models of the Leisure Constraint Negotiation Process in a Corporate Employee Recreation Setting', 145–63.

[61] S. Hudson and D. Gilbert, 'Tourism Constraints: The Neglected Dimension in Consumer Behaviour Research', *Journal of Travel and Tourism Marketing*, 8, 4 (1999), 69–78.

[62] Shaw and Whyte, 'An Analysis of the Hierarchical Model of Leisure Constraints: Using Fear of Violence as a Case Study'.

Serious Leisure, Social Identity and Sport Tourism

Ian Jones & B. Christine Green

Introduction

Much of the existing literature covering sport tourist participation examines such behaviour though the development of various classificatory systems, for example Standeven and DeKnop's [2] and Gammon and Robinson's [3] typologies of sport tourism, or Hall's [4] and Gibson's [5] classification of sport tourism activity into active and passive forms. Thus, for example, the individual may be classified as undertaking sport tourism in either a competitive (hard definition) or recreational (soft definition) context. Such approaches do have their strengths, and are useful tools with which to describe and measure sport tourism behaviour. Such classifications or typologies do, however, tend to have a number of weaknesses. Firstly, it is rare for participants to fall into such ideal-types that are proposed by such typologies. The arguments has been made that 'the trouble with typologies is that people rarely fit

B. Christine Green, Department of Kinesiology and Health Education, The University of Texas at Austin, 1 University Station #D3700, Austin, Texas 78758, USA. Correspondence to: E-mail: bcgreen@mail.utexas.edu.
Ian Jones, Department of Tourism, Leisure and Sport Management, University of Luton, Park Square, Luton, LU1 3JU.

them', [6] and that such typologies over-simplify human behaviour. Secondly, such approaches tend not to acknowledge the dynamic nature of such participation, instead presenting a static picture of involvement at a particular time. An example of this may be the sport tourist who experiences an activity for the first time as an incidental part of his or her trip, and enjoys the activity to the extent that it then becomes the primary focus of the visit. Finally, they demonstrate a tendency to examine the activity itself, rather than the meanings, norms and values of the individual undertaking the activity. Thus, as an example, there is little to differentiate the sport tourist who travels to watch an event for the very first time because they have been given a ticket, to the sport tourist who has devoted a considerable personal effort and commitment to the sport itself on a long-term basis. Jackson and Weed's [7] 'Sport Tourism Demand Continuum' goes some way to address some of the limitations of existing typologies, and to some extent reflects some of the points that will be made within this essay. There are also, however, inherent weaknesses within the continuum. One key weakness identified by Weed and Bull [8] is that the variety of behaviour patterns and motivations exhibited by different sport tourists undertaking the same activity renders such models at best over simplistic, especially given their argument that the sheer variety of sport tourist activity makes it a heterogeneous, rather than a homogenous phenomenon. Weed and Bull's Sport Tourism Participation Model [9] begins to address this issue, and focuses upon the meanings and values of the sport tourist experience for the participant, yet the need to categorize diverse behaviour seems to be still apparent within the sport tourism community. Gibson [10] acknowledges such over-emphasis on classifications of sport tourists, stating that 'I would urge that researchers need to move beyond profiling the active sport tourist into explanations of participation or non-participation. In doing this, we need to integrate concepts from the wider fields of leisure, tourism and sport studies.'

Both Hall [11] and Gibson [12] identify one such concept, that of 'Serious Leisure', as an appropriate framework with which to understand the behaviour of the committed sport tourist. Hall [13] originally suggested the concept of serious leisure to examine the active sport tourist, whilst Jones [14] and Gibson [15] initially acknowledged the usefulness of serious leisure to explore the sport fan. It seems, therefore, to be the case that the concept of serious leisure may provide insights into the behaviour of a variety of committed, or 'serious', sport tourist.

Serious Leisure

It could be argued that the term 'leisure' is, in contemporary society, now so broad ranging that it has little analytical usefulness as a concept with which to explain non-obligatory activities such as sport tourism. Long treated as a corollary of work, leisure has generally been associated with terms such as relaxation, recuperation, triviality, frivolity, and freedom from obligation, especially when compared to the seriousness, obligation, responsibility and importance of paid employment. Fox, for example, notes that amateur sport is characterized by such terms as 'unimportant', or 'impractical' when compared to the 'seriousness' of war, religion or business, or even 'fake' when compared to the rigour, commitment and importance assigned to professional sport [16]. When discussing the prospect of a 'leisure society', Clarke and Critcher also view work and leisure as dichotomous, suggesting that

> The prospect of the leisure society relies on a very sharp contrast being drawn between the realms of work and leisure. Work is represented as drudgery, approached with a grudging acceptance of that which must be done ... By contrast, leisure seems to offer the prospect of being all those things that work is not: the source of satisfactions, gratifications and pleasures. Where work is the realm of dull compulsion, leisure represents freedom, choice and creativity. Where work is what must be done, leisure is the pursuit of freely chosen self-interest [17].

Yet for many individuals, leisure activities such as sport tourism are of importance, and do involve obligation, commitment and responsibility, often to a level equivalent to, or exceeding, that assigned to those 'work-like' activities highlighted as 'important'. This raises the question of how contrasting activities can actually be classified under the single banner of 'leisure'. It seems clear that a conceptualisation of leisure that acknowledges that leisure may be – at times – closer to work than traditional conceptualisations of leisure is a more useful tool for examining such leisure behaviour. One such conceptualisation is that of Stebbins' theory of serious leisure.

The standard definition of serious leisure is that it is 'the systematic pursuit of an amateur, hobbyist or volunteer activity sufficiently substantial and interesting in nature for the participant to find a career there acquiring and expressing a combination of its special skills, knowledge, and experience' [18].

The nature of serious leisure can be demonstrated by contrasting it with what Stebbins refers to as 'casual leisure', or leisure that consists of 'immediately, intrinsically rewarding, relatively short-lived pleasurable activity requiring little or no special training to enjoy it' [19]. By identifying that certain leisure activities can be 'serious', Raisborough suggests that Stebbins's concept of serious leisure is able to 'challenge hedonist constructions of leisure; enables an exploration of deferred gratification and of participants' continual evaluation of costs and rewards; and, by envisioning leisure as "not-fun", allows leisure research to escape the conceptual burdens of enjoyment, freedom and celebrations of choice' [20].

Despite its obvious usefulness as a tool to examine certain forms of leisure participation, there has been little systematic research into serious leisure participation [21]. An examination of that research, however, demonstrates the diverse types of leisure activity that could be identified as 'serious'. These include Barbershop singing, [22] American Kennel Club membership, [23] membership of the Sea Cadets [24] and long distance running [25]. Overall, however, it can be argued that the concept of serious leisure has largely been overlooked within the leisure literature, [26] and almost completely ignored within the tourism literature [27]. Perhaps this is because, as Stebbins notes, 'At first blush, tourism and serious leisure would appear to go together about as well as pickles and ice cream, a seemingly incongruous, if not unappetizing, match on which most reasonable people would prefer to waste little of their precious thinking time' [28].

Two immediate sources of this incongruity can be identified. Firstly there is the apparent oxymoron of 'serious leisure', a term which combines the seemingly hedonistic, trivial, unobligated activity of 'leisure' with the connotations of importance and obligation produced by the term 'serious'. Secondly the use of the term 'serious' seems out of place when applied to the hedonistic activities often associated with tourist activities. Both leisure and tourism are associated with activity that is often based on the pursuit of 'pure pleasure' [29]. Yet, as will be demonstrated, serious leisure provides a useful theoretical concept to describe and explain certain sport tourism activities.

Characteristics of Serious Leisure

Serious leisure is defined by, and contrasted to, casual leisure through six distinctive qualities. These qualities may exist in all types of serious leisure, however not all serious leisure activities will demonstrate all six qualities. It is also the case that certain activities may fall somewhere between serious and casual, and the distinction between serious and casual leisure may be blurred.

Firstly, serious leisure activities generally involve some form of perseverance throughout the activity. Perseverance involves the negotiation of constraints such as embarrassment, danger and so on. Thus, serious leisure activities such as amateur dramatics will involve perseverance in learning lines and overcoming stage fright. The serious skier may have to persevere through fear, expense and the need to travel long distances to participate. Sports fans will have to persevere through times of consistent failure, and so on. Perseverance may range from the relatively minor, such as Stebbins' example of having to queue for local dishes as a quest of cultural tourism, [30] to the extremes of rock climbers or BASE jumpers persevering through fear of serious or even fatal injury. The range of perseverance noted can, however, be contrasted with casual leisure. The need to persevere in activities such as watching TV, reading, listening to music and so on is extremely limited, if such perseverance exists at all. The introduction of a need to persevere will result, in many casual leisure cases, in non-participation. Sport tourists persevere in the face of standard leisure constraints, and in the face of standard travel constraints (for example, time, distance, cost, cultural discomfort). Thus, serious sport tourists could be said to represent an extreme form of serious leisure.

Secondly, a long-term 'career' is developed through one's leisure pursuit, which includes stages of achievement or reward. The term 'career' is not used here in the vocational sense, but rather in terms of a progression throughout the activity in terms of encountering 'special contingencies, turning points and stages of achievement or involvement' [31]. Thus, the golfer may demonstrate a career that starts at the most basic level of participation, such as practising on the range. A career progression may be then to move to playing on a course, to achieving a high handicap, and to then reduce that handicap. The competitive golfer may then progress to local tournament play, and later travel to compete. Golf tourism is not limited to the competitive golfer, nor must one be competitive to be serious about one's leisure activity. Thus, the golf career may be highlighted by a 'Holy Grail' experience, such as the golfer being able to complete a round at St Andrews, or other revered courses. Again, this can be contrasted with casual leisure activities. It is highly unlikely that an individual will go through similar career stages in such activities as walking, sunbathing, reading, going to the cinema or other casual leisure activities. Such casual leisure activities may demonstrate changing patterns of participation, in that participants may change the manner in which they participate, but will show no clearly identifiable progression through stages of achievement. Progression through serious leisure careers is often assisted by professionals, in the form of tuition or coaching, or through peers and fellow participants. Thus, it would not be uncommon for the most serious golf tourists to advance their leisure careers through travel for instruction (for example, to attend a golf academy), for competition (for example, out-of-town tournament play), or to acquire valued experiences (for example, to play a famous course).

Stebbins' third characteristic of serious leisure is that significant personal effort is utilized to undertake that activity. This effort is based upon specially acquired skills or knowledge, and may be effort involved in preparation for, as well as participation in, the activity. Thus, a committed sports fan visiting a hall of fame or sports museum will need an understanding and interest in the history of the sport, its traditions and values to fully engage with the exhibits. The serious hill walker's physical effort will need to be augmented by an understanding of navigation, weather conditions, and so on. The acquisition of skills and knowledge will generally be based on a long-term effort by the individual to gather and digest information from books, specialist magazines, peers and tutors, and other forms of instruction. Indeed, the serious sport tourist must prepare for more than the sport activity; he or she must also prepare for the travel necessary to participate in the activity. The efforts of the serious sport tourist are significantly higher than either the non-travelling serious leisure participant or the casual sport tourist. The casual sport tourist, visiting the same attraction or undertaking the same activity may enjoy the experience, but in a more fleeting, transitory and superficial way, and may be unable to participate at all due to the lack of skill, knowledge or ability.

A fourth characteristic of serious leisure is the range of durable benefits that are an outcome of participation. Thus serious leisure may result in one or more of the following: the enhancement of the self-concept, self-actualisation, self-enrichment, self-expression, feelings of accomplishment, enhanced self-image and self-esteem, and social interaction. Interestingly, similar benefits have been shown to motivate tourists throughout their travel careers [32]. There is a further durable benefit of certain serious leisure activities, this being lasting physical products of the serious leisure activity itself, although this is less likely for sport tourism activities. This range of outcomes can be clearly contrasted with casual leisure, where a sense of enjoyment or entertainment is, arguably, the primary outcome. Many of these outcomes are a consequence of the strong identification that participants have with the activity, and the strong sense of social identity that is gained through serious leisure participation, which is outlined later.

The fifth and sixth characteristics of serious leisure are, we would suggest, strongly interrelated. The fifth characteristic of serious leisure is that of the unique ethos which exists within the activity. Unruh [33] suggests that a central component of this ethos is the 'social world' that participants become part of. Social worlds are defined as

> Large and highly permeable, amorphous and spatially transcendent forms of social organisation made up of people sharing common interests and sharing common channels of communication . . . Social worlds are not defined by their relation to the dominant culture, but by the production of a 'social object' such as sports, opera, card collections or gardens. Social worlds arise out of the co-ordinated efforts of people to create, distribute and evaluate social object [34].

The social world surrounding serious leisure activities tends not to have formal membership, yet organized groups will often exist with their own structure and hierarchy. Thus, serious leisure participants belong to a clearly identifiable group with its own norms, values, behaviours and even language. The social worlds of surfers, snowboarders and skateboarders are clearly recognizable examples of this unique ethos. 'Serious' surfers, for example, will be seen in the appropriate uniform (O'Neill, Salomon, Weird Fish) arrive in the standard form of transport (VW Combi) and talk in their own terminology, for example in talking about being 'stoked'. Serious kayakers may have specific stories, clothing, skills demonstrations, equipment displays and actions [35]. It is difficult for non-participants to enter this world, even briefly, and casual participants in such activities are generally unlikely to gain access. Tourism may become part of the unique ethos of the serious leisure participant, thus creating a subworld, [36] or perhaps a subculture, of serious leisure tourists.

This membership of sport tourism social worlds is strongly related to the sixth characteristic of serious leisure, that of subsequent social identification with the activity. Tajfel defines social identification as '[t]he individual's knowledge that he/she belongs to certain social groups together with some emotional and value significance to him/her of the group membership' [37].

Social identities are important for a variety of reasons. They provide the individual with a sense of belongingness or membership to a wider social group, a place within that environment, and the subsequent opportunity to use membership of that group to enhance feelings of self-worth and self-esteem. As we noted earlier, traditional social identities have been gained through ascribed groups such as gender, race, religion, and the largely ascribed identities obtained through work. However, as sport, leisure and tourism become more important to individuals through their 'serious' nature, then these contexts will subsequently form stronger, more valued social identities for those individuals. Again, this characteristic can be contrasted with casual leisure. It seems likely that it is only through serious, rather than casual, leisure that such identities are to be acquired. As Stebbins notes, casual leisure is 'too fleeting, mundane and commonplace for most people to find a distinctive identity there' [38]. Thus, reading, walking or watching television is generally not able to provide positive social identities.

Thus, we have been able to show the relevance of Stebbins' characteristics of serious leisure to sport tourism. As we noted, not all serious leisure contexts facilitate all six characteristics to the same extent. The characteristics demonstrated are largely due to the individual and the activity. Thus a snowboarder may be tied strongly to the unique ethos of the social world associated with snowboarding, whereas a hill walker who tends to walk as a solitary activity may have less of a tie to the unique ethos, but invests significant personal effort in the activity. Similarly, the perseverance associated with cultural tourism may be less than that for an amateur cyclist undertaking a stage of the *Tour de France.*

Types of Serious Leisure Activity

The characteristics of serious leisure outlined above may be found in different types of serious leisure activity. Stebbins has identified three broad types of serious leisure participation: amateurs, hobbyists and volunteers [39]. The characteristic features of each are outlined below:

Amateurs

Amateurs undertake activities where there is a professional counterpart. Rather than simply being an unpaid, less-able version of professionals, Stebbins [40] suggests that amateurs and professionals are part of a complex interdependent network, the Professional-Amateur-Public, (or PAP network), where the relationships between professional and amateur are closer than that between amateur and the public. Professionals set the benchmarks in terms of skills, techniques, clothes and behaviours, which are then aspired to by the amateur. The amateur football team undertaking a tour abroad would be an example of this type of serious leisure activity, as would the amateur golfer travelling to play championship courses abroad. Professionals create the benchmark of performance to which the amateur aspires. It is important to note that the term 'amateur' is not used pejoratively in this respect. In some cases, the distinction is not clear-cut in terms of ability, and certain occasions may see amateurs competing directly against professionals. Sport tourism amateurs exist in a variety of activities, for example the golfer cited above who travels to play a championship course, the cyclists who complete a single stage of the Tour de France, or the amateur sports team on tour. Arguably (although research is limited), amateurs will travel primarily for sporting reasons, rather than participate incidentally whilst on holiday, although amateurs may participate if the opportunity arises.

Hobbyists

Hobbyists have no professional counterpart, and thus could be said to exist within their own social world. Hobbyists are classified under five categories: collectors, makers and tinkerers, activity participants, sports and game players, and liberal arts enthusiasts. To examine sport tourism, the categories of activity participants and sport and game players are generally more important than those of collectors, makers and tinkerers, and liberal arts enthusiasts (although this is not to discount such categories as potentially related to sport tourism). Thus the sport tourist travelling to a Hall of Fame, the sports fan watching his or her team abroad, the individual who travels to a health resort, or the deep sea fisherman are all hobbyists.

Volunteers

Volunteers provide a service with no material gain. Two important categories of volunteering exist within the sport tourism/serious leisure framework. Volunteers in management and board work engage in administrative, organizational, policy and other committee work. Service volunteers perform such tasks as information-giving, stewarding and marshalling, and clerical functions. A further category, political and civic volunteering, has been identified, where volunteers become involved in citizens' movements, social advocacy, and political functions. Many sport and leisure activities are largely dependent on volunteer labour to exist. Events are particularly reliant on volunteers. Thus, volunteers may be a significant component of the sport tourism environment.

Serious Leisure, Sport Tourism and Social Identification

One key-defining characteristic of serious leisure is that it is able to provide participants with a sense of social identity. Traditional sources of social identity are those related to work, family or religion [41]. 'Serious' participation in sport or leisure is, however, able to provide a positive social identity for the participant that may otherwise be unavailable through work or other spheres [42]. As Gillespie *et al.* suggest, serious leisure is able to generate its own social identities, including patterns of time allocation, expenditures, family relationships and norms [43]. Shamir [44] suggests that a leisure-related identity becomes important when (1) it expresses and affirms the individual's talents and/or capabilities, (2) it provides the individual with some form of social recognition, and (3) it affirms the individual's central values and beliefs. Shamir also noted that the other characteristics of perseverance, personal effort, skill, training, and the unique ethos that surrounds such activities may serve to enhance the sense of social identity. Thus, the shift worker may, through participation in Masters swimming, develop a sense of social identity as a swimmer, or the accountant may acquire a social identity as a rock climber; identities that would otherwise be unavailable to such individuals. It would be expected, then, that one's social identity would be more highly valued and more central to one's self-identity for serious leisure participants than it would for casual participants. Correspondingly, the development of a leisure identity would be more important for serious leisure participants than for casual participants.

Developing a Serious Leisure Identity

A variety of authors have outlined the process of identity formation. Developing any social identity based upon serious leisure is generally more complex than just a sudden acquisition of that identity. Rather some form of 'social training' is necessary [45]. Although researchers have used differing terms for the stages of identity development, the general stages outlined are largely common to all. Levine and Moreland [46] have identified four general career stages whereby a sport-related identity may be developed: presocialization, recruitment, socialization and acceptance. Stebbins [47] has also noted a fifth, that of decline, or exit from that activity.

The first stage in developing any serious leisure identity is that of presocialization. This stage refers to the acquisition of knowledge by the individual about the specific serious leisure identity to which he or she aspires. This information may be gained through a variety of means, such as existing family or peer group participation in the activity itself, information gained from the media, or through personal contact with the social world surrounding the activity itself. It is during this stage that initial values and attitudes about both the activity and the associated identity are formed.

The next phase of developing a social identity is that of recruitment, or entry into the social world. This stage refers to the initial ingress into the social world, and is dependent upon the factors of opportunity to enter, motivation to enter and interest to enter [48]. This may occur locally. However, it may also occur as a consequence of a family holiday, for example, or incidental participation in a sport activity whilst travelling.

The third phase of developing a serious leisure identity is the socialization phase. Socialization refers to the ongoing process whereby the individual gains knowledge about the roles, norms and values associated with a serious leisure activity, and becomes assimilated as part of the social world. Iso-Ahola defines leisure socialization as 'a process by which basic leisure knowledge, attitudes, values, skills and motives are learned and internalized with the net result of socially relevant and psychologically rewarding leisure behaviour' [49].

It is during this stage that the individual learns about the unique ethos surrounding the serious leisure activity. Appropriate behaviours are learned, as is the terminology associated with the activity, the values of the group, and any other idiosyncratic features that distinguish the activity. During this process, the individual's commitment to the activity should increase [50] and sentiments towards the group will often be positive. For example, participants may feel a sense of pride or achievement based upon membership. Success during this stage will generally result in the individual reaching the fourth, and for many, final phase of the socialization process, that of acceptance, or identity confirmation.

Identity confirmation, rather than being an endpoint, is a continual process [51]. Participants continually interact within the social world of their chosen activity; showcasing not just their skill, but their knowledge of appropriate values and behaviours. Serious leisure participants would seem to be particularly concerned to align themselves with the unique ethos of their sport or activity.

Subculture, Social Worlds and the Unique Ethos of Serious Leisure

The term 'unique ethos' suggests Yinger's [52] conceptualization of subculture as a normative system used to set a group apart from a larger social world. Accordingly, each sport and leisure activity would have its own social world. Serious participants of a sport or activity would represent a distinct segment within that social world. They would adhere to a set of norms, values and behaviours that would differentiate them from the broader pool of casual participants. Crosset and Beal [53] argue that this is not a subculture; rather, it should be considered a subworld. They go on to argue that social worlds can be subdivided into qualitatively distinct subworlds, and that advancement in a sport is a function of a series of successful transitions from one subworld to another. Their description of transitions among subworlds seems to echo the discussion of 'careers' among serious leisure participants. However, two distinctions suggest the inadequacy of the concept of subworld to explain serious leisure participants. Firstly, the unique ethos of serious leisure participation represents the *shared ideas and values* of a group of people rather than merely the segment of people from a broader population. Secondly, these ideas and values are very often in opposition to those of the broader social world - that is, the world of casual participation - thus more closely align with classic notions of subculture [54].

A collective identity is central to subcultural membership [55]. In fact, the centrality of that identity is a distinguishing feature of serious leisure participants. Participants put forth significant effort to align themselves with the symbols, values and behaviours of the subculture. Yet participants vary in the success they have in presenting themselves as authentic members of the subculture [56]. Consequently, they also vary in their status within the subculture. Drawing on Bourdieu's concept of cultural capital, [57] Thornton coined the term, 'subcultural capital' as the currency measuring the value of individuals' knowledge, credibility, and identification with a subculture [58]. Unsurprisingly, self-presentation is core to the development of subcultural capital.

Once an individual acquires an important social identity, that identity is demonstrated to others through self-presentational behaviour. Self-presentation is defined as the individual's strategies and behaviours designed to manage the impressions that others form of them [59] (hence the term 'impression management' is often substituted). For example, Kane and Zink [60] have highlighted how kayakers wore logo-bearing clothing with logos related to both kayaking in general, but also destinations that had been visited. This was principally for other kayakers' benefit, as they - unlike the non-kayaking community - would be able to distinguish the 'symbolic capital' associated with such displays, thus providing the kayakers with significant subcultural capital. The use of self-presentational strategies by sports fans to demonstrate their allegiance to a successful team by wearing team shirts is a well-researched example of this phenomenon [61].

Commitment to Serious Leisure

The strong sense of social identification engendered by many serious leisure activities and their concomitant subcultures is useful to explain continued commitment. Three broad explanations for continued participation in 'serious' leisure can be highlighted, two of which are directly attributable to the serious nature of participation. Firstly, commitment to certain serious leisure activities can be explained using the 'profit hypothesis', [62] whereby the benefits of participation outweigh the costs of taking part. Thus, the skier who has a fear of heights or a dislike of the cold may negotiate such constraints as they feel that the thrill of the descent outweighs these factors (see Hinch, Jackson *et al.* for further discussion on constraint negotiation). The surfer who fails to master the art may continue to surf because of the social life that accompanies the activity. This explanation does, however, apply to casual leisure activities to some extent, although the 'costs' of casual leisure are arguably lower, and thus the threshold of 'profit' needed to experience a net reward is considerably lower. Secondly, commitment to other forms of serious leisure can be explained through the concept of 'social commitment', where individuals are tied to an activity by the expectations and needs of others, [63] either from inside or outside the subculture of the serious leisure activity. As Shamir suggests:

> Social commitment refers to the degree to which an individual's relationships to particular others depend upon being a given kind of person, i.e. occupying a particular position in a network of relationships, playing a particular role, and having a particular social identity. The person is socially committed to a role or an activity to the extent that extensive and intensive social relationships are built upon that role or activity [64].

Individuals that are strongly committed to a serious leisure activity may be committed thus by the needs and expectations of others, rather than any personal decisions. Thus, participation may be important to the family who have supported the individual and to whom withdrawal would be disappointing. Participation may be important to other participants when involvement is mutually dependent or when participants share transport costs. Alternatively, participants may be committed to the subculture and the social identification it provides. Indeed, Fairley and Gammon contend that commitment to a sport subculture is further reinforced by a sense of social nostalgia evoked by long time participation (see contribution by Fairley and Gammon in this volume).

Finally, a strong sense of social identification tends to lead to the individual undertaking compensatory behaviours to maintain and enhance their social identity, and subsequent participation in the activity [65]. These behaviours provide some explanation for continued participation in serious leisure activities when the profit/loss hypothesis or concept of social commitment is inappropriate. These behaviours include in-group favouritism, which can be defined as the preferential attitudes held towards fellow group members (that is, others within the same subculture). In-group favouritism may be further strengthened through those within the group seeing fellow group members as similar to each other, especially in terms of desirable traits. Thus, there can be an 'in-group homogeneity' effect, resulting in those within the group perceiving greater cohesiveness and solidarity amongst fellow members [66]. For example, strongly identified serious skiers should tend to view other skiers favourably. The consequences of such in-group favouritism are to protect and enhance self-esteem through the individual associating with what he or she perceives as a favourable group [67]. Thus, simply belonging to a group can be seen to have positive consequences for its members, even if there is no face-to-face interaction between members of the group. By contrast, non-members are often viewed in less positive terms, again, seemingly as an ego-enhancement or ego-protection process.

For example, snowboarders may be derogated by skiers in terms of their skills and abilities. A third consequence is that of a tendency to selectively focus upon positive aspects associated with a social identity. Thus the serious fan that travels to watch his or her team lose consistently may focus upon the actual experience of travelling, or the experience rather than the result. Each of these behaviours has a role in reinforcing commitment to a serious leisure activity [68]. Each behaviour also reinforces commitment to the subculture of that activity and may build subcultural capital.

Serious Leisure and Sport Tourism

It would seem that serious leisure, and travel to participate in serious leisure, are mutually reinforcing activities. Serious leisure finds an outlet in sport tourism, whilst sport tourism encourages serious leisure. The preceding sections discuss the ways in which social identity and subculture combine to support serious leisure participation. We argue here that travel further facilitates serious leisure participation in five key ways: (1) by offering a context through which to construct and/or confirm one's leisure identity, (2) by providing a time and place (and perhaps liminoid space) to interact with others sharing the ethos of one's chosen activity, (3) by providing a stage on which to parade and celebrate a valued social identity, (4) by creating another step in one's leisure career, and (5) by affording a means by which to signal one's career stage to others. Each is discussed below.

Context for Identity Construction and Confirmation

Serious sport tourism (that is, travel to participate in serious leisure) is able to provide individuals with a positive social identity. Serious leisure identities are, unlike those identities based upon race, gender and occupation, more easily chosen and achieved. Thus, serious leisure may provide social identities that would otherwise be unavailable to the individual. This may be beneficial to those requiring a diversion from day-to-day life, where the identities gained through work, family or leisure are unsatisfactory, or to those that simply aspire to an alternative social identity (see Gibson's essay on sport tourism as an ephemeral role, this volume). As Godbey suggests:

> While not everyone is satisfied with their jobs, those who suffer from dissatisfaction may not compensate for it during their leisure because of the choices they make during leisure ... It would appear, however, that if an individual chooses activities which produce meaning, the chance for major investment of the self, leisure has the potential to serve as such compensation [69].

The types of identity that can be obtained through serious sport tourism are varied, yet often overwhelmingly positive, providing both status and prestige for participants. Thus, the social identities associated with the serious skier, the surfer, the mountain climber, amateur footballer may all attract participants for whom the associated identity is an important motivating factor.

The ability of travel to facilitate a leisure identity is in large part based on the density of social interactions within the subculture. Both Becker [70] and Bourdieu [71] contend that social interactions are critical means to learn the values, norms and behaviours appropriate to membership in the subculture. Travel to participate in a sport or leisure activity puts one in extended contact with other participants (for further discussion see Fairley and Gammon's discussion on tour groups). Moreover, this contact occurs outside of everyday experience, and often includes more experienced members of the subculture. The elements of the subculture itself tend to break down traditional barriers, creating a strong sense of community. The liminoid [72] nature of the experience works to enhance the socialization process. Hence the quantity, quality and relative importance of these interactions are also enhanced. As a result, serious sport tourism can offer the serious leisure participant an intensive course in subcultural norms. Like the linguist that immerses him/herself in the native culture and makes dramatic improvements in language skill, the serious sport tourist can emerge with a stronger, more authentic leisure identity. Studies show that this occurs in a variety of leisure and tourism contexts across active and passive participant dimensions [73].

Related to this point, serious sport tourists may find their particular sport-related activity is an opportunity for self-actualisation and self-expression, outcomes that are not generally found in everyday life. Sport tourism as serious leisure allows the individual freedom for self-actualisation and self-expression in activities that are, to some extent, freely chosen, and that by their very nature allow achievement and realization of potential.

Space for Subcultural Interaction

As highlighted in the previous section, travel to participate in serious leisure can provide a space for participants to interact with one another based on their leisure identity. Serious golfers, for example, may go to Pebble Beach, California - home to a world famous resort and prestigious golf courses. In the course of everyday life, the serious golfer may play several times per week. However, golf activities (and the concomitant leisure identity) are interspersed with the demands of everyday life: work, family and other obligations. Consequently, the serious golfer is forced to shift amongst identities. In contrast, during a golf holiday, one's identity as a golfer remains central and is the identity presented to others. Thus, the tourist space encourages individuals to maintain their leisure identities and to interact based on those identities. However, the ability to identify members of a leisure subculture is not always as straightforward as the golf example suggests. Still, tourist contexts can also assist participants to identify like others by serving as a stage for parading and celebrating one's serious leisure identity.

Stage for Valued Identity

Serious leisure behaviour, like tourist behaviour more generally, can be understood in terms of both seeking and escaping [74]. Serious sport tourists are able to physically escape from their homes (and their home lives), and to seek out leisure experiences. Seeking and escaping can also be used to describe the role of social identity in these same contexts. That is, travel may help serious leisure participants to escape from enduring identities such as work role identities, and seek out identification with a serious leisure subculture [75].

The identity transformation described is further facilitated by the opportunity to communicate the valued leisure identity. Leisure, tourism and event settings are prime locations for projecting identity. Sport participants and fans alike wear clothing and other artefacts of the subculture. Conspicuous displays of subcultural capital are commonplace. The ubiquity, density and acceptability of subcultural elements such as language, humour, social interactions and other behaviours combine to create a place to parade and celebrate one's identity and place in the subculture [76]. The liminoid nature of the space provides fertile ground for these celebrations [77]. Participation in serious sport tourism settings requires subcultural capital, but that same participation can also become a source of subcultural capital.

Rung on the Leisure Career Ladder

One of the major tenets of serious leisure is the existence of a long-term leisure 'career' which includes stages of achievement or reward. In fact, Stebbins describes these stages as 'special contingencies, turning points and stages of achievement or involvement' [78]. Travel to participate easily falls into Stebbins' definition. Active sport tourists might move from competing in local competitions, to competing regionally, nationally or even internationally. Alternatively, serious divers might extend their career paths by collecting dives in various parts of the world. Passive sport tourists share similar careers. Fans of Australian Rules Football have been known to travel long hours to see their team play on the road. A pilgrimage to the Melbourne Cricket Ground (MCG), the mecca of Aussie Rules Football, adds another career notch for serious passive sport tourists [79]. Clearly, travel enhances the career path for serious leisure participants.

Signifier of Career Attainment

Whilst tourism experiences can serve as useful stages in the career development of serious leisure participants, once attained, these experiences also serve as powerful signifiers of career attainment. They are an important source of subcultural capital, signalling one's status firstly as an insider, and secondly, one's status within the subculture. According to Thornton, 'subcultural capital confers status on its owner in the eyes of the relevant beholder' [80]. Knowledge of places, events and attractions, knowledge of subcultural stories and lore, experience in the ritual and ceremony of the subculture's experience with the place, all contribute to the status of the serious sport tourist. When objectified, subcultural capital takes the form of souvenirs and/or photos from the activity and/or the destination. Tangible symbols of career attainment, such as awards, t-shirts and other items only available to participants carry even more value. In other words, travel to participate in serious leisure serves as an outward symbol of one's career stage, through the collection of tangible and intangible forms of subcultural capital.

Applications for Sport Tourism

The nexus of serious leisure, social identity and subculture provides a rich context through which to study sport tourism. As with any theoretical framework, the concept of serious leisure cannot explain all participation in sport tourism, however it is an appropriate framework with which to examine many facets of sport tourism activity. Firstly, it is useful to acknowledge the seriousness with which both active and passive sport tourists assign to their leisure, and the strong identities that can result from such participation. Secondly, the framework is useful to describe the subsequent commitment to the social identities and subcultures that are achieved through participation. Finally, the concept of sport tourism is also a useful framework with which to explore not only existing motivations for sport tourism participation, but also to identify potential benefits of 'serious' sport tourism participation for key social groups. Thus a number of benefits of serious sport tourism can accrue when adopted as a serious leisure activity.

Notes

[1] R. Stebbins, *Amateurs, Professionals and Serious Leisure* (Montreal: McGill-Queens University, 1992).
[2] J. Standeven and P. DeKnop, *Sport Tourism* (Champaign, IL: Human Kinetics,1999).
[3] S. Gammon and T. Robinson, 'Sport and Tourism: A Conceptual Framework', *Journal of Sport Tourism*, 4, 3 (1997), 8-24.
[4] C. Hall, 'Adventure, Sport and Health Tourism', in B. Weiler and C. Hall (eds), *Special Interest Tourism* (New York: Wiley, 1992), 1-14.
[5] H. Gibson, 'Active Sport Tourism: Who Participates?', *Leisure Studies*, 17, 2 (1998), 45-76.
[6] A. Bandura, 'Social Cognitive Theory of Moral Thought and Action', in W. Kurtines and J. Gewirtz (eds), *Handbook of Moral Behavior and Development* (Hillsdale, NJ: Erlbaum, 1991), 45-103.
[7] G. Jackson and M. Weed, 'The Sport Tourism Interrelationship', in B. Houlihan (ed.) *Sport in Society* (London: Sage, 2003), 235–51.
[8] M. Weed and C. Bull, *Sport Tourism: Participants, Policy and Providers* (Oxford: Butterworth Heinemann, 2004).
[9] Ibid.
[10] H. Gibson, 'Sport Tourism at a Crossroad? Considerations for the Future', in S. Gammon and J. Kurtzmann (eds), *Sport Tourism: Principles and Practice* (Eastbourne: Leisure Studies Association, 2002), 117.
[11] Hall, *Special Interest Tourism*.
[12] Gibson, 'Sport Tourism at a Crossroad? Considerations for the Future'.
[13] Hall, *Special Interest Tourism*.
[14] I. Jones, 'A Model of Serious Leisure: The Case of Football Fan Identification', *Leisure Studies*, 19, 4 (2000), 283-98.
[15] Gibson, 'Sport Tourism at a Crossroad? Considerations for the Future'.
[16] R. Fox, 'The So-Called Unreality of Sport', *Quest*, 34, 1 (1982), 1-11.

[17] J. Clarke and C. Critcher, *The Devil Makes Work: Leisure in Capitalist Britain* (Basingstoke: MacMillan, 1985), 2–3.

[18] Stebbins, *Amateurs, Professionals and Serious Leisure*, 3.

[19] R. Stebbins, 'Casual Leisure: A Conceptual Statement', *Leisure Studies*, 16, 1 (1997), 18.

[20] J. Raisborough, 'Research Note: The Concept of Serious Leisure and Women's Experiences of the Sea Cadet Corps', *Leisure Studies*, 18,1 (1999), 67.

[21] K. Roberts, *Leisure in Contemporary Society* (Oxford: CABI, 1999).

[22] R. Stebbins, 'Costs and Rewards in Barbershop Singing', *Leisure Studies*, 11, 2 (1992), 123-33.

[23] C. Baldwin and P. Norris, 'Exploring the Dimensions of Serious Leisure: "Love Me, Love My Dog"', *Journal of Leisure Research*, 31, 1 (1999), 1-17.

[24] Raisborough, 'Research Note: The Concept of Serious Leisure and Women's Experiences of the Sea Cadet Corps'.

[25] G. Yair, 'The Commitments to Long Distance Running and Levels of Activity: Personal or Structural?', *Journal of Leisure Research*, 22, 3 (1990), 213-27.

[26] K. Roberts, *Leisure in Contemporary Society* (Oxford: CABI, 1999).

[27] R. Stebbins, *New Directions in the Theory and Research of Serious Leisure* (Lewiston: Edwin Mellor, 2001), 71.

[28] Ibid., 71.

[29] Ibid., 71.

[30] Ibid., 51.

[31] Ibid., 6.

[32] P.L. Pearce and U. Lee, 'Developing the Travel Career Approach to Tourist Motivation', *Journal of Travel Research*, 43, 3 (2005), 226-37.

[33] D. Unruh, 'The Nature of Social Worlds', *Pacific Sociological Review*, 23, 3 (1980), 271-96.

[34] D. Unruh, *Invisible Lives: Social Worlds of the Aged* (Beverly Hills, CA: Sage, 1983) cited in T. Crosset and B. Beal, 'The Use of "Subculture" and "Subworld" in Ethnographic Works on Sport: A Discussion of Definitional Distinctions', *Sociology of Sport Journal*, 14, 1 (1997), 73-85.

[35] M. Kane and R. Zink, 'Package Adventure Tours: Markers in Serious Leisure Careers', *Leisure Studies*, 23, 4 (2004), 329-45.

[36] T. Crosset and B. Beal, 'The Use of "Subculture" and "Subworld" in Ethnographic Works on Sport: A Discussion of Definitional Distinctions', *Sociology of Sport Journal*, 14, 1 (1998), 1-22; P. Gahwiler and M.E. Havitz, 'Toward a Relational Understanding of Leisure Social Worlds, Involvement, Psychological Commitment, and Behavioral Loyalty', *Leisure Sciences*, 20, 1 (1998), 1-23.

[37] H. Tajfel, 'Social Psychology of Inter-group Relations', *Annual Review of Psychology*, 33 (1982), 31.

[38] Stebbins, *New Directions in the Theory and Research of Serious Leisure*, 7.

[39] Stebbins, 1992.

[40] Ibid.

[41] D. Gillespie, A. Leffler and E. Lerner, '"If It Weren't For My Hobby, I'd Have A Life": Dog Sports, Serious Leisure and Boundary Negotiations', *Leisure Studies*, 21, 3–4 (2002), 285-304.

[42] I. Jones and G. Symon, 'Lifelong Learning as Serious Leisure', *Leisure Studies*, 20, 4 (2001), 269-83; B.C. Green and L. Chalip, 'Sport Tourism As A Celebration Of Subculture: The Ethnography Of A Women's Football Tournament', *Annals of Tourism Research*, 25, 2 (1998), 275-91.

[43] Gillespie *et al.*, '"If It Weren't For My Hobby, I'd Have A Life": Dog Sports, Serious Leisure and Boundary Negotiations'.

[44] B. Shamir, 'Some Correlates of Leisure Identity Salience: Three Exploratory Studies', *Leisure Studies*, 24, 4 (1992), 301-23.

[45] I. Altman and M. Chemers, *Culture and Environment* (Belmont: Wadsworth, 1980); S. Widdecombe and R. Wooffitt, *The Language of Youth Subcultures* (Hemel Hempstead: Harvester Wheatsheaf, 1995).

[46] J. Levine and R. Moreland, 'Group Processes', in A. Tesser (ed.), *Advanced Social Psychology* (New York: McGraw-Hill, 1995), 419-65.

[47] Stebbins, *New Directions in the Theory and Research of Serious Leisure*.

[48] P. Donnelly and K. Young, 'The Construction and Confirmation of Identity in Sport Subcultures', *Sociology of Sport Journal*, 5, 3 (1988), 223-40.

[49] S. Iso-Ahola, *Social Psychological Perspectives on Leisure* (Boston: Charles Thomas, 1980), 132.

[50] Levine and Moreland, 'Group Processes'.

[51] Donnelly and Young, 'The Construction and Confirmation of Identity in Sport Subcultures'.

[52] M. Yinger, 'Contraculture and Subculture', *American Sociological Review*, 25, 5 (1960), 625-35.

[53] Crosset and Beal, 'The Use of "Subculture" and "Subworld" in Ethnographic Works on Sport: A Discussion of Definitional Distinctions'.

[54] D.O. Arnold (ed.), *Subcultures* (Berkeley, CA: The Glendessary Press, 1970). M.M. Gordon, 'The Concept of Sub-Culture and its Application', in K. Gelder and S. Thornton (eds), *The Subcultures Reader* (London: Routledge, 1997), 40-3. A.K. Cohen, 'A General Theory of Subcultures', in Gelder and Thornton, *The Subcultures* Reader, 44-54. J. Irwin, 'Notes on the Status of the Concept Subculture', in Gelder and Thornton, *The Subcultures Reader*, 66-70.

[55] D. Hebdige, *Subculture: The Meaning of Style* (London: Routledge, 1979).

[56] Donnelly and Young, 'The Construction and Confirmation of Identity in Sport Subcultures'. J.W. Schouten and J.H. McAlexander, 'Subcultures of Consumption: An Ethnography of the New Bikers', *Journal of Consumer Research*, 22, 1 (1995), 43-61.

[57] P. Bourdieu, *Distinction: A Critique of the Judgement of Taste* (London: Routledge, 1984).

[58] S. Thornton, *Club Cultures: Music, Media and Subcultural Capital* (Cambridge: Polity, 1995).

[59] B. Schlenker, *Impression Management* (Monterey, CA: Brooks/Cole, 1980).

[60] Kane and Zink, 'Package Adventure Tours: Markers in Serious Leisure Careers'.

[61] R. Cialdini, R. Borden, A. Thorne, M. Walker, S. Freeman and L. Sloan, 'Basking in Reflected Glory; Three (Football) Field Studies', *Journal of Personality and Social Psychology*, 34, 3 (1976), 366-75, M. Lee, 'Self-Esteem and Social Identity in Basketball Fans', *Journal of Sports Behaviour*, 8, 4 (1985), 210-23, D. Wann and N. Branscombe, 'Die-Hard and Fair Weather Fans: Effects of Identification on BIRGing and CORFing Tendencies', *Journal of Sport and Social Issues*, 14, 2 (1990), 103-17.

[62] Stebbins, 1992.

[63] Shamir, 'Some Correlates of Leisure Identity Salience: Three Exploratory Studies'.

[64] Ibid.

[65] I. Jones, 'A Model of Serious Leisure Identification: The Case of Football Fandom', *Leisure Studies*, 19, 4 (2000), 283-98.

[66] B. Simon and T. Pettigrew, 'Social Identity and Perceived Group Homogeneity: Evidence for the In-group Homogeneity Effect', *European Journal of Social Psychology*, 20 (1990), 269-86.

[67] P. Oakes and J. Turner, 'Social Categorisation and Inter-group Behaviour: Does Minimal Inter-group Discrimination Make Social Identity More Positive?', *European Journal of Social Psychology*, 10 (1980), 295-301.

[68] Jones, 'A Model of Serious Leisure Identification: The Case of Football Fandom'.

[69] G. Godbey, *Leisure in Your Life* (Pennsylvania: Ventura, 1994).

[70] H.S. Becker, *Outsiders: Studies in the Sociology of Deviance* (London: Free Press, 1963).

[71] Bourdieu, *Distinction: A Critique of the Judgement of Taste*.

[72] V. Turner, *From Ritual to Theatre: The Human Seriousness of Play* (New York: Performing Arts Journal Publications, 1982).

[73] G. Crawford, 'The Career of the Sport Supporter: The Case of the Manchester Storm', *Sociology*, 37, 219-37. D.B. Holt, 'How Consumers Consume: A Typology of Consumption Practices', *Journal of Consumer Research*, 22, (1995), 1-16. J.H. McAlexander and J.W. Shouten,

'Brandfests: Servicescapes for the Cultivation of Brand Equity', in J.F. Sherry Jr. (ed.), *Servicescapes* (Chicago: American Marketing Association, 1998), 377-401.

[74] S.E. Iso-Ahola, 'Motivation for Leisure', in E.L. Jackson and T.L. Burton (eds.), *Understanding Leisure and Recreations: Shaping the Past, Charting the Future* (State College, PA: Venture, 1989), 247-80.

[75] E.D. Ross and S.E. Iso-Ahola, 'Sightseeing Tourists' Motivation and Satisfaction', *Annals of Tourism Research*, 18 (1991), 226-37.

[76] P. Donnelly, 'Subcultures in Sport, Resilience and Transformation', in A. Ingham and J. Loy (eds), *Sport in Social Development, Traditions, Transitions, and Transformations* (Champaign, IL: Human Kinetics, 1993), 119-45. Green and Chalip, 'Sport Tourism as the Celebration of Subculture'. W.M. Leonard and L.R. Schmitt, 'Sport-Identity as a Side Bet: Towards Explaining Commitment From an Interactionist Perspective', *International Review for the Sociology of Sport*, 22, 4 (1987), 249-61.

[77] B.C. Green, 'Leveraging Subculture And Identity To Promote Sport Events', *Sport Management Review*, 4 (2001), 1-20.

[78] Stebbins, *New Directions in the Theory and Research of Serious Leisure*.

[79] S. Fairley, 'In Search of Relived Social Experience: Group-Based Nostalgia Sport Tourism', *Journal of Sport Management*, 17, 3 (2003), 284-304.

[80] Thornton, *The Subcultures Reader*.

Something Lived, Something Learned: Nostalgia's Expanding Role in Sport Tourism

Sheranne Fairley & Sean Gammon

> Memory's dog-teeth, lovely detritus smoothed out and laid up. And always the feeling comes that it was better then. Whatever it was people and places, the sweet taste of things. And this one, wave-borne and wave-washed, was part of all that. (*Nostalgia* by Charles Wright) [1]

Introduction

Nostalgia's role in sport tourism is multifaceted and stems from the nostalgic appeal of sport, tourism and related social experience. Two broad conceptualizations of nostalgia in sport tourism have been used: nostalgia for sport place or artefact, and nostalgia for social experience. The former conceptualization of nostalgia has viewed nostalgia as that which relates to the heritage of sport(s) including sport halls of fame, museums

---

Sheranne Fairley, Department of Sport Management, Isenberg School of Management, University of Massachusetts Amherst, Amherst, MA 01003, USA. Correspondence to: sfairley@sportmgt.umass.edu

and historical artefacts. The latter conceptualization has suggested that sport tourism need not be restricted to nostalgia that is generated by only attractions or objects, but can be generated by wanting to relive a social experience. Within these two broad conceptualizations nostalgia acts in many ways: as motive, as socialization tool, and forms an integral part of the norms and rituals of various social worlds.

This essay begins with a description of nostalgia and how it has been used in studies of sport, tourism and sport tourism. We then identify and consider the multiple roles of nostalgia in generating and shaping the sport tourism experience.

What is Nostalgia?

Nostalgia is a concept that has been used widely in the social sciences to understand and describe various aspects of human cognition and behaviour. While various definitions of nostalgia exist, broadly speaking, nostalgia can be defined as a yearning to return to or relive a past period. Various restrictions have been applied to definitions of nostalgia relating to the foci of reference and temporal frame. While it has been argued that individuals cannot experience nostalgic feelings for periods through which they have not lived, Holbrook suggests that if an object is embedded within a particular culture, nostalgia for the object can be learned [2]. Nostalgia relies on memory as one cannot have a yearning to relive a past period that they cannot remember (whether the experience is real or imagined). Others argue that memories that generate nostalgia are not restricted to periods that one has directly lived through. Instead, events and the associated meaning can be learned. Learning of past events (or events where one was absent) is enabled by the portrayal of events or objects through modern media technology. Additionally, individuals can learn of nostalgic recollections through forms of socialization such as the passing on of stories which have nostalgic appeal. Using a modified version of Holbrook and Schindler's definition of nostalgia [3], Fairley defined nostalgia as 'a preference (general liking, positive attitude or favourable affect) towards objects (people, places, experiences or things) from when one was younger or from times about which one has learned vicariously, perhaps through socialization or the media' [4]. This definition of nostalgia will be used to understand nostalgia sport tourism throughout this essay.

Nostalgia and Identity

Nostalgia is inextricably linked to one's identity [5], and thus is often indicative of how one views and defines oneself in the past, present, and/or future. Belk states 'our memories constitute our lives, they are us' [6]. Therefore, memories which form the basis of nostalgic recollections serve to remind us of who we are [7]. An individual's identity is composed of both a personal and social component. Consequently, memories that an individual holds include both self and collective memories that reflect an individual's identification with, and belongingness to, a particular social group. As a large amount of an individual's identity is derived from their social surroundings [8], it is not surprising that an individual's memories may relate to the groups to which they have a strong identification. That is, individual's memories stem from the groups with which they psychologically recognize themselves as belonging to [9].

In many instances we try and relive pasts that are not our own but that are related to a group to which we feel a sense of belongingness. In particular, individuals extend their identity by including an imagined past related to what they believe the past eras of a group or subculture entail. Although individuals have not lived through this past themselves, they interpret the past uniquely, and then insist on the authenticity of the memories as if they were their own. As Mead states, 'the past (or some meaningful structure of the past, is as hypothetical as the future', but nonetheless individuals insist on the authenticity of their memories [10].

Memories belong not just to an individual or direct social group, but can also be interpreted in the context of a wider collective. This collective identity can be usefully understood in terms of social worlds and subcultures. Social worlds are powerful social entities created around a common activity that governs values, attitudes and norms [11]. Donnelly defines a subculture as 'a collectivity of groups and individuals who possess common cultural characteristics and who interact with each other, or who have the potential and the ability to interact with each other either directly or symbolically (i.e., through such media as magazines and newsletters)' [12]. Memories that form the basis of nostalgic recollections essentially stem from each level of the subculture: the individual, social group or the wider subculture. While individuals do not necessarily differentiate between the different levels, some memories may be universal within a subculture, whereas others may pertain to a group or individual within the subculture. However, the memories do not necessarily remain at any one level as identity and memories are not static, but are continuously evolving entities.

It is often claimed that nostalgia is used by individuals as a form of identity maintenance. Various authors have suggested different ways in which the nostalgic recollections are used. For example, Aden suggests that nostalgic recollections are used as a form of *temporal escape* [13], while Belk claims that these recollections can be used as a means of *temporal enlargement* [14]. In the case of identity threat, nostalgic recollections allow individuals who are dissatisfied with a particular aspect of an identity to utilize memories which contain a more positive aspect of (or experience with) that identity and thereby temporally escape the identity threat [15]. Similarly, Belk suggests that individuals use nostalgic recollections to temporarily bolster their identity by reliving past experiences related to that particular identity [16]. As both sport and tourism represent salient personal and collective identities for many, it is not surprising that memories of sport and tourism form the basis of nostalgic recollections.

Sport and Nostalgia

Both sport and tourism have been identified as potent instigators of nostalgia [17], as they both represent salient personal and collective life-markers that can, over time, be vigorously edited and generously gilded. In the case of sport, participant and spectator past events can evoke strong senses of nostalgia that help instil meaning, identity and stability triggered by current life uncertainties and/or anxieties [18]. Recollections of personal athletic/sporting achievements (genuine or otherwise) may not only ward off the existential threat of what the dreaded future might hold, but can also help bolster and positively reinforce an individual's self concept; as John McEnroe so eloquently put it: 'The older I get – the better I was'. To gaze back, albeit selectively, to a time and age when an individual was young, active, fit and healthy may act as a partial remedy to the fearful future, whilst also acting as a means of devaluing the present by comparing it with a superior past. Similarly, bygone sporting events experienced by the spectator take on a more noble and honest quality. For many, sport 'back then' represented the way the game was originally meant to be played; the players were real personalities whose abilities were 'God given' as opposed to the vital training and dietary regimes that the current 'manufactured' professionals adhere to. Such debasing of the present is not new as each generation juxtaposes a reconstructed past with an inferior present and an even poorer future [19]. Whether directed specifically at sport or at society as a whole, the protection and glorification of what has gone before is clearly not a new practice, primarily because it can help protect and reinforce an entire generation's self esteem. There is little doubt that the youth of today will, in years to come, fondly squint back to the simplicity and superiority of the first twenty years of the twenty-first century. As Pearson succinctly observes, 'The grumbling of older generations against the folly of the youth – in which the rising generation is accused of breaking with "timeless" traditions of the past – has all the appearance of being a "timeless" phenomenon itself' [20].

While participant and spectator events have long been acknowledged as instigators of nostalgic recollections, the role of volunteering at sport events as a catalyst for nostalgia is more recent [21]. Fairley and Kellett identified nostalgic recollections of volunteering at previous sport events, as well as nostalgic recollections of the history and tradition of the Olympic Games as motives for volunteerism.

Sport in all its guises can be an appropriate and accessible receptacle in which to place important personal and collective nostalgic recollections. There exists a strong emotional ownership with the great sporting feats of yesteryear. How truly exceptional those feats were is of course a matter of some conjecture, though the accuracy of the recollection appears less important than the bittersweet feeling(s) it evokes. Sport marketers have capitalized on the nostalgic appeal of sport by offering merchandise that encourages fans to be nostalgic. For example, baseball cards, halls of fame and sport museums provide a catalyst to remind individuals to focus on the past.

Tourism and Nostalgia

Tourism is also a great source of nostalgia, whether it be personal sentimental recollections of past vacations[22] or as a commodity sold by an industry, keen to profit from the past. Much like in sport, tourism experiences can be powerful sources of nostalgia; for they too can ward off, albeit palliatively, the negative feelings of both the present and future. Recalling idyllic childhood holidays of yesteryear can be a convenient and effective method in which to frame a safer, simpler and superior past. Predictably, the efficacious nature of tourism in generating powerful nostalgic experiences has not been lost on those responsible for managing and creating tourist attractions [23]. Heritage visiting in particular has been acknowledged as a potent generator of nostalgia [24]. Whether it be in the retrospective display of both architecture and subservience connected to past eras displayed at many hotels, or in the proliferation of historical attractions which are carefully designed and targeted at the hopeless nostalgic, the message is clear: there is future profit to be made from past events.

Sport Tourism and Nostalgia

The identification of nostalgia as being potentially an enlightening phenomenon in which to study sport tourism is relatively new [25], though it had been implicitly acknowledged earlier through the identification of sport tourism attractions some five years earlier [26]. The earliest reference to nostalgia sport tourism was Redmond [27]. It was, however Heather Gibson who took the lead from Redmond, first coined the term nostalgia sport tourism, explaining that it:

> involves visiting famous sports-related attractions. Visits to the sports halls of fame such as the Basketball Hall of Fame in Springfield, Massachusetts, sports museums such as the NASCAR Museum in Charlotte, North Carolina and famous sporting venues such as the Olympic Stadia in Barcelona and Atlanta fall into this category [28].

While the majority of research on sport tourism has followed Gibson's definition and thus focused on the visiting of sport halls of fame, museums and stadia, it has more recently been found that nostalgia has wider utility in the context of sport tourism. Specifically, it has been suggested that nostalgia sport tourism need not be generated solely from fixed monuments and artefacts, but also from social experience [29]. Thus, the definition of what constitutes 'nostalgia sport tourism' has broadened from that initially posited to include group-based social experience.

Given the size and breadth of this market it was suggested that nostalgia sport tourism be considered (along with active and event sport tourism) as one of the three major types of sport tourism. Chalip highlights that there is substantial overlap and convergence between the three categories, and emphasises the need for sport and destination marketers to consider each type in the mix of sport tourism opportunities offered [30]. While Chalip views this overlap as a challenge for sport and destination marketers, this tripartite split has come under criticism from Weed and Bull [31]. While travelling to actively participate in sport or to watch sport seem reasonably well-defined categories, Weed and Bull suggest that nostalgia sport tourism appears less distinct; relying heavily on the aforementioned first two categories. Whilst at first glance nostalgia sport tourism may seem to sit incongruously with the other two types it does illustrate the inter-relationship that all three categories have with each other (for further discussion see Gibson's essay, this volume). This should not be considered a problem or weakness but rather as an example of the fluidity and complexity of the subject, that to demarcate individuals in to one single category is unrealistic and restrictive. Moreover, it illustrates the growth of sport-based tourist attractions that rely heavily on the presentation and representation of sporting history. Weed and Bull further question the importance of nostalgia sport tourism. Specifically, they suggest that it is unlikely that tourists will travel in order to actively or passively engage in nostalgia sport tourism as their primary reason:

> in only the smallest minority of cases will a visit to a sports museum or hall of fame be the prime purpose of the trip involving an overnight stay. Such 'sports tourism pilgrims' (Gammon, 2002) do exist, but are far outnumbered in relation to tourism involving an overnight stay, by those visiting the area for other reasons [32].

This second criticism is very much dependent upon two issues: what constitutes a tourist, and what constitutes nostalgia in the context of sport tourism. First, definitional debates have a long history, especially those concerning the differentiation between tourist and excursionist [33]. Whilst it is accepted that such distinctions are useful in identifying visitor profiles, it must be taken on board that sport tourism is a broad church that includes both recreational and competitive sport – as well as the broader interpretations of tourism [34]. Consequently in the realms of sport tourism the excursionist is perceived as a certain type of tourist – but a tourist all the same. To dismiss the excursionist as inconsequential or unimportant because they do not include an overnight stay ignores the possible economic, environmental and social impacts they may generate [35]. Preliminary evidence suggests that excursionists are prepared to travel considerable distances in which to specifically visit sport-related attractions [36]. It may be a little ambitious to label them 'sport tourist pilgrims' but the fact that their journeys and motives were primarily driven by the expectation of visiting a sporting attraction suggests that they represent a fascinating and important segment of sport tourism.

Second, nostalgia sport tourism is not entirely concocted of sport-related attractions but represents a diverse and complex area of study that can be broadly categorized into nostalgia for place or artefact (object based) elements as well as nostalgia for social experience (group-based) events [37]. Object-based nostalgia refers to objects, music, scents, products and possessions which are responsible for triggering nostalgically affected recollections [38]. In contrast social nostalgia concerns stimuli attached to friends, family members, picnics, birthday parties, reunions and lost loved ones [39]. More specifically object-based nostalgia sport tourism can be further categorized into attractions and events associated with heritage, tours and cruises, fantasy and thematically-designed retail outlets. Unsurprisingly heritage represents the largest category of the five, including sport museums, halls of fame, retro heritage events and masters/seniors competitions. The sport museum has become, especially in North America and Europe, a significant contributor to the broader tourist attraction market. For example, FC Barcelona's football museum is the most visited museum in the city; boasting over a million visits annually, whilst the museums at Wimbledon (tennis) and at Lords (cricket) have become serious players in London's tourism attraction portfolio. In addition there are ambitious plans for a National Sports Museum in New York (opening in 2006) that aims to be:

> the first world-class, interactive sports museum dedicated to the celebration of all sports and their significance in our lives and culture. As a 'nation's definitive museum of sports', The National Sports Museum is the place for domestic and international visitors to experience the thrill and history of sports throughout the ages and throughout the world [40].

Sport museums can act as persuasive instigators of nostalgia primarily because they tend not to just honour the elite but also display any miscellaneous heritage connected to the sport – no matter how seemingly trivial [41]. Consequently, they can trigger both collective and personal recollections tied to individuals' specific biographies [42]. Similarly, sport halls of fame are both a consequence and instigator of nostalgia, though the artefacts displayed in these attractions differ from those shown in museums, in that they are a celebration specifically aimed at the exceptional and/or gifted. The operative word here is 'fame', as to qualify entry as an exhibit an individual must have achieved positive notoriety within their sport. For the visitor, especially the ardent fan, the experience of such attractions has been equated to the quasi-religious; where heroes are immortalized through the enshrinement of their records and personal sporting paraphernalia. Such historical framing can both fuel and confirm the nostalgic tendencies of those who choose to visit.

In practice, although there are clear differences between the two attractions it is not uncommon that each will incorporate characteristics of the other. For example it is not unusual for museums to include mini halls of fame amongst their other exhibits (National Football Museum: Preston, UK) and for halls of fame to integrate regular museum exhibits (National Baseball Hall of Fame: Cooperstown, US). It is also important to point out that these types of attractions, like many others, are not solely designed for the ardent nostalgic but will appeal to a range of visitor whose interest may be grounded more in history, education, entertainment or simple curiosity.

The nostalgic event on the other hand offers a far more uncompromising nostalgic take on the past. Here, in some vain attempt to confirm a golden sporting era(s), the past is resurrected and celebrated by bringing back the 'great' players so they can perform for us once again. The popularity and success of both European and American golf senior tours is testament to this phenomena which undoubtedly feeds off all forms of nostalgia; both lived and unlived [43]. Similarly, the relatively recent success of the Delta tour of champions, which celebrates seniors tennis, illustrates that there is a growing market who want to see John McEnroe, Jim Courier, Pat Cash *et al.* play one more time. They do not hit the ball as hard and are clearly not as athletic as they used to be, but this seems not to detract from the 'authenticity' of the event, even the use of the latest technology (rackets, shoes, et cetera) is overlooked and excused. In contrast, The Heritage Classic event in Canada in 2003 offered a more themed and romantic interpretation of the past that generated collective nostalgia, focusing primarily on Canadian identity. The event involved two hockey matches (both between the Edmonton Oilers and the Montreal Canadiens); one a National Hockey League match and the other a game made up from retired national hockey heroes from the 1970s and 1980s (referred to as the Heritage Classic Megastars Alumni Game). The main draw was the appearance of Wayne Gretzky who was to lead the Oilers wearing the famous No. 99 jersey, a sight not seen for fifteen years. To add extra romance both games were to be played outdoors on a rink constructed within the Commonwealth stadium in Edmonton in front of approximately 60,000 spectators. Holding the event outdoors was ostensibly designed to celebrate the 86th anniversary of the founding of the NHL, but in reality it was a method of framing the spectacle in the past; reminding both players and spectators of the way the game was originally played – and perhaps the way it still should be [44].

The stadium tour has also been alluded to as an example of nostalgia-based sport tourism[45] as they (stadia) represent huge emotional receptacles that contain in their very fabric the highs and lows of every matched played. For many, the tour represents an opportunity to be reminded of the great deeds of yesterday while offering an 'authentic' insight into areas otherwise preserved for the very privileged [46]. In some cases a stadium tour will also incorporate a visit to an on-site museum and as a consequence (for example, The Nou Camp in Barcelona) be accepted as an integral part of a city's tourist attractions [47].

Themed sport cruises on the other hand offer the chance for customers to play sport (for example, golf) at a number of destinations. The experience is given a nostalgic twist when back on board ship the passengers have the opportunity to be entertained and/or coached by famous golf ex-professionals. Alternatively sport-themed retail outlets such as those associated with bars and restaurants create a nostalgic environment through related memorabilia, music and the playing of old sports footage.

Sport fantasy camps illustrate the complex and multi-faceted nature of nostalgia whilst also acting as a bridge between experiences which are object-based and those which are socially determined (the social perspective will be explained in more detail in the following section). They offer a chance for the average person to directly interact with important sports people, places and events from their pasts. The appeal of such camps can be identified through the promotion of one or more of the following:[48]

- *The Event*: where the interest lies in the desire to be connected with a famous event, such as the World Series, the Olympic Games and the Tour de France.
- *The Stadia/Facility*: where the aspiration is to experience a famous and/or meaningful sporting location, (for example, Fenway Park, Shea Stadium) or in the opportunity to train at the same facility as the professionals.

- *The Team/Club*: usually connected with a supporter or fan of a club or of a particular famous team (for example, Chicago Cubs, Cincinatti Reds, and Detroit Tigers).
- *The Players and Coaches*: where the fantasy revolves around famous individuals. These can be either players from the past or famous coaches.
- *The Sport*: motivation is generated through a general interest in the chosen sport as a whole. These camps tend to focus primarily upon educating the attendees, so usually (though not exclusively) attract younger individuals who wish to improve their game. The fantasy here, revolves around the opportunity to play and to be coached in your favourite sport along with other like-minded enthusiasts. They are not fantasy camps in the traditional sense, that is, they rarely deal with the history of the game.

The object-based nostalgia emanates from the place and facilities in which the camps are based. Moreover the ex-professionals may also be determined (though this is unclear) as objects – or perhaps living, moving artefacts – by the fee-paying campers. However the social experience is a key feature of the fantasy camp [49]. This can be seen from both the attendees' perspective, who have an opportunity to relive and concoct personal and collective sporting memories amongst like-minded individuals, and from the ex-players themselves who have a chance to meet up with old comrades and become once again the stars they once were – or should have been [50]. In addition it is not unusual for participants to return annually to the same camps, meet up with 'old' friends and reflect upon previous deeds and experiences. Indeed, the camaraderie and intensity of the friendships made at these events may add up to what can only be described as the ultimate liminoid experience

Nostalgia for Liminoid Space

Just as nostalgic recollections of sport and/or tourism act as a catalyst for sport tourism, so to do the memories of direct experience within smaller social groups. In other words, the memories that generate nostalgia sport tourism are not limited to experiences of sport, or to experiences of place, but can be generated by the unique social experience that sport and tourism engender. As sport provides a fundamentally social experience for many [51], it is not surprising that individuals derive memories from the smaller social groups to which they belong. While the previous section considered nostalgia relating primarily to sport and tourism, the following section describes nostalgia generated from social experience.

Studies of sport participants [52], sport fans [53], and sport volunteers[54] in the context of tourism have noted that the camaraderie that develops and exists between likeminded participants is an important part of the experience (see Green and Jones' essay, this volume). In a participant context, Green and Chalip suggest that the sense of community developed among individuals who travel to a sport event transgresses everyday social norms [55]. In particular, Green and Chalip found that participants at a women's football tournament abandoned traditional elements of social class including feminine stereotypes. This abandonment was enabled in part by a strong sense of community among participants, and the opportunity to parade and celebrate a shared subcultural identity. The process by which individuals momentarily neglect their differences, accept each other as social equals, and come to behave as a unitary group exhibits what Turner[56] refers to as a liminoid state of communitas, and what Norbeck[57] refers to as a rite of reversal. This 'state of being' is referred to as a rite of reversal as the structured, institutionalized roles and statuses of everyday life are reversed to a state of anti-structure where individuals act as social equals.

A similar transgression of social norms, and heightened sense of community has been found in studies of sport fans who travel to follow a team both domestically [58], and internationally [59]. In understanding the behaviour of fans who travel to follow an Australian professional football team, Fairley found that fans accept each other as social equals, which is enabled by a shared sense of identity based on team fanship. Individuals are often cognizant of this transgression and are conscious of how their behaviour differs from that of everyday life, with participants continually noting the diversity within the social groups in which they travel. For example, one participant in Fairley's study[60] stated that the group was comprised of 'people from all walks of life, with all different interests'. The same participant went on to say that 'you don't get much of that [diversity] these days', thus implying a desire to relive or return to the type of social experience that is enabled by a liminoid state. This is also true in an international setting. For example, Giulianotti notes a similar transgression in describing those who travel overseas to follow a team; however he interprets the behaviour in terms of carnival:

> An appropriate way of depicting the culture of these international fans overseas is through the metaphor of 'carnival'. Behaviourally, carnivals are characterized by an abandonment to hedonistic excess, and the psycho-social jouissance of eating, drinking, singing, joking, swearing, wearing of stylized attire and costumes, engaging in elaborate social interplay, enjoying sexual activity, etc. For these indulgences to occur, carnival can only function as 'authorized transgression': 'the modern mass-carnival is limited in space: it is reserved for certain places, certain streets, or framed by the television screen' (Eco 1984, 6) [61].

Similar to Turner's liminoid state of communitas [62], the notion of carnival brings along with it a collapse of social boundaries related to every-day roles such as social class, ethnicity and religion [63]. This transgression of social class has also been identified as part of the tourism experience [64]. In describing the nature of a tourism experience, Graburn refers to individuals leaving their lives to participate in non-ordinary experiences [65]. Sport and tourism are conducive to such conditions as both provide settings where individuals are able to escape the pressures of every-day life. As sport provides a salient aspect of identity for many it provides an opportunity to escape from the stresses and pressures of everyday life to celebrate a common identity. Given the structured nature of society, the improbability of tourist behaviour in a non-tourist setting [66], and the improbability of sport fan behaviour in a non-sport setting provokes nostalgia for these experiences. The focus of nostalgic recollections born from sport tourism is not necessarily related to the actual activities engaged in, but to the state of communitas that the experience engenders.

The absence of traditional status markers during a state of communitas provides a setting where socializing and socialization are made easier. In discussing the experiences of sport event participants who travelled to compete in a women's football tournament, Green and Chalip emphasize how shared subcultural identity and the transgression of social norms that occurs eases attempts at starting conversation with other participants [67]. Similarly, Fairley notes that group formation and the socialization of new members into a group is made easier by the liminoid state with which the trip takes place [68]. Various authors have highlighted a similar dissolution of social norms and breakdown of social barriers that expedite group formation during a tourist experience. For example, Gorman discusses how the transgression of social norms can hasten the process of group formation [69]. Nostalgic recollections play an integral role in the socializing and socialization that occurs. When repeat trip participants come together to take part in a trip, memories of past trips become particularly salient. As repeat participants discuss these memories and share stories with each other and also with new participants, newcomers become aware of the activities that are important to the group to the point where they are able to relive past trips vicariously. In fact, by the end of the trip newcomers can vividly recount stories of past trips that they were not on, and often use these stories as a basis to compare the trip that they had. Not only does the telling of stories and folklore from previous trips act to socialize newcomers into the group, but it also acts to reinforce and strengthen the nostalgic recollections in the minds of the group members that are telling the stories to other existing group members. While united by shared experience, group members each hold fragments of the overall experience in their minds. When the group reunites and memories of past trips are shared, the fragments coalesce to reinforce and remind of the collective memory of the group. Quiroga suggests a number of characteristics of group tours that influence the formation and development of the group, including a shared setting for development, proximity of members during the trip, the brief existence of the group, shared circumstances and shared experience [70]. She suggests that group interaction, group size, the physical environment and group cohesion are key aspects affecting the formation and development of tour groups. One key aspect is the physical environment provided by the mode of travel to the destination.

The sport tourism experience separates participants in both time and space from their everyday lives. The nostalgic recollections are not limited to what takes place at the destination, or at the sport venue. Of equal importance is the travel experience itself and the group interaction that occurs en route to the destination. Although bus travel is not the most comfortable, time efficient, or in some cases, economical mode of travel, it is the preferred choice for various sport tourism groups. The bus is the preferred travel mode choice, not for its aesthetic appeal, but because it allows group members to socialize and share stories of past trips. It provides a setting that separates group members from non-group members. The actual travel experience itself can play a central role in the nostalgic recollections of a sport tourism experience – especially when travel is by means of a closed medium such as a bus.

Even though participants hold memories of how uncomfortable, or time consuming, bus travel was on previous trips, the social experience that it provides is valued enough to outweigh the negative aspects. Fairley found that bus travel in particular provides a closed medium which expedites the formation and closeness of a group [71]. Bus travel has been shown to be particularly conducive to group formation and interaction as it isolates the group from the outside world. This is consistent with work on group processes suggesting that situations resulting in crisis, confrontation, danger and/or group isolation expedite group formation [72]. Gorman found that the isolation in both time and space of a tour group on a bus acts to break down traditional boundaries such as social status, race and ethnicity [73]. Thus, the bus helps facilitate the liminoid state of communitas. Other authors have asserted that coach tours act as a closed medium, which provide physical and psychological distance between participants and the outside world [74]. Likewise, Schmidt identifies the temporary role that a tourist adopts through separating his or her every-day life in terms of 'role segregation' and labels the tourist as 'a marginal person, temporarily without affiliation, except to tourism' [75]. This is not strictly the case for sport tourists, as in many instances sport tourists maintain their affiliation with at least one aspect of the sport they represent during the trip, as well as to tourism. The sport tourist's personal identity is masked by anonymity; however, the identity as a supporter of a particular team, or as a participant in a particular event, is still salient. Sport tourists are therefore able to parade and celebrate a common identity during the sport tourism experience, which is aided by the fact that it occurs in liminoid space. Nostalgia is not just for the *sport* or the *travel* experience, but also for the camaraderie and friendships that occurs in liminoid space.

Nostalgia sport tourism is not limited to those who travel to participate in or watch sport. Nostalgia has been noted as an important motive for a volunteer sport tourism experience [76]. While nostalgia relating to visiting the home of the modern Olympic Games was noted as a motive (or a form of pilgrimage) for travelling to volunteer at the Athens Olympic Games, what was more important was nostalgia relating to previous experiences of volunteering at the Sydney Olympic Games. In particular, nostalgic recollections of experiences had during the Sydney Olympic Games were key in deciding to travel to volunteer at the Athens Olympic Games. Similar to the work on sport fans and sport participants, the experiences that individuals sought to relive were not about sport, or place, but about the camaraderie and friendship that the experience provided. Thus, further emphasizing the focus of nostalgic recollections is not necessarily related to the actual activities engaged in, but to the camaraderie and sense of community that the experience engenders.

Just as nostalgic memories related to the subcultural identity of a sport or particular team act as a catalyst for sport tourism, so to do the memories of experiences that individuals experience within smaller social groups. As sport provides a fundamentally social experience for many, it is not surprising that individuals derive memories from the smaller social groups to which they belong.

Conclusions and Future Directions

The definition of nostalgia sport tourism has expanded considerably over the last decade. The original conceptualization of nostalgia sport tourism included travel to sport halls of fames, museums and to see historical artefacts. This definition has recently been extended. Nostalgia's role in sport tourism not only includes travel to place or artefact, but extends to an individual's own experiences with sport, and to group-based social experiences which sport and tourism provide. In this essay nostalgia sport tourism is considered congruously with travel to visit place and artefact, travel to participate in physical activity, travel to watch sport, and travel to volunteer at sport events. The interrelationships between nostalgia and these different forms of tourism should be further studied.

Research in sport tourism continues to highlight the key role that nostalgia plays in sport tourism. The use of qualitative research in further describing nostalgia's relationship with sport tourism is crucial. The recent studies that have highlighted nostalgia's extensive role in sport tourism were not purposefully designed to examine nostalgia, but rather, nostalgia emerged as a key variable. This demonstrates the critical need for qualitative research to gain a more in-depth understanding of nostalgia's multiple roles in sport tourism.

Future research should explore the multiple roles that nostalgia plays in different sport tourism contexts. It would also be useful to identify elements that act as a catalyst for nostalgic recollections related to sport tourism – whether they be related to sport, tourism, social experience, or some other variable. While memories of the liminoid state that the sport tourism experience provides has been identified as a key point of reference for nostalgic recollection, further research should examine the different aspects of sport tourism experience that facilitate liminoid space. Sport and destination marketers should use nostalgic appeals to encourage individuals to participate in sport tourism experiences – to visit a sport related place or artefact, to participate in physical activity, to attend a sport event, or to volunteer at a sport event.

Notes

[1] C. Wright, *A Short History of the Shadows* (New York: Farrar, Straus and Giroux), 36.
[2] M.B. Holbrook, 'Nostalgia and Consumption Preferences: Some Emerging Patterns of Consumer Tastes', *Journal of Consumer Research*, 20, 2 (1993), 245–56.
[3] M.B. Holbrook and R.M. Schindler, 'Echoes of the Dear Departed Past: Some Work in Progress on Nostalgia', *Advances in Consumer Research*, 18 (1991), 330–3.
[4] S. Fairley, 'In Search of Relived Social Experience: Group-Based Nostalgia Sport Tourism', *Journal of Sport Management*, 17, 3 (2003), 288.
[5] F. Davis, *Yearning for Yesterday: A Sociology of Nostalgia* (New York: Free Press, 1979).

[6] R.W. Belk, 'The Role of Possessions in Constructing and Maintaining a Sense of Past', *Advances in Consumer Research*, 17 (1990), 674.

[7] C.R. Barcley and P. DeCooke, 'Ordinary Everyday Memory: Some of the Things of Which Selves are Made', in U. Neisser and E. Winogard (eds), *Remembering Reconsidered: Ecological and Traditional Approaches to the Study of Memory* (New York: Cambridge University Press, 1988), pp.91–125; Belk, 'The Role of Possessions in Constructing and Maintaining a Sense of Past'.

[8] H. Tajfel and J.C. Turner, 'The Social Identity Theory of Intergroup Behavior', in W.G. Austin and S. Worchel (eds), *The Psychology of Intergroup Relations* (Chicago: Nelson Hall, 1986), pp.7–24.

[9] C.B. Bhattacharya, H. Rao and M.A. Glynn, 'Understanding the Bond of Identification: An Investigation of its Correlates Among Art Museum Members', *Journal of Marketing*, 59, 4 (1995), 46–57.

[10] G.H. Mead, *The Philosophy of the Present* (LaSalle, IL: Open Court, 1932), p.12.

[11] D.R. Unruh, 'The Nature of Social Worlds', *Pacific Sociological Review*, 23, 3 (1980), 271–96.

[12] P. Donnelly, 'Towards a Definition of Sport Subcultures', in M. Hart and S. Birrell (eds), *Sport in the Sociocultural Process* (Dubuque, Iowa: Wm. C Brown Company Publishers, 1981), p.570.

[13] R.C. Aden, 'Nostalgic Communication as Temporal Escape: "When it was a Game" Reconstruction of a Baseball Work Community', *Western Journal of Communication*, 59, 1 (1995), 20–38.

[14] Belk, 'The Role of Possessions in Constructing and Maintaining a Sense of Past'.

[15] Aden, 'Nostalgic Communication as Temporal Escape'.

[16] Belk, 'The Role of Possessions in Constructing and Maintaining a Sense of Past'.

[17] G. Dann, 'Tourism: The Nostalgia Industry of the Future', in W. Theobald (ed.), *Global Tourism* (Oxford: Butterworth Heinemann, 1994), pp.55–67; J.F. Healey, 'An Exploration of the Relationship Between Memory and Sport', *Sociology of Sport Journal*, 8, 3 (1991), 213–27.

[18] C. Sedikides, T. Wildscut and D. Baden, 'Nostalgia. Conceptual Issues and Existential Functions', in J. Greenberg (ed.), *Handbook of Experimental Existential Psychology* (New York: Guilford Publications, 2004), pp.200–14; H.S. Schwartz, 'Anti-social Actions of Committed Organizational Participants: An Existential Psychoanalytic Perspective', *Organization Studies*, 8, 4 (1987), 327–40.

[19] G. Pearson, *Hooligan. A History of Respectable Fears* (London: Macmillan, 1983), pp.219–20.

[20] Ibid.

[21] S. Fairley and P. Kellett, 'Volunteering Abroad: Motives for Travel to Volunteer at the Athens Olympic Games', Manuscript submitted for publication: *Journal of Sport Management* (2005).

[22] F. Inglis, *The Delicious History of the Holiday* (London: Routledge, 2000).

[23] Dann, 'Tourism: The Nostalgia Industry of the Future'; R. Hewison, *The Heritage Industry: Britain in a Climate of Decline* (London: Methuen, 1987); D. MacCannell, *The Tourist: A New Theory of the Leisure Class* (London: University of California Press, 1999).

[24] C. Goulding, 'Heritage, Nostalgia, and the "Grey Consumer"', *Journal of Marketing Practice: Applied Marketing Science*, 5, 6 (1999), 177–99; C. Goulding, 'Romancing the Past: Heritage Visiting and the Nostalgic Consumer', *Psychology & Marketing*, 18, 6 (2001), 565–92.

[25] H. Gibson, 'Sport Tourism: A Critical Analysis of Research', *Sport Management Review*, 1, 1 (1998), 45–76.

[26] Sport Tourism International Council, 'Categories of Sport Tourism', *Journal of Sport Tourism*, 1, 1 (1993), 1–2.

[27] G. Redmond, 'A Plethora of Shrines: Sport in the Museum and the Hall of Fame', *Quest*, 19, Winter (1973), 41–8.

[28] H. Gibson, 'Active Sport Tourism, Who Participates?' *Leisure Studies*, 17, 2 (1998), 157.

[29] Fairley, 'In Search of Relived Social Experience'.

[30] L.Chalip, 'Sport and Tourism: Capitalising on the Linkage', in D. Kluka and G. Schilling (eds), *The Business of Sport* (Oxford, UK: Meyer & Meyer, 2001), pp.77–89.

[31] M.Weed and C. Bull, *Sports Tourism: Participants, Policy and Providers* (Oxford: Elsevier, 2004), p.70.

[32] Ibid.

[33] C. Goeldner and J.R.B. Ritchie, *Tourism: Principles, Practices and Philosophies* (New York: John Wiley & Sons, 2003).

[34] H. Gibson, *Sport Management: Contemporary Sport Management* (Leeds: Human Kinetics, 2004); T. Hinch and J. Higham, *Sport Tourism Development* (Clevedon: Channel View Publications, 2004).

[35] H. Gibson, C. Willming and A. Holdnak, 'Small-scale Event Sport Tourism: College Sport as a Tourist Attraction', *Tourism Management*, 24, 2 (2003), 181–90; H. Nogawa, Y. Yamaguchi and Y. Hagi, 'An Empirical Research Study on Japanese Sport Tourism in Sport-for-All Events: Case studies of a Single-Night Event and a Multiple-Night Event', *Journal of Travel Research*, 35, 2 (1996), 46–54.

[36] S. Gammon and V. Fear, *Sport Tourism Development and the Stadia Tour: 'For the Real Millennium Experience'* (Pre Olympic Conference, Rhodes: Org. STIC, 2004); A. Wilson, 'The Relationship Between Consumer Role Socialization and Nostalgia Sport Tourism: A Symbolic Interactionist Perspective' (unpublished Masters thesis, University of Florida, Gainesville, 2004).

[37] Fairley, 'In Search of Relived Social Experience', 288.

[38] S.L. Holak and W.J. Havlena, 'Feelings, Fantasies, and Memories: An Examination of the Emotional Components of Nostalgia', *Journal of Business Research*, 42 (1998), 217–26; C. Sedikides, T. Wildscut and D. Baden, 'Nostalgia. Conceptual Issues and Existential Functions', in J. Greenberg (ed.), *Handbook of Experimental Existential Psychology* (New York: Guilford Publications, 2004), pp.200–14.

[39] Ibid.

[40] The National Sports Museum, http://www.thesportsmuseum.com/. (Accessed Oct. 2004.)

[41] S. Gammon, 'Fantasy, Nostalgia and The Pursuit of What Never Was', in S. Gammon and J. Kurtzman (eds), *Sport Tourism: Principles and Practice* (Eastbourne: LSA Publications, 2002), pp.61–71; G. Redmond, 'A Plethora of Shrines: Sport in the Museum and the Hall of Fame', *Quest*, 19, Winter (1973), 41–8.

[42] E. Snyder, 'Sociology of Nostalgia: Halls of Fame and Museums in America', *Sociology of Sport Journal*, 8, 3 (1991), 228–38.

[43] Holbrook, 'Nostalgia and Consumption Preferences: Some Emerging Patterns of Consumer Tastes'.

[44] Gammon, 'Fantasy, Nostalgia and The Pursuit of What Never Was'; K. Yorio, 'On Frozen Pond', *Sporting News*, 227, 48 (2003), 20–2.

[45] Gibson, *Sport Management: Contemporary Sport Management*.

[46] C. Gaffney and J. Bale, 'Sensing the Stadium', in P. Vertinsky and J. Bale (eds), *Sites of Sport: Space, Place, Experience* (London: Routledge, 2004), pp.25–39; S. Gammon, 'Secular Pilgrimage and Sport Tourism', in B. Ritchie and D. Adair (eds), *Sport Tourism: Interrelationships, Impacts and Issues* (Clevedon: Channel View Publications, 2004), pp.30–46.

[47] G. John, 'Stadia and Tourism', in S. Gammon, S. Kurtzman and J. Kurtzman (eds), *Sport Tourism: Principles and Practice* (Eastbourne: LSA Publications, 2002), pp.53–61.

[48] Gammon, 'Fantasy, Nostalgia and The Pursuit of What Never Was'.

[49] H. Schlossberg, *Sports Marketing* (Oxford: Blackwell, 1996).

[50] Gammon, 'Fantasy, Nostalgia and The Pursuit of What Never Was'.

[51] D.B. Holt, 'How Consumers Consume: A Typology of Consumption Practices', *Journal of Consumer Research*, 22, 1 (1995), 1–16.

[52] B.C. Green and L. Chalip, 'Sport Tourism as the Celebration of Subculture', *Annals of Tourism Research*, 25, 2 (1998), 275–91.

[53] Fairley, 'In Search of Relived Social Experience'; R. Giulianotti, 'Football and the Politics of Carnival: An Ethnographic Study of Scotland Football Fans in Sweden', *International Review for the Sociology of Sport*, 30, 2 (1995), 191–223.

[54] Fairley and Kellett, 'Volunteering Abroad: Motives for Travel to Volunteer at the Athens Olympic Games'.

[55] Green and Chalip, 'Sport Tourism as the Celebration of Subculture'.

[56] V. Turner, *Dramas, Fields, and Metaphors* (New York: Cornell University Press, 1974).

[57] E. Norbeck, 'The Anthropological Study of Human Play', *Rice University Studies*, 60, 3 (1974), 1–8.

[58] Fairley, 'In Search of Relived Social Experience'.

[59] Giulianotti, 'Football and the Politics of Carnival'.

[60] Fairley, 'In Search of Relived Social Experience', 292.

[61] Giulianotti, 'Football and the Politics of Carnival', 194.

[62] Turner, *Dramas, Fields, and Metaphors*.

[63] R. Da Matta, *Carnival, Rogues and Heroes* (Notre Dame: University of Notre Dame Press, 1991); V.V. Ivanov, 'The Semiotic Theory of Carnival as the Inversion of Bipolar Opposites', in T.A. Sebeok (ed.), *Carnival!* (New York: Mouton, 1984), pp.11–35.

[64] B. Gorman, 'Seven Days, Five Countries: The Making of a Group', *Urban Life*, 7, 4 (1979), 469–91; J.W. Lett Jr., 'Ludic and Liminoid Aspects of Charter Yacht Tourism in the Caribbean', *Annals of Tourism Research*, 10, 1 (1983), 35–56.

[65] N. Graburn, 'Tourism: The Sacred Journey', in V. Smith (ed.), *Hosts and Guests: The Anthropology of Tourism* (Philadelphia: University of Pennsylvania Press, 1977), pp.17–31.

[66] Lett, 'Ludic and Liminoid Aspects of Charter Yacht Tourism in the Caribbean'.

[67] Green and Chalip, 'Sport Tourism as the Celebration of Subculture'.

[68] Fairley, 'In Search of Relived Social Experience'.

[69] Gorman, 'Seven Days, Five Countries: The Making of a Group'.

[70] I. Quiroga, 'Characteristics of Package Tours in Europe', *Annals of Tourism Research*, 17, 2 (1990), 185–207.

[71] Fairley, 'In Search of Relived Social Experience'.

[72] G.C. Homans, *The Human Group* (New York: Harcourt, Brace & World, 1950).

[73] Gorman, 'Seven Days, Five Countries: The Making of a Group'.

[74] C. Holloway, 'The Guided Tour: A Sociological Approach', *Annals of Tourism Research*, 8, 3 (1981), 377–402; Quiroga, 'Characteristics of Package Tours in Europe'.

[75] C. Schmidt, 'The Guided Tour: Insulated Adventure', *Urban Life*, 7, 4 (1979), 459.

[76] Fairley and Kellett, 'Volunteering Abroad: Motives for Travel to Volunteer at the Athens Olympic Games'.

Towards an Understanding of 'Why Sport Tourists Do What They Do'

Heather Gibson

Introduction

One of the ongoing issues in sport tourism research has been how to define and classify different types of sport tourism. The debate has generally centred on the dual concepts of passive and active involvement in sport-related travel, passive usually connoting watching sport and active referring to participating in sport [1]. Following Redmond's discussion about the growth in the popularity of sports-themed vacations such as visits to sports halls of fame and museums, fantasy camps and sports cruises, I suggested the possibility of a third form, that of nostalgia sport tourism [2]. In mainstream tourism, nostalgia has been increasingly used as a theme for destinations and marketing over the past ten years [3], and preliminary investigations in sport tourism suggest that nostalgia may be part of the experience for tourists (see Fairley and Gammon's essay) [4].

Nonetheless, while the debate on what defines sport tourism seems to have abated somewhat, the more important issue remains: how do we understand and explain sport tourism? The quest to provide some direction to resolve this issue was

Heather J. Gibson, Department of Tourism, Recreation and Sport Management, University of Florida, PO Box 118208, Gainesville, FL 32608-8208, USA. Correspondence to: hgibson@hhp.ulf.edu the impetus for this collection. In this essay I will tackle part of this issue and suggest a framework for classifying and understanding why people choose different forms of sport tourism. The suggested framework draws upon role theory from sociology and its application in tourism studies in the form of tourist roles. I will also adopt an interdisciplinary perspective drawing upon social psychology in accounting for the role of motivation and life span and sociology in terms of understanding the influence of socio-cultural factors such as gender, race and social class on sport tourism choices.

Role Theory and Tourist Roles

Ralph Turner explained that a role is a collection of behaviours associated with a social status rather than a position, and that individuals enact roles rather than occupy them [5]. Role theory is largely located in sociology and is one of the oldest paradigms used to understand the workings of society, although as Gerhardt cautions [6], traditional conceptualisations of roles have been critiqued as conservative because they purport social conformity and the acceptance of social inequality. Certainly, early role theorists viewed society from a socially deterministic perspective with norms and behaviours located outside of the individual. As such, roles were regarded as a collection of behaviours that were both external and constraining to those enacting them [7]. For example, Linton suggested, 'a role includes the attitudes, values and behaviour ascribed by the society to any and all persons occupying this status' [8]. In contrast to this social fact approach to roles where the interaction between individuals and social structure is de-emphasized [9], a more interpretive approach to role theory has been developed and is of more utility in understanding leisure roles such as various forms of sport tourism, especially since the inherent nature of these roles is that they are chosen voluntarily.

With the growing recognition of the actor as an active agent in sociology, theorists have suggested that enacting a role may be more about consistency in behaviours rather than absolute conformity and that there are opportunities for individuals to incorporate some individuality into role enactment [10]. By integrating more psychological dimensions into understanding behaviour, Zurcher suggests that by conceptualising role enactment more as a process than conformity, it is possible to understand the relationship between role-playing and the development of identity [11]. Indeed, Goffman explained that behaviour is part of the person-role formula, which is not totally constrained or totally free [12]. The extent to which a role shapes an individual's behaviour may be related to the degree of involvement he or she has with that role. If an individual is highly involved in a role it is likely that the role is a major part of his or her identity. Similarly, low involvement with a role is likely to result in avoiding or downplaying it. This idea of involvement or specialization in a role will be revisited later in this essay, as it is a concept of particular utility to understanding leisure and tourism roles.

Zurcher's thesis regarding the idea of ephemeral roles is another perspective from role theory that has potential applications to understanding sport tourism behaviour [13]. Zurcher identified two components of self that are influential in role adoption: 'self as object', which is the part of the self that is most responsive to the influence of others in role selection, and 'self as process', which refers to the influence of the individual's own preferences regarding a role. Understanding why people choose to enact certain roles in relation to these components of self, Zurcher invoked Mills' concept of a vocabulary of motive, the idea that individuals develop justifications or reasons for enacting roles which they articulate to others [14]. Ultimately the vocabulary of motives becomes part of an individual's self-concept, and as such is viewed as an internalised vocabulary of motive. Thus, future role choices are usually consistent with these vocabularies and the roles individuals play have some level of cohesion, although not always as there are instances of role conflict [15].

Zurcher as a sociologist did not wholeheartedly dismiss the influence of power and social structure on role selection as he recognized that choices of roles might not be as voluntaristic as this explanation seems to suggest [16]; but his ideas endorse more action on the part of the individual in role selection than the social fact approach. He identified four aspects of role selection that should be considered when understanding why people enact the roles they do: a) the internalised vocabulary of motive which is routinely adapted to meet changing needs; b) the operating dominant role which is the set of behaviours currently central in a person's life. These roles are usually associated with statuses such as worker or family member and it is possible that individuals have two dominant roles that might conflict. It is generally assumed however, that most internalised vocabulary of motives will be satisfied by dominant role enactment. However, this satisfaction may not be complete and an individual may select new roles to fill these needs; c) each individual also holds a model dominant role. This role may be one that previously was the operating dominant role or it may be a fantasy or referent role. As such, it serves as a model for selecting new roles, or d) ephemeral roles. An ephemeral role is a temporary or peripheral role chosen by individuals to satisfy needs not met by the operating dominant role. In the ideal world, individuals should perceive the operating dominant role as the major source of satisfaction for their internalised vocabularies of motive; however, ephemeral roles provide ancillary satisfaction more akin to the familiar or fantasy model dominant roles. Thus, leisure or tourist roles can be conceptualised as ephemeral roles in that they are temporary or peripheral roles that provide individuals with the opportunity to satisfy different needs not met in their everyday lives. Indeed, Zurcher studied a group of friends who met weekly to play poker, noting that this leisure context was regarded as an ephemeral role for the participants [17]. Furthermore, as Wahlers and Etzel suggested in relation to touristic behaviour, that understanding tourist choices should be contextualised in a person's home environment, particularly the notion of lifestyle stimulation. Thus, they postulate, the need to escape from under-stimulating or over-stimulating situations may be the key for seeking facets not found in the home environment and as such may provide the impetus to choose certain vacation behaviours [18]. If we begin to understand leisure and tourism choices in relation to conceptions of the self and vocabularies of motive we can see that such choices are not merely haphazard but are grounded in underlying needs that certain sets of behaviour can fulfil or be perceived as being able to fulfil.

Tourist Roles

In tourism studies role theory has been applied to tourist classification schemes since the 1970s. Erik Cohen was one of the first to suggest that it is futile to look for one type of tourist and that different types of tourist exist [19]. Using the premise that a role is a collection of behaviours associated with a status, he identified four different tourist roles that can be distinguished by the degree of novelty and familiarity tourists enacting a particular role seek in their vacation behaviours. The four tourist roles are located on a continuum of familiarity to strangeness or novelty with organized mass tourists largely experiencing their vacations from within their 'environmental bubble of the familiar', to the independent mass tourists where the vacation experience is less pre-planned but still emphasizes familiarity; to the explorer where vacation activities involve more novelty, to the drifter where novel experiences predominate and they show a disdain for mass tourist behaviours.

Throughout the 1960s, this disdain for mass tourism experiences spawned the authenticity debate whereby academics discussed and continue to discuss the 'realness' or the authenticity of touristic experiences [20]. The relevance of this debate to our discussion is that Cohen not only suggested that there is more than one type of tourist, but that tourists are not all motivated by a search for authenticity [21]. Some are motivated by recreation and diversion. In 1979, he proposed that choices of tourist role should be understood in relation to the meaning that an experience has for the individual. His typology categorizes five modes of touristic experience distinguished by the degree to which travel is motivated by a 'quest for centre'. This idea of seeking qualities that are different from those present in everyday can be related back to Zurcher's proposition that individuals adopt ephemeral roles to satisfy needs not met by dominant roles [22]. Thus, in the vacation space where roles are generally chosen with a high degree of autonomy, we could hypothesize that whether a tourist chooses the recreational or diversionary modes or experimental or existential modes can be traced back to their internalised vocabulary of motive, and ultimately such an approach might be used to understand why individuals choose to take part in certain types of sport tourism.

Over time, various scholars have extended Cohen's work and have developed several tourist role typologies [23]. Pearce was the first to use quantitative methods to investigate the existence of travel-related roles. He tested the role differentiation and role interrelatedness of fifteen travel-related roles including the Jet-setter, Holiday-maker, the Overseas Student and the Traveller. He demonstrated the conceptual distinctiveness of each role by asking a sample of one hundred participants to evaluate each of the roles according to twenty travel-related behaviours. Employing fuzzy set analysis he found that not all of the roles were equally well defined [24]. The roles of Jet-setter and the Tourist were distinctive, whereas, roles such as the Traveller, Overseas

Student, and International Athlete were the least clearly defined. To test the interrelatedness of these roles, Pearce used multi-dimensional scaling analysis. He identified five clusters: Environmental Travel, High Contact Travel, Exploitative Travel, Pleasure First Travel and Spiritual Travel. The roles of Migrant and International Athlete were not classified as belonging to any of the five clusters. Yiannakis and Gibson hypothesized that some of the 'fuzziness' and difficulties classifying roles experienced by Pearce was due to the fact that his fifteen travel-related roles were not all tourist roles, that is, the distinction between leisure-based travel and travel for other reasons was not made [25].

In 1986, Andrew Yiannakis developed the first version of the Tourist Role Preference Scale (TRPS). He worked from the assumption, like Cohen and Smith before him, that tourism is a specialized form of leisure [26]. Hence, the roles contained in the TRPS operationalised different types of tourism in terms of the primary behaviours associated with a particular role. In subsequent work with Gibson and later with Murdy the TRPS was refined [27]. The TRPS has a number of applications to understanding sport tourism behaviour. Firstly, the TRPS contains a role that was originally labelled the sportlover and was later renamed the active sport tourist [28]. This role is comprised of the behaviours 'when I go on vacation I like to stay physically active and to take part in my favourite sports'. Secondly, like Pearce, Yiannakis and Gibson tested the distinctiveness and interrelatedness of the tourist roles in the TRPS. They identified three underlying dimensions that seem to distinguish different roles from each other. These dimensions were a preference for familiarity or novelty (similar to Cohen, 1972); a preference for structure or independence; and a preference for tranquillity or stimulation [29]. By analysing tourist roles in three-dimensional space it was possible to see what types of roles are distinct and which ones are similar to each other. This finding is valuable to understanding mainstream tourism in general as well as sport tourism in particular.

Ryan suggested that with increased diversity in the tourism industry the tourist is faced with an array of choices and it is conceivable that 'the tourist knowingly slips from role to role' [30]. However, Gibson and Yiannakis found that while individuals may choose to enact multiple roles on vacation, they appear to choose tourist roles with similar characteristics such as familiarity or structure or risk and they appear to adopt at least one dominant role [31]. By understanding the underlying dimensions behind tourist roles it is possible to identify the type of roles that cluster together. In sport tourism, this has particular utility as studies have shown that some sport tourists are uni-dimensional in their behaviours choosing to be purely active, event or nostalgia sport tourists, whereas others take part in two or more types of sport tourism during one trip. For example, an individual might be both an event and a nostalgia sport tourist if they choose to go on a stadium tour as well as attend a game at the stadium as part of a single trip. So in this instance is their trip classified as nostalgia or event sport tourism? Indeed, it is possible that sport tourists will also take part in other types of tourism while on a trip, in fact, communities hosting sport tourists hope that this will be the case [32]. Thus, it is conceivable that an event sport tourist will also visit an historical attraction or go shopping in a community hosting a particular sports event.

Furthermore, beyond the basic understanding of behavioural choice that such tourist role typologies provide, utilizing our knowledge about the underlying dimensions of such behaviour also has the potential to expand our understanding of sport tourism behaviour. For example, why do some golf tourists choose to vacation at a mass tourism destination like Walt Disney World, whereas others shun such a destination in favour of the more natural links style courses of the United Kingdom or Ireland? Why are some people more likely to attend mega events that involve long haul travel as in the case of the 2000 Olympic Games in Sydney or the jointly hosted World Cup Soccer tournament in Korea and Japan? Certainly, concepts such as cultural and psychological distance inherent in the dimensions underlying different tourist roles might shed light on this. For example, tourists who seek familiarity in destinations may be less likely to travel to mega events hosted by destinations such as China (Olympic Games 2008) or Korea (World Cup 2002) because they are perceived as more culturally dissimilar to their own countries than events held in mainland Europe, such as the 2006 World Cup Soccer to be held in Germany. Of course, this assumption is written from the view of the traditional western tourist-generating regions of North America and Europe and may change as more people from the Asian Pacific countries are predicted to travel internationally in the next decade [33].

Another application of the ideas of familiarity and novelty pertains to understanding which tourists are more and less risk adverse when it comes to travelling in uncertain times. Using Cohen's tourist role typology, Lepp and Gibson found that individuals who opted for the explorer or drifter roles (that is, preferred more novelty in their travels) were less averse to international travel than organized and independent mass tourists (that is, prefer more familiarity in their travels) [34]. Certainly, the organizers of sporting mega events have been forced to consider the possibility of terrorism at their events over the last few years. As such it will be important to understand which tourists will travel during uncertain times and which tourists are deterred by the threat of tourism as this will be crucial to the success of such events [35]. We also know that tourist role preference is related to life course stage, gender, social class and motivation and that risk aversion can differ with age [36].

Placing Tourist Roles into the Life Context

Cohen suggested that tourism motivation should be understood in terms of how it relates to individuals' long-term psychological needs and life plans [37]. In leisure studies the proposition that leisure choices are related to stage in the life course or family life cycle is well documented [38]. In tourism research the influence of life stage and family life cycle on travel choice has been observed over the years; however, until recently, systematic study of this relationship has been scarce. Indeed, Hall laments the lack of understanding that exists regarding why, for example, youth and early-adult adults are particularly attracted to adventure and sport tourism while older adults seem to prefer health travel. He argues 'substantial research still needs to be conducted on the pattern of involvement that an individual will have in specialized travel activities over time and the degree to which activity displacement occurs given various functions of age and education' [39].

Throughout the 1990s, various scholars investigated the influence of family life cycle stage on choice of tourist behaviour [40]. Lawson used a modernized family life cycle model to investigate the tourist behaviours of international visitors to New Zealand. He found that over the eight stages of the family life cycle that the amount of discretionary income and the presence and age of children were particularly influential. Thus, for example, vacations for young singles were characterized as being cheap, active and lengthy compared to full nest ones where the presence of small children and limited discretionary income resulted in 'relax with granny' type vacations. Lawson concluded that there appears to be a relationship between vacation activities and the age of the adults and children in the travel group. Similarly, Bojanic used a modernized family life cycle model to examine a sample of Americans who had travelled to Europe. He also found that vacation activities, presence and age of children, and discretionary income were influential in shaping vacation styles. For example, during the bachelor stage (young singles) vacations were characterized by adventure and excitement and a preference for nightlife and beaches. While, among married couples and couples with children, the availability of nightlife declined in significance and the type of accommodations and restaurants available in a destination became more important. Bojanic and Warnick also found that resorts could be segmented on the basis of family life cycle. In a study of a ski resort in New England (US) they found that most of the patrons were under the age of 45, married with children. Few skiers outside of this lifecycle stage visited the resort. They suggested that such a homogenous consumer base can be both an advantage and a disadvantage. The advantage lies in that services can be tailored to meet the needs of this segment and new clients who have similar backgrounds may be attracted to the resort. The disadvantage is that an image as a family destination may deter other potential consumers and if something happens to this one segment, then a resort can be left without any customers.

A critique of the studies discussed so far is that they are cross sectional in nature. While it is accepted that cross sectional data can be used to approximate life course and family life cycle, there have been some concerns that such studies explain age differences and not age change, and that cohort effects and socio-historical time are not accounted for [41]. Oppermann used longitudinal data to address some of these critiques [42]. Oppermann traced the life long travel patterns of German tourists. He found similar travel patterns across nine stages of the family life cycle as noted by Lawson and Bojanic. Discretionary income and the presence and age of children were generally related to choices of travel style. However, a cohort analysis of the data revealed that there might also be some generational differences in travel choices with younger people being more experienced travellers at an earlier age than previous generations. Indeed, some studies have adopted a generational analysis to examine the effects of cohort on travel choices [43]. While there appear to be some cohort differences, life stage appears to be a more powerful factor in determining vacation choice.

In a study that combined a family life cycle approach with motivation theory, Ryan examined the influence of life stage among a group of British tourists [44]. Using Beard and Ragheb's leisure motivation scale and a family life cycle analysis, Ryan found that life stage consistently emerged as an important predictor of travel choice and that motivations for travel differed by age, marital status and social class. For example, married couples were more likely to seek relaxation in a vacation than non-married people who were motivated by social needs, while the addition of motivation theory into a family life cycle analysis of travel behaviour furthers our understanding of travel behaviour. However, even when a modernized family life cycle model is used, the relevance of family life cycle models in societies where the diversity of family types is pervasive has been questioned and some scholars have suggested that a life cycle perspective that accounts for individuals' socio-psychological needs, the context of their lives and the society in which they live might be more appropriate. Since 1988, in my work with Yiannakis, we have framed our work on patterns of change and stability in tourist role preference on Levinson *et al.*'s model of the adult life cycle [45]. We have found that there appear to be three overall patterns in tourist role preference over the life course, with preference for some roles decreasing with age (roles characterized by physicality, risk and thrill), preference for some roles increasing over the life course (roles characterized by culture, history and familiarity), and some roles varying in their popularity over the life course (roles such as the independent mass tourist).

Studies of sport participation over the life course tend to show a decline in active participation with age [46]. Likewise in our study of the active sport tourist role over the life course we found that preference for this role was less popular among older individuals [47], although participation in active sport tourism did not disappear entirely. We hypothesized that this may be related to continued participation in golf tourism among individuals, particularly men in late adulthood. Moreover, recent studies on participation in amateur sports competitions such as the Master's or Senior Games show that there is an avid group of middle-aged and older athletes who travel to take part in these events [48]. Preliminary findings from these studies suggest that a range of reasons including competition, social belongingness and enjoyment motivates these active sport tourists. Placing participation in sport tourism within a life span context allows us to understand both the social, as well as the psychological, aspects of aging. In using a Levinsonian framework [49], we were able to link preference for different tourist roles to socio-psychological needs [50]. In relation to the active sport tourist role for men, in our study participation in active sport tourism appeared to be related to a combination of satisfied and unsatisfied needs. The unsatisfied needs included the need for play, sexual needs and home and family. Whereas they reported that their needs for clear goals and control over their lives were satisfied. For female active sport tourists, the combined effects of unsatisfied needs related to health, need for control and sexual needs with satisfied needs for home and family and escaping the everyday appeared to underlie their choice of vacation behaviour. Using a form of time series analysis called ARIMA (autoregressive integrated moving average) we found that the cross correlation functions appear to suggest that socio-psychological needs are 'leading indicators' of tourist role preference and, as such, support the contention that to understand sport tourism behaviour we need to address both social and psychological factors.

Motivation and Tourism

It has long been recognized that travel provides individuals with opportunities to satisfy a variety of socio-psychological needs. Indeed, such a supposition supports Zurcher's thesis that individuals choose ephemeral roles to satisfy needs not met by their everyday roles [51]. Moreover, as noted previously, Wahlers and Etzel found that individuals choose vacation environments which match their optimal level of stimulation, often compensating for the lack of stimulation or over stimulation in their everyday lives [52]. There has been a range of work on tourism and motivation over the years, although perhaps the most widely-cited study is Crompton's [53]. He identified seven socio-psychological motives or push factors, including escape and relaxation, and two cultural motives or pull factors as being pertinent to travel choices. He postulated that one of the common misconceptions in the tourism industry is that potential tourists are influenced in their travel choices by the attributes of a destination or what he and Dann call pull factors [54], when in fact, push factors or, socio-psychological needs may be more important, an idea that has a long history in social psychology.

Psychologists such as Murray and Maslow have long postulated that behaviour is a function of needs; indeed, much of their work has provided the theoretical foundation for studies that have investigated the relationship between leisure or tourism and need satisfaction [55]. A third motivation model that of Berlyne' concept of optimal level of stimulation has also guided work in leisure and tourism [56]. All of these theories are based on the supposition that motives or needs rooted in the basic physiological and socio-psychological needs underpin all behaviour. Moreover, these needs are not static; they rise and fall over time and as such may explain why the same person chooses to engage in different behaviours at different times. If this idea is related back to tourist role preference, understanding the needs that are associated with certain roles may provide greater insights into sport tourism behaviour and choices. For example, Pearce and Caltabiano applied Maslow's theory to a study of tourism experiences [57]. They found that vacation satisfaction was associated with the degree to which the needs for self-actualisation, belongingness and physiology were met by the experience, whereas individuals who were dissatisfied with their vacations tended to report unsatisfied primary needs such as safety and security. The authors linked Maslow's needs hierarchy to travel experience and proposed that more experienced travellers might be more apt to be motivated by higher order needs than less experienced travellers. In refining this idea of a travel career, Pearce used the analogy of a ladder whereby tourists move up the ladder as they become more experienced travellers and were thus likely to be motivated by higher order needs such as belongingness, self-esteem and self-actualisation [58].

Involvement or Specialization in an Activity

While the travel career ladder (TCL) has been the subject of much debate and refinement, in 1995 Pearce suggested conceptualising it within a life span model [59]. Certainly, the idea of linking needs, previous travel experience and life stage to touristic behaviour and destination choices makes conceptual sense. Holden applied the TCL to understand the dynamic nature of motivation among skiers and snowboarders [60]. He used the TCL as an indicator of skill level and experience in snowboarding and skiing. Holden found that advanced skiers and snowboarders were motivated by thrills and self-esteem, whereas those with intermediate level skills reported that the social aspects of the sports were more important. Invoking the idea that level of experience in a sport or as a tourist is related to differences in motivation is analogous to studies that have incorporated various conceptions of involvement, specialization or skilled consumption into their explanations of leisure, tourism and sport behaviour. Similar to Holden, Richards found that advanced level skiers sought challenging attributes in the ski destinations they selected, whereas less experienced skiers focused more on type of accommodation and price. Richard's study was framed in Gratton's concept of skilled consumption, which postulates that more skilled participants in a sport will seek a certain level of challenge to meet their skill level and if they do not meet this challenge then they are likely to be bored and dissatisfied with their vacation experience [61].

This discussion on skill level and involvement is also related to other concepts used in leisure, sport and tourism research to understand different participation patterns. The theory of consumer involvement originating in social psychology and consumer behaviour has been applied to studies of tourism, outdoor recreation, and sport tourism, among others [62]. The supposition behind these studies is that as level of involvement in an activity grows, then patterns of behaviour such as purchasing of equipment, frequency of participation and motivations will change. A similar theory is that of recreation specialization which posits that as an individual's experience in an activity increases then they will move from a general participant to a specialist and as a result their consumption behaviours and identification with the activity will also change [63]. Stebbins' concept of serious leisure further develops these ideas of involvement, career and identification with an activity [64]. Stebbins posits that participation in an activity can constitute a major source of identity for an individual and subsequently this will reinforce his or her behavioural choices in other areas of their lives.

This brings us full circle in support of Goffman's idea of the person-role formula outlined at the beginning of this essay [65]. Goffman posits that the degree to which an individual is involved in a role will shape his or her identity accordingly. Thus, individuals who are highly involved in a role will use it as a major source of identity and conceivably, as the literature discussed in this section shows, will be differently motivated to take part in various activities. Thus, as Crandall argued, while motivation theories can help us understand behaviour, in our case sport tourism behaviour, motivation is complex and it is not merely a matter of matching needs to behaviours [66]. We need to recognize the interactive nature of motivation, role, life stage and social structure. There has already been some discussion about the role of motivation in the sport tourism literature. Gammon and Robinson suggest that sport tourists can be distinguished by the extent to which sport is the primary or secondary reason for their trip, sport tourists being those where sport is primary and tourism sportists where it is secondary [67]. Again, the level of involvement in a sport may be linked to these different motivation patterns. In a study of nostalgia sport tourists Wilson found that the common tourist motivations of escape, spending time with family and novelty, were more important than nostalgia in shaping their travel decisions, although for men nostalgia was found to be more of an important motive for their trip than for women [68]. Similarly, adopting a gender differences approach, McGehee *et al.* investigated the influence of gender on tourist motivation [69]. They found that women were more likely to be motivated by culture, opportunities for family bonding and prestige, while men placed more importance on sports and adventure. This idea of gender difference in motivations lends further support to my contention that we need to address the interplay between sociology and social psychology to further our understanding of sport tourist behaviours.

The Influence of Social Structure: Gender, Class and Race

Gender

In sport sociology there is a substantial body of work documenting the participation and non-participation patterns of girls and women in sport. Like tourism, much of the early work used role theory to frame the analysis. For example, Greendorfer and Lewko focused on differences in gender role socialization to explain the different participation patterns of males and females in sport [70]. Role conflict was another angle taken to explain non-participation, the idea being that participation in sport roles conflicted with traditional expectations associated with female roles [71]. Gerhardt's caution about the conservative nature of role theory can be observed in the change of focus in sport sociology during the 1980s [72].

Using critical theories, researchers such as Birrell and Richter, Cole, and Hargreaves, showed how gender role socialization tends to marginalize girls' and women's participation in sport [73]. While, girls' and women's participation in sport and physical activity has increased in the US since the passage of Title IX in the 1970s, (federal legislation mandating equal access to sport in terms of funding, facilities, equipment et cetera in organizations receiving government funding), the values and attitudes that suggest that some sports are more acceptable for females than others is still pervasive [74]. For example, Scratton *et al.* found that women's participation in a team sport such as soccer still tends to be discouraged and disparaged [75]. Women are confined to the fitness activities such as aerobics [76]. The common conclusion from these studies is that the dominant value system sanctions participation in the 'traditionally feminine' sports and activities and restricts access to arenas where financial rewards and other benefits of participation accrue, such as access to business networking through playing golf.

A consistent theme in tourism research is that men and women tend to travel differently [77]. For example, McGehee *et al.* found that women preferred spending time with family and cultural experiences on vacation, whereas men sought opportunities for sport and adventure [78]. These findings are supported by the literature on family decision-making and vacations. In trips where men are the primary planner, sports and physical activity tend to be emphasised [79]. Indeed, in a study of nostalgia sport tourists visiting Wrigley Field, home of the Chicago Cubs Baseball team, Wilson found that men were more likely to report that the stadium and its history were primary pull factors behind their visit, whereas women were more motivated by the chances for family bonding likely to accrue from the trip [80].

There is little work on the gendered nature of sport tourism [81]. One form of sport tourism, skiing, has received the most attention. Williams and Lattey, and Williams and Fidgeon, examined women's participation and non-participation in skiing using a constraints perspective [82]. They found that intrapersonal constraints such as the sport being too dangerous or cold were the biggest barriers for women. Such attitudes are likely to be related to the wider gender role socialization practices pertaining to women's participation in sport, thus Shaw, Bonen and McCabe's recommendation, that socio-structural influences such as gender and race might be more powerful than constraints, should be heeded [83]. Indeed, skiing tends to be a very white (Caucasian) and middle-class pursuit, thus attention to the influence of race and class on sport tourism participation seems to be warranted [84].

Race

The study of the influence on race and sport has largely focused on the experiences of African Americans in the US, although this focus is gradually changing as the Hispanic population continues to grow [85]. While there is a large body of work on race and sport, in tourism studies the influence of race and ethnicity on travel and tourism has received little attention. Some studies have addressed the issue of discrimination [86]. The Travel Industry Association reports show that African Americans are quite active travellers, taking upwards of 70 million trips annually. Willming found that in relation to sport tourism, African Americans tended to be event sport tourists rather than active sport tourists. She also found that many of these event sport tourists had experienced discrimination in the course of their event attendance. The issue of discrimination and its effect on participation has received much attention in the field of leisure studies. For example, researchers have found that patterns of recreation participation are significantly influenced by the threat of discrimination, so much so that the wilderness remains overwhelmingly white [87]. Work in sport tourism has not addressed the issue of race and ethnicity as yet, the one exception being Hinch and Higham's work on the Arctic Winter Games in Canada, where the indigenous peoples use the games to showcase their culture [88].

Social Class

Another influence of social structure that has received little attention in sport tourism research is social class. In sport sociology and leisure studies, the influence of class has been examined, and topics such as the democratization of activities such as golf over the twentieth century, and the influence of class-based subculture on encouraging or inhibiting participation in certain activities has also been addressed [89]. I suggest that future work in sport tourism address the interactive effects of class, race and gender. This would not only increase our understanding of the influence of social structure on participation and move us beyond treating these dimensions as demographic variables in identifying the profile of a sport tourist, but also, by adopting more critical perspectives on class, race and gender from sociology, we could start addressing issues such as discrimination and exclusion which have largely been absent from our work [90].

Conclusion

In this essay I have proposed an interdisciplinary model drawing on concepts from sociology, social psychology and life span developmental psychology to try and understand why sport tourists choose certain types of behaviours. I have suggested that role theory and its applications in tourism studies could be used to not only classify different types of sport tourists, but to identify the underlying dimensions that are likely to accompany each classification. For example, if we look at one typology in sport tourism, that of Gammon and Robinson's sport tourist and tourism sportist, this classification is based on motivation, the extent to which sport is the primary purpose of the trip [91]. Conceivably, using statistics such as discriminant analysis or cluster analysis, it would be possible (with the appropriate independent variables) to identify other characteristics in addition to the primacy of sport as the purpose of a trip. For example, gender, life stage, class, race and ethnicity in addition to motivation might distinguish why some people are sport tourists and others are tourism sportists.

One could then ask the question, 'why would we need to know such information?' I have critiqued the state of the knowledge in sport tourism as being too dominated by profile work [92]. My suggestions above could easily be used to create more profiles. I suggest that we need to go further than merely identifying the characteristics of certain types of sport tourists and ask the question 'why do they do what they do?' This is where the different theoretical approaches I have suggested can be applied. For example, Zurcher's [93] ideas of ephemeral roles could be combined with

Goffman's [94] ideas about degree of involvement and we could understand how serious participation in a form of sport tourism might provide a major source of identity for individuals and provide them with a sense of community, which might be lacking in other parts of their lives, or compliments their everyday life roles. The work on participation in senior games or Masters Games underscores some of the benefits of participation for mid-life and older adults [95]. Using Stebbins' ideas of serious leisure, we might also trace a career of participation in a certain form of sport tourism [96]. Gibson *et al.* in a study of college football fans found that some of them not only travel miles to follow their team, but that being a University of Florida Gator fan is a major part of their lives and a source of identity and social capital [97].

Equally, more critical perspectives from sociology could be used to critique patterns of sport tourism participation on the basis of inequalities. Is it by chance that many forms of active sport tourism in particular are full of white, middle-class participants? Alternatively, such critical theories can be used to not only understand participation patterns, but also to identify unequal distributions of positive and negative impacts from hosting mega events or building sports infrastructure as a means of urban regeneration (see Silk and Amis's essay).

In terms of practical applications, having more of an understanding of why people do what they do can be used to provide better facilities and services and also to more effectively market products to potential clientele. Going beyond profiles that identify various demographic characteristics such as gender or age, and understanding the underlying dimensions behind these demographics, can provide powerful insights into potential target markets.

Thus, in this essay I have outlined some concepts that could be used to further our understanding of sport tourism participation patterns. An approach that incorporates motivation, social structure and the roles individuals play in their lives can provide a comprehensive understanding of behaviour. Obviously, there are other factors that could be added to this model; certainly some of the essays in this collection point to other potential influences such as nostalgia, subculture, satisfaction with service quality, or images held about particular destinations which can all play a part in understanding behaviour. The key point underpinning this essay and this collection is to encourage scholars to draw upon relevant conceptual models to help us better understand sport tourism.

Notes

[1] T. Hinch and J. Higham, 'Sport Tourism: A Framework for Research', *International Journal of Tourism Research*, 3, 1 (2001a), 45–58. C. Hall, 'Adventure, Sport and Health Tourism', in B. Weiler and C.M. Hall (eds), *Special Interest Tourism* (London: Bellhaven Press, 1992), pp.141–58. J. Standevan and P. De Knop, *Sport Tourism* (Champaign, IL: Human Kinetics, 1999).

[2] G. Redmond, 'Changing Styles of Sports Tourism: Industry/Consumer Interactions in Canada, the USA and Europe', in M. Sinclair and M. Stabler (eds), *The Tourism Industry: An*

International Analysis (Wallingford: CAB International, 1991), pp.107–20. H. Gibson, 'Sport Tourism: A Critical Analysis of Research', *Sport Management Review*, 1, 1 (1998a), 45–76.

[3] G. Dann, 'Tourism: The Nostalgia Industry of the Future', in W. Theobold (ed.), *Global Tourism: The Next Decade* (Oxford: Butterworth-Heinemann, 1994), pp.56–67. J. Urry, *The Tourist Gaze* (London: Sage, 1990).

[4] S. Fairley, 'In Search of Relived Social Experience: Group-based Nostalgia Sport Tourism', *Journal of Sport Management*, 17, 3 (2003), 284–304. A. Wilson, 'The Relationship Between Consumer Role Socialization and Nostalgia Sport Tourism: A Symbolic Interactionist Perspective' (unpublished Master's thesis, University of Florida, Gainesville, 2004).

[5] R. Turner, 'Role-taking, Role Standpoint, and Reference-group Behaviour', *American Journal of Sociology*, 61, September (1956), 316–28.

[6] U. Gerhardt, 'Toward a Critical Analysis of Role', *Social Problems*, 27, 5 (1980), 556–69.

[7] A. Birenbaum, 'Toward a Theory of Role Acquisition', *Sociological Theory*, 2 (1984), 315–28.

[8] R. Linton, *The Cultural Background of Personality* (New York: D Appleton Century Co., 1945), 113.

[9] E. Durkheim, *The Division of Labour in Society* (translated by George Simpson) (New York: Free Press, 1893/1960).

[10] Turner, 'Role-taking, Role Standpoint, and Reference-group Behaviour'.

[11] L. Zurcher, 'Role Selection: The Influence of Internalised Vocabularies of Motive', *Symbolic Interaction*, 2, 2 (1979), 45–62.

[12] E. Goffman, *Frame Analysis: An Essay on the Organisation of Experience* (New York: Harper & Row, 1974).

[13] Zurcher, 'Role Selection'.

[14] C. Mills, 'Situated Actions and Vocabularies of Motive', *American Sociological Review*, 5, 6 (1940), 904–13.

[15] R. Merton, 'The Role-set: Problems in Sociological Theory', *British Journal of Sociology*, 8, June (1957), 106–20. E. Van de Vliert, 'A Three Step Theory of Role Conflict Resolution', *Journal of Social Psychology*, 113 (1981), 77–83.

[16] Zurcher, 'Role Selection'.

[17] L. Zurcher, 'The "Friendly" Poker Game: A Study of an Ephemeral Role', *Social Forces*, 49, 2 (1970), 173–86.

[18] R. Wahlers and M. Etzel, 'Vacation Preference as a Manifestation of Optimal Stimulation and Lifestyle Experience', *Journal of Leisure Research*, 17, 4 (1985), 283–95. S. Iso-Ahola, 'Toward a Social Psychology of Recreational Travel', *Leisure Studies*, 2, 1 (1983), 45–56.

[19] E. Cohen, 'Toward a Sociology of International Tourism', *Social Research*, 39, 1 (1972), 164–82. E. Cohen, 'Who is a Tourist?: A Conceptual Clarification', *Sociological Review*, 22, 4 (1974), 527–55.

[20] D. Boorstin, *The Image: A Guide to Pseudo-Events in America* (New York: Harper & Row, 1961). D. MacCannell, *The Tourist: A New Theory of the Leisure Class* (New York: Schocken Books, 1976).

[21] E. Cohen, 'A Phenomenology of Tourist Experiences', *Sociology*, 13, 2 (1979), 179–201.

[22] Zurcher, 'Role Selection'.

[23] P. Pearce, *The Social Psychology of Tourist Behaviour* (Oxford, UK: Pergamon, 1982). P. Pearce, 'A Systematic Comparison of Travel-related Roles', *Human Relations*, 38, 11 (1985), 1001–1011. C. Mo, D. Howard and M. Havitz, 'Testing an International Tourist Role Typology', *Annals of Tourism Research*, 20, 2 (1993), 319–35. A. Yiannakis, *The Ephemeral Role of the Tourist: Some Correlates of Tourist Role Preference*. Paper presented at the NASSS Conference, Las Vegas, Nevada, Oct. 1986. A. Yiannakis and H. Gibson, 'Roles Tourists Play', *Annals of Tourism Research*, 19, 2 (1992), 287–303.

[24] M. Smithson, 'Notes on Fuzzy Set Analysis' (unpublished manuscript, Department of Behavioural Sciences, James Cook University, 1980).

[25] Yiannakis and Gibson, 'Roles Tourists Play'.

[26] Yiannakis, *The Ephemeral Role of the Tourist*. Cohen, 'Toward a Sociology of International Tourism'. V. Smith (ed.), *Hosts and Guests: The Anthropology of Tourism* (Philadelphia, PA: University of Pennsylvania Press, 1977).

[27] H. Gibson, 'Tourist Roles: Stability and Change Over the Life Cycle' (unpublished Master's thesis, University of Connecticut, Storrs, 1989). H. Gibson, 'Some Predictors of Tourist Role Preference for Men and Women over the Adult Life Course' (unpublished Doctoral Dissertation, University of Connecticut, Storrs, 1994). A. Yiannakis and H. Gibson, *Tourist Role Preference and Need Satisfaction: Some Continuities and Discontinuities over the Life Course.* Paper presented at the Leisure Studies Association Conference, Brighton, England, 29 June–3 July 1988. Yiannakis and Gibson, 'Roles Tourists Play'. J. Murdy, 'Predicting Tourist Roles Across The Life Course' (unpublished Doctoral Dissertation, University of Connecticut, Storrs, 2001).

[28] H. Gibson and A. Yiannakis, 'Tourist Roles: Needs and the Life Course', *Annals of Tourism Research*, 29, 2 (2002), 358–83.

[29] Pearce, 'A Systematic Comparison of Travel-related Roles'. Yiannakis and Gibson, 'Roles Tourists Play'. Cohen, 'Toward a Sociology of International Tourism'.

[30] C. Ryan, *The Tourist Experience: A New Introduction* (London: Cassell, 1997), p.41.

[31] Gibson and Yiannakis, 'Tourist Roles: Needs and the Life Course'.

[32] H. Gibson, C. Willming and A. Holdnak, 'Small-scale Event Sport Tourism: College Sport as a Tourist Attraction', *Tourism Management*, 24 (2003), 181–90. J. Higham and T. Hinch, 'Sport, Space and Time: Effects of the Otago Highlanders' Franchise on Tourism', *Journal of Sport Management*, 17 (2003), 235–57.

[33] C. Goeldner and J.R.B. Ritchie, *Tourism: Principles, Practices and Philosophies* (New York: John Wiley & Sons, 2003), p.560.

[34] Cohen, 'Toward a Sociology of International Tourism'. A. Lepp and H. Gibson, 'Tourist Roles, Perceived Risk and International Tourism', *Annals of Tourism Research*, 30, 3 (2003), 606–24.

[35] N. Kim and L. Chalip, 'Why Travel to the FIFA World Cup?', *Tourism Management*, 25, 695–707. K. Toohey, T. Taylor and C. Lee, 'The FIFA World Cup 2002: The Effects of Terrorism on Sport Tourists', *Journal of Sport Tourism*, 8, 3 (2003), 167–85.

[36] E. Cohen, 'The Sociology of Tourism: Approaches, Issues and Findings', *Annual Review of Sociology*, 10 (1984), 373–92. Gibson, 'Tourist Roles: Stability and Change Over the Life Cycle'. Gibson, 'Some Predictors of Tourist Role Preference for Men and Women over the Adult Life Course'. Yiannakis and Gibson, *Tourist Role Preference and Need Satisfaction: Some Continuities and Discontinuities over the Life Course*. Gibson and Yiannakis, 'Tourist Roles: Needs and the Life Course'. H. Gibson, 'Thrill Seeking vacations: A Lifespan Perspective', *Loisir et Societe/Society and Leisure*, 19, 2, 2 (1996), 439–58.

[37] Cohen, 'The Sociology of Tourism: Approaches, Issues and Findings'.

[38] J. Kelly, *Leisure* (Englewood Cliffs, NJ: Prentice-Hall, 1982). D. Kleiber and J. Kelly, 'Leisure, Socialization and the Life Cycle', in S. Iso-Ahola (ed.), *Social Psychological Perspectives on Leisure and Recreation* (Springfield, IL: Charles C. Thomas, 1980), pp.91–138. S. Parker, *The Sociology of Leisure* (London,: George Allen Unwin, 1976). R. Rapoport and R. Rapoport, *Leisure and the Family Life Cycle* (London: Routledge and Kegan Paul, 1975).

[39] Hall, 'Adventure, Sport and Health Tourism', p.152.

[40] R. Lawson, 'Patterns of Tourist Expenditure and Types of Vacation Across the Family Life Cycle'. *Journal of Travel Research*, 29, Spring (1991), 12–18. D. Bojanic, 'A Look at a Modernized Family Life Cycle and Overseas Travel', *Journal of Travel and Tourism Marketing*, 1, 1 (1992), 61–79. D. Bojanic and R. Warnick, 'Segmenting the Market for Winter Vacations', *Journal of Travel and Tourism Marketing*, 4, 4 (1995), 85–95. D. Fodness, 'The Impact of Family Life Cycle on the Vacation Decision-making Process', *Journal of Travel Research*, 31, 3 (1992),

8–13. M. Oppermann, 'Family Life Cycle and Cohort Effects: A Study of Travel Patterns of German Residents', *Journal of Travel and Tourism Marketing*, 4, 1 (1995a), 23–44. M. Oppermann, 'Travel Life Cycle', *Annals of Tourism Research*, 22, 3 (1995b), 535–52. M. Oppermann, 'Travel Life Cycles – A Multi-temporal Perspective of Changing Travel Patterns', *Journal of Travel and Tourism Marketing*, 4, 3 (1995c), 101–109.

[41] E. Babbie, *The Practice of Social Research* (7th edition) (Belmont, CA: Wadsworth Publishing Co, 1995). V. Freysinger, 'Life Span and Life Course Perspective on Leisure', In E. Jackson and T. Burton (eds), *Leisure Studies: Prospects for the Twenty-first Century* (State College, PA: Venture Publishing, 1999), pp.253–70.

[42] Oppermann, 'Family Life Cycle and Cohort Effects: A Study of Travel Patterns of German Residents'. Oppermann, 'Travel Life Cycle'. Oppermann, 'Travel Life Cycles – A Multi-temporal Perspective of Changing Travel Patterns'. Lawson, 'Patterns of Tourist Expenditure and Types of Vacation Across the Family Life Cycle'. Bojanic, 'A Look at a Modernized Family Life Cycle and Overseas Travel'.

[43] R. Warnick, 'Domestic Travel: Back to the future – The Impact of an Ageing US Population on Domestic Travel Trends', in *The Annual Review of Travel* (New York: American Express Travel Related Services, 1993), pp.73–90. L. Pennington-Gray, J. Fridgen and D. Stynes, 'Cohort Segmentation: An Application to Tourism', *Leisure Sciences*, 25, 4 (2003) 341–62.

[44] C. Ryan, 'Islands, Beaches and Life-stage Marketing', in M. Conlin and T. Baum (eds), *Island Tourism: Management Principles and Practice* (New York: John Wiley and Sons, 1995), pp.79–93. J. Beard and M. Ragheb, 'Measuring Leisure Motivation', *Journal of Leisure Research*, 15, 3 (1983), 219–28.

[45] D. Levinson, C. Darrow, E. Klein, N. Levinson and B. McKee, *The Seasons of a Man's Life* (New York: Knopf, 1978). D. Levinson, *The Seasons of a Woman's Life* (New York: Knopf, 1996). Gibson, 'Tourist Roles: Stability and Change Over the Life Cycle'. Gibson, 'Some Predictors of Tourist Role Preference for Men and Women over the Adult Life Course'. Yiannakis and Gibson, *Tourist Role Preference and Need Satisfaction: Some Continuities and Discontinuities over the Life Course*. Gibson and Yiannakis, 'Tourist Roles: Needs and the Adult Life Course'. Gibson, 'Thrill Seeking vacations: A Lifespan Perspective'.

[46] B. McPherson, 'Sport Participation Across the Life Cycle: A Review of the Literature and Suggestions for Future Research', *Sociology of Sport Journal*, 1, 3 (1984), 213–30.

[47] H. Gibson, S. Attle and A. Yiannakis, 'Segmenting the Sport Tourist Market: A Lifespan Perspective', *Journal of Vacation Marketing*, 4, 1 (1998), 52–64. Gibson and Yiannakis, 'Tourist Roles: Needs and the Adult Life Course'.

[48] R. Dionigi, 'Leisure and Identity Management in Later Life: Understanding Competitive Sport Participation among Older Adults', *World Leisure* 44, 3 (2002), 4–15. H. Gibson, K. Kensinger and C. Ashton-Shaeffer, *Senior Games: Docile Bodies or Resignified Subjectivities*. Paper presented at the 2004 Pre Olympic Congress, Thessalonkiki, Greece, 6–12 Aug. 2004. B. Trauer, C. Ryan and T. Lockyer, 'The South Pacific Masters' Games – Competitor Involvement and Games Development: Implications for Management and Tourism', *Journal of Sport Tourism*, 8, 4 (2003), 270–83.

[49] Levinson, Darrow, Klein, Levinson and McKee, *The Seasons of a Man's Life*. Levinson, *The Seasons of a Woman's Life*. Gibson, 'Tourist Roles: Stability and Change Over the Life Cycle'. Gibson, 'Some Predictors of Tourist Role Preference for Men and Women over the Adult Life Course'. Yiannakis and Gibson, *Tourist Role Preference and Need Satisfaction: Some Continuities and Discontinuities over the Life Course*. Gibson and Yiannakis, 'Tourist Roles: Needs and the Adult Life Course'. Gibson, 'Thrill Seeking vacations: A Lifespan Perspective'.

[50] Gibson and Yiannakis, 'Tourist Roles: Needs and the Adult Life Course'.

[51] Zurcher, 'Role Selection'.

[52] Wahlers and Etzel, 'Vacation Preference as a Manifestation of Optimal Stimulation and Lifestyle Experience'.

[53] J. Crompton, 'Motivations for Pleasure Vacation', *Annals of Tourism Research*, 6, 4 (1979), 408–24.

[54] G. Dann, 'Anomie, Ego-enhancement and Tourism', *Annals of Tourism Research*, 4, 4 (1977), 184–94.

[55] H. Murray, *Exploration and Personality* (New York: Oxford University Press, 1938). A. Maslow, 'A Theory of Human Motivation', *Psychological Review*, 50 (1943), 370–96. J. Lounsbury and J. Polik, 'Leisure Needs and Vacation Satisfaction', *Leisure Sciences*, 14, 2 (1992), 105–19. G. Romsa, P. Bondy and M. Blenman, 'Modeling Retiree's Life Satisfaction Levels: The Role of Recreational, Life Cycle and Socio-environmental Elements', *Journal of Leisure Research*, 17, 1 (1985), 29–39. C. Ryan and I. Glendon, 'Application of Leisure Motivation Scale to Tourism', *Annals of Tourism Research*, 25, 1 (1998), 169–84.

[56] D. Berlyne, *Conflict, Arousal and Curiosity* (New York: McGraw-Hill Inc., 1960). Iso-Ahola, 'Toward a Social Psychology of Recreational Travel'. Wahlers and Etzel, 'Vacation Preference as a Manifestation of Optimal Stimulation and Lifestyle Experience'.

[57] P. Pearce and M. Caltabiano, 'Inferring Travel Motivation from Travelers' Experience', *Journal of Travel Research*, 22, 2 (1983), 16–20. Maslow, 'A Theory of Human Motivation'.

[58] P. Pearce, *The Ulysses Factor: Evaluating Visitors in Tourist Settings* (New York: Springer-Verlag, 1988).

[59] C. Ryan, 'The Travel Career Ladder: An Appraisal', *Annals of Tourism Research*, 25, 4 (1998), 936–57. P. Pearce, 'Pleasure Travel Motivation', in R. McIntosh, C. Goeldner and J. Brent Ritchie (eds), *Tourism: Principles, Practices, Philosophies* (7th Edition) (New York: John Wiley and Sons, Inc, 1995), pp.165–90.

[60] A. Holden, 'Understanding Skier's Motivation using Pearce's "Travel Career" Construct', *Annals of Tourism Research*, 26, 2 (1999), 435–57.

[61] G. Richards, 'Skilled Consumption and UK Ski Holidays', *Tourism Management*, 17, 1 (1996), 25–34. Holden, 'Understanding Skier's Motivation using Pearce's "Travel Career" Construct'. C. Gratton, *Consumer Behaviour in Tourism: A Psycho-economic Approach*. Paper presented at the Tourism Research into the 1990s Conference, Durham, UK, Dec. 1990.

[62] H. Assael, *Consumer Behavior and Marketing Action* (3rd edn) (Boston, MA: Kent Publishing Company, 1987). P. Bloch, D. Sherrell and N. Ridgeway, 'Consumer Search: An Extended Framework', *Journal of Consumer Research*, 13, 1 (1986), 119–26. A. Broderick and R. Mueller, 'A Theoretical and Empirical Exegesis of the Consumer Involvement Construct: The Psychology of the Food Shopper', *Journal of Marketing Theory and Practice*, 7, 4 (1999), 97–108. X. Lehto, J. O'Leary and A. Morrison, 'The Effect of Prior Experience on Vacation Behaviour', *Annals of Tourism Research*, 31, 4 (2004), 801–18. K. Bricker and D. Kerstetter, 'Level of Specialization and Place Attachment: An Exploratory Study of White Water Recreation', *Leisure Sciences*, 22, 4 (2000), 233–57. H. Gibson, S. Williams and L. Pennington-Gray, 'Destination Images and Benefits Sought from an International Ski and Snowboard Trip: A Follow-up Study', in E. Fors (ed.), *Proceedings of the European Association for Sport Management Congress* (Stockholm, Sweden: College of Physical Education, 10–13 Sept. 2003), pp.167–9. N. McGehee, Y. Yoon and D. Cárdenas, 'Involvement and Travel for Recreational Runners in North Carolina', *Journal of Sport Management*, 17, 3 (2003), 305–24.

[63] H. Bryan, 'Leisure Value Systems and Recreational Specialization: The Case of Trout Fishermen', *Journal of Leisure Research*, 9, 3 (1977), 174–87. H. Bryan, 'Recreation Specialization Revisited', *Journal of Leisure Research*, 32, 1 (2000), 18–21.

[64] R. Stebbins, 'Serious Leisure: A Conceptual Statement', *Pacific Sociological Review*, 25, 2 (1982), 251–72. R. Stebbins, *Amateurs, Professionals, and Serious Leisure* (Montreal: McGill Queen's University Press, 1992).

[65] Goffman, *Frame Analysis: An Essay on the Organisation of Experience.*

[66] R. Crandall, 'Motivations for Leisure', *Journal of Leisure Research*, 12, 1 (1980), 45–54.

[67] S. Gammon and T. Robinson, 'Sport and Tourism: A Conceptual Framework', *Journal of Sport Tourism*, 8 (2003), 21–6.

[68] Wilson, 'The Relationship Between Consumer Role Socialization and Nostalgia Sport Tourism: A Symbolic Interactionist Perspective'.

[69] N.G. McGehee, L. Loker-Murphy and M. Uysal, 'The Australian International Pleasure Travel Market: Motivations from a Gendered Perspective', *The Journal of Tourism Studies*, 7, 1 (1996), 45–57.

[70] S. Greendorfer and J. Lewko, 'Role of Family Members in Sport Socialization of Children', *Research Quarterly*, 49, 2 (1978), 146–52.

[71] G. Sage and S. Loudermilk, 'The Female Athlete and Role Conflict', *Research Quarterly*, 50, 1 (1979), 88–96.

[72] Gerhardt, 'Toward a Critical Analysis of Role'.

[73] S. Birrell and D.M. Richter, 'Is a Diamond Forever? Feminist Transformations of Sport', *Women Studies International Forum*, 10, 4 (1987), 395–409. C. Cole, 'Resisting the Canon: Feminist Cultural Studies, Sport and Technologies of the Body', *Journal of Sport and Social Issues*, 17, 2 (1993), 77–97. J. Hargreaves, *Sporting Females: Critical Issues in the History and Sociology of Women's Sports* (London: Routledge, 1994).

[74] M.J. Kane, 'The Post Title IX Female Athlete in the Media', *Journal of Physical Education, Recreation and Dance*, 60 (March 1989), 58–62.

[75] S. Scraton, K. Fasting, G. Pfister and A. Brunuel, 'It's Still a Man's Game? The Experiences of Top-level European Women Footballers', *International Review for the Sociology of Sport*, 34, 2 (1999), 99–111.

[76] P. Markula, 'Firm but Shapely, Fit but Sexy, Strong but Thin: The Postmodern Aerobicizing Female Bodies', *Sociology of Sport Journal*, 12, 4 (1995), 424–53. J. Frederick, M. Havitz and S. Shaw, 'Social Comparison in Aerobic Exercise Classes: Propositions for Analyzing Motives and Participation', *Leisure Sciences*, 16, 3 (1994), 161–76.

[77] L.F. Anderson and M.A. Littrell, 'Souvenir Purchase Behavior of Women Tourists', *Annals of Tourism Research*, 22, 2 (1995), 328–48. K. Butler, 'Independence for Western Women through Tourism', *Annals of Tourism Research*, 22, 2 (1995), 487–9. F. Jordan and H. Gibson, *Whose Space is it Anyway? The Experiences of Solo Women Travellers.* Paper presented at the Royal Geographical Society, Institute of British Geographers Conference, Sussex, UK, Jan. 2000.

[78] McGehee, Loker-Murphy and Uysal, 'The Australian International Pleasure Travel Market: Motivations from a Gendered Perspective'.

[79] C. Nichols and D. Snepenger, 'Family Decision-making and Tourism Behaviour and Attitudes', *Journal of Travel Research*, Spring (1988), 2–6.

[80] Wilson, ' The Relationship Between Consumer Role Socialization and Nostalgia Sport Tourism: A Symbolic Interactionist Perspective'.

[81] B.C. Green and L. Chalip, 'Sport Tourism as the Celebration of Subculture', *Annals of Tourism Research*, 25, 2 (1998), 275–92.

[82] S. Hudson, 'The Segmentation of Potential Tourists: Constraint Differences between Men and Women', *Journal of Travel Research*, 38, 4 (2000), 363–9. P. Williams and C. Lattey, 'Skiing Constraints for Women', *Journal of Travel Research*, 32, 2 (1994), 21–5. P. Williams and P. Fidgeon, 'Addressing Participation Constraint: A Case Study of Potential Skiers', *Tourism Management*, 21 (2000), 379–93.

[83] S. Shaw, A. Bonen and J. McCabe, 'Do More Constraints Mean Less Leisure? Examining the Relationship between Constraints and Participation', *Journal of Leisure Research*, 23, 4 (1991), 286–300.

[84] A. Gilbert-Coleman, 'The Unbearable Whiteness of Skiing', *Pacific Historical Review*, 65, 4 (1996), 583–614. Williams and Fidgeon, 'Addressing Participation Constraint: A Case Study of Potential Skiers'.

[85] H. Edwards, *The Sociology of Sport* (Homewood, IL: Dorsey, 1973). A. Guttman, *Whole New Ball Game: An Interpretation of American Sports* (Chapel Hill, NC: University of North Carolina Press, 1988). J. Gramman, *Ethnicity, Race and Outdoor Recreation: A Review of Trends, Policy and Research* (Miscellaneous Paper R-96-1) (Vicksburg, MS: US Army Engineer Waterways Experiment Station, 1996).

[86] S.F. Philipp, 'Racial Differences in the Perceived Attractiveness of Tourism Destinations', *Journal of Leisure Research*, 25, 3 (1993), 290–305. S.F. Philipp, 'Race and Tourism Choice: A Legacy of Discrimination?', *Annals of Tourism Research*, 21, 3 (1994), 479–88. C. Willming, 'Leisure-Travel Behaviors of African Americans and Perceived Racial Discrimination' (unpublished Doctoral dissertation, University of Florida, Gainesville, 2001). TIA, *The Minority Traveler* (Washington, DC: Travel Industry Association of America, 2000).

[87] M. Floyd and J. Gramann, 'Perceptions of Discrimination in a Recreation Context', *Journal of Leisure Research*, 27, 2 (1995), 192–9. R.F. Washburne, 'Black Under-participation in Wildland Recreation: Alternative Explanations', *Leisure Sciences*, 1, 2 (1978), 175–89. P. West, 'The Tyranny of Metaphor: Interracial Relations, Minority Recreation and the Wildland-urban Interface', in W. Ewert, D. Chavez and A. Magill (eds), *Culture, Conflict and Communication in the Wildland-urban Interface* (Boulder, CO: Westview Press, 1993), pp.109–15.

[88] T. Hinch and J. Higham, *Sport, Culture and Tourism: The Arctic Winter Games*. Paper presented at the Leisure Studies Association Annual Conference, University of Luton, UK, 17–19 July 2001.

[89] P. Donnelly, 'Democratization Revisited: Seven Theses on the Democratization of Sport and Active Leisure', *Loisir et Societe/Society and Leisure*, 16, 2 (1993), 413–34. D. Wynne, 'Leisure, Lifestyle and the Construction of Social Position', *Leisure Studies*, 9, 1 (1990), 21–34.

[90] H. Gibson, 'Active Sport Tourism: Who Participates?', *Leisure Studies*, 17, 2 (1998), 155–70.

[91] Gammon and Robinson, 'Sport and Tourism: A Conceptual Framework'.

[92] H. Gibson, 'Moving Beyond the "what is and who" of Sport Tourism to Understanding "why"', *Journal of Sport Tourism*, 9, 3 (2004), 247–65.

[93] Zurcher, 'Role Selection'.

[94] Goffman, *Frame Analysis: An Essay on the Organisation of Experience*.

[95] Dionigi, 'Leisure and Identity Management in Later Life: Understanding Competitive Sport Participation among Older Adults'. Gibson, Kensinger and Ashton-Shaeffer, *Senior Games: Docile Bodies or Resignified Subjectivities*. Trauer, Ryan and Lockyer, 'The South Pacific Masters' Games – Competitor Involvement and Games Development: Implications for Management and Tourism'.

[96] Stebbins, 'Serious Leisure: A Conceptual Statement'. Stebbins, *Amateurs, Professionals, and Serious Leisure*.

[97] H. Gibson, C. Willming and A. Holdnak, '"We're Gators not just a Gator fan:" Serious Leisure, Social Identity and University of Florida Football', *Journal of Leisure Research*, 14, 4 (2002), 397–425.

Building Sport Event Tourism into the Destination Brand: Foundations for a General Theory

Laurence Chalip & Carla A. Costa

Introduction

Brand development and brand management have become core foci of modern marketing[1]. A strong brand is thought to add saliency to products and services, to impart perceptions of quality and value, and thereby to cultivate market share and customer loyalty[2]. Consequently, branding provides a focus for marketing – one that can be evaluated in terms of the degree to which marketing activities conserve or increase brand equity[3]. It is not surprising, therefore, that cities and regions are increasingly turning to brand agencies to help them formulate and communicate a coherent brand[4]. Maureen Atkinson, a senior partner with one such agency, commented, 'A brand is a type of shorthand for a product. With city branding, what you try to do is create that shorthand so that when people think of your city, they automatically think of what is best about it'[5].

Laurence Chalip, Department of Kinesiology and Health Education, The University of Texas at Austin, 1 University Station #D3700, Austin, Texas 78758, USA. Correspondence to: lchalip@mail.utexas.edu

Thus, a brand is more than the place name or logo; it refers to the overall impression that the destination creates in the minds of potential tourists, including its functional and symbolic elements. The brand encompasses the destination's physical attributes, services, attractions, name, logo, reputation, and the benefits that those provide the visitor. A recognizable brand facilitates a tourist's choice of destination because it encapsulates what the destination has to offer. Branding a city or a region in order to promote tourism requires that available attractions and activities be identified and, if necessary, augmented or enhanced in a manner that is consistent with the brand image that the destination seeks to convey[6].

Special events, particularly sport events, are being used by destination marketers with increasing frequency to enhance the host destination's brand[7]. Advocates of brand equity as a core marketing objective contend that destinations should only choose to host events that can contribute to the saliency or value of the destination's brand[8]. This is consistent with the attitudes of both destination and event marketers, who expect events to generate attention for the destination through advertising, publicity and word-of-mouth before, during and after the event has taken place[9]. Yet, event and destination marketers report that events are poorly used in destination branding, largely because the means and bases for building events into destination branding strategies are poorly understood[10].

This essay begins by examining the fundamental tenets of branding. It then describes the general principles for incorporating events into a destination branding strategy. It next considers the place of sport events relative to cultural events in the destination's event portfolio. It also considers the ways that sport events complement other sport attractions and activities at the destination. The essay concludes by suggesting future directions for theory, research and practice.

Building Events into Destination Branding

Although the words 'brand' and 'branding' are often found in tourism research, destination image (rather than destination brand) has commonly been the focus of tourism researchers. In fact, 'brand' and 'image' are rarely differentiated in tourism research, and are often used interchangeably. Conversely, in the marketing literature, the term 'image' is often associated with 'brand' and 'branding', but image and brand are not treated as synonymous. Rather, a brand's image is thought to be a component of its overall equity, and image building is one task in building a brand. However, even that relationship is misleading insomuch as the term 'image' is typically defined and operationalized differently in tourism research than it is by marketing researchers who study brands and brand equity. In order to explore the ways that events can be built into destination branding, it is therefore useful to begin by comparing destination image with destination brand.

Destination Image versus Destination Brand

Studies of destination image derive from the sense that image is a key factor in tourism development[11]. This makes intuitive sense. When a tourist is planning a holiday[12] or evaluating one already taken[13] it seems reasonable to expect that the tourist will have a mental image of the destinations that might be visited and destinations that have already been visited. Simple introspection of one's own travel planning and evaluation processes makes this notion appealing. Further, there is some support in consumer research for the expectation that consumers' images of products play a role in consumption choice[14].

Given the intuitive appeal of the notion that destinations invoke images, and of the expectation that those images can make a difference in tourist decision making, there has been a great deal of interest in measuring destination images. Several methods have been used to identify the relevant dimensions of destination image, including multidimensional scaling[15], repertory grid[16], mapping[17], correspondence analysis[18], adjective elicitation[19], and exploratory factor analysis[20]. The difficulty with each of these approaches is that the results depend on the stimuli chosen by the researcher. Even the same technique using different items or applied to different destinations can yield unique results. This makes it difficult to generalize results or to formulate cumulative theory. Consequently, there has been some effort to synthesize the various findings into a more general framework. One approach specifies the categories of image to be measured and then standardizes the techniques to be applied[21]. Another employs a taxonomy of measurement techniques recommended for particular image categories[22].

The effort to identify and model destination images has been inductive. Tourists' descriptors or ratings have been analysed *post hoc*; theory building has been *ex post facto* and minimal. There has, however, been some effort to import concepts from psychology to impose added structure. For example, it has been suggested that some image dimensions are cognitive (that is, those that describe objective aspects of the destination, such as the degree of its natural or built environment), while others are affective (that is, those that describe judgments about the destination, such as its convenience or value)[23]. It is argued that by differentiating types of dimensions, the differing psychological processes associated with affect versus cognition can then be invoked to generate expectations for how the different dimensions will affect tourist behaviour and choice.

The combination of multiple methods and inductive epistemologies has fostered identification of a wide array of destination image dimensions and characteristics. Many of these might not have been elicited if the nature and range of dimensions and characteristics had been constrained to those that could be derived deductively from *a priori* theory. On the other hand, the focus on image has not readily encompassed benefits[24] and values[25], and has consequently limited the marketing utility of resulting models.

In contrast, the study of brands has been grounded from the outset in models of consumer cognition that are derived from psychological theory[26]. The consumer is conceived as a rational actor who evaluates products in order to maximize the value (in economic jargon: 'utility') obtained from all goods and services purchased. Accordingly, affect is a consequence of the utility associated with a product, and utility derives from the consumer's (rational) evaluation of the product. Utility is grounded in the consumer's values and the benefits the consumer perceives the product to offer. One reason this approach is appealing to marketers is that it is consistent with fundamental economic tenets of consumer behaviour, which hold that consumers are rational utility maximizers. Cognitive psychology has been an appealing basis for exploring consumers' evaluations of products because it provides the requisite theory to map consumers' processes of judgment and choice. If consumer reasoning can be modelled, then marketers could have the knowledge necessary to affect consumers' judgments and choices.

Schema theory has served as the most fundamental psychological theory on which to found theories of brands[27]. A schema is a cognitive representation of expectations about a domain[28]. Destinations and sport events are both domains. According to schema theory, consumers' expectations about destinations and events will include suppositions about each – including the attributes, the level of those attributes, the importance of those attributes, and the variability of those attributes.

Schemas are thought to be hierarchically organized. The theory holds that consumers have a general schema for sport events and a general schema for destinations. At a more specific level, consumers have a schema for each sport event and for each destination. In the absence of specific information about a particular event or destination, expectations from the general schema can be used to render expectations for the particular case. When a new event or destination is encountered it is assimilated to the existing general schema if its characteristics are not strongly discrepant with the schema. Similarly, when new information about an event or destination is encountered it is assimilated to the existing event or destination schema if the information is not highly discrepant with the schema. On the other hand, if the event, destination or information is highly discrepant with a schema, then the discrepant example or information is accommodated as the schema is restructured to incorporate the example or information. This could require substantial reorganization of the schema, or it might merely require that a new subcategory be formed.

If one accepts the presupposition that it is heuristically useful to study consumers as if they were rational utility maximizers, then schema theory provides a useful basis for modelling consumer judgment and choice. Schema theory can be used to model expectations for a particular brand and the utilities associated with those expectations. Thus, the phrase 'brand image' refers to attributes, the benefits those attributes confer, and the utilities associated with those attributes given the consumer's values. Whether the dimensions inductively derived in destination image studies are suitable proxies for brand attributes is not clear, as the paradigm from which destination image dimensions derive is markedly different from the consumer psychology paradigm that grounds brand image studies. Nevertheless, destination attributes and destination image share the common objective that each seeks to be a representation of what is in the consumer's mind. In that sense, it is not unreasonable to expect that the two are related, even if they are not isomorphic. What the concept of destination brand offers that destination image does not is a more elaborated specification of the necessary relationships among attributes, benefits, values and choice. From the standpoint of endeavouring to model the effects of events on consumer perceptions of the destination, the brand concept has the distinct advantage that it is sufficiently well grounded theoretically for a reasoned analysis.

Destination Brands and Destination Branding

The destination's brand is not its name, logo, slogan or any other marketing device. Rather, these represent the brand. They are intended to invoke a brand image, which is a schema in the sense that it is a hierarchically related set of associations in memory. The schema consists of nodes that are connected through a network of associations. Each node is a piece of information stored in memory, and the number and strength of associations among nodes determines the schema's structure. Since some nodes may be present in more than one schema, it is possible for schemas to become associated with one another, and even for one schema to invoke another. The process by which nodes are activated when a schema is brought into working memory is called 'spreading activation'[29]. The activation of a node stimulates activation of associated nodes. Spreading activation favours nodes that are most closely associated with the source of activation. Destination branding consists of fostering spreading activation to nodes that the marketer most wants associated with the destination brand. To do so, the marketer first identifies the most desirable and relevant nodes, and then works to create and strengthen the associations among them. The desirability of particular nodes depends on: (1) the attributes that target market segments value (because of the benefits target market segments expect those attributes to bestow), and (2) the degree to which those nodes will favourably differentiate the destination from competing destinations.

To illustrate, consider Figure 1. The Figure depicts a hypothetical network of associations for two competing holiday destinations, the Costa del Sol (in southern Spain) and the Côte d'Azur (in southern France). In this example, the association network for each destination is equally complex – consisting of fourteen activated relationships. Both include sun, beaches, music, spas and yachting. The key point of differentiation is that the Costa del Sol is seen to offer a more exciting nightlife, and consequently more exhilaration, while the Côte d'Azur offers greater prestige as a consequence of its more glamorous nightlife and shopping.

So, let us consider how each destination might use an event to enhance or change its image among the market segment represented in the figure. Let's also consider how each destination might use an event to enhance its strategic position in that market. If either destination were to use an event to strengthen its brand image, it would choose one with a brand association network that includes one or more nodes comparable to those in the destination's association network. Thus, either destination would benefit by hosting a regatta or an event that features its sunny beaches, such as a triathlon. If the event were noticed by this target market, then the association between the destination and the relevant nodes (yachting, in the case of the regatta, or beaches and sun, in the case of the triathlon) would be strengthened. However, neither event would differentiate one

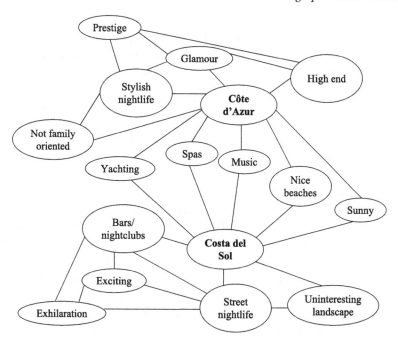

Figure 1 Hypothetical Brand Association Network for Two Competing Beach Destinations in South-western Mediterranean Europe.

destination from the other. If the Costa del Sol sought to strengthen its point of differentiation, then it might choose to host an event that accentuates its street nightlife, such as a night-time road rally. In contrast, the Côte d'Azur could accentuate its more glamorous image by hosting a glamorous event, such as a high profile international horse race. In a similar fashion, either destination could use a sport event to redress its weakness. The Costa del Sol could seek to change the 'uninteresting landscape' node by hosting an event that would showcase picturesque landscapes, such as the area where its mountains meet the sea. An orienteering event might be appropriate for that purpose. Similarly, the Côte d'Azur could seek to change the 'not family oriented' node by hosting an event for children, such as a youth soccer tournament. Finally, either destination could seek to add a node. For example, the Costa del Sol might endeavour to create a node that represents its flamenco traditions by hosting a flamenco dancing competition.

The basic techniques are clear: Identify the destination brand's association network in the target market. Also identify the association network of competing destinations. Then host events that can reinforce, change or add desirable nodes or associations. What has not yet been described is how to use an event to obtain the desired effect on a destination's brand.

The Strategic Use of Sport Events When the Event has a Distinct Brand Image

When seeking to use an event to help brand the destination, the first challenge for the destination marketer is to determine what the event can contribute to the brand. This depends largely on the degree to which the event has a distinct brand image in one or more of the destination's source markets. For example, popular events like World Cup soccer, the Super Bowl, the Olympic Games, and the America's Cup have strong brand images in their host destinations' source markets. When an event has a well-established brand of its own, then the event name, logo or slogan will activate an event-specific network of nodes and associations. By pairing the event's brand with the destination brand, the expectation is that elements of the event brand will transfer to the destination's brand, and vice versa. This is a form of co-branding[30].

Co-branding has enjoyed substantial growth in recent years because it can be an effective way to reinforce or change a brand image[31]. From the standpoint of the destination marketer, the objective is to transfer desired portions of the event brand to the destination, and not to transfer any undesirable aspects of the event brand to the destination. Consider a recent study of the effects of the Gold Coast IndyCar race on the image of the Gold Coast in long-haul and short-haul markets[32]. Race media did not enhance dimensions of image that would drive tourism from the short-haul market. Worse yet, in both markets, race media (advertising and telecast) depressed viewers' ratings of the Gold Coast's natural environment, despite the vital role that the Gold Coast's natural environment (particularly its beaches) plays in the destination's marketing. The event's noisy and technological image was incompatible with the beneficent natural environment image that the Gold Coast seeks to project.

The co-branding effect depends on associating the event brand with the destination brand[33]. Typically, that requires the two brands to be featured jointly in advertising and/or media about the event or the destination. The effective use of event brands in destination advertising is rare, although Australia's use of the Sydney Olympics is an instructive exception[34]. It is also uncommon for the destination to be featured during a sport event. After all, the media focus is on the sport, not the host destination. A recent study of the Women's Final Four (a high profile basketball championship in the United States) nicely illustrates the problem[35]. Throughout the 11 hours and 45 minutes of the event telecast, visuals of the host city appeared for less than 3.5 minutes. Further, visuals of the city were not accompanied by mentions of the city name, and were so generic that audiences could not have distinguished them as representing the host city. However, the event logo received 28.6 minutes of exposure. This provided some exposure for the host city insomuch as the city name and the silhouette of its leading tourism icon were both incorporated into the logo.

The IndyCar race and the Women's Final Four demonstrate that the mere presence of an event at the destination can have little impact or even a negative impact on the host destination's brand. In order for there to be an effect, destination marketers must plan strategically to create the transfer of brand image that they seek[36]. This requires that they build the event into the destination's marketing communications, and that they work with event organizers to build the destination into event advertising and publicity. In order to obtain adequate pairings of the destination with the event, the destination's name and/or icons need to be built into the event logo, and destination visuals need to be built into event media. This could include contract stipulations about camera placements, camera angles and the use of video postcards. It might also include stipulations about commentary in relation to destination visuals.

However, merely pairing the event and the destination is insufficient. In order to prevent negative transfer and to initiate positive transfer, the nature of associations that are highlighted matters. In other words, the market's attention needs to be focused on the desired associations (and away from undesired associations). Research suggests that a desired association can be produced by drawing the consumer's attention to the presence of the desired node or relationship in the event brand when pairing the event with the destination[37]. This could be done verbally or by visually pairing relevant event and destination visuals. As an example of verbal pairing, if the Côte d'Azur were to host a high-profile international horse race as a means to strengthen the glamour aspect of its brand, then mentions of the race's glamour in close proximity to mentions or visuals of the destination would highlight the association. As an example of visual pairing, if the Côte d'Azur were to use a youth soccer tournament to generate a more family-friendly image, close pairings of visuals of the city with visuals of young people playing at the tournament would cultivate the desired association. The value of using both verbal and visual pairings is suggested by work showing that each invokes a different memory process[38].

Consumers may not respond favourably to the pairing of an event and the destination. The level of perceived match between two brands plays a significant role in the ways that each is perceived when they are paired[39]. The pairing and, consequently, each brand are appraised more favourably when the two brands are perceived to be well matched than when they are perceived to be poorly matched – even if both brands are individually liked. A match-up seems to facilitate processing of the association between the two brands. If a tourist's schema for a destination were inconsistent with their schema for an event hosted at the destination, then the association could not be represented in memory. Consequently, the association would not be processed, and the event would fail to reinforce or enhance the host destination's brand. The inability to process the association could, however, trigger negative affect, thus causing a less favourable global evaluation of the two brands.

From the standpoints of theory and professional practice, the match-up requirement suffers two deficiencies. First, there are no explicit bases for determining whether a match-up exists. In research settings, match-up has simply been asserted on *a priori* grounds (for example, a spokesperson for cosmetics should be attractive) or it has been determined pragmatically (for example, people say they do not think the brands are well matched). Although schema theory is invoked to explain the need for a match, schema theory has not been employed to specify the criteria required to render a match. Second, by calling for a close match at the outset, the match-up requirement suggests that co-branding is suitable for reinforcing a brand image, but not for changing a brand image. Dissimilarity between the event brand and the destination brand would render a poor match, and would therefore have negative consequences for the intended transfer of brand image. This would be unfortunate insomuch as changing the destination brand is often a reason that destination marketers seek to host events[40]. Further, it is clear that properly managed event communications can render a change in destination image[41].

Schema theory suggests that the relevance of initial perceptions of match should wane if pairing the event and destination brands will take place over a long period of time during which target markets will obtain multiple exposures to the pairing[42]. Recall that schemas are abstract sets of relationships that are changed as a consequence of learning[43]. Multiple exposures to a seemingly mismatched pairing will normally engender some accommodation of the schema so that the pairing can be processed in memory.

Nevertheless, the effect of pairings is not always benign, as the example of the IndyCar race cited above demonstrates. The ways that pairings of event and destination are interpreted matter. The interpretations that are prompted through event and destination communications are pivotal because they prime the relevant schemata and direct consumers' attention. When the event is intended to nurture a change in the host destination's brand, then the consumer's capacity to accommodate new nodes will be facilitated if communications suggest the pathways by which to link the desired event nodes to the destination. For example, when highlighting event nodes to be transferred to the destination, it may be useful to note at least one attribute or benefit that the event and destination can be said to share in common. The common attribute or benefit represents a point of articulation between the event and the destination, thus establishing a pathway through which to connect the new nodes. Repetition of the connections helps to strengthen the pathways along which activation will spread when either brand is evoked in future.

The more complex the event's brand, the more nodes can be transferred to the destination. Thus, it is theoretically possible to formulate a number of different brand objectives when hosting an event with a distinct brand image. Once the desired elements of brand transfer are identified, then tactics for highlighting the desired associations both verbally and visually can be formulated for event and destination advertising and publicity, as well as for telecasts and commentary during the event.

Co-branding or Brand Extension?

Most events do not have a distinct brand image. Some are so closely associated with their host destination that the event brand cannot be disentangled from the destination brand. These events developed their brands under the host destination brand, and often bear the host destination's name. For example, the New York City Marathon is now one of the world's largest marathon events, boasting over 36,000 runners and substantial coverage in domestic and international media. Yet the event had humble beginnings in 1970 with only 55 finishers, a budget of $1,000 and little media attention. The race was developed by linking its brand closely to the New York City brand – a strategy that was advanced in 1976 by altering the route so that the race could cover all five New York City boroughs: Staten Island, Brooklyn, Queens, the

Bronx and Manhattan. (The race was previously run in Central Park.) There are comparable examples of event brands that have been nurtured by and tied to the host destination brand. Consider, for example, the Tour de France, the Melbourne Cup and the Henley Royal Regatta.

Co-branding is not at issue with events of this type because the event is inextricably linked with its host destination. Events of this type are akin to brand extensions. The important aspect is not that the event name includes the host destination's name; the important aspect is that the event is explicitly part of the destination's brand range. Indeed, an event can be a destination brand extension even if it is not named for the destination. For example, the Rose Bowl is one of the most significant post-season games in American college football. Its brand is tied to that of the host city, Pasadena, California. The tie is made tangible in two ways: The stadium in which the event is held is called 'The Rose Bowl', and each year the pre-game festivities include the Tournament of Roses Parade during which floats pass through the city. Like the football game, the parade obtains national and international media attention.

The event's links to its facility and an associated street festival illustrates an essential point about brand extensions: Brand extensions are perceived more favourably when there is consistency between concepts and features represented by other products sharing the same brand[44]. In other words, an event that is marketed under its host destination's brand will be received more favourably if it is conceptually consistent with other elements in the destination's product and service mix, and if other elements in the mix share a common feature with the event. In the case of the Rose Bowl, giving the same name to the event and its stadium reinforces a conceptual linkage, and the pre-event festival (that is, the parade) exemplifies a shared feature (that is, a related event).

The fundamental advantage of events that can be treated as brand extensions is that they are closely tied to the host destination's brand. The connection between the event and the destination is intrinsic to the relationship. When events of this type are favourably received by the market, the destination's market share should increase as a consequence of tourists' enhanced perceptions of the destination's brand image and values[45]. As an extension of the destination's brand, any benefits that tourists recognize in the event also become benefits associated with the destination[46]. The principles of brand image transfer in the case of a brand extension are comparable to those in co-branding because the psychological mechanisms are the same.

The marketing communications challenge is different, however. Whereas co-branding required that two independent brands be linked, brand extension requires that the event's inclusion in the destination's product and service mix should appear rational. In other words, it needs to be shown that the event fits with other attractions and activities offered at the destination. This can be attained if marketing communications highlight the event's consistency with core destination benefits (for example, prestige, exhilaration, play) as well as features the event shares with other attractions or activities at the destination[47]. Advertising jingles and slogans can be an effective means to underscore the consistent benefits or shared features[48].

As destination brand extensions, events bear a unique risk, particularly if the event develops a significant brand of its own. A popular event can obtain substantial media coverage and a consequently salient position in consumers' imaginations – so much so that the destination's brand could be overwhelmed by the event brand. For example, the name 'Wimbledon' is better known internationally for the tennis event than for the event's host city. Similarly, the 24 Hours at Le Mans, an auto race held in and around Le Mans (France) since 1923, has eclipsed its host destination's brand. The event grew up under the destination's brand, and bears the destination name. Although Le Mans is a picturesque Loire Valley locale, its name has come to represent the race more than the place. The effect is consequential insomuch as the event has therefore been able to uncouple itself from the destination, as demonstrated by the introduction of an 'American Le Mans Series' in the United States.

The Wimbledon and Le Mans examples illustrate the importance of managing the destination brand in concert with the event brand. Growth in the event's brand equity should be reflected by growth in the host destination's brand equity. As events grow, destination marketers need to build them into their marketing strategies, and they need to take tactical advantage of events when planning the destination's marketing communications campaign. If suitably incorporated into destination marketing, events can play a role in building the destination's brand. On the other hand, if destination marketers fail to capitalize on the destination marketing opportunities that events provide, the destination's brand could be diluted or eclipsed.

Sport Events as Destination Features

The popular wisdom among event and destination marketers is that an event must have or create a distinct brand if it is going to be a useful tool for destination branding[49]. If true, this would be discouraging news for destination marketers who seek to make aggressive use of events to build their destination's brand. The majority of events do not obtain sufficient exposure in tourist markets to cultivate a distinct brand image, and those that do are typically costly[50]. However, examination of the literature on branding suggests that it is not essential for an event to have a distinct brand image in order to contribute to its host destination's brand. An event can serve as a brand feature[51].

In this instance, an event that lacks salience in source markets might nonetheless serve as a tangible example of destination brand attributes. For example, Fort Stockton (a rural community in west Texas) annually hosts 'Water Carnival', a festival that features aquatic sports and activities. The event has scant brand equity beyond Fort Stockton's neighbouring communities. However, for those who consider visiting the community, the event's celebratory atmosphere exemplifies the community's tag-line, 'The Friendliest Town in Texas'.

Events that begin as destination features can develop sufficient brand equity in source markets to become brand extensions. Consider the Henley-on-Todd Regatta in Alice Springs (Australia). The event began in 1962 as an expression of the humour and improvisation that local residents employ to cope with the rigours of living in Australia's outback. The fact that the nearest navigable body of water is 1,500 kilometres away has never been an impediment to hosting the regatta. Contestants race bottomless boats through the dry sands of the Todd riverbed. Over the years, word of the event has spread, often through the effort of marketers who have helped to obtain publicity for the event. The regatta now attracts international competitors and international media.

The growth of the Henley-on-Todd brand has elevated its contribution to the Alice Springs brand, and has helped to expand tourism to the community. However, establishing the brand in source markets is not necessary for an event to make a contribution to the destination's brand. Lightning Ridge is a small community at the edge of the Australian outback, over 700 kilometres from the nearest large Australian city. Yet the town has nurtured a growing tourist trade, and it has used a unique sport event as a noteworthy destination feature. The town positions itself as an historic community – one that represents the rigours of mining opal in traditional outback Australia. Like Alice Springs, it has developed an event that serves as a tangible expression of outback life and values: The Lightning Ridge Great Goat Race. Drivers sit in a sulky harnessed to the goat that races them down the town's main street. The event has insufficient brand equity in the town's key source markets (the capital cities of Australia's states), but it is sufficiently renowned that tourists planning an outback holiday often learn of it and explore the potential of adding Lightning Ridge to their itinerary.

Events like Fort Stockton's Water Carnival and the Lightning Ridge Great Goat Race are unlikely to obtain media attention in their host destinations' source markets. Their value to the destination's brand is their capacity to provide tangible representation of attributes and benefits that destination marketers seek to communicate about the destination brand. Consequently, the most effective means for using them in marketing communications are similar to those used to promote brand extensions. Destination advertising or publicity that includes mentions or visuals of the event should also suggest attributes or benefits of the destination brand that the event illustrates.

Choosing an Approach

Sport events vary in the role they can play in destination branding. Some will be co-brands, some will serve as brand extensions, and some will be brand features. Others may play no role. There are numerous competitions, tournaments, and invitationals that serve as attractions for enthusiasts and their families, but that have little relevance to the host destination's brand. The destination marketer must decide which role an event should play, and must then construct a marketing

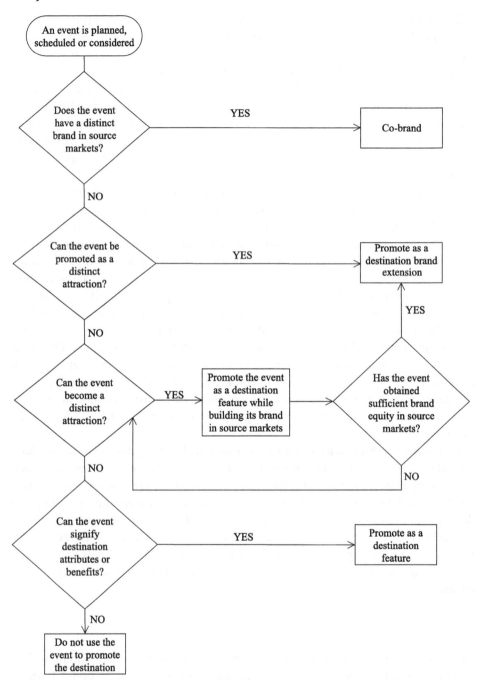

Figure 2 Flow Chart for Identifying the Role for Events in Destination Branding.

strategy that uses the event in a manner that is appropriate to its role. Figure 2 provides a flow-chart to serve as a guide for deciding the appropriate role for an event in branding the destination.

Sport Events in the Destination's Events Portfolio

Destination marketers who seek to use events to build their brand must construct a portfolio of events[52]. A single event – even one with a high profile – has only a passing effect on the destination brand[53]. In order to sustain the impact of events on the destination's brand, it is necessary to host events throughout the year and to find means to create synergy among them.

Sport events are rarely the only events in a destination's portfolio. Cultural events featuring music, food, art or other cultural activities are also vital components of events portfolios. In addition to determining the role that an event can play in destination branding, the destination marketer must choose which events to include in a portfolio. From the standpoints of sport event tourism and destination branding, it is pertinent to determine what role sport events can play relative to one another and relative to cultural events.

The effect of events on a destination's brand depends substantially on the reach and frequency of event mentions and visuals[54]. For an event's brand to affect the destination's brand, consumers must pay sufficient attention to be exposed to the associations that are being primed. Since each event appeals primarily to those consumers who have an interest in the entertainment or activity that the event offers, only those consumers with that interest are likely to be exposed to associations between the event and destination brands. Thus, the reach of the event portfolio depends on the diversity of market segments that will be reached via the portfolio. The more varied the array of sport and cultural events in the portfolio, the greater the total reach.

This is not to suggest that the portfolio should simply be a diverse potpourri of events. Since each event should enhance or reinforce the destination brand, only those events that are best suited to that task should be included in the portfolio. Some events are better suited to building a particular aspect of the destination brand than are others. Which aspect each event can serve depends on the event's brand, category and features. Each event in the portfolio should complement or reinforce the branding benefits bestowed by other events in the portfolio.

The degree to which events complement one another is also a function of their contribution to the total number of exposures to the brand message that target market segments obtain. Each event lasts a relatively short period of time. By including a range of events that will enable brand messages to reach target market segments throughout the year, the frequency of exposures and the consequent branding impact will be elevated.

Events can also act as hooks for one another[55]. A target market segment that normally pays attention only to particular sport events is likely to miss the brand messages being communicated by other sport events or by cultural events. However, when events of different types are bundled together, destination marketers can focus the attention of target markets onto brand messages to which they would not otherwise be exposed. Event organizers often do add subsidiary events as a means to increase the size of their market, the length of the event, and the event's consequent economic and media impacts[56]. For example, the Gold Coast IndyCar race is preceded by a week-long festival of social events and subsidiary auto races. The collection of events has been dubbed 'The Indy Carnival'. Similarly, the Preakness (the second horse race in America's 'Triple Crown') has been expanded from a single day to a week-long collection of events called 'The Preakness Celebration'. In addition to the horse race (which culminates the week's activities), seventeen events were scheduled for Preakness Celebration in 2005. These included concerts, running events, visits to significant horse racing sites and even a flower show. By bundling the events into a mega-celebration, the opportunity is created to reach market segments with brand messages they might not otherwise receive.

Sport Events and Sport Tourism

In the foregoing presentation, it was noted that utilization of sport events as extensions or allies of the destination brand can require that a logical connection between the destination's brand and the event brand be demonstrated. Other sport attractions and activities at the destination are likely to provide a workable basis for making that demonstration because they can signal that the event fits with the destination's product and service mix. For example, Fort Lauderdale, Florida is home to the International Swimming Hall of Fame (ISHOF). Not coincidentally, Fort Lauderdale often hosts national and international swimming competitions. The ISHOF is commonly mentioned or shown in swimming event advertising and publicity. This supports the swimming events' effects on Fort Lauderdale's brand while also promoting the ISHOF as an attraction for tourists who are interested in swimming.

Events can similarly be linked to participation opportunities. For example, it is a simple matter to demonstrate the match between the Quick Silver Pro (a surfing competition on the Gold Coast of Australia) and the host destination. The destination's 42 kilometres of white sand beaches are popular with surfers of all abilities.

This is not to suggest that only other sport attractions and activities are appropriate bases for demonstrating an event's match to the destination. A match is demonstrated by highlighting one or more nodes that are shared in the two brands' networks of associations. Sport activities and sport attractions at the destination are likely to share relevant associations with a sport event because they share the sport category, but they are unlikely to be the only activities or attractions that share associations with the event. Destination marketers can cross-leverage sport elements at the destination, but the contribution of sport events to the destination's brand will be greatest when their brand relevance is not constrained only to sport.

The Future of Sport Event Tourism in Destination Branding

The study of brands and branding has grown substantially in recent years. Nevertheless, there is a great deal to be learned about the uses and effects of events in destination branding. In particular, the voluminous work on destination image needs to be more thoroughly integrated into a branding framework. Our models of how destination brands are formed and changed need to be more fully elaborated, and the effects of brands on tourists' judgment and choice need to be modelled.

The expectation that there should be a match between event brands and destination brands remains one of the most vexing stipulations of current theory. We need to determine what is required to create a match, and we need to identify the strategic means to use apparent mismatches to foster desired changes in the host destination's brand. We need to explore the processes by which associations with an event brand affect the destination brand image, and we need to determine how those processes vary as a function of the event's role – as a co-brand, a brand extension or a brand feature.

The necessary work is complicated further by the fact that destinations may obtain little exposure from events[57], and the exposures that are obtained can render negative effects[58]. It is insufficient to determine how to elevate the number of exposures that events provide their host destinations; it is insufficient to determine how to optimize positive brand associations; it is insufficient to determine how to minimize negative brand associations. All three aspects must be studied in concert. We need to determine how to obtain and frame exposures in a manner that will engender desired brand associations but will not also import unfavourable brand associations. Further, we need to do so with reference to the effects of the consumer's focus of attention. The same association with the same framing might have a different effect in marketing communications for the destination than it has in marketing communications for the event because the schemas that are primed in the two instances can vary[59]. Thus, the context in which the event and the destination are paired may moderate the effects. We need to find out.

The role of an event in destination branding could change as the event's brand becomes sufficiently distinctive. As we have seen, this is not without risk as an event's brand can dilute or eclipse the destination brand. The most effective means to coordinate the event and destination brands over time need to be identified. This includes building event brands (for example, from destination features to destination brand extensions), as well as building the destination brand as the event's brand develops.

Finally, we need to put sport events into their broader context. The effect of individual events needs to be considered with reference to the overall event portfolio and with reference to the destination's mix of products and services, particularly other sport products and services. The impact of any one event depends on the ways it is leveraged[60]. The destination's events portfolio and its product and service mix provide the raw material for event leverage. The branding challenge is to craft the tactics for effective leverage.

Notes

[1] K.L. Keller, *Strategic Brand Management: Building, Measuring, and Managing Brand Equity* (Upper Saddle River, NJ: Prentice Hall, 1998).

[2] D.A. Aaker, *Building Strong Brands* (New York: Free Press, 1996).

[3] L. de Chernatony, *From Vision to Brand Evaluation: Strategically Building and Sustaining Brands* (Oxford: Butterworth-Heinemann, 2001).

[4] R. Mortimer, 'Creating Regional Appeal', *Brand Strategy*, 162, 1 (2001), 24–5.

[5] K. Finucan, 'What Brand Are You?', Planning, 68, 8 (2002), 11.

[6] G. Hankinson, 'Location Branding: A Study of the Branding Practices of 12 English Cities', *Brand Management*, 9, 2 (2001), 127–42. N. Morgan and A. Pritchard, 'Meeting the Destination Branding Challenge', in N. Morgan, A. Pritchard and R. Pride (eds), *Destination Branding: Creating the Unique Destination Proposition* (Amsterdam: Elsevier, 2004), pp.59–78.

[7] G. Brown, L. Chalip, L. Jago and T. Mules, 'Developing Brand Australia: Examining the Role of Events', in N. Morgan, A. Pritchard and R. Pride (eds), *Destination Branding: Creating the Unique Destination Proposition* (Amsterdam: Elsevier, 2004), pp.279–305. A. Smith, 'Reimaging the City: The Value of Sport Initiatives', *Annals of Tourism Research*, 32, 1 (2005), 217–36.

[8] T. Ambler and C. Styles, 'Brand Development versus New Product Development: Toward a Process Model of Extension Decisions', *Journal of Product and Brand Management*, 6, 4 (1997), 222–34. L. Chalip, 'Beyond Impact: A General Model for Sport Event Leverage', in B.W. Ritchie and D. Adair (eds), *Sport Tourism: Interrelationships, Impacts and Issues* (Clevedon: Channel View, 2004), pp.226–52.

[9] L. Jago, L. Chalip, G. Brown, T. Mules and S. Ali, 'Building Events into Destination Branding: Insights from Experts', *Event Management*, 8, 1 (2003), 3–14.

[10] Ibid.

[11] G.J. Ashworth, 'Products, Places and Promotion: Destination Images in the Analysis of the Tourism Industry', in T. Sinclair and M.J. Stabler (eds), *The Tourism Industry: An International Analysis* (Wallingford: CAB International, 1991), pp.121–42. J. Hunt, 'Image as a Factor in Tourism Development', *Journal of Travel Research*, 13, 3 (1975), 1–7.

[12] J. Crompton, 'An Assessment of the Image of Mexico as a Vacation Destination and the Influence of Geographical Location Upon that Image', *Journal of Travel Research*, 17, 4 (1979), 18–24. B. Goodall, 'Understanding Holiday Choice', in C. Cooper (ed.), *Progress in Tourism, Recreation and Hospitality Management* (London: Belhaven Press, 1991), pp.58–77.

[13] L. Andreu, J. Bigne and C. Cooper, 'Projected and Perceived Image of Spain as a Tourist Destination for British Travellers', *Journal of Travel and Tourism Marketing*, 9, 4 (2000), 47–67. A. Beerli and J.D. Martin, 'Factors Influencing Destination Image', *Annals of Tourism Research*, 31, 3 (2004), 657–81.

[14] E. Dichter, 'What Is an Image?' *Journal of Consumer Research*, 13, 4 (1985), 455–72. W.H. Reynolds, 'The Role of the Consumer in Image Building', *California Management Review*, 7, 3 (1965), 69–76.

[15] W.C. Gartner, 'Tourism Image: Attribute Measurement of State Tourism Products Using Multidimensional Scaling Techniques', *Journal of Travel Research*, 28, 2 (1989), 16–20. J.N. Goodrich, 'A New Approach to Image Analysis through Multidimensional Scaling', *Journal of Travel Research*, 17, 2 (1978), 2–7.

[16] J. Embacher and F. Buttle, 'A Repertory Grid Analysis of Austria's Image as a Summer Vacation Destination', *Journal of Travel Research*, 28, 3 (1989), 3–23. D. Walmsley and M. Young, 'Evaluative Images and Tourism: The Use of Personal Constructs to Describe the Structure of Destination Images', *Journal of Travel Research*, 36, 3 (1998), 65–9.

[17] J.A. Mazanec, 'Image Measurement with Self-Organizing Maps: A Tentative Application to Austrian Tour Operators', *Revue du Turisme*, 49, 3 (1994), 9–18.

[18] R.J. Calantone, C.A. di Benedetto, A. Hakam and D.C. Bojanic, 'Multiple Multinational Tourism Positioning Using Correspondence Analysis', *Journal of Travel Research*, 28, 2 (1989), 25–32.

[19] M.D. Reilly, 'Free Elicitation of Descriptive Adjectives for Tourism Image Assessment', *Journal of Travel Research*, 28, 4 (1990), 21–6.

[20] C.P. Borchgrvink and B.J. Knutson, 'Norway Seen from Abroad: Perceptions of Norway and Norwegian Tourism: An Image Study', *Journal of Hospitality and Leisure Marketing*, 4, 4 (1997), 25–48. J.L. Crompton, 'An Assessment of the Image of Mexico as a Vacation Destination and the Influence of Geographical Location upon the Image', *Journal of Travel Research*, 18, 4 (1979), 18–23. M. Oppermann, 'Convention Destination Images Analysis of Association Meeting Planners', *Tourism Management*, 17, 3 (1996), 175–182.

[21] C.M. Echtner and J.R.B. Ritchie, 'The Meaning and Measurement of Destination Image', *Journal of Tourism Studies*, 2, 2 (1991), 2–12.

[22] M.G. Gallarza, I. Gil Saura and H. Calderon Garcia, 'Destination Image: Towards a Conceptual Framework', *Annals of Tourism Research*, 29, 1 (2002), 56–78.

[23] S. Baloglu and K. McCleary, 'A Model of Destination Image Formation', *Annals of Tourism Research*, 26, 4 (1999), 868–97. Beerli and Martin, 'Factors Influencing Destination Image'.

[24] I. Frochot, 'A Benefit Segmentation of Tourists in Rural Areas: A Scottish Perspective', *Tourism Management*, 26, 3 (2005), 335–46. C. Goosens, 'Tourism Information and Pleasure Motivation', *Annals of Tourism Research*, 27, 2 (2000), 301–21.

[25] J.A. Chandler, 'Comparing Visitor Profiles at Heritage Tourism Destinations in Eastern North Carolina', *Journal of Travel and Tourism Marketing*, 16, 1 (2004), 51–61. T.E. Muller, 'Using Personal Values to Define Segments in an International Tourism Market', *International Marketing Review*, 8, 1 (1991), 57–70.

[26] Aaker, *Building Strong Brands*. Keller, *Strategic Brand Management*.

[27] K.A. Braun-LaTour and M.S. LaTour, 'Assessing the Long-Term Impact of a Consistent Advertising Campaign on Consumer Memory', *Journal of Advertising*, 33, 2 (2004), 49–61. J. Gregan-Paxton, 'The Role of Abstract and Specific Knowledge in the Formation of Product Judgments: An Analogical Learning Perspective', *Journal of Consumer Psychology*, 11, 3 (2001), 141–58. M. Sujan and J.R. Bettman, 'The Effects of Brand Positioning Strategies on Consumers' Brand and Category Perceptions: Some Insights from Schema Research', *Journal of Marketing Research*, 26, 4 (1989), 454–67.

[28] M.W. Baldwin, 'Relational Schemas and the Processing of Social Information', *Psychological Bulletin*, 112, 3 (1992), 461–84. A. Iran-Nejad and A. Winsler, 'Bartlett's Schema Theory and Modern Accounts of Learning and Remembering', *Journal of Mind and Behavior*, 21, 1 (2000), 5–35. J.R. Milligan, 'Schema Learning Theory: An Approach to Perceptual Learning', *Review of Educational Research*, 49, 2 (1979), 197–207.

[29] J. Anderson, *The Architecture of Cognition* (Cambridge, MA: Harvard University Press, 1983).

[30] Brown et al., 'Developing Brand Australia: Examining the Role of Events'.

[31] A.R. Rao and R.W. Ruekert, 'Brand Alliances as Signals of Product Quality', *Sloan Management Review*, 36, 1 (1994), 87–97. B.L. Simonin and J.A. Ruth, 'Is a Company Known by the Company It Keeps? Assessing the Spillover Effects of Brand Alliances on Brand Attitudes', *Journal of Marketing Research*, 35, 1 (1998), 30–42. B. Spethman and K. Benezra, 'Co-brand or be Damned', *Brandweek*, 35, 45 (1994), 20–5.

[32] L. Chalip, B.C. Green and B. Hill, 'Effects of Sport Event Media on Destination Image and Intention to Visit', *Journal of Sport Management*, 17, 3 (2003), 214–34.

[33] Jago *et al.*, 'Building Events into Destination Branding: Insights from Experts'. J. Motion, S. Leitch and R.J. Brodie, 'Equity in Corporate Co-branding: The Case of Adidas and the All Blacks', *European Journal of Marketing*, 37, 7–8 (2003), 1080–94.

[34] Brown *et al.*, 'Developing Brand Australia: Examining the Role of Events'.

[35] B.C. Green, C. Costa and M. Fitzgerald, 'Marketing the Host City: Analyzing Exposure Generated by a Sport Event', *International Journal of Sports Marketing and Sponsorship*, 4, 4 (2003), 335–52.

[36] K.L. Keller, 'Brand Synthesis: The Multidimensionality of Brand Knowledge', *Journal of Consumer Research*, 29, 4 (2003), 595–600.

[37] J. Kim and C.T. Allen, 'An Investigation of the Mediational Mechanisms Underlying Attitudinal Conditioning', *Journal of Marketing Research*, 33, 3 (1996), 318–28. S. Van Auken and A.J. Adams, 'Across- versus Within-class Comparative Advertising: Insights into Prestige Class Anchoring', *Psychology and Marketing*, 16, 5 (1999), 429–50.

[38] E. Tulving and D.L. Schaacter, 'Priming and Human Memory', *Science*, 247, 4940 (1990), 301–6.

[39] S.E. Koernig and A.L. Page, 'What if Your Dentist Looked Like Tom Cruise? Applying the Match-up Hypothesis to a Service Encounter', *Psychology and Marketing*, 19, 1 (2002), 91–110. S.R. McDaniel, 'An Investigation of Match-up Effects in Sport Sponsorship Advertising: The Implications of Consumer Advertising Schemas', *Psychology and Marketing*, 16 (1999), 163–84. B.D. Till and M. Busler, 'The Match-up Hypothesis: Physical Attractiveness, Expertise, and the Role of Fit on Brand Attitude, Purchase Intent and Brand Beliefs', *Journal of Advertising*, 29, 3 (2000), 1–13.

[40] B. Bramwell, 'Strategic Planning Before and After a Mega-Event', *Tourism Management*, 18, 3 (1997), 167–76. L. van den Berg, E. Braun and A.H.J. Otgaar, *Sports and City Marketing in European Cities* (Rotterdam: euricur, 2000).

[41] L. Chalip, 'The Politics of Olympic Theatre: New Zealand and Korean Cross-National Relations', in Seoul Olympic Sports Promotion Foundation (ed.), *Toward One World Beyond All Barriers, Vol. 1* (Seoul: Poong Nam, 1990), pp.408–33. S.S. Kim and A.M. Morrison, 'Change of Images of South Korea among Foreign Tourists after the 2002 FIFA World Cup', *Tourism Management*, 26, 2 (2005), 233–47.

[42] Braun-LaTour and LaTour, 'Assessing the Long-Term Impact of a Consistent Advertising Campaign on Consumer Memory'.

[43] D.P. Ausubel, *The Acquisition and Retention of Knowledge: A Cognitive View* (Boston: Kluwer, 2000). D.R. Shanks, *The Psychology of Associative Learning* (New York: Cambridge University Press, 1995).

[44] C.W. Park, S. Milberg and R. Lawson, 'Evaluation of Brand Extensions: The Role of Product Feature Similarity and Brand Concept Consistency', *Journal of Consumer Research*, 18, 2 (1991), 185–93.

[45] V. Swaminathan, R.J. Fox and S.K. Reddy, 'The Impact of Brand Extension Introduction on Choice', *Journal of Marketing*, 65, 4 (2001), 1–15. E.M. Tauber, 'Brand Leverage: Strategy for Growth in a Cost Control World', *Journal of Advertising Research*, 28, 4 (1988), 26–30.

[46] T. Meyvis and C. Janiszewski, 'When Are Broader Brands Stronger Brands? An Accessibility Perspective on the Success of Brand Extensions', *Journal of Consumer Research*, 31, 2 (2004), 346–57. M. Supphellen, Ø. Eismann and L.E. Hem, 'Can Advertisements for Brand Extensions Revitalize Flagship Products? An Experiment', *International Journal of Advertising*, 23, 2 (2004), 173–96.

[47] J.Y. Kim, 'Communication Message Strategies for Brand Extensions', *Journal of Product and Brand Management*, 12, 7 (2003), 462–76.

[48] K. Pryor and R.J. Brodie, 'How Advertising Slogans can Prime Evaluations of Brand Extensions: Further Empirical Results', *Journal of Product and Brand Management*, 7, 6 (1998), 497–508.

[49] Jago et al., 'Building Events into Destination Branding: Insights from Experts'.

[50] D. Whitson and D. Macintosh, 'The Global Circus: International Sport, Tourism, and the Marketing of Cities', *Journal of Sport and Social Issues*, 20, 3 (1996), 278–97.

[51] R.J. Meyer and A. Sathi, 'A Multiattribute Model of Consumer Choice During Product Learning', *Marketing Science*, 4, 1 (1985), 41–61. S. Ahang and A.B. Markman, 'Processing

Product Unique Features: Alignability and Involvement in Preference Construction', *Journal of Consumer Psychology*, 11, 1 (2001), 13–27.

[52] Jago *et al.*, 'Building Events into Destination Branding: Insights from Experts'.

[53] J. Ritchie and B. Smith, 'The Impact of a Mega-Event on Host Region Awareness: A Longitudinal Study', *Journal of Travel Research*, 13, 2 (1991), 14–20.

[54] H. Kamin, 'Advertising Reach and Frequency', *Journal of Advertising Research*, 18, 1 (1978), 21–5. P.J. Kreshel, K.M. Lancaster and M.A. Toomey, 'How Leading Advertising Agencies Perceive Effective Reach and Frequency', *Journal of Advertising*, 14, 3 (1985), 32–9.

[55] B. Garcia, 'Enhancing Sport Marketing through Cultural and Arts Programs: Lessons from the Sydney 2000 Olympic Arts Festivals', *Sport Management Review*, 4, 2 (2001), 193–219.

[56] Chalip, 'Beyond Impact: A General Model for Sport Event Leverage'. Jago *et al.*, 'Building Events into Destination Branding: Insights from Experts'.

[57] Green *et al.*, 'Marketing the Host City: Analyzing Exposure Generated by a Sport Event'.

[58] Chalip *et al.*, 'Effects of Sport Event Media on Destination Image and Intention to Visit'.

[59] K.S. Coulter, 'The Effects of Affective Responses to Media Context on Advertising Evaluations', *Journal of Advertising*, 27, 4 (1998), 41–51. Y. Yi, 'Cognitive and Affective Priming Effects of the Context for Print Advertisements', *Journal of Advertising*, 19, 2 (1990), 40–8.

[60] Chalip, 'Beyond Impact: A General Model for Sport Event Leverage'.

Sport Tourism as an Attraction for Managing Seasonality

James Higham

Introduction

The New Zealand Rugby Union (NZRU) expects the British and Irish Lions rugby tour of New Zealand in 2005 to be the biggest sports event that New Zealand has ever hosted. This is a significant claim given that New Zealand has hosted the Commonwealth Games (Christchurch 1974 and Auckland 1990), America's Cup (Auckland 1995 and 2000) and co-hosted (with Australia) the 1987 Rugby and 1992 Cricket world cups. It is also significant given that treating regular season or sport team tours as an 'event' is a recent occurrence. The New Zealand Rugby Union anticipates that 20,000 rugby supporters from England, Scotland, Wales and Ireland will travel in support of the Lions on their five-week tour of New Zealand, a figure similar to the number of fans who followed the Lions on tour in Australia in 2001 [2]

This scenario lends weight to the view that sports can, and often do, function as tourist attractions [3]. However, the management implications of consciously treating sport as a tourist attraction are yet to be comprehensively explored. Conceptualizing

James Higham, Department of Tourism, School of Business, University of Otago, PO Box 56, Dunedin, New Zealand. Correspondence to: jhigham@business.otago.ac.nz sport as a tourist attraction represents a paradigmatic shift for sport managers. Yet doing so may offer insights into niche tourism markets of relevance to specific sports, and the communication of information and/or imagery to those markets. This may allow sports managers to target specific markets that lie beyond their geographic regions that sports teams represent. Sports, like most tourism attractions, change with the seasons. Thus, the conceptualization of sport as a tourist attraction cannot be divorced from the challenges of managing a seasonal phenomenon. An understanding of the seasonal context of sport is required in order to influence and, where possible, manage temporal patterns of demand for tourism attractions. This essay explores the ways in which sport may function as a tourist attraction, and the relationship between sports attractions and seasonality of tourist demand. The relevance of these theoretical discussions is then illustrated through the application of tourism attraction theory to the sport of rugby union in New Zealand.

Tourism and Sport Attractions

The fact that many sports attract tourists as spectators is well established [4]. The uncertainty of outcome associated with sport competition, for instance, may be viewed as an aspect of authentic tourist experience. This is particularly evident in the case of high profile sports contests such as English football's FA Cup. It is also true of hallmark sports events, those in which the particular sports event is synonymous with the specific location in which is takes place [5]. Prominent examples include the Wimbledon tennis championship, the Indianapolis 500 motor race, and the Kentucky Derby horse race. It is also true that sport generates diverse and heterogeneous flows of travellers [6] that may include, in addition to spectators, athletes, media, sponsors, team personnel and representatives of national or international sports organizations [7]. The manner in which sports function as tourist attractions, in reality, extends far beyond world championship sports competitions and hallmark sports events. Indeed it might be argued that all sports offer the potential to function in varying ways, and to varying degrees, as tourist attractions.

Given the significance of sport as a generator of tourism it is surprising that sport related tourism has received so little dedicated attention in terms of empirical research and the development of theory. The theoretical basis for conceptualizing sport as a tourist attraction has only recently been considered in detail [8]. Leiper's systems approach to tourist attractions provides a useful means for doing this [9]. Leiper defines a tourist attraction as 'a system comprising three elements: a tourist or human element, a nucleus or central element, and a marker or informative element. A tourist attraction comes into existence when the three elements are connected' [10].

The first component of Leiper's attraction system is the human element that is represented by people who travel in the pursuit of leisure. Leiper highlights several aspects of the human element of tourist attractions. He observes that the essence of touristic behaviour involves a search for satisfying leisure via suitable attractions or, to be more precise, a search for personal (*in situ*) experiences of the nuclear elements of attraction systems. In order to facilitate this process, attraction markers or informative elements perform a critical role in connecting tourists with the nuclear elements being sought for personal experience. It is noteworthy that this process is not automatically productive. Thus, tourists' needs are not always satisfied due to the reality that attraction systems may be functional or dysfunctional, to varying degrees [11].

The second element of Leiper's tourist attraction system is the nucleus, which refers to the site where the tourist experience is produced and consumed. Leiper recognizes that the nucleus may play a variety of roles in the tourist experience, which he describes in terms of the nuclear mix and hierarchy. The nuclear mix refers to the combination of attractions that a tourist may wish to experience at the tourist destination. In most cases leisure travellers will visit a diverse range of attractions while at a destination. The attraction hierarchy indicates that some attraction nuclei are more important than others in influencing both the decision to travel and the planning of visitor experiences. Primary attractions are those that directly or immediately influence a visitor's decision to travel to a destination. Secondary attractions are known to the tourist prior to their visit but are not significant in the decision to travel, or the planning of the travel itinerary. Tertiary attractions are not known to the traveller prior to their visit but may be experienced when the visitor is at the destination [12].

The third element of the attraction system consists of markers, which are items of information about any phenomenon that is a potential tourist attraction [13]. Attraction markers may be contiguous or on-site when specifically related to the attraction, or associated with the attraction nucleus. Alternatively attraction markers may be detached or removed from the nucleus. Thus attractions may be 'marked' for tourists through media coverage, indirect association with generic advertising campaigns, or through the commercial activities of sponsors. In both cases markers may be positioned consciously or unconsciously to function as part of the attraction system.

Leiper's systems approach to defining tourist attractions has been applied specifically to the study of sport [14]. Hinch and Higham observe that the human element of sport attractions is distinctive in its diversity [15]. It includes forms as varied as event-based sports, team and individual sports, active involvement in competitive or recreational sports and spectatorship. Thus, it is apparent that sports attractions offer the potential to generate diverse and heterogeneous flows of travellers. Most obvious, and most thoroughly addressed in the tourism literature, are sports events that may generate significant spectator interest. Sports events such as the Masters golf championships have been discussed in terms of their tourism attraction functions [16]. But so, too, to varying degrees do all range of sports that are contested at international, national and regional levels of competition. Thus the human element of spectator sports may include such varied niche markets as dedicated sports fans [17], aficionados [18], and occasional sport spectators [19]. Furthermore sports managers may specifically target casual sport spectators. This niche market includes inbound tourists who may seek to experience sport as a unique element of the cultural experience of a destination.

However, the human element of sport tourism attractions extends far beyond spectator-driven sports events. Participant events (for example city marathons and Masters Games) may also function as tourist attractions and, in doing so, offer quite distinct human elements. Other manifestations of the human element of sport tourism attractions may include professional athletes, player/team management staff, media, sponsors and other corporate interests, and representatives of sports organizations. Indeed these human elements of the sport tourism attraction system are more readily estimated (indeed often confirmed) in advance of sports contests, than the more discretionary nature of spectator interest [20].

The nuclear element of the tourism attraction system as it applies to sport reflects established sport tourism typologies associated with multiple sport trips and categories of sport tourists motivations [21]. The tourism attraction hierarchy is evident in sport tourism insofar as travellers may be motivated by:

1. a particular sports attraction,
2. a combination of sporting and non-sporting attractions, and
3. non-sport attractions, where destination experiences/activities include sport.

The attraction system, therefore, recognizes that sport may function as a tourist attraction in a variety of ways for a variety of people. Appreciating the place of sport within a destination's nuclear mix and hierarchy of attractions, as it relates to different tourist market segments, has significant sport and tourism management implications. These include important aspects of tourism such as the diversity of niche travel markets, the magnitude of travel flows, timing of visits and visitor behaviour. The nuclear mix and attraction hierarchy also links closely to seasonal patterns of sport tourism.

The prominence of sport in commercial and media markets indicates that sport attractions are served by an equally diverse range of attraction markers. Examples of conscious attraction markers featuring sport are common. Typically, they take the form of advertisements showing visitors involved in destination specific sports activities and events. Unconscious detached markers are even more pervasive. At the forefront of these are televised broadcasts of elite sporting competitions and advertisements featuring sports in recognizable destinations. Broadcast listeners and viewers have the location marked for them as a tourist attraction, which may influence future travel decisions [22]. Additionally, the significance of the popular media as sport tourism markers is matched by few other tourist activities.

With the professionalization of many sports there have developed significant sport sponsorship interests that may function as unconscious detached markers. In such cases the roles that sponsors perform as attraction markers may support or counter tourism development interests. This is evident in sponsorship associated with local/regional, national and transnational corporate interests. However, the extent to which potential for conflict between global processes and local meanings associated with sport varies between each. The potential for disjuncture, or 'lack of fit' in the global/local nexus [23] must be understood and negotiated. The sponsorship of elite athletes and professional sports teams may also link closely to the roles of tourism attraction markers, and contribute to the uniqueness and profile of tourism destinations. Thus, the application of Leiper's systems approach to conceptualizing tourist attractions demonstrates the fundamental similarities that sport shares with other types of tourist attractions.

Sport Attractions and Seasonality

Seasonal variation in tourism phenomena represents a universal challenge in the management of tourist attractions. It is important to consider issues, challenges and opportunities relating to seasonality as they apply to sport-based tourism attractions. Both sport and tourism are characterized by seasonality and the respective sport and tourism seasons may interact with each other in a variety of ways [24]. In the context of tourism, seasonality has been defined as 'a temporal imbalance in the phenomenon of tourism' [25]. The prevailing view of tourism seasonality is that it is a problem that should be resolved by destination and attraction managers. Advocates of this position point out that tourism seasonality has many negative effects [26]. They relate to 'underutilisation of capacity at one end of the scale and congestion, environmental damage and a negative impact on the quality of the tourism product at the other' [27].

At a general level, tourism seasonality has been attributed to 'natural' and 'institutional' factors [28]. Natural seasonality refers to regular temporal variations in natural phenomena, particularly those associated with cyclical climatic changes throughout the year [29]. 'Climate and weather conditions ... influence how satisfying particular recreational outings will be (as determined by) air temperature, humidity, precipitation, cloudiness, amount of daylight, visibility, wind, water temperature, and snow and ice cover' [30]. By contrast, institutional factors reflect the social norms and practices of society [31]. These include religious, cultural, social and economic practices as epitomized by religious, school and work holidays. Two of the most prevalent institutional constraints on the scheduling of sports travel are school and work commitments [32]. While tradition also plays a large part in the timing of holidays, changing religious views, social norms, transportation options and technological advances may moderate these influences.

Butler identifies three additional causes of seasonality [33]. The first of these is social pressure or fashion. As an example, media attention given to celebrities at yachting regattas and horse racing events may drive demand for sport tourism experiences. Inertia or tradition is a second seasonality factor. People who have traditionally taken holidays at a particular time of year commonly continue to do so, even when the factors that once determined the timing of holidays (such as school terms/semesters) have ceased to apply. Thirdly, the scheduling of sporting seasons is recognized as a factor in its own right. Butler makes the case that sport's seasons have a direct impact on tourism seasons [34]. Winter sports such as skiing, snowboarding and snowmobiling are perhaps the most obvious examples, but summer-based activities such as surfing and golf also influence travel patterns as tourists search for the best seasonal conditions for the pursuit of their sporting interests. Thus, while many sports are seasonal phenomena by virtue of variations in climatic conditions, sport seasonality clearly also fits within the category of 'institutional' factors influencing tourism seasonality.

The Dynamic Nature of Sport and Tourism Seasonality

While the factors that influence seasonal patterns of sport tourism are complex, their basic relationship is relatively straightforward. Sport tourism managers may influence patterns of seasonality by modifying supply attributes through strategies such as the development of climatically-controlled sports facilities [35]. They may also modify institutional and natural factors on the demand side through such strategies as promotions that seek to counter or dispel negative perceptions that may exist within latent tourism markets vis-à-vis sport participation outside the main sports season.

A significant part of the dynamic evolution of sport over the past thirty years has been the expansion of traditional sporting seasons. The reasons for this development include technological innovations (for example in clothing and protective equipment) and changing social conditions. One significant factor influencing seasonal dynamics in sport has been the professionalization (or semi-professionalization) of sports at elite and non-elite levels of competition. In conjunction with this trend, partnerships with broadcast media have generated pressures to increase the length of competition seasons [36]. In many cases the professional development of numerous sports has had the consequence that teams compete virtually year round [37]. This has either largely eliminated or at the very least significantly altered the notion of sport seasonality.

European football is one of many examples that illustrate this trend. The professional football season in Europe has been transformed through the parallel development of domestic and international club competitions. Thus, football has evolved from a domestic winter competition into a combination of domestic and international club championships (league and knockout competitions) that takes place through a hierarchy of concurrent championship competitions across most of the calendar year (Table 1). Table 1 denotes the seasonal parameters of scheduled competitions that involve English football clubs and, in the case of Euro 2004, the England national team. Table 1 does not include training, pre-season and promotional tours or, for example, the games played by England (against Japan and Iceland) in June 2004 in preparation for the Euro 2004 championship. These respective competitions involve different clubs and are, therefore, characterized by distinct spectator catchments as well as different regional, national and/or European-wide spatial travel flows.

Other examples exist where sports seasons have been altered to revolve around the summer rather than winter months to exploit favourable playing conditions, enhance

Table 1 English Football Competition Seasons (2003–04)*

Month	Jan				Feb				Mar				Apr				May				Jun				Jul				Aug				Sep				Oct				Nov				Dec		
Week No.	1	2	3	4	5	6	7	8	9	10	11	12	13	14	15	16	17	18	19	20	21	22	23	24	25	26	27	28	29	30	31	32	33	34	35	36	37	38	39	40	41	42	43	44	45	46	47	48	49	50	51	52

Competitions charted (as horizontal bars): Champions League, UEFA Cup, FA Cup, League Cup, Premier League, Division 1, Division 2, Division 3, Euro 2004, UEFA/Champions League Qualification.

*Scheduled competitions only (i.e., does not include training, pre-season and promotional tours).

the spectator experience and, perhaps as a consequence, promote the sport as a tourist attraction. Similarly, the realignment of competition seasons to facilitate global (northern and southern hemisphere) competitions has or is currently being explored. 'Super League' effectively involved the realignment of Rugby League from a winter to a summer sport in the United Kingdom and France as part of a strategy to develop a global competition season involving championship-winning teams from the northern and southern hemispheres. Similar initiatives are now being explored in Rugby Union to align national and franchise (regional or club) competitions in a global season [38]. The extended nature of concurrent league and championship competitions in English rugby union also illustrates the increasingly congested calendar associated with this sport (Table 2).

Differential Influence Across the Hierarchy of Sport Attractions

The degree to which a sporting activity influences tourism seasonality is in part determined by the placement of sport within the hierarchy of attractions that the traveller seeks to experience [39]. Trip behaviour varies based on how prominently sport features in the travel motivations of the traveller. Where sport is the principal focus of the trip (that is, the primary attraction), travellers demonstrate a greater propensity to travel in the tourism 'off-season' [40]. More casual sport tourists (that is, those who see sport as a secondary or tertiary attraction) show higher levels of seasonal variation in their travels [41]. Where sport is the primary motivation, sport tourists are likely to be more willing to negotiate institutional and natural constraints that might otherwise be considered insurmountable by casual sport tourists [42].

Strategic Responses to Sport Tourism Seasonality

Specific sports and sporting competitions are characterized by their own patterns of seasonality. By capitalizing on these unique characteristics it is possible to manipulate seasonal patterns of travel to experience a sport attraction [43]. Two types of sport-based product mix strategies are particularly prominent in attempts to modify patterns of tourist seasonality at sport attractions. The first is the introduction of sporting events during off-peak and shoulder tourism seasons, and the second is the introduction of new or improved sport facilities and programmes [44]. The introduction of new sports events or competitions, and/or bidding for contestable sports events and championships, are common strategies for altering seasonal patterns of tourism [45]. Many sports events do not require large capital expenditures, are relatively transportable and can be targeted to specific market segments. Sports events may offer the additional advantage of utilizing existing facilities and infrastructure at off-peak time periods within the sports calendar. Tables 1 and 2. offer examples of relevance in the scheduling of the Euro 2004 football championship and England international rugby tours (respectively).

Table 2 English Rugby Union Competition Seasons (2002–03)*

Month	Jan				Feb					Mar				Apr					May				Jun				Jul					Aug					Sep				Oct					Nov				Dec			
Week No.	1	2	3	4	5	6	7	8	9	10	11	12	13	14	15	16	17	18	19	20	21	22	23	24	25	26	27	28	29	30	31	32	33	34	35	36	37	38	39	40	41	42	43	44	45	46	47	48	49	50	51	52

Competition bars:

- **Six Nations** (Feb–Mar)
- **Heineken Cup (European)** (Jan–May)
- **Zurich Premiereship** (Jan–May; Aug–Dec)
- **National League 1** (Jan–May; Aug–Dec)
- **National League 2** (Jan–May; Aug–Dec)
- **National League 3** (Jan–May; Aug–Dec)
- **Int'l Tours** (Jun–Jul)
- **Rugby World Cup** (Oct–Nov)
- **Heineken** (Dec)

*Scheduled competitions only (i.e., does not include training, pre-season and promotional tours). Does not include domestic or international rugby sevens competitions.

Product diversification designed to modify seasonal visitation can also take the form of the physical development of sport attractions. In a sport context, an example of this strategy is the development of all weather resorts, such as Centerparcs in Europe, which provide year round sport-based facilities for family groups [46]. Golf developments have also been used effectively to modify seasonal arrivals at tourism attractions [47]. For product diversification strategies to work there needs to be a corresponding market demand. The development of the Rugby Super 12 competition in 1996 specifically targeted new rugby spectator niche markets [48]. The NZRU branding values for Rugby Super 12 centre on entertainment [49]. This brand was deliberately positioned to attract new rugby spectator markets, most particularly female, mature and family groups.

In a tourist seasonality context, there are a number of market segments that are traditionally recognized as having fewer constraints relating to the timing of travel. These groups include senior, conference, incentive, affinity and special interest markets [50]. While there are many market segments of importance in terms of sport tourism seasonality, one of the most promising is the special interest segment [51]. Individuals who are passionate about a given sport are more motivated to overcome temporal travel constraints than other tourists [52]. These market segments may include passionate sports fans, members of sport subcultures and sport aficionados [53].

The Case of Rugby Union in New Zealand

Rugby Union serves as much more than a popular participation and spectator sport in New Zealand. It has been variously described as a symbol of nationhood and a defining element of New Zealand culture [54]. Jackson, Batty and Scherer describe the All Blacks (the New Zealand rugby team) as 'one of the most dominant symbols of New Zealand culture and identity' [55]. Rugby Union has long been a vector for domestic and international travel as club, provincial and national teams have travelled in search of competition [56]. Higham and Hinch observe that the fundamental association between rugby and tourism is found on scoreboards and changing room doors which are typically labelled 'home' (the home team) and 'away' (the visiting team), or 'hosts' and 'visitors' [57]. These terms highlight the interrelationship between sport and tourism.

The Evolution of Rugby Union as a Tourist Attraction in New Zealand

The history of rugby union (rugby) is steeped in the traditions of amateurism and playing for the love of the game. For a century rugby in New Zealand was based upon local club and domestic provincial competitions. The winter season was occasionally complemented by inbound international or outbound tours by the All Blacks and various other national representative teams such as New Zealand Māori. By the 1980s a form of semi-professional rugby had emerged in New Zealand [58]. While some players argued in favour of remuneration for the career-like commitment of players to the sport, this move was initiated by provincial unions that sought to retain and attract elite players to their provinces. Advocates of amateur rugby referred to this state of semi-professionalism as 'shamateurism'. In 1995 this structure changed significantly when the sport was professionalized [59]. The development of two professional competitions which were inaugurated in 1996 brought substantial changes to the institutional framework for rugby in New Zealand [60].

In 1995 the amateur status of rugby union ended due in large part to the haemorrhaging of players to the rival professional code (Rugby League) [61]. During the Rugby World Cup in 1995 the national unions of South Africa, New Zealand and Australia defied the International Rugby Board (IRB) and formed SANZAR (South Africa, New Zealand, Australia Rugby) to create a professional Southern Hemisphere rugby board. The development of SANZAR, and the administrative structure of Rugby Super 12, is unlike other professional sports leagues. The creation of SANZAR was the result of the mutual interests and dialogue that emerged in 1995 between the national unions of South Africa, Australia and New Zealand, and News Corporation (part of Rupert Murdoch's media empire). The former sought to form a professional rugby competition in the interests of player retention to be achieved by offering competitive salaries. The interests of News Corporation lay in exclusive broadcasting rights to Rugby Union in South Africa, Australia and New Zealand [62]. The investment of $US550 million over ten years (1996–2005) by News Corporation was a significant incentive to the development of professional rugby union. This negotiation, and the development of a short-lived rival World Rugby Corporation (WRC), gave rise to a period of upheaval and conflict over the structure and organization of professional rugby in the southern hemisphere, referred to as 'the rugby war' [63].

The SANZAR negotiations with News Corporation resulted in the creation of two professional competitions, the Tri-Nations and Rugby Super 12, initially for a period of ten years (1996–2005) [64]. The Tri-Nations is a mid-season series of international matches between the three member nations, contested annually in June–August. It involves home and away games between each of the three member nations. The Super 12 competition, by contrast is contested between five New Zealand, four South African and three Australian-based regional teams.

Three common structures exist for professional team sport leagues: (a) all franchises are owned or partially owned by the league, (b) each franchise is privately held and is admitted to the league, or (c) each franchise is a club that is admitted to the league. Super 12 differs from most models as its structure is rooted in the amateur competitions that preceded it. Each franchise is owned by its respective national union. Twelve teams were formed to compete in Rugby Super 12 as selected sides based around the models that had long been used for inter-provincial competitions within these unions. The administration of each Super 12 team is performed by provincial or state administrations. In New Zealand this process saw the amalgamation of twenty seven provincial unions into five Super 12 franchise regions. Amateur rugby clubs within each region are also part of the administrative provenance of the same organization that fields the Super 12 team. These clubs do not compete in the league, nor are they comparable to 'minor league teams' as they are known in American baseball, although they do represent the core of the sports developmental base. As such, the Super 12 competition may be expanded after 2005 to include additional teams, or altered in other ways, if agreed by the SANZAR member unions in consultation with News Corporation [65].

The introduction of these professional competitions required that careful consideration be given to the scheduling of different levels of competition, leading to considerable reorganization of the New Zealand rugby calendar. Prior to 1996 the domestic rugby season took place in local club competitions and three divisions of provincial competition (including promotion/relegation). The domestic provincial championship began in July following the completion of the club season. The national provincial championship was (until 1992) completed in eight weeks of round robin competition including mid-week (Tuesday or Wednesday) fixtures (no semi-finals/final format). Tables 3 and 4 illustrate the seasonal reorganization that was required to accommodate the introduction of two professional competitions in 1996.

Conceptualizing Rugby Union as a Tourist Attraction

The recent evolution of professional rugby union in New Zealand has changed and, it is argued here, so too the way the sport functions as a tourist attraction. Prior to the professionalization of rugby union in 1996 the human element of the sport was generally twofold: amateur players and provincial supporters, very few of whom travelled in support of their provincial teams. Since 1996 the human element of rugby union has diversified and expanded considerably. In terms of professional and semi-professional players the human element of rugby union in New Zealand now includes a squad of up to thirty-six All Blacks, 125 professional Super 12 players (twenty-five per franchise) and twenty-seven provincial unions (in three divisions) each supporting squads of 26–30 players (these player resources are not mutually exclusive). In addition, the NZRU manages Under 17, New Zealand secondary schools, Under 19 and Under 21 (years) squads through national high performance programmes (referred to as 'Academies'). The human element of rugby union then goes beyond the athletes themselves to include team staff (coaches, team management, fitness trainers and medical staff), media, sponsors, and provincial and national administrators (marketing managers are employed by all Super 12 franchises).

The greatest potential for rugby union to generate significant recurrent flows of travellers lies with the spectator catchments associated with different teams competing in different domestic and international competitions. Higham and Hinch note that changes to the sport attraction have affected the spatial and temporal tourism impacts and opportunities associated with rugby union [66]. The more powerful the sport attraction, the greater the propensity and the further people will be willing to travel to experience it. 'Attractiveness', therefore, has a direct bearing on the size of markets that are drawn to experience a sport attraction. The 'attractiveness' of rugby union has been

Table 3 NZRU Competition Structure (–1996)

Month	Jan				Feb				Mar					Apr				May				Jun					Jul				Aug					Sep				Oct				Nov					Dec			
Week No.	1	2	3	4	5	6	7	8	9	10	11	12	13	14	15	16	17	18	19	20	21	22	23	24	25	26	27	28	29	30	31	32	33	34	35	36	37	38	39	40	41	42	43	44	45	46	47	48	49	50	51	52

Bars shown in the chart:

- **All Blacks**: weeks 22–26 (Jun) and weeks 42–47 (Oct–Nov)
- **Club**: weeks 15–25 (Apr–Jun)
- **NPC 1st Div**: weeks 27–37
- **NPC 2nd Div**: weeks 27–35
- **NPC 3rd Div**: weeks 27–35

Source: New Zealand Rugby Almanak, 1990–95.

Table 4 NZRU Competition Structure (1996–2005). Premier and Domestic 1 with Current Super 12 (12 Teams)

Month	Jan				Feb				Mar					Apr				May					Jun				Jul					Aug					Sep					Oct				Nov				Dec			
Week No.	1	2	3	4	5	6	7	8	9	10	11	12	13	14	15	16	17	18	19	20	21	22	23	24	25	26	27	28	29	30	31	32	33	34	35	36	37	38	39	40	41	42	43	44	45	46	47	48	49	50	51	52

Super 12

Club

All Blacks

NPC 1st Div

NPC 2nd Div

NPC 3rd Div

All Blacks

Source: New Zealand Rugby Union (2003).

enhanced through the professionalization of the sport, although the power of the attraction varies between competitions. The attractiveness of touring national teams such as the All Blacks and, as illustrated at the start of this chapter, the British and Irish Lions, is greatest, offering the potential to generate significant international travel flows.

It has been noted that Rugby Super 12 is branded as a fast, skilful and spectacular form of rugby [67]. As such, it has been successful in generating and attracting diverse spectator markets. The human element of Rugby Super 12 includes national and regional flows of spectators who may perceive Super 12 as being a primary, secondary or tertiary attraction [68]. The potential for Super 12 to function as a primary tourist attraction is greatest when neighbouring franchise teams play each other (such as the Canterbury Crusaders versus Otago Highlanders). The human element of Super 12 extends to secondary and casual sport tourism markets (including international tourists whose travel itineraries coincide with Super 12 games at a destination). The potential for international tourists to perceive Super 12 to be a visitor attraction is implied when travel guidebooks such as *Lonely Planet* feature Super 12 teams as part of the suite of attractions at New Zealand regional destinations. Part of this attraction lies in the fact that rugby union represents a deeply entrenched aspect of national culture which casual sport tourists may choose to experience first hand while visiting New Zealand.

The National Provincial Championship (NPC) is branded by the NZRU as the heartland domestic competition and is associated with brand images that emphasize heritage, tradition and provincial parochialism. As such it usually generates local and intra-provincial spectator interest. Exceptions to this rule include local derby fixtures (such as Auckland versus Waikato and Canterbury versus Otago) and fixtures that carry special heritage value (such as Otago versus Southland) and/or significance within the context of the competition season (semi-finals/final, promotion/relegation and Ranfurly Shield challenges) [69]. In these instances the potential for provincial rugby to generate inter-provincial travel flows associated with player, team management, spectator and media markets is significant. This is recognized by Air New Zealand (the national airline) which is the major sponsor of the NPC.

The attraction nuclei associated with rugby union have also expanded, diversified and otherwise been enhanced by professionalism. In the context of rugby union the sites where tourist experiences are produced and consumed centre on the stadia that host international, Super 12 and provincial games. The enhancement of stadium facilities at Super 12 franchise headquarters, including lighting required for the televising of night sport, was a condition of the News Corporations agreement with SANZAR. Stadia exist within a location hierarchy that is dynamic and competitive [70]. Prior to 1990 the major stadia in New Zealand remained in a state largely unchanged for over fifty years. Stadia such as Athletic Park (Wellington) and Carisbrook (Dunedin) were widely criticized by sports people, administrators and media alike, as being outdated, inadequate and potentially dangerous. Since 1991, in direct response to the emerging professionalization of rugby union in New Zealand, a period of intense stadium development has taken place. The location hierarchy for stadium-based sports has, as a consequence, become highly contested, with significant implications for the status of stadia as tourism attractions.

Law indicates that the greatest potential for stadia to function as tourism attractions exists in cases where stadia are developed in close proximity to related attractions (that is, nuclear mix), tourism services and infrastructure [71]. These stadia now form part of the new urban landscape that exists in nodal entertainment enclaves and function as 'tourist precincts' (see Silk and Amis's essay) [72]. As group-specific combinations of spatially related attractions and facilities, these may be referred to as 'complexes' [73]. The status of stadium attraction nuclei are enhanced when facility developments are planned in coordination with entertainment, tourism and service sector interests. It is not surprising, therefore, that there is a trend to integrate contemporary stadium developments with malls, plazas, hotels and other sport and entertainment facilities, such as theme parks, halls of fame and cinemas [74].

The development of modern stadia has also been influential in advancing service sector, tourism and economic development interests at sport tourism destinations [75]. The development of Westpac Trust Stadium (Wellington) in 1999 and Waikato Stadium (Hamilton) in 2002 are examples of stadia that have been developed recently in inner city sites, with immediate proximity to central transport nodes and other urban entertainment facilities. These developments confirm the important roles that stadia may serve relating to the status of urban sports attractions and economic development.

In the context of rugby union in New Zealand the status of attraction nuclei have been influenced by associated developments relating to leisure travel such as the integration of stadium developments with tourist services and infrastructure, as well as visitor attractions including sports halls of fame and sports museums (see Fairley and Gammon's essay). The servicing of visitor needs relating to niche travel markets that are attracted to stadium sports has recently expanded to include the development of corporate and meeting facilities, media reporting and television broadcast resources. National and regional coaching and training facilities (such as the Adidas New Zealand Rugby Institute) have also been to the fore in the recent development of attractions that cater for, and influence, the contemporary mobilities of professional athletes and officials.

The potential for rugby union nuclei to function as attraction markers is yet to be fully explored in New Zealand. Primarily stadia and the sports contests that they host offer the potential to mark specific sport attractions as being unique. Media reporting, and the national and/or international television broadcasting of professional sports, perhaps offer the greatest potential for this to be achieved. That said, the redevelopment or relocation of existing stadia has generally resulted in the loss of unique elements of the tourist attraction. Technological developments such as video screens, virtual advertising and floodlighting have been widely imposed on modern stadia in New Zealand. This course of development has significantly altered the overall sports experiences of both competitors and spectators, and also contributed to the standardization of stadium facilities.

One important implication for the manner in which stadia function as attraction markers has been compromise of the cultural mosaic that makes stadium and visitor attractions unique. The potential for unique stadium design to function as contiguous attraction markers and distinctive elements of a destination has been compromised in some cases. Exceptions to this rule include the naming of new stadium facilities after local sports legends (such as the Hadlee Stand, Jade Stadium), and the development or retention of facilities that are historically linked to a unique sports heritage. As an example, the 'Terrace' at Carisbrook (Dunedin) functions as a contiguous attraction marker due to its strong association with the University of Otago, as it is from the Terrace that students have traditionally watched rugby matches in their own colourful and entertaining style. This association has been entrenched through the projection of the Terrace 'bar' facility to a national audience via a television advertisement for Speights beer (a major sponsor of the Otago NPC team).

Marketing, advertising and sponsorship offer important opportunities relating to the projection of unique tourism attraction imagery. Marketing campaigns associated with Super 12 franchises are commonly aligned with tourist attraction imagery that highlights the local/regional differentiation of tourism destinations. The Otago Highlanders advertising campaigns generally focus on the colonial history of the region that the team represents, utilizing imagery that draws upon the Scottish heritage of the region (most notably Larnach's Castle). The same is particularly true of the marketing campaigns associated with the Canterbury (Crusaders) and Waikato (Chiefs) Super 12 franchises. These promotions function as detached attraction markers.

The emergence of transnational sport marketing in rugby union since the professionalization of the sport also demonstrates great relevance to the status of rugby union as a tourist attraction. The dominant example in the New Zealand rugby context is the sponsorship of the All Blacks in a NZ$120 million/ five-year deal (1999–2004) negotiated between the NZRU and Adidas. Alongside this, iconic All Black players such as Jeff Wilson (Nike) and Jonah Lomu (Adidas) have been introduced to global markets through their associations with transnational corporate sponsors.

Jackson, Batty and Scherer argue that the strong links between rugby and national culture in New Zealand, as well as the economic and cultural currency associated with global media exposure of the All Blacks in the professional era, were particularly attractive to Adidas [76]. They observe that 'Adidas used several different strategies in order to . . . construct the image of a long-standing relationship between the (Adidas) brand and the All Blacks' [77]. These included the release of new products, such as a redesigned All Black jersey (which emphasizes traditional features and elements of design derived from the All Black jerseys of the 1920s), television and radio advertisements, event promotions and follow-up print media promotions.

One key aspect of the Adidas sponsorship was the use of the All Black haka (Māori ceremonial dance used in New Zealand rugby – particularly by national, representative and school rugby teams – as a pre-match challenge), and Māori imagery in an international advertising campaign that was used in seventy countries worldwide. This Adidas advertisement 'utilised a black and white cinematographic technique to merge images of traditional Māori warriors with contemporary All Black stars' [78]. The use of this important Māori cultural ritual in the Adidas global advertising campaign is an example of rugby sponsorship that may function as an attraction marker.

However, it should also be noted that the impacts of global corporate forces on local sports cultures and tourist experiences are not well understood. Jackson *et al.* refer to the 'Adidasification of the New Zealand All Blacks', which has involved corporatization of New Zealand identity and contested indigenous Māori cultural identity [79]. This has resulted in Māori resistance to the use of the haka by Adidas which is seen as an inappropriate use of Māori artefacts, icons and imagery [80]. Jackson *et al.* highlight the potential for disjuncture, or 'lack of fit between global processes and local cultures', giving rise to conflict and resistance when transnational corporate interests seek to impose themselves upon the New Zealand cultural landscape [81].

Rugby Union, Sport and Tourism Seasonality

While rugby union may function as a tourist attraction, the potential that the sport offers in this regard varies with time of year due to the seasonal nature of the sport. As such this potential has changed as the seasonal context of rugby union competitions has evolved. The competition structure and seasonal context of rugby union in New Zealand has changed periodically in recent decades, [82] and continues to change [83]. The introduction of the NPC in 1976, and the transition to professionalism in 1995 have heralded periods of transformation (Tables 3 and 4) [84].

Tables 5–6 indicate ongoing change to the seasonal context of rugby union in New Zealand. The original ten-year agreement negotiated by SANZAR and News Corporation expires at the end of the 2005 season, and is currently being renegotiated with New Corporation and other television/media broadcast interests. Tables 5–6. project the continuing evolution of rugby competition seasons, as outlined in the NZRU *Competitions Review* [85]. Table 5 illustrates the proposed introduction of an All Black (international) competition season (including the Tri-Nations championship) immediately following the Super 12 season, and continuing over an annual five month season. The represents an expansion of interests in international brand projection and revenue generation with implications for travel mobility [86]. It also heralds a move towards the alignment of a global season allowing southern hemisphere (namely Tri-Nations) and European nations to compete in a global international season in the September–November quarter [87]. This will render the All Blacks ineligible to play in the annual NPC competition, which may detract from the status of that competition as a tourist attraction [88].

The continuing expansion of the New Zealand rugby season is evident in Tables 3–6. Table 6, for example, depicts an expansion of the Super 12 competition to accommodate three news teams (Super 15). This is intended to generate new travel markets, and penetrate new supporter and media markets associated with any new teams that are introduced to the competition (possibly a proposed Pacific Island team comprised of

Table 5 Proposed NZRU Competition Structure (2006–). Premier and Domestic 1 with Current Super 12 (12 Teams)

Month	Jan				Feb				Mar					Apr				May					Jun					Jul					Aug					Sep					Oct				Nov				Dec			
Week No.	1	2	3	4	5	6	7	8	9	10	11	12	13	14	15	16	17	18	19	20	21	22	23	24	25	26	27	28	29	30	31	32	33	34	35	36	37	38	39	40	41	42	43	44	45	46	47	48	49	50	51	52

Super 12

All Blacks

Premier

Domestic 1

Club

Source: New Zealand Rugby Union (2003).

Table 6 Proposed NZRU Competition Structure (2006–). Premier and Domestic 1 with Expanded Super 12 (15 Teams)

Month	Jan				Feb				Mar				Apr				May				Jun				Jul				Aug				Sep				Oct				Nov				Dec		
Week No.	1	2	3	4	5	6	7	8	9	10	11	12	13	14	15	16	17	18	19	20	21	22	23	24	25	26	27	28	29	30	31	32	33	34	35	36	37	38	39	40	41	42	43	44	45	46	47	48	49	50	51	52

Super 12

All Blacks

Premier

Domestic 1

Club

Source: New Zealand Rugby Union (2003).

players selected from Fiji, Samoa and Tonga). This development will result in a longer Super 15 season than is currently the case (Table 6), although the seasonal context of this competition will remain largely unchanged as the entertainment value of Rugby Super 12 is maximized by this seasonal (late summer/autumn) placement [89]. Atmosphere and entertainment values are promoted by weather conducive to skilful play and these factors formed part of the plan to attract 'new' rugby watchers to attend games [90]. This confirms Kreutzwiser's observation of the link between climate/weather conditions and levels of satisfaction with sport and tourist experiences [91]. It explains in part the success of Super 12 as a tourist attraction in terms of market range, match attendance, atmosphere, sponsorship and merchandise sales.

Conclusion

The search for competition and/or desirable locations in which to engage ones sporting interests are inescapable aspects of sport. As such sport is inevitably associated with tourism. This applies in varying degrees to all sports, across the various levels of sport competition and across all forms of engagement in sports. As such sports may be an important part of the suite of attractions at a tourism destination, although sports have rarely been conceived or managed as such. Conceptualizing sport as a tourist attraction represents a paradigmatic shift for sport managers. Leiper's tourist attraction system provides a theoretical framework that may be applied to the study of sport as a tourist attraction [92]. Viewing sport as a tourist attraction allows sport managers to target specific markets that lie beyond the geographic regions that sports teams represent. 'Targeted promotions that correspond to primary, secondary and tertiary levels of the attraction hierarchy are likely to be significantly more successful than the traditional approach of treating non-local sport patrons as a single homogeneous group' [93].

This framework also provides insights into the dynamic relationship between sports attractions and tourism seasonality. Sports may offer unique opportunities to ameliorate or modify seasonal patterns of tourist demand. This may be achieved by lengthening competition seasons for spectator sports and scheduling sport events and competitions during tourism shoulder seasons. Such initiatives, if successful, may be harnessed to generate demand for secondary and/or tertiary sports attractions at the destination and, indeed, non-sport visitor activities and attractions. It is useful for sport administrators to recognize the three elements of the attraction system: the human element, attraction nucleus and markers, as they relate to sport. It is also important that sport managers, perhaps in collaboration with tourism destination managers, consciously seek to connect these three parts if, to use the words of Leiper, the attraction system is to be functional [94]. The most effective ways of achieving this connectivity might be a fruitful avenue of future research.

Acknowledgements

The theoretical discussions presented in this chapter are derived from work published by Hinch and Higham (2001) and Higham and Hinch (2002) [95].

Notes

[1] N. Leiper, 'Tourist Attraction Systems', *Annals of Tourism Research*, 17, 3 (1990), 371–2.

[2] G. John, 'Stadia and Tourism', in S. Gammon and J. Kurtzman (eds), *Sport Tourism: Principles and Practice* (Eastbourne, UK: Leisure Studies Association, LSA Publication Number 76, 2002), pp.53–60.

[3] G. Redmond, 'Points of Increasing Contact: Sport and Tourism in the Modern World', in A. Tomlinson (ed.), *Sport in Society: Policy, Politics and Culture* (Eastbourne, UK: Leisure Studies Association, 1990), pp.158–67.

[4] Redmond, 'Points of Increasing Contact: Sport and Tourism in the Modern World'; L. Delpy, Editorial, *Journal of Vacation Marketing*, 4, 1 (1998), 4–5; T.D. Hinch and J.E.S. Higham, 'Sport Tourism: A Framework for Research', *The International Journal of Tourism Research*, 3, 1 (2001), 45–58.

[5] J. Allen, W. O'Toole, I. McDonnell and R. Harris, *Festival & Special Event Management* (Sydney: John Wiley & Sons Australia Ltd., 2000).

[6] M. Weed and C. Bull, *Sports Tourism: Participants, Policy and Practice* (Oxford: Elsevier Butterworth Heinemann, 2004).

[7] C. Gratton, S. Shibli and R. Coleman, 'The Economics of Sport Tourism at Major Sports Events', in J.E.S. Higham (ed.), *Sport Tourism Destinations: Issues, Opportunities and Analysis* (Oxford: Elsevier Butterworth Heinemann, 2004), 233–47.

[8] Hinch and Higham, 'Sport Tourism: A Framework for Research'; J.E.S. Higham and T.D. Hinch, 'Sport, Space and Time: Effects of the Otago Highlanders Franchise on Tourism', *Journal of Sport Management*, 17, 3 (2003), 235–57; T.D. Hinch and J.E.S. Higham, *Sport Tourism Development* (Clevedon: Channel View Publications, 2004).

[9] Leiper, 'Tourist Attraction Systems'.

[10] Ibid.

[11] Ibid.

[12] Ibid.

[13] Ibid.

[14] Hinch and Higham, *Sport Tourism Development*.

[15] Ibid.

[16] Redmond, 'Points of Increasing Contact: Sport and Tourism in the Modern World'.

[17] B. Stewart, 'Fab Club', *Australian Leisure Management*, (Oct./Nov. 2001), 16–19.

[18] R.W. Butler, 'The Influence of Sport on Destination Development: The Example of Golf at St. Andrews, Scotland', in J.E.S. Higham (ed.), *Sport Tourism Destinations: Issues, Opportunities and Analysis* (Oxford: Elsevier Butterworth-Heinemann, 2004), 274–82.

[19] J. Standeven and P. De Knop, *Sport Tourism* (Champaign, IL: Human Kinetics, 1999).

[20] Gratton, Shibli and Coleman, 'The Economics of Sport Tourism at Major Sports Events'.

[21] Standeven and De Knop, *Sport Tourism*; S. Gammon and J. Kurtzman (eds), *Sport Tourism: Principles and Practice* (Eastbourne, UK: Leisure Studies Association, LSA Publication Number 76, 2002), pp.53–60.

[22] Leiper, 'Tourist Attraction Systems'.

[23] S.J. Jackson, R. Batty and J. Scherer, 'Transnational Sports Marketing at the Global/Local Nexus: The Adidasification of the New Zealand All Blacks', *International Journal of Sports Marketing and Sponsorship*, 3, 2 (2001), 185–201.

[24] R.W. Butler, 'Seasonality in Tourism: Issues and Problems', in A.V. Seaton (ed.), *Tourism: The State of the Art* (Chichester: John Wiley and Sons, 1994), pp.332–9.

[25] R.W. Butler, 'Seasonality in Tourism: Issues and Implications', in T. Baum and S. Lundtorp (eds), *Seasonality in Tourism* (London: Pergamon, 2001), pp.5–23 (p.5).

[26] J.B. Allcock, 'Seasonality', in S.F. Witt and L. Moutinho (eds), *Tourism Marketing and Management Handbook* (Englewood Cliffs: Prentice Hall, 1989), pp.387–92; A. Jefferson,

'Smoothing Out the Ups and Downs in Demand', *British Hotelier and Restaurateur*, (July/Aug. 1986), 24–5; E. Laws, *Marketing: Service and Quality Management Perspectives* (Cheltenham: Stanley Thornes Publishers, 1991); A. Lockwood and Y. Guerrier, 'Labour Shortages in the International Hotel Industry', *Travel and Tourism Analyst*, 6 (1990), 17–35; A. Poon, 'All-inclusive Resorts', *Travel and Tourism Analyst*, 2 (1993), 54–68.

[27] J. McEnnif, 'Seasonality of Tourism Demand in the European Community', *Travel and Tourism Analyst*, 3 (1992), 67–88, (p.68).

[28] R.R.V. BarOn, *Seasonality in Tourism: A Guide to the Analysis of Seasonality and Trends for Policy Making* (London: Economist Intelligence Unit, 1975); R. Hartman, 'Tourism, Seasonality and Social Change', *Leisure Studies*, 5, 1 (1986), 25–33; D.C. Frechtling, *Practical Tourism Forecasting* (Oxford: Butterworth-Heinemann, 1996).

[29] Butler, 'Seasonality in Tourism: Issues and Problems'; Allcock, 'Seasonality'.

[30] R. Kreutzwiser, 'Supply', in G. Wall (ed.), *Outdoor Recreation in Canada* (Toronto: John Wiley & Sons, 1989), pp.19–42; (pp.29–30).

[31] T.D. Hinch and G. Hickey, 'Tourism Attractions and Seasonality: Spatial Relationships in Alberta', in K. MacKay and K.R. Boyd (eds), *Tourism for All Seasons: Using Research to Meet the Challenge of Seasonality*. Conference Proceedings of the Travel and Tourism Research Association – Canada Chapter, Ottawa, Canada, 1996, pp.69–76.

[32] Butler, 'Seasonality in Tourism: Issues and Problems'; McEnnif, 'Seasonality of Tourism Demand in the European Community'.

[33] Butler, 'Seasonality in Tourism: Issues and Problems'; Butler, 'Seasonality in Tourism: Issues and Implications'.

[34] Butler, 'Seasonality in Tourism: Issues and Implications'.

[35] J.E.S. Higham and T.D. Hinch, 'Sport, Tourism and Seasons: The Challenges and Potential of Overcoming Seasonality in the Sport and Tourism Sectors', *Tourism Management*, 23, 2 (2002), 175–85.

[36] B.D. McPherson, J.E. Curtis and J.W. Loy, *The Social Significance of Sport: An Introduction to the Sociology of Sport* (Champaign, IL: Human Kinetics Books, 1989).

[37] Higham and Hinch, 'Sport, Tourism and Seasons: The Challenges and Potential of Overcoming Seasonality in the Sport and Tourism Sectors'.

[38] New Zealand Rugby Union, *New Zealand Rugby Union Competitions Review 2003*. Unpublished report (Wellington, New Zealand: New Zealand Rugby Union, 2003).

[39] Hinch and Higham, *Sport Tourism Development*.

[40] World Tourism Organization and International Olympic Committee, *Sport and Tourism: Sport Activities During the Outbound Holidays of the Germans, the Dutch and the French* (Madrid, Spain: Report published by the World Tourism Organization and International Olympic Committee, 2001).

[41] Hinch and Higham, *Sport Tourism Development*.

[42] T.D. Hinch, G. Hickey, G. Jackson and E.L. Jackson, 'Seasonal Visitation at Fort Edmonton Park: An Empirical Analysis Using a Leisure Constraints Framework', in T. Baum and S. Lundtorp (eds), *Seasonality in Tourism* (London: Pergamon, 2001), pp.173–86.

[43] Higham and Hinch, 'Sport, Tourism and Seasons'.

[44] Hinch and Higham, *Sport Tourism Development*.

[45] T.D. Hinch and E.L. Jackson, 'Leisure Constraints Research: Its Value as a Framework for Understanding Tourism Seasonality', *Current Issues in Tourism*, 3, 2 (2000), 87–106.

[46] Hinch and Higham, *Sport Tourism Development*.

[47] T. Baum and L. Hagen, 'Responses to Seasonality: The Experiences of Peripheral Destinations', *International Journal of Tourism Research*, 1 (1999), 299–312; (p.309).

[48] Higham and Hinch, 'Sport, Space and Time'.

[49] New Zealand Rugby Union, *NZRFU Brand Values and Positioning Articulation*. Unpublished report (Wellington, New Zealand: New Zealand Rugby Union, 1998).

[50] Baum and Hagen, 'Responses to Seasonality'.

[51] C.M. Hall and B. Weiler (eds), *Special Interest Tourism* (London: Belhaven Press, 1992).

[52] Hinch and Higham, *Sport Tourism Development*.

[53] Ibid.

[54] P. Bush, *The Game for all New Zealand* (Auckland: Moa Publications, 1986); C. Laidlaw, 'Rugby's Rip van Winkle Awakes', *Otago Daily Times* (Oct. 1998), 9; F. Macdonald, *The Game of our Lives* (Auckland: Penguin Books (NZ) Ltd, 1996).

[55] Jackson, Batty and Scherer, 'Transnational Sports Marketing at the Global/Local Nexus', 194.

[56] Macdonald, *The Game of our Lives*.

[57] Higham and Hinch, 'Sport, Space and Time'.

[58] Jackson, Batty and Scherer, 'Transnational Sports Marketing at the Global/Local Nexus'.

[59] Ibid.

[60] P.D. Owen and C.R. Weatherston, *Professionalization of New Zealand Rugby Union: Historical Background, Structural Changes and Competitive Balance* (Dunedin: University of Otago, Department of Economics, Economics Discussion Papers No. 0214, 2002).

[61] P. Fitzsimmons, *The Rugby War* (Sydney: Harper Sports, 1996).

[62] A. Smith, 'Civil War in England: The Clubs, the RFU, and the Impact of Professionalism on Rugby Union, 1995–99', in A. Smith and D. Porter (eds), *Amateurs and Professionals in Post-war British Sport* (London: Frank Cass Publishers, 2000), pp.146–88.

[63] Fitzsimmons, *The Rugby War*.

[64] New Zealand Rugby Union, *History of the Super 12* [Electronic version]. URL: http://www.nzrugby.com/nzrfu/Pages/Super12/s12histf.htm. Retrieved 23 Feb. 2002.

[65] Higham and Hinch, 'Sport, Space and Time'.

[66] Ibid.

[67] New Zealand Rugby Union, *History of the Super 12*.

[68] Higham and Hinch, 'Sport, Space and Time'.

[69] The Ranfurly Shield is a trophy held by one provincial union and defended during the provincial championship in fixtures taking place at the home ground of the holders of the shield (until defeated by a successful challenger).

[70] J. Bale, *Sports Geography* (London: E & FN Spon, 1989).

[71] C.M. Law, *Urban Tourism: The Visitor Economy and the Growth of Large Cities* (London: Continuum, 2002).

[72] Leiper, 'Tourist Attraction Systems'.

[73] A.G.J. Dietvorst, 'Tourist Behaviour and the Importance of Time-Space Analysis', in G.J. Ashworth and A.G.J. Dietvorst (eds), *Tourism and Spatial Transformations: Implications for Policy and Planning* (Wallingford, UK: CAB International, 1995).

[74] T. Stevens, 'Stadia and Tourism Related Facilities', *Travel and Tourism Analyst*, 2 (2001), 59–73.

[75] Ibid; W. Schaffer and L. Davidson, *Economic Impact of the Falcons on Atlanta: 1984* (Suwanee, GA.: The Atlanta Falcons, 1985).

[76] Jackson, Batty and Scherer, 'Transnational Sports Marketing at the Global/Local Nexus'.

[77] Ibid, 191.

[78] Ibid.

[79] Jackson, Batty and Scherer, 'Transnational Sports Marketing at the Global/Local Nexus'.

[80] S.J. Jackson and B. Hokowhitu, 'Sport, Tribes and Technology: The New Zealand All Blacks Haka and the Politics of Identity', *Journal of Sport and Social Issues*, 26, 2 (2002), 125–39.

[81] Jackson, Batty and Scherer, 'Transnational Sports Marketing at the Global/Local Nexus', 197.

[82] Ibid., 194.

[83] New Zealand Rugby Union, *New Zealand Rugby Union Competitions Review 2003*.

[84] Higham and Hinch, 'Sport, Space and Time'; Jackson, Batty and Scherer, 'Transnational Sports Marketing at the Global/Local Nexus', 194.

[85] New Zealand Rugby Union, *New Zealand Rugby Union Competitions Review 2003*.

[86] Ibid.

[87] Ibid.

[88] Ibid.

[89] Higham and Hinch, 'Sport, Tourism and Seasons'.

[90] New Zealand Rugby Union, *NZRFU brand values and positioning articulation*.

[91] Kreutzwiser, 'Supply'.

[92] Leiper, 'Tourist Attraction Systems'.

[93] Hinch and Higham, *Sport Tourism Development*, p.128.

[94] Leiper, 'Tourist Attraction Systems'.

[95] Hinch and Higham, 'Sport Tourism: A Framework for Research'; Higham and Hinch, 'Sport, Tourism and Seasons'.

Host and Guest Relations and Sport Tourism

Elizabeth Fredline

Introduction

It is important that any discussion of sport tourism considers the population of the host region and takes into account how tourists' enjoyment of the sport and recreation facilities at a destination may impact upon the quality of life of local residents. As with any human activity there is a range of potential positive and negative impacts associated with sport tourism, and an understanding of these is useful in informing the tourism planning and management function within both public and private sectors.

There are two reasons why it is imperative that governments manage the impacts of sport tourism on the host community. Firstly, there is a moral obligation for governments to attempt to ensure sustainability in any activity they promote and support, and that such activity does not have negative implications for the quality of life of local residents. Secondly, and more pragmatically, local residents often play an important part in sport tourism, and in many instances, the commercial success of the

Elizabeth Fredline, Senior Research Fellow, Research Development Unit, RMIT University, GPO Box 2476V, Melbourne 3001, Australia. Correspondence to: liz.fredline@rmit.edu.au product is dependant on a supportive and involved local community. Such support will wane if residents perceive the negative impacts to outweigh the positives.

A growing awareness amongst public sector managers of the need to manage social impacts has lead to the recent embracement of the concept of Triple Bottom Line reporting. This term, originally coined by John Elkington [1]. refers to the importance of considering not only the economic impacts of any endeavour, but also to consider the social and environmental issues associated with it.

Empirical research on the impacts of sport tourism on host communities is limited, but substantial insight can be drawn from the literature documenting the impacts of tourism activity more generally. This essay will present a review of the social impacts of tourism literature with a view to identifying the range of potential positive and negative impacts of sport tourism. It will then examine the theoretical frameworks that have been used to explain variation in impact across and within regions.

Strategies used by hosts to deal with tourists will be explored as will the issue of user conflicts with regard to recreational facilities. Finally, the essay will conclude with a discussion of the future research needs of this emerging sub-field as it relates to the socio-cultural impacts of sport tourism.

Social Impacts of Tourism

Although it has not been specifically addressed in the literature, there appear to be two alternative approaches to defining the social impacts of tourism. Some authors include only the impacts that could not be regarded as fitting into any other category, that is, are neither economic nor environmental, while others more broadly consider any impact on society as being within the social domain. For example, Mathieson and Wall suggest that 'social impacts of tourism refer to the changes in quality of life of residents of tourist destinations' and using this definition, the social aspects of economic and environmental change must be deemed as being in scope [2]. For example, the contribution made by tourism to employment levels is typically considered to be an economic impact, but it clearly has social implications as well. Similarly, an environmental impact of tourism, such as damage to sensitive environmental areas, is also likely to affect the quality of life for local residents by reducing the amenity it provides to them.

The use of these alternative definitions seems to be related to three main assessment techniques that have been previously employed in the evaluation of social impacts. By far the most common method measures impacts through host community perceptions [3]. In this type of study, a sample of local residents is asked to report their perceptions of specific impacts of tourism on their quality of life via a questionnaire. The questionnaire method allows the inclusion of a large number of impacts (within reason) and therefore these studies typically adopt the broader definition of 'social' impacts.

Another method, which has been occasionally employed, is the use of Contingent Valuation (CV) and related techniques such as Choice Modelling. These techniques attempt to assign monetary values to social impacts by asking residents about how much they are willing to pay to ensure or avoid some aspects of tourism development [4]. A quasi-experimental design is used in this type of research and thus there are limits on the number of variables (impacts) and levels of those impacts, which can be manipulated. For this reason a narrow definition of social impacts is typically adopted, and even then, only a few impacts can be tested at one time.

In an example of this type of study, Lindberg, Andersson and Dellaert modelled the impacts of new slope development in a ski resort in terms of residents' reactions to the potential social gains (increased tourism employment) and social losses (increased risk of landslides) [5]. They also took account of recreational benefits that would accrue differently across the community depending on the extent to which the residents participated in skiing as a recreational pastime. The questionnaire asked residents who perceived the proposed development positively about how much additional taxation they were willing to pay to ensure that the new slopes were developed. Where residents opposed the proposed development they were asked to nominate the level of tax cut that would be required for them to accept the new slopes. The conclusion of the study was that overall social losses outweighed potential social gains in this case study.

The final method has parallels with a technique developed in urban planning referred to as Social Impact Assessment (SIA). Originally this method was aimed at 'assessing or estimating, in advance, the social consequences that are likely to flow from specific policy actions or project development' and it is often used in justifying proposed tourism development [6]. However, examples of academic research that fit this description within the tourism literature have instead adopted a post-development evaluation perspective. They have identified key indicators of social impact and described the changes that can be attributed to the tourism activity. For example, Hall, Selwood and McKewon documented some of the social impacts of the 1987 America's Cup in Fremantle, Western Australia, including increases in crime and prostitution [7].

However, by far the bulk of the literature has adopted the first approach, the measurement of impacts of tourism as perceived by local residents. This approach has advantages and disadvantages. First, it is clearly a subjective measure and responses to the survey will be framed within the respondent's value and attitude set. Therefore, a respondent may, either consciously or subconsciously, over or under rate the actual impacts in an effort to present a picture that is consistent with their overall representation of the tourism activity. However, many of the impacts, particularly the specifically 'social' impacts, cannot be effectively measured in any other way. As an example, there is no objective way of measuring the exciting atmosphere that is generated in a community that plays host to a major sporting event, such as the Olympic Games. Even when impacts can be objectively assessed, for example the increase in noise generated by sport tourism, any objective measure must then be compared with a researcher-defined optimum level. There seems to be an assumption that the impact is uniform across the community, and that all local residents will perceive it in a similar way. However, empirical research has shown that, in some contexts, although many residents perceive increased noise as a negative impact, some actually see it in a positive light as a contribution to the excitement associated with some sporting events [8]. Therefore, use of the host community perception approach to assessing the social impacts of tourism allows exploration of the variation within a community, which can lead to a better understanding of the differential impact amongst community subgroups.

Characteristics of Sport Tourism

There is a broad array of activities that can be regarded as sport tourism and there are many ways to define the concept. However, in terms of the impact on the host community, it may be more useful to think of a number of different continua that can be used to describe sport related activity undertaken while away from home. And it is not only the characteristics of the sport tourism activity that will influence the level of impact on the host region. There is interplay between the characteristics of the activity and the participants it attracts, with the characteristics of the host destination. Table 1 presents a series of descriptors, presented as semantic differentials, which describe some of the factors that may affect level of impact.

When the activity is small scale, frequent and spatially diffuse, a low level but continual impact occurs which, over time, residents are likely to adapt to, especially if the activity is consistent with local values and residents can also gain advantage through participation. However, a large scale one off event is likely to be more disruptive, but also bring more economic, entertainment and excitement benefits. Intuitively, a large, well developed, urban area will cope better with the impacts of tourism; however, the residents of a small regional or rural area, which has fewer industrial bases, may be more eager to attract the economic benefits of sport tourism, and therefore be more prepared to accept any negative externalities. Management of

Table 1 Variables which Affect the Impact of Sport Tourism on the Host Community

	Small Scale	Large Scale
The Activity is...	Frequent (daily or weekly)	Rare (one off event)
	Free	Expensive to participate in
	Spatially diffuse	Spatially concentrated
	Consistent with local values	Inconsistent with local values
The participants are...	Actively involved	Passively involved (spectators)
	Tourists and locals	Tourists only
	Non elite	Elite
	Socially and culturally similar to locals	Socially and culturally different to locals
The destination is...	Small, regional or rural	Large, urban
	Environmentally sensitive	Environmentally robust
	Relatively undeveloped	Relatively well developed
The tourism is...	Well managed	Poorly managed

impacts is clearly a critical component in ameliorating the costs and promoting the benefits of tourism.

Tourism Impacts

Using the broader definition of social impacts referred to earlier, that is, any impact that has a social dimension, leads to the identification of an enormous array of possible effects. It is therefore useful to summarize them into a classification scheme. For some time it has been popular to think about tourism impacts in three domains: economic, environmental and social [9]; and recently, tourism researchers have borrowed the term the 'triple bottom line' from company accounting, to refer to this trilogy. Ritchie identified six impact domains in the context of event tourism, but these are also useful for examining the potential impacts of tourism more generally [10]. Recent work in the area of sport event impact assessment has merged these two approaches by examining impacts within the triple bottom line framework with an additional focus on longer term effects on image [11]. Table 2 summarizes the overlap between these classification schemes. Each type of impact may have both positive and negative manifestations, and the magnitude of the impact is likely to be substantially affected by management intervention. Some of the impacts of tourism may be

Table 2 Classification of Impacts

Triple Bottom Line Approach[9]	Ritchie[10]	Fredline, Raybould, Jago and Deery[11]	Examples of impacts that could be classified into each category
Economic	Economic	Economic	Contribution to Gross Regional Product Generation of income Employment Changes in the structure of the local economy Stimulation of entrepreneurial activity Opportunity costs Upward pressure on prices/property values
Physical	Physical	Environmental	Pressure on sensitive natural areas Pollution and litter Pressure on existing urban infrastructure e.g. Traffic, crowding, noise, public transport Influence on new infrastructure development
Social	Socio-cultural Psychological Political	Social	Influence on social structure Influence on culture and values (Demonstration Effect) Outcomes of intercultural interaction Political outcomes Influence on individual psychological well being
	Tourism/ Commercial	Long Term Image • Media Exposure • Destination Image • Business Promotion	Changes in tourism flows Changes in investment patterns and business opportunities

perceived differently within a community as they effectively redistribute resources resulting in some subgroups reaping rewards at the expense of others.

Sport Tourism Impacts

Economic.

The economic impacts of sport tourism are unlikely to be substantially different from those associated with other forms of tourism, although there is some evidence to suggest that sport tourists (particularly spectating sport tourists) yield higher returns than the average 'holiday' visitor because they tend to spend more per day [12]. Some forms of sport tourism may also be more likely to deliver economic benefits to non-urban areas where regional economic development is desirable [13].

Physical and environmental impacts

Physical and environmental impacts will depend to some extent on the characteristics of the region that is playing host to the activity. Where sport is undertaken in a potentially sensitive natural area, environmental damage may result. For example bushwalking, horse or mountain bike riding, and other activities in pristine natural environments may have minimal impact if traffic is low, but as activity increases then impacts such as pollution, erosion and disruption to flora and fauna are likely to escalate. In urban environments it can be more difficult to attribute environmental and physical change specifically to tourism; however, any activity that temporarily increases the population of an area, is likely to place increased pressure on existing infrastructure such as roads and public transport, particularly in the case of a large-scale sporting event, which may also contribute to unwelcome levels of noise and crowding.

On the positive side, the growth of sport tourism in a destination can promote the development of infrastructure that may also be utilized by local residents. Large-scale sporting events tend to promote the development of new sporting venues and the longer-term benefits of these depend on the extent to which they can be effectively utilized to the advantage of locals.

Social impacts

In terms of 'social' impacts of sport tourism (using the narrower definition) the hosting of major sporting events is often associated with a sense of pride and self-actualisation amongst the resident population. They may also provide opportunities for entertainment and community or family togetherness. The demonstration effect of hosting sport activity may also be a catalyst for promoting sporting activity amongst the local community, which may have long-term implications for fitness levels and health.

On the negative side, there are examples of situations where the demonstration effect may be perceived as detrimental, for example, sport fans behaving in a rowdy or delinquent manner, which is negative in itself but may also have some affect on the behaviour of local residents. Intercultural interaction can manifest itself negatively, especially when international sporting teams are competing and nationalistic sentiments are strong. Also, individuals or community subgroups may experience reductions in their psychological well being, especially if they perceive a loss of control over their environment, and an injustice in the way tourism impacts are managed.

It is not possible to fully document the myriad of possible impacts because of the unique characteristics of each destination and sport tourism activity. It is important though to understand why some regions are differently impacted than others, and also why impacts are perceived differently amongst some communities and community subgroups. Some insight can be drawn from sociological theory.

Theoretical Bases for Understanding the Impacts of Tourism

The literature relating to the impacts of tourism on host communities has generally taken one of two approaches. The earliest studies adopted a macro perspective assuming a level of homogeneity within the resident population. These studies examine residents' reactions to tourism in terms of variables that characterize the region as a whole. This type of study has been described as 'extrinsic' because they look only at the community as a single entity [14]. In many of the more recent studies, the emphasis has switched to the exploration of the inherent heterogeneity within geographically-defined communities. These 'intrinsic' studies aim to understand why some subgroups of residents perceive the impacts of tourism differently than others.

Extrinsic Models of Community Impact

A sub sector of extrinsic models are often also referred to as stage-based models because they describe how resident reactions to tourism change in response to changes in the magnitude and characteristics of tourism to the host region. One of the earliest models was Doxey's Irridex [15], which suggested that the attitudes of the host community toward tourists will pass through a series of stages including euphoria, apathy, annoyance and antagonism. The implication is that, over time, the hosts will be exposed to continued (and probably increasing) levels of negative impact.

Butler's well renowned Tourist Area Cycle of Evolution similarly implies that as the number of tourists increases, the impact on the host community is likely to intensify, and that escalating annoyance is a possible outcome [16]. However, he suggests that a thorough explanation of resident reaction is far more complex, and consideration must be given not only to the characteristics of the tourism, but also to the characteristics of the hosts and their region.

These early models seem to ignore the potential for residents to adapt to the impacts of increasing tourism, which appears likely given that more recent studies have found high levels of support in destinations with advanced tourism development such as Hawaii and Australia's Gold Coast [17]. However, the models are highly valuable to the extent that they have been instrumental in raising awareness of the importance of managing the impacts of tourism to avoid eventual antagonism.

In these extrinsic models, there are several variables that are considered likely to explain differences in host community perceptions of tourism. These include the stage of development; that is, whether tourism is in an exploration, involvement, development, consolidation, stagnation, rejuvenation or declining phase [18]. Also, the seasonality of the tourism activity is thought to be relevant; whether visitation levels are fairly uniform over an annual period or whether they are concentrated into specific tourism seasons. The host/guest ratio, and the cultural distance between hosts and guests are also considered to be relevant, together giving an indication of the tourism-carrying capacity of the region [19]. This is defined as the point beyond which the tourism resources of a community become overloaded and, therefore, if this point is exceeded negative impacts and negative community perceptions are likely to result [20]. Unfortunately the limited empirical work in this area has been, by necessity, case based, and frequently using substantially different methods which impedes comparison. A larger body of work exploring intrinsic variables means that this variation is better understood.

Intrinsic Models of Community Impact

The intrinsic models attempt to explain why some residents within a community have higher levels of support for tourism activity than others. A substantial body of literature has accumulated in recent decades and some of the relevant variables have been clearly identified, as summarized in Table 3.

While early intrinsic studies shed substantial light on the variables that appeared to explain variance in resident perceptions of tourism, they tended to be descriptive and atheoretical, and it is only relatively recently that an attempt has been made to explain the variation in light of existing sociological and psychological theory.

Table 3 Variables which Explain Intrinsic Variation in Resident Perceptions of Impacts

Variable	Relationship
Financial benefit from tourism (through employment or ownership of a business that benefits from tourism)	Residents who benefit financially from tourism perceive higher levels of social benefit.
Identification with the Theme	Residents who enjoy the theme of the tourism/event perceive higher levels of social benefit.
Contact (usually defined by residential proximity)	Residents who come into closer physical contact with tourism perceive both costs and benefits more highly.
Values	Residents who have social values that are consistent with development tend to perceive higher levels of social benefit.

Ap [21] employed social exchange theory, in an effort to understand how residents may feel and behave in the context of tourism [22]. The theory describes behaviour in terms of exchanges, suggesting that residents engage in tourism exchanges such as working in or owning a business in the sector, sharing community resources with tourists, and utilizing new resources developed because of tourism. They then weigh up the costs and benefits of these exchanges and their overall perception will be the result of an internal cost benefit analysis. That is, if they believe that on balance, the benefits of tourism outweigh the costs, they will form a positive attitude toward tourism and may engage in supportive behaviours. If however they perceive the costs to outweigh the benefits, they will hold negative attitudes toward tourism and may attempt to withdraw from the relationship.

Pearce, Moscardo and Ross [23] have drawn upon social representation theory [24], which describes how values and attitudes toward a phenomenon are shared within a community. Social representations are 'systems of preconceptions, images and values' about a phenomenon [25]. Representations are the mechanisms people use to try to understand the world around them. When information on an unfamiliar object or event is encountered, past experience and prior knowledge of something that is seen as similar is used as a reference point. It is argued that representations are resistant to change, because they form a frame of reference through which new information is interpreted. Echabe and Rovira found that people had more accurate recall of facts that were consistent with their representation, and tended to 'modify' facts that were inconsistent [26].

The 'social' element refers to the fact that these representations are shared by social groups and help facilitate communication. In the context of tourism, the theory suggests that residents have representations of tourism which underpin their perceptions of impact, and that these representations are informed by direct experiences, social interaction and other information sources such as the media.

These two theories are not inconsistent, in fact there are substantial parallels, but social representation theory allows for non-rational reactions to tourism that are based on personal and social values, while social exchange tends to assume rational information processing. Social representation theory also acknowledges the fact that representations are socially transmitted making it possible for people who have less experience with a phenomenon to adopt a representation that is presented to them by their social group or through the media.

A third theory that has been advanced in this regard by Lindberg and Johnson [27] is the expectancy-value model [28]. This model suggest that there is an interaction between the importance that residents place on certain outcomes (values) and the degree to which they believe tourism contributes to these outcomes (expectancy). Like social exchange, this model does not appear to allow for residents who act as cognitive misers; that is, they do not care enough about an issue to think deeply about it. Rather, they assume a representation that is consistent with the norms of their social groups.

However, while social representation theory is more appealing than the alternatives in terms of its ability to accommodate different levels of interest in tourism amongst various resident sub-groups and the transmission of representations from person to person; this additional complexity also makes it far more difficult to test. There is substantial progress yet to be made in substantiating the validity and reliability of existing measures of social impact, and then in more fully understanding the variation within communities and between different communities.

The next section summarizes a series of studies that have been undertaken to explore residents' reactions to the hosting of large-scale sporting events. These studies have taken place in developed western destinations, and therefore the results cannot necessarily be generalized to other contexts, but the results nonetheless provide insight into the potential impacts of sporting events and sport tourism more generally.

Empirical Research

A series of studies have been undertaken on a range of large-scale sporting events in Australia using similar methods. Some of the results from four of these studies are reported here to give some insight into the range of impacts identified, and the perception of impacts of different types of event in different communities. A brief overview of the four case studies reported on is provided below.

The 2002 Australian Formula One Grand Prix. The Australian Formula One Grand Prix has been hosted in Melbourne every year sine 1996. Melbourne is a large (by Australian standards) state capital city with a population of approximately 3.6 million [29]. The event is hosted close to the city, approximately four kilometres south of the centre on a street circuit, in and around a large city park. Thus, there is substantial effort required in erection and dismantling of the necessary infrastructure. This creates substantial disruption in the vicinity and restricts access to the park for a period of the year.

The 2003 Australian Open Tennis Tournament. The Australian Open was first hosted in Melbourne in 1905, and thus it is a long-standing tradition in the city. The event is one of the Grand Slam tournaments on the international tennis circuit, and is therefore regarded as a prestigious event. It is staged in a purpose-built facility, The National Tennis Centre, close to the city and there is substantial infrastructure supporting the event precinct including parking and public transport.

The 2003 Rugby World Cup – Brisbane Matches. The Rugby World Cup is held every four years, but as it rotates between host regions it is effectively a one-off event. The 2003 event was hosted by the Australian Rugby Union (ARU) and matches were held across the nation in ten different cities. Brisbane is the capital city of Queensland and has a population of about 1.7 million residents [30]. The city hosted seven pool matches and two quarter finals over a period of approximately four weeks.

The 2003 Rugby World Cup – Townsville Matches. Townsville is the second largest city in Queensland situated in the north of the state, approximately 1,500 kilometres north of Brisbane. It is a much smaller city with a population of approximately 140,000 residents, and it serves as the regional centre for North Queensland, an area that is fairly reliant on agriculture and mining. The northern regions of Queensland are also important tourism destinations; however, Townsville itself attracts fewer tourists than more popular areas to the north (for example Cairns) and to the south (for example, the Whitsunday Islands, gateway to the Great Barrier Reef).

Method

In each of the case studies, a random selection of local residents was surveyed, either using a self-completion questionnaire administered through the postal system or via a telephone interview. The instrument was developed over time. The earliest studies used a scale with forty-five items, but subsequent studies have used a compressed scale derived from analysis of the previously collected data. More details on the scale development process are documented elsewhere [31]. The compressed impact scale, which comprised twelve items, initially asked respondents to agree or disagree with a statement about a potential impact of the event. If they agreed, they were then asked to rate the level of impact on their personal quality of life, and the impact on the community as a whole.

Results

Table 4 shows the mean personal and community level ratings for each of the events on each of the potential impacts. There is a fairly consistent pattern in the responses, which is to be expected given that the events were all similar in theme (that is, mainstream, large-scale, spectator sport events) and the communities examined all had similar cultural backgrounds. However, there are some differences that are worthy of further attention. The respondents in Townsville perceived a substantially higher level of community benefit from the RWC with regard to pride, entertainment opportunities, regional showcasing and economic impact. This is most likely to be related to the characteristics of this city in comparison to the other regions. Given Townsville's much smaller population, and its status as a remote regional centre rather than a state capital city, residents there would have fewer opportunities for sport-related entertainment, and feelings of pride and self-actualisation associated with playing host to a major event. Both Melbourne and Brisbane host several other international sporting events on a regular basis, thus any individual experience is less unique for residents of those communities. Also, Townsville's ambitions to attract more inbound tourism probably create awareness amongst local residents of the value of short- and long-term economic benefits of the hosting of events.

   With regard to costs, none of these events attracted substantial mean ratings for any of the negative impacts except the Grand Prix, where local residents appear to be somewhat concerned about disruption, community injustice and the impact on the environment. This is likely to be a function of the fact that the Grand Prix is the only one of these events not staged in a permanent venue. The race track has to be built and dismantled for each event creating substantial disruption in the vicinity for about three months each year and denying local residents access to an important recreational venue. This undoubtedly fuels the perception that the event is unjust because those

Table 4 Comparison of Perceived Impacts of Events

EVENT	Australian F1 Grand Prix		Australian Open Tennis		Rugby World Cup		Rugby World Cup	
Host Region	Melbourne		Melbourne		Brisbane		Townsville	
Year	2002		2003		2003		2003	
Frequency of Event	Annual		Annual		One-Off		One-Off	
Scale	45 items#		12 items		12 items		12 items	
Administration method	Self completion postal survey		Telephone interview		Telephone interview		Telephone interview	
Sample size	279		300		306		303	
Perceived Impacts	Personal	Community	Personal	Community	Personal	Community	Personal	Community
The Event made local residents feel more proud of their city and made them feel good about themselves and their community.	0.8#	1.2#	0.6	1.2	0.8	1.2	0.9	1.7
The Event promoted development and better maintenance of public facilities such as roads, parks, sporting facilities, and/or public transport.	0.7#	1.4#	0.3	0.7	0.2	0.7	0.3	0.7
The Event gave residents an opportunity to attend an interesting event, have fun with their family and friends, and interact with new people.	0.6#	1.3#	0.9	1.5	0.9	1.4	0.8	1.9
The Event showcased the region in a positive light. This helps to promote a better opinion of our region and encourages future tourism and/or business investment.	0.5#	1.4#	0.5	1.5	0.4	1.2	0.6	2.1
The Event was good for the community because the money that visitors spent when they came for the Event helps to stimulate the economy, stimulates employment opportunities, and is good for local business.	0.4#	1.5#	0.4	1.5	0.3	1.5	0.5	2.0

(continued)

Statement								
The Event was associated with some people behaving inappropriately, perhaps in a rowdy and delinquent way, or engaging in excessive drinking or drug use or other criminal behaviour.	−0.1#	−0.3#	0.0	0.0	0.0	−0.2	0.0	−0.2
The Event led to increases in the price of some things such as some goods and services and property values and/or rental costs.	−0.1#	0.0#	0.0	−0.1	0.0	−0.1	−0.1	−0.1
The Event had a negative impact on the environment through excessive litter and/or pollution and/or damage to natural areas.	−0.2#	−0.5#	0.0	0.0	−0.1	0.0	0.0	0.0
The Event was unfair to ordinary residents, and the costs and benefits were distributed unfairly across the community.	−0.2#	−0.7#	0.0	0.0	−0.1	−0.1	0.0	−0.1
The Event was a waste of public money, that is, too much public money was spent on the event that would be better spent on other public activities.	−0.3#	−0.4#	0.0	0.0	−0.1	0.0	0.0	−0.1
The Event disrupted the lives of local residents and created inconvenience. While the event was on problems like traffic congestion, parking difficulties and excessive noise were worse than usual.	−0.4#	−1.1#	0.0	−0.1	−0.3	−0.3	−0.1	−0.2
The Event denied local residents access to public facilities, that is, roads, parks, sporting facilities, public transport and/or other facilities were less available to local residents because of closure or overcrowding.	*	*	0.0	−0.1	−0.2	−0.2	−0.1	−0.1

these scores represent the average response to multiple items.
*no equivalent impact measured.

who reside further away from the event site are not as exposed to the localized negative externalities such as increased traffic congestion, parking problems and excessive noise. In terms of environmental damage, it seems logical that a motor sport event would be perceived as being more detrimental to the environment than tennis or rugby.

Strategies used by Hosts to Deal with Tourists

At the micro, or individual level, some insight has been shed on the different ways in which residents may adapt their lifestyles to cope with tourism. Dogan suggested five behavioural responses including resistance, retreatism, boundary maintenance, revitalization and adoption, which could be employed by residents to cope with tourism activity in their community [32]. Ap and Crompton developed a simple scale for measuring residents' behavioural responses to tourism based on Dogan's categories [33]. They reduced the options to four levels because of difficulties in operationalizing the distinctions between all the responses, the eventual response options being embracement, tolerance, adjustment and withdrawal.

Subsequent research suggests that residents can identify with these reactions [34]. In a case study comparison of the Gold Coast Indy Car Race 1998 and the Melbourne Grand Prix 1999, local residents reported behaviours consistent with these four responses. About one quarter of the sample reported that they embraced their event (through attending it or related functions, or by becoming involved in the public celebration). Over 40 per cent reported tolerance (which is associated with no behavioural change), and about 15 per cent reported minor adjustments to cope with the inconveniences. Finally, approximately 20 per cent of the sample reported withdrawal which manifested itself by retreating to the confines of their homes for the duration of the event or by electing to leave the area altogether.

At a macro level, public sector tourism management organizations can employ a range of strategies to reduce the negative impacts of tourism on the host community, but only if they are aware of the issues. Until recently, such organizations have shown little interest in the evaluation of tourism impacts beyond an assessment of the economic benefits which is frequently undertaken to justify substantial public investment (particularly in large-scale sporting events). However, recent embracement of the concept of triple bottom line reporting amongst the public sector should hopefully promote more social and environmental impact assessment and extend awareness of the issues that need to be considered. Such information will be useful in informing the sustainable management of existing sport tourism activity within a region, and in selecting appropriate new forms of sport tourism to promote within a destination.

User Conflicts

One of the potential impacts of sport tourism is the impact of increased demand on natural areas and sporting and other tourism infrastructure. Beaches may become overcrowded, sporting venues, which are normally accessible to the public, may be restricted for a specific event, and roads may be closed for a motor race or a marathon. While there is the potential that increasing demand will lead to increased supply of built facilities through public or private sector investment in sporting facilities, there is still the possibility that residents will perceive that tourism has reduced their amenity with regard to certain facilities.

The empirical research suggests that one of the important intrinsic predictors of overall perceptions of the impacts of tourism is utilization of affected recreation facilities. In the case of the Australian Formula One Grand Prix, the event takes place in a large recreational park which is the home of numerous sporting venues providing facilities for basketball, netball, badminton, squash, table tennis, cricket, football, soccer, baseball, hockey, lawn bowls and tennis. There is also a golf course and driving range, and a lake for boating. The erection and dismantling of event infrastructure restricts access to the park before, during and after the event. Residents who frequently used the park for recreational purposes (at least once a week) were found to have significantly more negative perceptions of the social impact of the Grand Prix than did those who were not frequent users of the park. This is consistent will findings from previous research by Keogh who found that residents who were frequent users of a recreational area were more concerned about tourist use of that area because of the potential reduction in amenity to them [35].

Conclusion

Given the perceived benefits of tourism, particularly the economic impacts, it is likely that tourism will continue to be encouraged in many destinations by both public and private sector organizations [36]. As noted in Table 1, one of the key influences on the level of impact of tourism is likely to be the management strategies employed in an effort to maximize the benefits and minimize the costs associated with the activity, and it is only through research, and an increased understanding of the most effective management techniques, that sustainability can be achieved.

Social impact assessment has progressed considerably in the last two decades and yet there is still much work to be done. More work is required to ensure the validity of the measures and this could be at least partially achieved through triangulation, by simultaneously employing more than one of the methods referred to at the beginning of this paper. Additionally, more empirical work is required, to better understand the extrinsic sources of variation in social impact.

There has been a long history of evaluation of the economic impacts of tourism, and these techniques have been embraced by government in an effort to justify the promotion of tourism. However, it is only very recently that governments have also indicated an interest in assessing the broader range of impacts including environmental, social and longer-term impacts. The triple bottom line approach, represents a step forward for tourism impact management, not only because it considers broader issues, but because it can also consider the trade-offs between impacts of different types. For example, a large-scale motor sport event may attract numerous high-spend international visitors leading to substantial economic benefits but may also cause extensive social disruption and environmental damage. A smaller, participant-oriented sport activity, may not generate as much revenue, but is unlikely to have the same level of social and environmental cost.

Techniques that attempt to synthesize the various impacts of tourism into an overall assessment, are in their infancy, and need substantial development. Once this has occurred they will be extremely useful in identifying the best types of sport tourism for destination managers to pursue.

Notes

[1] J. Elkington, *The Ecology of Tomorrow's World* (New York: Halsted Press, 1981).

[2] A. Mathieson, and G. Wall, *Tourism: Economic, Physical and Social Impacts* (London: Longman, 1982), p.137.

[3] J. Ap and J.L. Crompton, 'Developing and Testing a Tourism Impact Scale', *Journal of Travel Research*, 37, 2 (1998), 120–30; C. Ryan and D. Montgomery, 'The Attitudes of Bakewell Residents to Tourism and Issues in Community Responsive Tourism', *Tourism Management*, 15, 5 (1994), 358–69; E. Fredline and B. Faulkner, 'Residents' Reactions to the Staging of Major Motorsport Events Within Their Communities: A Cluster Analysis', *Event Management*, 7, 2 (2002), 103–14.

[4] K. Lindberg and R. Johnson, 'The Economic Values of Tourism's Social Impacts', *Annals of Tourism Research*, 24, 1(1997), 90–116; K. Lindberg, B. Dellaert and C. Rassing, 'Resident Tradeoffs: A Choice Modelling Approach', *Annals of Tourism Research*, 26, 3 (1999), 554–69; K. Lindberg, T. Andersson and B. Dellaert, 'Tourism Development: Assessing Social Gains and Losses', *Annals of Tourism Research*, 28, 4 (2001), 1010–30.

[5] Lindberg, Andersson and Dellaert, 'Tourism Development: Assessing Social Gains and Losses', 1010–30.

[6] R. Burdge and F. Vanclay, 'Social Impact Assessment: A Contribution to the State of the Art Series', *Impact Assessment*, 14, 1 (1996), 59.

[7] C. M. Hall, J. Selwood and E. McKewon, 'Hedonists, Ladies and Larrikins: Crime, Prostitution and the 1987 America's Cup', *Visions in Leisure and Business*, 14, 3 (1996), 28–51.

[8] E. Fredline, 'Host Community Reactions to Major Sporting Events: The Gold Coast Indy and the Australian Formula One Grand Prix in Melbourne' (unpublished Doctoral Thesis, Griffith University, Gold Coast, 2000).

[9] Mathieson and Wall, *Tourism: Economic, Physical and Social Impacts*; C.M. Hall, *Hallmark Tourist Events: Impacts, Management and Planning* (London: Bethaven Press, 1992).

[10] J. Ritchie, 'Assessing the Impact of Hallmark Events: Conceptual and Research Issues', *Journal of Travel Research*, 22, 1 (1984), 2–11.

[11] E. Fredline, M. Raybould, L. Jago and M. Deery, 'Triple Bottom Line Event Evaluation: Progress Toward a Technique to Assist in Planning and Managing Events in a Sustainable Manner'. Paper presented at the *Tourism State of the Art II Conference*, Glasgow, June 2004.

[12] Bureau of Tourism Research, *International Visitor Survey* (Canberra: BTR, 2003). (This conclusion is based on Australian tourism expenditure data estimates and may not be generalizable to other destinations.)

[13] See Mules and Dwyer, this volume, for more discussion on economic impacts.

[14] B. Faulkner and C. Tideswell, 'A Framework for Monitoring Community Impacts of Tourism', *Journal of Sustainable Tourism*, 5, 1 (1997), 3–28.

[15] G.V. Doxey, 'A Causation Theory of Visitor Resident Irritants: Methodology and Research Inferences', in *Travel and Tourism Research Association Sixth Annual Conference Proceedings*, (San Diego, CA: TTRA 1975), pp.195–8.

[16] R.W. Butler, 'The Concept of a Tourist Area Cycle of Evolution: Implications for Management of Resources', *Canadian Geographer*, 24, 1 (1980), 5–12.

[17] J. Lui and T. Var, 'Resident Attitudes Toward Tourism Impacts in Hawaii', *Annals of Tourism Research*, 13, 2 (1986), 193–214; Faulkner and Tideswell, 'A Framework for Monitoring Community Impacts of Tourism', 3–28.

[18] Butler, 'The Concept of a Tourist Area Cycle of Evolution', 5–12.

[19] R.W. Butler, 'Tourism as an Agent of Social Change', *Proceedings of the International Geographical Union's Working Group on the Geography of Tourism and Recreation* (Ontario, Canada: Trent University, 1975), pp.85–90.

[20] H. Coccossis and A. Parpairis, 'Tourism and the Environment: Some Observations on the Concept of Carrying Capacity', in H. Briassoulis (ed.), *Tourism and the Environment: Regional, Economic and Policy Issues* (Dordrecht: Kluwer Academic Publications, 1992), pp.23–33.

[21] J. Ap, 'Residents' Perceptions on Tourism Impacts', *Annals of Tourism Research*, 19, 4 (1992), 665–90.

[22] R. Emerson, 'Exchange Theory. Part 1: A Psychological Basis for Social Exchange', in J. Berger, M. Zelditch and B. Anderson (eds), *Sociological Theories in Progress* (New York: Houghton-Mifflin, 1972), pp.38–87.

[23] P.L. Pearce, G. Moscardo and G. F. Ross, *Tourism Community Relationships* (Oxford: Pergamon, 1996).

[24] S. Moscovici, 'On Social Representations', in J. P. Forgas (ed.), *Social Cognition: Perspectives on Everyday Understanding* (London: Academic Press, 1981), pp. 181–209.

[25] S. Moscovici, 'The Coming Era of Social Representations', in J.P. Codol and J.P. Leyens (eds), *Cognitive Approaches to Social Behavior* (The Hague: Nijhoff, 1982), p.122.

[26] A. Echabe and D. Rovira, 'Social Representations and Memory', *European Journal of Social Psychology*, 19 (1989), 543–51.

[27] Lindberg and Johnson, 'The Economic Values of Tourism's Social Impacts', 90–116.

[28] A.H. Eagly and S. Chaiken, *The Psychology of Attitudes* (Orlando, Florida: Harcourt Brace Jovanovich, 1993).

[29] Australian Bureau of Statistics, *Australian Demographic Statistics* (Canberra: ABS, 2003).

[30] Ibid.

[31] E. Fredline, L. Jago and M. Deery, 'The Development of a Generic Scale to Measure the Social Impacts of Events', *Event Management*, 8, 1 (2003), 23–37.

[32] H.Z. Dogan, 'Forms of Adjustment: Sociocultural Impacts of Tourism', *Annals of Tourism Research*, 16, 2 (1989), 216–36.

[33] J. Ap and J. L. Crompton, 'Residents' Strategies for Responding to Tourism Impacts', *Journal of Travel Research*, 32, 1 (1993), 47–50.

[34] Fredline, 'Host Community Reactions to Major Sporting Events: The Gold Coast Indy and the Australian Formula One Grand Prix in Melbourne'.

[35] B. Keogh, 'Public Participation in Community Tourism Planning', *Annals of Tourism Research*, 17, 3 (1990), 449–65.

[36] See Mules and Dwyer in this volume for more on economic impacts.

Sport Tourism, Cityscapes and Cultural Politics

Michael Silk & John Amis

Practical and academic interest in sport tourism has grown exponentially in recent years. Largely due to the democratization of sport and tourism [1], an increased prominence and understanding of the technological, ideological and cultural levers of globalization, and a corresponding rise of a late capitalist consumer culture centred on symbolic images, sport tourism has been thrust into the cross-currents of contemporary social analysis. This growth has been met with a number of volumes that have begun to make sense of these recent developments [2]. Perhaps most critically interrogated in the work of Tom Hinch and James Higham [3], sport tourism has become influential in the construction of aspects of local, regional, national, and, or global policy, and is firmly entrenched within many university curricula [4].

Recently, in a special issue of the *Journal of Sport Management*, Heather Gibson [5], while reflecting on this rapid growth, reiterated her earlier calls for theoretically grounded, interdisciplinary, sport tourism studies – necessary, she believed, in order

Michael Silk, Physical Cultural Studies, Department of Kinesiology, University of Maryland, College Park, Maryland, 20742, USA. Correspondence to: msilk@umd.edu to overcome the unhelpful disciplinary divisions that inhibit advances in many academic disciplines [6]. Within this essay, we embrace Gibson's logic and develop arguments that are emblematic of a shift to a more theoretically-grounded understanding of the drivers and outcomes of sport tourism. Specifically, we add to the growing discourse on the ways in which sport tourism has affected, and has in turn been affected by, the definition and utilization of space and place.

With its roots in wider theoretical embrace of the contributions of a spatial understanding [7], particularly with respect to sporting cultures, economies and experiences [8], the academic domain of sport tourism has, relatively recently, begun to address how sport tourism becomes manifest in space and how such manifestations may be influenced by tourism developments [9]. Certainly, these contributions have provided for a more insightful, dense and critical interrogation of the impact of the production and consumption of sport tourism. However, and likely due to the relative infancy of the field, there has yet to be adequate theoretical and empirical consideration of the tourist-oriented, carefully orchestrated, contouring of city spaces as sites of social struggle in which dominant power relations can be constructed, contested and reproduced. This is despite recognition elsewhere of various neglected issues related to tourism capital, commodification of place, state regulation, labour and entrepreneurship [10].

Given the paucity of work in this area, and following this promising lead for the future of sport tourism research, our focus is explicitly spatial, focusing on transformations in place – transformations that have in part taken place due to the emergence of new relationships between cities and a global economy. In this regard, we are interested in issues related to space, place, culture, commodification and nostalgia within the realm of sport tourism. Within our own work, these issues are, for the most part, although not exclusively, anchored within a cultural studies approach that celebrates interdisciplinarity and a multi-methodological focus. Thus, drawing mostly on, and indeed operating in the boundaries between, cultural geography, media studies, sociology, urban studies, political economy, organizational studies and history, we illustrate these issues through brief sketches of two cities, Baltimore and Memphis, both of which serve as poignant exemplars of the processes that have moulded cities under late capitalism. Specifically, through a study of the physical and imagined spaces of these two cities, we investigate the responses to a declining manufacturing base and increasing economic polarization through the creation of 'tourist bubbles' [11] to facilitate the regeneration of increasingly desolate urban areas. Prominent in this analysis is the utilization of sport and entertainment, and particularly the investment of new infrastructure, to anchor these neatly defined, and physically bounded, spaces of play. Doreen Massey [12] has clearly articulated that any such study must locate analysis of the local within the uneven dynamic of capitalist society, an approach that allows for the unearthing of the particularities and differences of the local in relation to the dynamics of the spatial economy. As such, prior to presenting our empirical findings, we provide an account of transformations in place in relation to spatial reconfigurations.

Spaces of Late Capitalist Production and Consumption

Within the relatively recent past, scholars have begun to recognize, interpret and incorporate into their patterns of thinking the spatiality of human life in much the same way that others have traditionally interpreted history and society[13]. A reinvigorated critical perspective associated with an explicitly spatial imagination has infused the study of history and society with new modes of thinking and interpretation. Initially taken up within cultural geography, and influenced through engagement with cultural studies and postmodern thought, it is no longer possible to think through notions of culture without consideration of its moorings in space. As Edward Soja has suggested, at the turn of the twenty-first century 'there is a renewed awareness of the simultaneity and interwoven complexity of the social, historical and spatial dimensions of our lives, their inseparability and often problematic interdependence'[14].

With respect to the contemporary city, a spatial perspective points towards the relationships that cities have with a new global, or network economy[15]. Given the partial unbundling, or at least weakening, of the national as a spatial unit due to privatization, deregulation, technological advances in communications, and the associated strengthening of globalization, there have come about conditions for the ascendance of other spatial scales[16]. Perhaps most famously captured within the work of Saskia Sassen, these changes in the global flows of production, commodities and information have amounted to a new spatial expression of the logic of accumulation[17]. This has impacted upon the relationship that cities, or places, have to the spatial expression of late capitalism – in both physical and imagined transformations that emerge as a result of the multiple and contradictory relationships with the network economy. From the early 1970s, many Western cities have taken on a new morphology more closely aligned to the symbolic regimes of production and consumption underpinning the late capitalist economy[18], the emergence of which was bolstered by the breaking down of the national bargain – the rolling back of the Keynesian welfare state, and the emergence of post-Fordist patterns of production and consumption[19]. Faced with the triple problems of deindustrialization, a falling tax base and declining public expenditure[20], cities have engaged in a competitive process of economic restructuring to reposition and represent themselves as centres for international finance, information and communication services, and consumption[21].

Central to the successful implementation of such strategic repositioning for many cities has been the perceived need to attract affluent individuals, both as residents (see Florida, 2002) and more notably for the purposes of this text, tourists. This has led to an unprecedented level of inter-city competition for business and indeed sporting events[22] as civic leaders have sought to revive formerly industrial cities on the back of new economies based on tourism, entertainment and culture[23]. In many instances, civic leadership has responded to deindustrialization with a series of investments that would set the stage for new residential development designed to attract older baby boomers and young professionals to urban lifestyles amid the new entertainment opportunities in downtown areas [24]. Clearly, the rationale behind reorienting the cityspace around spectacular spaces of consumption – most notably shopping malls, themed restaurants, hotels, bars, theme parks, mega-complexes for professional sport franchises, gentrified housing, conference complexes and waterfront pleasure domes [25] – is to dramatically redefine the city for residents and potential visitors, repairing the 'pockmarks' of the dilapidated and obsolete urban core [26].

The shift from a welfare oriented, inwardly focused city, to one directed to the securing of outside individual and corporate investment, has been termed urban imagineering by Short and colleagues [27]. Urban imagineering involves the active efforts to adopt an entrepreneurial stance to attract mobile capital and thereby refurbish and refine both the built urban environment and the imagined spaces of identity [28]. This 'spectacularization of urban space', [29] gives a greater importance to promoting the positive, unique and differential amenity and service attributes of a city; in this way the entire urban core is looked upon as a recreational environment and as a tourism resource [30]. Based around the manufacturing and promotion of a positive brand identity for a city, this 'symbolic commodification of place' [31] is designed to appeal to and attract tourists wanting to visit this must-see destination. The repositioning of cities, often involving intensified place-competition between cities, regions, states and nations then [32], is not only an activity involving investment and land use, it is also very importantly an effort at image creation or preservation – a representation of reality [33]. Britton, for example invokes the term 'tourism production system' to address the activities involved in investing places and spaces with social meaning and representations that allow them to be incorporated into the production process associated with tourism and capital generation [34]. However, and while such transformations can be aesthetically appealing, we cannot just accept these spaces without questioning their representations of urban life, lest we risk succumbing to a visually seductive, privatized public culture [35].

In *Whose* Interests? Sporting the Tourist Bubble

While cities may have shed their industrial fibre, the turn to a 'visually seductive' tourist culture, negates the mid-twentieth-century processes of suburbanization and the perception of the inner city as unsafe areas of unchecked blight, racial strife, criminality and deviance [36]. In this way, and perhaps as the Janus face of tourist development, it is important to think of cityspace as polarized or segregated – a divided city, a container of multiple narratives within the context of transformation in the predominant mode of social regulation [37]. As such, and to attract middle-class residents, suburban consumers, corporate investors and tourists into downtown areas, these spaces of consumption are often specially-designed, sanitized, entertainment districts concentrated in small areas. As physically bounded 'tourist bubbles' [38], such areas effectively cordon off and cosset the desired visitor while simultaneously warding off the threatening 'native' [39]. Through the creation of an image of style, safety and entertainment, fears can be eased and reluctance about visiting the downtown reduced. As such, the presentation of a faux-like downtown works to negate the unpredictability of preconceived urban experiences [40]. In this way, the tourist bubble can provide a sophisticated façade [41] that belies the structural inequalities in the contemporary cityscape, often becoming manifest in polarized labour markets, extreme economic disparities, and racially differentiated housing and schooling provision.

Initially anchored by festival marketplaces which failed to produce the desired outcomes, and bolstered by the real estate boom of the early 1990s, cities turned to new forms of entertainment and tourist facilities to assist downtown development – sporting properties assumed increased importance within these processes [42]. While sports venue projects do not necessarily generate regional growth and often-involve large subsidies, city leaders hoped that these facilities would bring residents, businesses and tourists to downtown areas and create a positive impact on the downtown economy [43]. With sporting events having arguably eclipsed other forms of mega-event, they have thus assumed increased significance in global city promotion and urban renewal strategies [44]. Consequently, the construction of new facilities devoted to tourism and entertainment has transformed the built environment of many cities [45]. Indeed, the social institution of sport and local sporting character are part of the fabric of place identity and the fortunes of sporting performance are frequently invoked in various dimensions of place representation [46]. Within the United States, the resources devoted to this reconstruction are impressive. More than $2 billion was spent annually in the early 1990s on sports facilities and convention centres alone [47], and the pace of construction has undoubtedly quickened since then [48].

To attract tourists, it is thus important for a city, often through sport, to project an identity that can transform ordinary places and times into extraordinary tourist worlds – something not easily accomplished for formerly mercantile and industrial cities [49] (see Harrison–Hill and Chalip, Marketing Sport Tourism: Creating Synergy between Sport and Destination). This involves directing attention to those who are currently responsible for the contouring of the urban environment. Clearly, the production of city narratives do not emerge from nowhere, rather they are produced, reproduced and reified by those 'public' and 'private' actors with responsibility for making decisions regarding the physical and imagined landscape of contemporary cityspaces [50]. Furthermore, the reach of the neo-liberal governmental agenda has been operationalized and institutionalized within the production of cityspace [51] – a new urban politics in which the responsibility for regenerating inner-city areas thus falls increasingly on the shoulders of public-private concerns and coalitions [52].

The enhanced role of the private sector in the regeneration of the city further complicates the complexion of those responsible for physically and symbolically designing 'cityspace'. Indeed, Sheller and Urry suggest that powerful, mobile, networks are refolding what was once known as public and private to the degree that the distinction between public and private domains has become all but meaningless [53]. Exemplified in Sack and Johnson's [54] account of the role of city elites in bringing the Volvo International Tennis Tournament to New Haven, Connecticut, this has meant that democratic politics have largely been removed from the development of infrastructure, tourism and environment to the degree that what the electorate may actually prefer is frequently rendered of little importance [55]. Rather, a shift of power from democratic local governing regimes to semi-autonomous public/private authorities has fragmented urban politics into a constellation of public/private institutions that operate largely independently from democracy and with little public accountability [56]. Indeed, the governance of such spatial fragments amid an era of 'place marketing' can be seen as part of a 'revanchist' urban vernacular that suspends commitment to extend social justice to the whole of society, compelling the poor and disposed to be tightly disciplined through a range of legal and architectural methods [57].

The careful orchestration of cityspace then brings to the fore questions surrounding the manipulation of place identity by public/private agencies pursuing strategies promoting the advantages of their cities within the processes and rhetoric of global competition [58]. In this respect, key questions emerge within the practices of urban regeneration with respect to *whose* aesthetics really count, *who* benefits, *whose* collective memory is being performed, and *whose* interests are being furthered [59]. To address these questions, we turn to two poignant exemplars of cities that have responded to the spatial logic of accumulation through the creation of sport-anchored tourist bubbles. In so doing, we aim to highlight the very active reconstitution of cityspace, the strategizing of key agencies to create, regulate and govern the sanitized spaces of play, and provide a marker for the conclusion which centres on the problems inherent in, and issues that arise from, such urban regeneration. Initially, we provide a brief sketch of Baltimore that highlights the processes and strategizing undertaken within the city to transform its image as the 'armpit of the east' [60] to one centred on image alone, an image designed to attract and nurture corporate, touristic and desired resident investment.

Sketch One: Baltimore – 'The Rot Beneath the Sporting Glitter'

According to David Harvey, Baltimore is emblematic of the conditions that have moulded cities under late capitalism [61]. Baltimore has been credited with having undergone a startling urban renaissance, a redevelopment that has been widely lauded as a model for urban regeneration [62]. Baltimore has earned this reputation with projects such as the Charles Center, the Inner Harbor, the Digital Harbor and Oriole Park at Camden Yards that have attracted the 'creative class' [63], tourists, and international media attention to the city's once moribund central business district (CBD), and gentrified surrounding neighbourhoods. These redevelopment efforts have been promoted by an alliance of the city's business community and political leadership, particularly the administration of Mayor William Donald Schaefer (1971–86), and financed through public–private partnerships in which the city and state governments have absorbed most of the financial risk while the private sector has reaped most of the profits [64]. Further, and fully bound within a new urban politics in which civic responsibility is assuaged in favour of public–private concerns and coalitions [65], segments of the Baltimore urban core were designated in 1994 as an Empowerment Zone (EZ) by the President's Community Enterprise Board.

The most prominent criteria for selection as an EZ area was economic distress couched in a language of decentralization, exurbanization and commercial flight [66]. The Empowerment Zone and Enterprise Community (EC) initiative was designed to revitalize urban communities through the creation of partnerships, the leveraging of private investment, the utilization of federal grant funding from the Departments of Agriculture and Housing and Urban Development, and significant federal tax incentives in the form of tax credits, tax deductions for businesses locating within these areas and tax exempt private facility bonds for those businesses in EZ/EC areas [67].

The origins of Baltimore's decline can be traced back to the not atypical post-WWII experiences of urban deindustrialization and depopulation. Initial redevelopment of the CBD started in the 1950s with the $180 million Charles Center office and retail complex, which was targeted towards white-collar professional corporations in the legal, finance, insurance and real estate industries [68]. Business leaders then turned their focus toward the Inner Harbour, which had been a 'cradle' of the city's development and long been a centre for Baltimore's industrial, warehousing and wholesaling activities, but had fallen into disuse and decay by 1960 and was characterized as an area of urban blight [69]. The potential of the Inner Harbor began to be realized following the election of Mayor Schaefer in 1971, whose campaign and administration focused on the redevelopment of downtown and the Inner Harbor [70]. Within a short time, the Inner Harbor began to be transformed into a consumption space, notably with the berthing of the U.S.S. Constellation, an early nineteenth-century US Navy ship, in 1972. The relocation of the Baltimore City Fair, attended by 2 million people, from Charles Center to the Inner Harbor in 1973, and the completion of the Maryland Science Center (1974) and the 27-story World Trade Center (1977) provided further momentum [71].

The next round of development, overcoming opposition from citizens who wanted to preserve the waterfront for public use, became manifest in the Inner Harbor's flagship projects: the Harborplace festival mall, National Aquarium, Hyatt Regency Hotel and Baltimore Convention Center [72]. Baltimore was praised in the media as having undergone an 'urban renaissance', with the London *Sunday Times* claiming in 1987 that 'the decay of old Baltimore slowed, halted, then turned back' [73]. Seeking to perpetuate this image, the Strategic Management Committee [74] published *The Renaissance Continues: A 20 Year Strategy for Downtown Baltimore*. This vision of Baltimore in 2010 projected the downtown area as 'a place for people', a place of 'opportunity', 'uncommonly liveable', 'easy to get to' and 'especially attractive' for residents and tourists to consume from a diverse array of leisure options offered around Baltimore's Inner Harbor:

> The rich tapestry of visitor attractions and services clustered near the harbour and the twice expanded Convention Center contribute mightily to the region's well-being. Downtown's cultural, entertainment and recreational attractions have become a magnet to visitors from around the world, and to many new businesses as well. The city's fine facilities such as the Sports Stadiums, Performing Arts Center and Christopher Columbus Center of Marine Research and Exploration have joined the fine National Aquarium and Marine Mammal Pavilion, City Life Museums, Science

Center, IMAX, Maritime Museum, theatres, concert halls, art institutions and other new and traditional attractions to form a mass of activity generators in a very favourable relationship to one another and to supporting services and facilities [75].

Of particular interest in this essay is the perceived role of sporting facilities in anchoring such urban regeneration strategies. According to Ritzer, consumers 'grow bored easily' with consumption environments. As such Baltimore had to create 'increasingly spectacular displays and a continual escalation of efforts to lure consumers' [76]. In order to differentiate itself from other cities and ensure the freshness of the consumption environment, in the late 1980s Baltimore unveiled plans for the construction of a baseball stadium in Camden Yards [77]. Located on the western fringe of the Inner Harbor, Camden Station and Warehouse were closed and abandoned in the early 1970s as industrial production in the city waned – an image that was inconsistent with the newly developed tourist-oriented Inner Harbor space of consumption. Bound with a concern over the potential relocation of the Orioles Baseball team (following the 1984 departure of the National Football League's Colts to Indianapolis) and the wilting Memorial Stadium, the city was desperate to find a new home for its remaining major league franchise. By architecturally incorporating the Camden Yards Warehouse within the retro-design of the ground, the stadium provided Baltimore with an imageable landmark that caught the attention of baseball fans and players, professional sports owners, the general public and architectural critics.

The construction of the publicly financed $210 million stadium not only provided a solution to the potential perceived loss of the city's major league status, but provided an opportunity to extend the tourist bubble westwards. This has been manifest in the creation of the Baltimore 'Westside', an area of the downtown anchored by the Camden Yards ballpark, the M&T Bank Stadium (home of the NFL franchise, the Baltimore Ravens), the Hippodrome Theatre, the new Centerpoint retail complex, and a number of newly renovated upscale apartment buildings and hotel complexes. Connecting to the Inner Harbour along the Pratt Street tourist corridor, flanked by the Baltimore Convention centre, these developments extend the Inner Harbour retail and commercial zone approximately one mile westwards to the University of Maryland Medical School and Hospital. These medical, consumer, sporting and tourist oriented facilities, so desired by civic leadership, are buffered by, somewhat ironically, the Martin Luther King expressway which acts as a physical boundary between the tourist bubble and those 'threatening natives' located a few blocks further west [78].

Harvey proposed that Baltimore's Inner Harbour functions as a sophisticated mask that invites us to participate in a spectacle [79]. However, he warned that, 'like any mask, it can beguile and distract in engaging ways, but at some point we want to know what lies behind it. If the mask cracks or is violently torn off, the terrible face of Baltimore's impoverishment may appear.' [80] Harvey's reasoning demonstrates the counter-side of gentrification and the need for more critical analyses of such investments within (and beyond) the sport tourism literatures. For if, as Friedman and colleagues, following Harvey [81], propose, we tear off this façade, the rot beneath the sporting glitter is all too evident. Such processes of urban renewal, for all their glittering façades, can actually be emblematic of the potential pitfalls of state capitalism [82]. In this sense, Baltimore's aesthetic rejuvenation is a veneer – quite literally in some run down and deserted neighbourhoods in which city workers are creating an illusion of occupancy by placing 'pictures of urban stability' in the form of life-sized photographs of windows and doors glued to plywood that camouflage boarded up houses [83] – masking the city's deep-rooted structural problems. It is a strategy designed to favour civic image over improved citizen welfare in which the city and state governments have absorbed most of the financial risk while the private sector has reaped the benefits [84].

Furthermore, those citizens who previously resided within these areas are becoming increasingly disconnected from their urban environment. In many neighbourhoods, owners who once accepted rent-subsidized tenants are either refurbishing units to be sold or rented at an increased rate [85]. The desire to attract and connect the 'creative class' to the new urban core [86], the concomitant decline in available public housing and the city's ceiling on Section Eight (a Federal government housing assistance programme for low income families) rental spending [87], has meant that many former residents are having to move to the city's periphery, away from the service oriented jobs on which the core ironically thrives. Worse still, many such displaced individuals find themselves in boarding houses, on the street, or in areas in which the city's blight – drug abuse, prostitution, and homelessness [88] – is far from hidden and in full view.

The sketch above exemplifies the ways that sport and entertainment infrastructure have been used to attempt to transform the image of a city's downtown core and place a city within the circuits of tourist promotion [89]. The disruption to, and relocation of, a populous deemed superfluous – even dangerous – to the planned urban regeneration demonstrates the counter-side of gentrification and the need for more critical analyses of such investments [90]. We now turn to another, more recent, example of a city that is striving to follow a similar path, Memphis.

Sketch Two: Memphis – Come Downtown and Play

Harvey [91] proposed that the perceived success of the Inner Harbor has led to other cities revitalizing their own waterfronts through entertainment and recreation facilities that are similar to Harborplace [92] – Memphis is one such city. Located in the mid-South and with an economy that was once prosperously centred on the cotton industry and Mississippi River but became increasingly fragmented through the course of the twentieth century, Memphis has entered into a range of new relationships emerging from the expression and logics of the spatial reach of capital – indeed Memphis can be termed a prototypical 'comeback' city [93]. Like Baltimore, the downtown core of Memphis has been transformed from a derelict, 'evacuated' [94] and dangerous space (at least in media fuelled perception) to one centred, according to *The New York Times*, on 'amusements for 26 year olds with advanced degrees' [95]. Through a dramatic effort of redevelopment, Memphis has attempted to reposition itself as a site for consumption and leisure services. Within the strategizing of key groups involved in these processes, notably architects, media organizations, the sports industry, and public/private 'officials', much of the urban core of downtown Memphis has been transformed into a recreational environment and tourism resource [96] that promotes the positive, unique and differential amenity and service attributes of the city [97]. As articulated by the City Center Commission's 'Planning for Growth' strategic planning process, the overall vision for the downtown is to 'transform the areas from a 9-to-5 business district to a 24-hour entertainment, sports and cultural centre' [98].

In the midst of a $2.3 billion downtown redevelopment programme, the new fully-integrated urban core comprises a central business district, with office buildings, residential areas, specialized shops, restaurants, luxury hotels, riverfront redevelopment, and a 28-block, clearly delineated, 'Sports and Entertainment District' (SED) [99]. A key component of this redevelopment, and exemplary of the exacerbated role of sporting and leisure forms, practices and experiences within the processes of urban renewal [100], there has been heavy investment in sport and entertainment infrastructure. Summarized in the advertising by-line, 'come downtown and play', the SED has been conjured as a safe, sanitized and surveillance-dominated place of play anchored by the Peabody Place, FedExForum, Beale Street and Autozone Park (but also including other entertainment venues such as the traditional Peabody Hotel and Orpheum Theatre, and various restaurants and bars).

All four of these major amenities are emblematic of a city that has cultivated the efficacy of particular imagery in an attempt to attract capital, particularly tourist capital. For example, Peabody Place is described by the developer Belz Enterprises as a project that,

> covers eight city blocks in total, with restored historic buildings, a 15-story modern office tower, top-notch apartments, prestigious offices, popular restaurants and gathering places. In all, more than two million square feet connected by skywalks, corridors and trolley stations make Peabody Place a virtual city within a city. And with over 1.1 million residents and over eight million visitors annually, Memphis' metropolitan area is perfectly suited for the project – the largest mixed-use urban development in the South [101].

The high-end shopping, twenty two-screen cinema, and middle-class restaurants are overtly aimed at attracting an educated clientele with a significant disposable income (who are predominantly white); the overt surveillance, signs instructing what constitutes unacceptable dress, cruising regulations, mounted or walking police patrols, zero-tolerance policing, the physical removal of 'undesirable' (read homeless) populations [102] and private security guards charged with continually breaking up and moving on the (inevitably black) groups of youths that gather, result in a venue that is far-removed from a traditional down-town Memphis 'gathering place'. Beale Street, the 'centre of music exchange from the 1880s to the 1960s ... the heart of African-American society where residents went to shop, bank, and of course, sing' [103] has also been transformed. The substantial renovation of the early 1980s was an early attempt to make the street more attractive to tourists, and today the neon signs and heavy police presence are tell-tale symbols of an area that, while undoubtedly still drawing on the musical heritage of the region, has been quite sanitized and securitized to attract tourists – a process emblematic of the increased governance and regulation of the contemporary tourist-oriented cityscape [104].

The other two dominant features of the SED are brand new sporting arenas. Autozone Park, home to the AAA Memphis Redbirds, was opened in 2000 at a total development cost of $161 million (including the attached office space, housing, parking garage and school) [105]. Frequently described – particularly in the local media! – as 'the most beautiful minor league ballpark in America', the attempt to draw upon nostalgic notions of a bygone age can be viewed as similar to the rationale behind the architecture of Baltimore's Camden Yards. While important in terms of the initial reimagining of the downtown core, the impact of Autozone Park will likely be dwarfed by FedExForum, set to open in September 2004 at a cost of $250 million. Built initially as part of the agreement to attract the NBA's Grizzlies from Vancouver, FedExForum has been constructed – presciently or fortuitously – at the intersection of Beale Street and Highway 61, locally known as 'The Blues Highway' because of its route through several towns notable for their musical heritage. The Memphis Grizzlies senior management have embraced this opportunity to imbricate the organization in Memphis' cultural history by theming the arena throughout – from restaurant outlets to luxury boxes to the housing of the Smithsonian Rock n' Soul Museum – with music. Similarly, the overt attempts to position the organization as a good corporate citizen – reified through the donation of $5 million to fund Grizzlies House, a residence for families of patients at St Jude Children's Research Hospital, and prominent role of the franchise and individual players in other local charitable causes – have overshadowed the disruption that the building of the Forum brought to local people and businesses located in one of the poorest parts of Tennessee [106] and the use of the taxpayers' money to build a facility that is operated by – and which revenue streams benefit – a private enterprise.

Revitalization of the Memphis downtown area is not restricted to the SED. Located one mile north of the 'tourist bubble', the iconic Pyramid Arena is a 32 story, stainless steel pyramid that pays homage to the city's Egyptian namesake. Located on the banks of the Mississippi river, the structure is the third largest pyramid in the world, taller than the Statue of Liberty and the Taj Mahal, seats 21,000 and boasts half-a-million square feet of internal usable space [107]. Memphis' former basketball and entertainment venue, now deemed somewhat anachronistic with the unveiling of FedExForum, the future of the Pyramid has generated much debate in the local media. Adjacent to one of the city's most affluent and desirable residential areas, Mud Island, the Pyramid occupies a key role in the continued development of the north end of the downtown area. This part of the city – known as the Pinch District and also home to St Jude Children's Research Hospital, the Cook Convention Center/Cannon Center for the Performing Arts, and new higher-income housing – is linked to the SED by a trolley system that runs through an area that is somewhat desolate and deserted. The city has already undertaken steps towards addressing this by revising the downtown trolley system that links the downtown core with the Pyramid Arena with the intent of establishing a 'tourist corridor' between the Pyramid, Mud Island and SED.

Important in the revitalization of this tourist corridor has been the creation of a public/private partnership, the Riverfront Development Corporation, who in turn have hired New York-based architectural consulting group Cooper Robertson and Partners to create a waterfront destination that will showcase the Mississippi river and provide a new 'front door' to the city. Based on the selective mimicry of a series of waterfront and promenade precedents, especially developments in Baltimore's Inner Harbor, Sydney Harbour, Brooklyn Heights Promenade in New York City, The Embarcadero in San Francisco, the efforts to bring Barcelona 'closer to the water', and Parisian Boulevards, the development plans propose a reconnection between the river and the public realm [108]. These include creating a downtown harbour, with private commercial development modelled on the 'ESPN type zone and environment similar to that found in Baltimore's Inner Harbor' [109]. There will also be a land bridge between the Mud Island housing development and the downtown core and removal of a number of buildings that currently obscure the downtown from the river, a strategy that will connect the 'desirable' and affluent Mud Island residents to the downtown core [110].

Another major player in the redevelopment of the downtown area is Memphis 2005, a private/public agglomeration born out of Memphis' designation as an EC in 1994 and a Renewal Community in 2002. A central element of the Memphis 2005 agglomeration is hospitality and tourist development, a strategy that aims to 'develop and promote world class amenities which attract visitors from the region, nation, and world to Memphis to stay longer, spend more and return often ... develop new or improved facilities for the performing and cultural arts, museums, libraries and sports related events as the focal point ... [and] build new sports and exercise venues on the riverfront or in proximity to other attractions' [111]. As with Baltimore, the strategic repositioning of the city within the global market, the physical and symbolic transformations within the downtown core, the emphasis on sporting properties as a central element within the tourism economy, and the concomitant surveillance and regulation of these spaces, provides an emblematic example of the transformations in cityspace.

Coda: Towards a Critical Sport Tourism

Baltimore and Memphis are clearly 'mobilizing the spectacle' [112], as an expression of late capitalist image power relations [113], capitalizing upon sporting and entertainment investments to create tourist-oriented landscapes for sale within the global marketplace. Of course, space is always contested [114], and tourist space is no different. However, the sketches above point to the relative power and capacity of particular groups, the new urban imagineers, to physically define and proffer meanings about place, meanings that often become abstracted from local culture, mask the complexities and contradictions of everyday life, and are translated into marketable cultural meanings beyond the borders of the place in which they are rooted [115]. There are some obvious parallels between the two cities – the deployment of sporting properties, the use of the different bodies of water, and the desire to extend the tourist bubble beyond its original borders. However, and rather than succumbing to this visually seductive privatized public culture [116], within this suggestive conclusion we question these representations of urban life, pointing to concerns that have emerged from our brief sketches of these two cities, and that we feel need to be embraced by those within the sport tourism field.

There has been a clear shift in those groups responsible for contouring cityscape under the rubrics of privatism, in which even those remaining (pseudo)-public authorities are operating under the ideology of capital accumulation [117]. A shift of power from democratic local governing regimes to these semi-autonomous public/private authorities has fragmented urban politics into a constellation of public/private institutions that operate largely independently from democracy and with little public accountability [118]. This has meant that democratic politics have largely been removed from the development of infrastructure, tourism and environment to the degree that what the electorate may actually prefer is rendered of little importance. In this sense, the governance of such spatial fragments amid an era of 'place marketing' can be seen as part of a revanchist urban vernacular that suspends commitment to extend social justice to the whole of society, compelling the poor and ill-disposed to be tightly disciplined through a range of legal and architectural methods [119].

This raises very important questions in regard to the problematic of the seduction of new sporting and tourist-oriented infrastructure as the panacea to urban ills. As spectacular urban environments are (re)constructed and cultural capital gained, a critical sport tourism needs to ask who benefits, and concomitantly, whose interests are retarded? Anchoring urban development in core components such as sport is clearly part of an initiative deployed to 'physically' rebuild the 'threatening' urban core as a safe, sanitized, consumption-oriented space, a process that involves both an internal and external re-imagining of the city's popular image and meaning. However, in the creation of a 'fantasy city' [120], the spaces of (sporting) consumption often present an unreal perception of city life and shields both suburbanites and tourists from the city's continuing urban problems. Thus, as a solution to post-war processes of deindustrialization and suburbanization, we should question whether the reimaging and rebuilding of the urban core does actually overcome intensifying urban decay, manifested in increased crime and drug-use, the often media-fuelled demonizing of certain populations, rising levels of poverty and ill-health, decreasing employment, and polarized housing and education. Furthermore, questions over the long-term impact of such investment and the relative contribution that adding spaces of (sporting) consumption will have on a region's stability need to be posed and interrogated. Detroit, for example, has added two new sports stadia and a performing arts complex in recent years, but these have not been sufficient to offset the detrimental effects of deteriorating outer neighbourhoods, high property taxes and poor schools that have resulted in a net decline in population between 2000 and 2003 of 4.2 per cent [121]. According to Bruce Katz, director of the Center on Urban and Metropolitan Policy at the Brookings

Institution in Washington, city leaders should focus on long-term improvements such as better schools rather than relying on (superficial) amenities such as new sports stadium that can provide a temporary lift but fail to address underlying problems [122].

Given the perceived functions of heritage environments in the amassing of symbolic capital, drawing tourist spending and providing settings for entertainment, relaxation and consumption [123], it is of little surprise that heritage has become an extremely important resource for international tourism [124]. However, the marketing of heritage is often problematic, for what is marketed as 'history' is often just one selected, revised or performed *version* of the past, a version that can bear only partial resemblance to supposedly authentic histories of place [125]. Heritage, as a cultural product, is clearly an economic resource; one imagined, defined, articulated and exploited everywhere as a primary component of strategies to promote tourism, economic development and urban regeneration [126]. Such narratives of heritage communicate *the* local to the global network and provide a mechanism whereby city authorities can refashion sites and direct the tourist gaze towards a (limited) range of interpretations [127]. The commodification of 'pastness' often provides an emphasis of style over substance, an interpretation of the past manipulated in the interests of capital or dominant social norms – a process argued to have intensified within the dictates of the late capitalist consumption economy [128]. While it is recognized that different people will experience heritage environments differently – such environments are polysemic, and will be experienced and consumed differently [129] – the important question for sport tourism concerns the relative power to control historical knowledge, the power to disseminate such knowledge [130], and the distortion or staging of the 'authentic' in the name of capital [131].

Within such processes, the particularities of place [132] are often capitalized upon, indeed exploited, within the (re)production of 'difference' and 'authenticity'. In the sketches provided above, 'difference' was clearly central within efforts to reimage the urban core. Juxtaposed alongside signature and spectacular newer architectural forms, Memphis capitalizes upon certain particularities of place based around food (barbecue), music (Beale Street) and culture (in the form of the Civil Rights museum). Baltimore offers similar, albeit slightly different peculiarities: food (crab cakes), the original new-old stadia in the form of Camden Yards, the National Aquarium and perhaps the first mall to anchor a downtown redevelopment. Yet tourism can be largely parasitic upon culture; the economic commodification of various particularities of place, such as historic buildings, communities, architectures and so on, may so trivialize local culture that it can result in the destruction of the heritage resource which is its *raison d'etre* [133].

Of particular importance in sport tourism is the somewhat worrying tendencies toward serial replication and standardization of signature forms. Leaving Las Vegas behind as a somewhat obvious example, and not mentioning the neo-Nevadian landscapes of the Lake Las Vegas resort built as a pseudo-Tuscan replica, such repetition is clearly felt within the more banal, the everyday, the local. Ritzer, for example, proposed that cities have to continuously add new amenities and experiences to 're-enchanted' tourist places to overcome problems such as the loss of novelty, replication of local peculiarities in distant places, and increased competition with other cities [134]. While this has been an impetus for the constant upgrading of the tourist bubble, it has also, paradoxically, meant that such spaces are becoming increasingly standardized and characterized by chains of themed outlets, restaurants and experiences [135]. Harvey, in relation to Barcelona (a particularly telling example given the mimicry of the city within the Memphis Riverfront Development Corporation's plans), warns that as opportunities present themselves on the basis of symbolic capital, an irresistible lure draws more and more homogenizing multinational commodification in its wake [136]. In contemporary Western cities then, such as Memphis and Baltimore, which are engaged in aspirant efforts to ensure they are plugged into new spatial units and forms, the later stages of urban development can begin to look exactly like every other city. These processes are characterized by the emergence of multinational stores, experiences or services replacing local shops, gentrification that removes long-term residential populations and destroys older urban fabric, and the lure of sporting forms that have little or no connection to the city – all of which contribute to the loss, or indeed palpable weakening, of marks of history, tradition and distinction [137]. In this way, standardization and the loss of distinctiveness undermines the very marketing images being portrayed through the medium of urban heritage [138].

Clearly, critical sport tourism has an agenda above and beyond our preliminary and suggestive observations drawn from the sketches of two cities engaged in reorienting their economies around sport tourism. As an academic sub-field, sport tourism finds itself increasingly at the forefront of the cross-currents of contemporary social analysis. Through articulating sport tourism with economic, historical, political, technological, aesthetic, cultural (gendered, racialized, sexualized and so on) contexts, as well as offering critical methodologies for understanding the particularities of lived experiences [139], a critical sport tourism can avoid acontextual and ahistorical accounts of specific sport tourist landscapes and address the social struggle around the production and maintenance [140] of the multifarious sites of sport tourism. Scholars then are increasingly going to find themselves articulating sport tourism within a wider cultural politics, centred around, but not limited to, the oft-interconnected and at times contradictory, vectors of globalization, inequality, power, politics, economics, terror, peace, policy, social needs, identities and neo-liberalism. Those scholars who position themselves within critical sport tourism will thus be in a position to address concerns above and beyond those that force a focus on the aesthetic or the visually seductive and which make broad generalizations that are often complicit with contemporary regimes of power and truth. Rather, through adopting an approach grounded within cultural studies, and deploying a theoretical and methodological arsenal appropriate to the key social problems of our time, the future direction of critical sport tourism offers potential for a progressive politics that can interrogate the lived power relations that operate in, and through, tourist spaces, places and cultures. If the field fails to make such connections, and fails to articulate sport tourism as an element of the cultural terrain within wider cultural politics [141], then sport tourism's 'growth' will likely be acquiescent with what eminent sociologist Zygman Bauman [142] suggests is an intellectualism that 'lauds conformity and promotes conformity'. Such an approach avoids the most pressing social problems and produces a politics that offers nothing but more of the same [143]. Rather, a critical sport tourism is one that becomes meaningful when it can 'connect private troubles and public concerns, extending its critical, performative, and utopian impulses to address urgent social issues in the interests of promoting change . . . [It] involves using theory as a resource to think and act, learning how to situate texts within historical and institutional contexts, and creating the conditions for collective struggles over resources and power' [144]. In this way, a productive, meaningful, and necessarily interdisciplinary critical sport tourism will foster a 'spirit in opposition, rather than in accommodation' and intellectuals committed to the critical interrogation of sport tourism will not 'be mistaken for an anonymous functionary or careful bureaucrat' [145].

Notes

[1] T. Hinch and J. Higham, *Sport Tourism Development* (Clevedon: Channel View Publications, 2004).
[2] Ibid.; S. Hudson, *Sport and Adventure Tourism* (Binghampton, NY: Haworth Press, 2003); B. Ritchie and D. Adair *Sport Tourism: Interrelationships, Impacts and Issues* (Clevedon, UK: Channel View, 2003). K. Swart, 'An Assessment of Sport Tourism Curriculum Offerings at Academic Institutions', *Journal of Sports Tourism*, 6, 1 (2002), 5–9.
[3] Hinch and Higham, *Sport Tourism Development*; J. Higham and T. Hinch, 'Sport, Space, and Time: Effects of the Otago Highlanders Franchise on Tourism', *Journal of Sport Management*, 17, 2 (2003), 235–57.
[4] H. Gibson, 'Sport Tourism: An Introduction to the Special Issue', *Journal of Sport Management*, 17, 1 (2003), 205–13.
[5] Ibid.; H. Gibson, 'Sport Tourism at a Crossroad? Considerations for the Future', in S. Garmon and J. Kurtzman (eds), *Sport Tourism: Principles and Practice* (Eastbourne, UK: LSA Publications No. 76, 2002), pp.123–40); H. Gibson, 'Sport Tourism: A Critical Analysis of Research', *Sport Management Review*, 1, 1 (1998), 45–76.
[6] J. Kincheloe, 'Describing the Bricolage: Conceptualizing a New Rigor in Qualitative Research', *Qualitative Inquiry*, 7, 6 (2002), 679–92.
[7] D. Harvey, *The Condition of Postmodernity*, (Oxford: Blackwell, 1989); H. Lefevbre, *The Production of Space* (translation D. Nicholson-Smith) (Oxford: Blackwell, 1991); E. Soja, *Postmodern Geographies: The Reassertion of Space in Critical Social Theory* (London: Verso, 1989).
[8] I. Borden, *Skateboarding, Space & the City: Architecture & the Body* (Oxford: Berg, 2001). M. Lowes, *Indy dreams and Urban Nightmares: Speed Merchants, Spectacle, and the Struggle over Public Space in the World-Class City* (Toronto: University of Toronto Press, 2002). M. Silk, 'Bangsa Malaysia: Global Sport, the City & the Refurbishment of Local Identities', *Media, Culture & Society*, 24, 6 (2002), 775–94; M. Silk, 'A Tale of Two Cities: The Social Production of Sterile Sporting Space', *Journal of Sport and Social Issues*, x, x (2004), 1–30; C. Van Ingen, 'Geographies of Gender, Sexuality and Race', *International Review for the Sociology of Sport*, 38, 2 (2003), 201–16; R. Wilcox and D. Andrews, 'Sport in the City: Cultural, Economic and Political Portraits', in R. Wilcox, D. Andrews, R. Pitter and R. Irwin (eds), *Sporting Dystopias: The Making and Meanings of Urban Sport Cultures* (New York: SUNY Press, 2003), pp.1–16.
[9] Hinch and Higham, *Sport Tourism Development*.

[10] S. Britton, 'Tourism, Capital and Place: Towards a Critical Geography of Tourism', *Environment and Planning D: Society and Space*, 9, 4 (1991), 451–78; C. Hall, *Tourism and Politics: Policy, Power and Place* (Chichester: John Wiley, 1994); I. Ateljevic, 'Circuits of Tourism: Stepping Beyond the "Production / Consumption" Dichotomy', *Tourism Geographies*, 2, 4 (2000), 369–88.

[11] D. Judd, 'Constructing the Tourist Bubble', in S. Fainstein and D. Judd (eds), *The Tourist City* (New Haven, CT: Yale, 1999), pp.35–53.

[12] D. Massey, 'Understanding Cities', *City*, 4, 1 (2000), 135–44.

[13] See especially Harvey, *The Condition of Postmodernity*; D. Harvey, *Spaces of Hope* (Boulder: University of Colorado Press, 2000); D. Harvey, *Spaces of Capital: Towards a Critical Geography.* (London and New York: Routledge, 2001); S. Lash and J. Urry, *Economies of Signs and Space* (London: Sage, 1994); S. Lash and J. Urry, *The End of Organized Capitalism* (Madison: University of Wisconsin Press, 2000). H. Lefevbre, *Writings on Cities / Henri Lefevbre* (translated by E. Kofman and E. Lebas) (Oxford: Blackwell, 1996); E. Soja *Thirdspace: Journeys to Los Angeles and Other Real-and-Imagined Spaces* (Oxford: Blackwell, 1996); E. Soja *Postmetropolis: Critical Studies of Cities and Regions* (Oxford: Blackwell, 2000).

[14] Soja, *Postmetropolis*, p.7.

[15] M. Castells, *The Rise of the Network Society* (Oxford: Blackwell, 1996).

[16] M. Hardt and A. Negri, *Empire* (Cambridge: MA: Harvard University Press, 2000).

[17] S. Sassen, *The Global City* (New Jersey: Princeton University Press, 1991); S. Sassen, 'Whose City is it? Globalization and the Formation of New Claims', in F.J. Lechner (d.), *The Globalization Reader* (Malden, MA: Blackwell, 2001), pp.70–6.

[18] F. Jameson, *Postmodernism or, the Cultural Logic of Late Capitalism* (Durham, NC: Duke, 1991).

[19] G. MacLeod, M. Raco and K. Ward, 'Negotiating the Contemporary City', *Urban Studies*, 40, 9 (2003), 1655–71; R. Walks, 'The Social Ecology of the Post-Fordist/Global City? Economic Restructuring and Socio-Spatial Polarisation in the Toronto Urban Regional', *Urban Studies*, 38, 3 (2003), 407–47.

[20] M. Goodwin, 'The City as Commodity: The Contested Spaces of Urban Development', in G. Kearns and C. Philo (eds), *Selling Places: The City as Cultural Capital, Past and Present* (Oxford: Pergamon, 1993), pp.145–62.

[21] M. Gottdiener, 'Lefebvre and the Bias of Academic Urbanism: What can we Learn from the New Urban Analysis?', *City*, 4, 1 (2000), 93–100; MacLeod *et al.*, 'Negotiating the Contemporary City'; Sassen, *The Global City*; Sassen, 'Whose City is it?'; D. Whitson and D. Macintosh, 'The Global Circus: International Sport, Tourism and the Marketing of Cities', *Journal of Sport and Social Issues*, 20, 3 (1996), 239–57.

[22] H. Savitch and P. Kantor, 'Urban Strategies for a Global Era: A Cross National Comparison', *American Behavioral Scientist*, 46, 8 (2003), 1002–33.

[23] Gottdiener, Lefebvre and the Bias of Academic Urbanism; D. Judd and D. Simpson, 'Reconstructing the Local State: The Role of External Constituencies in Building Urban Tourism', *American Behavioral Scientist*, 46, 8 (2003), 1056–69.

[24] R. Turner and M. Rosentraub, 'Tourism, Sports and the Centrality of Cities', *Journal of Urban Affairs*, 24, 5 (2002), 487–92.

[25] Gottdiener, 'Lefebvre and the Bias of Academic Urbanism'.

[26] MacLeod *et al.*, 'Negotiating the Contemporary City'.

[27] J. Short, C. Breitbach, S. Buckman and J. Essex, 'From World Cities to Gateway Cities: Extending the Boundaries of Globalization Theory', *City*, 4, 3 (2003), 317–40.

[28] K. Robins, 'Tradition and Transition: National Culture in its Global Context', in J. Corner and S. Harvey (eds), *Enterprise and Heritage* (London: Routledge, 1991).

[29] A. Bélanger, 'Sport Venues and the Spectacularization of Urban Spaces in North America: The Case of the Molson Center in Montreal', *International Review for the Sociology of Sport*, 35, 3 (2000), 378–97.

[30] M. Jansen-Verbeke, 'Inner Cities and Urban Tourism in the Netherlands: New Challenges for Local Authorities', in P. Bramham, I. Henrey, H. Mommas and H. Van Der Poel (eds), *Leisure and Urban Processes: Critical Studies of Leisure Policy in Western European Cities* (London: Routledge, 1989).

[31] Whitson and Macintosh, 'The Global Circus'.

[32] G. Kearns and C. Philo, *Selling Places: The City as Cultural Capital, Past and Present* (Oxford: Pergamon, 1993); D. Rowe and P. McGuirk, 'Drunk for Three Weeks: Sporting Success and the City Image', *International Review for the Sociology of Sport*, 34, 1 (2002), 125–42.

[33] M. Pagano and A. Bowman, *Cityscapes and Capital: The Politics of Urban Development* (Baltimore: The John Hopkins University Press, 1995).

[34] Britton, 'Tourism, Capital and Place'.

[35] S. Zukin, *The Culture of Cities* (Oxford: Blackwell, 1995).

[36] M. Friedman, D. Andrews and M. Silk, 'Sport and the Façade of Redevelopment in the Postindustrial City', *Sociology of Sport Journal*, 21, 2 (2004), 119–39; Judd, 'Constructing the Tourist Bubble'.

[37] Walks, 'The Social Ecology of the Post-Fordist/Global City?'.

[38] Judd, 'Constructing the Tourist Bubble', p.53.

[39] S. Fanstein and D. Gladstone, 'Evaluating Urban Tourism', in S. Fanstein and D. Gladstone (eds), *The Tourist City* (New Haven, CT: Yale, 1999), pp.21–34; Friedman *et al.*, 'Sport and the Façade of Redevelopment in the Postindustrial City'; Harvey, *Spaces of Capital*.

[40] Turner and Rosentraub, *Tourism*

[41] Freidman *et al.*, *Sport*; Harvey, *Spaces of Capital*; J. Richards. *Facadism*. (London & New York: Routledge, 1994).

[42] M. Rosentraub. *Major League Losers: The Real Cost of Sports and Who's Paying For It* (2nd ed.). (New York: Basic Books, 1999).

[43] Turner and Rosentraub, 'Tourism, Sports and the Centrality of Cities'.

[44] B. Chalkey and S. Essex, 'Urban Development through Hosting International Events: A History of the Olympic Games', *Planning Perspectives*, 14, 4 (1999), 369–94.

[45] Judd and Simpson, 'Reconstructing the Local State'.

[46] P. McGuirk and D. Rowe, 'Defining Moments and Refining Myths in the Making of Place Identity: The Newcastle Knights and the Australian Rugby League Grand Final', *Australian Geographical Studies*, 39, 1 (2001), 52–66.

[47] P. Eisinger, 'The Politics of Bread and Circuses: Building the City for the Visitor Class', *Urban Affairs Review*, 35, 3 (1999), 316–33.

[48] Judd, 'Constructing the Tourist Bubble'; Judd and Simpson, 'Reconstructing the Local State'.

[49] D. Judd, 'The Rise of the New Walled Cities', in H. Liggett and D. Perry (eds), *Spatial Practices: Critical Explorations in Social/Spatial Theory* (Thousand Oaks, CA: Sage, 1995), pp.144–66; MacLeod *et al.*, 'Negotiating the Contemporary City'.

[50] R. De Cillia, M. Reisgel and R. Wodak, 'The Discursive Construction of National Identities', *Discourse and Society*, 10, 2 (1999), 19–173; W.R. Scott, *Institutions and Organizations* (Thousand Oaks, CA: Sage Publications, 1995).

[51] MacLeod *et al.*, 'Negotiating the Contemporary City'; N. Rose, 'Government and Control', *British Journal of Criminology*, 40, 2 (2000), 321–39.

[52] M. Edwards, 'Wealth Creation and Poverty Creation: Global-Local Interactions in the Economy of London', *City*, 6, 1 (2001), 25–42; K. Ward, 'Coalitions in Urban Regeneration: A Regime Approach', *Environment and Planning A*, 29, 8 (1997), 1493–1506.

[53] M. Sheller and J. Urry, 'Mobile Transformations of Public and Private Life', *Theory, Culture & Society*, 20, 3 (2003), 107–25.

[54] A. Sack and A. Johnson, 'Politics, Economic Development and the Volvo International Tennis Tournament', *Journal of Sport Management*, 10, 1 (1996), 1–14.

[55] Judd and Simpson, 'Reconstructing the Local State'.

[56] Ibid; Sack and Johnson, 'Politics, Economic Development and the Volvo International Tennis Tournament'.

[57] MacLeod *et al.*, 'Negotiating the Contemporary City'; N. Smith, 'Guiliani Time: The Revanchist 1990s', *Social Text*, 57, 1 (1998), 1–20.

[58] McGuirk and Rowe, 'Defining Moments and Refining Myths in the Making of Place Identity'.

[59] Harvey, *Spaces of Capital*; B. Graham, 'Heritage as Knowledge: Capital or Culture?', *Urban Studies*, 39, 5–6 (2002), 1003–17.

[60] Harvey, *Spaces of Capital*.

[61] Ibid.

[62] Ibid.; R. Hula, 'The Two Baltimores', in D. Judd and M. Parkinson (eds), *Leadership and Urban Regeneration: Cities in North America and Europe* (Newbury Park, CA: Sage, 1990), pp.191–215; M. Levine, 'Tourism, Urban Redevelopment, and the "World-Class" City: The Cases of Baltimore and Montreal', in C. Andrew, P. Armstrong and A. Lapierre (eds), *World-Class Cities: Can Canada Play?* (Ottawa: University of Ottawa, 1999), pp.421–50.

[63] R. Florida, *The Rise of the Creative Class* (New York: Basic Books, 2002).

[64] Harvey, *Spaces of Capital*; K. Schimmel, A. Ingham and J. Howell, 'Professional Team Sport and the American City: Urban Politics and Franchise Relocation', In A. Ingham and J. Loy (eds), *Sport in Social Development: Traditions, Transitions, and Transformations* (Champaign, IL: Human Kinetics, 1993), pp.211–44.

[65] Edwards, 'Wealth Creation and Poverty Creation'; Sheller and Urry, 'Mobile Transformations of Public and Private Life'; Ward, 'Coalitions in Urban Regeneration'.

[66] J. Bockmeyer, 'A Culture of Distrust: The Impact of Local Political Culture on Participation in the Detroit EZ', *Urban Studies*, 37, 13 (2000), 2417–40.

[67] United States Department of Health and Human Services, Empowerment Zones and Enterprise Communities Programs. Available at: http://www2.acf.hhs.gov/programs/ocs/ez-ec/info.htm (accessed 25 March 2004).

[68] Harvey, *Spaces of Capital*; Hula, 'The Two Baltimores'; P. Wagner, 'The Construction of Urban Tourism Space: Baltimore's Inner Harbor, 1964–1990' (unpublished Master's thesis, University of Maryland, College Park, 1994).

[69] Morton Hoffman and Company, *Economic and Market Analysis, Inner Harbor Area, Baltimore, Maryland* (Baltimore, MD: Author, 1964); see also Wagner, 'The Construction of Urban Tourism Space'.

[70] Hula, 'The Two Baltimores'.

[71] Ibid; Wagner, 'The Construction of Urban Tourism Space'.

[72] Harvey, *Spaces of Capital*; Hula, 'The Two Baltimores'; Wagner, 'The Construction of Urban Tourism Space'.

[73] Harvey, *Spaces of Capital*, p.139.

[74] Friedman *et al.*, 'Sport and the Façade of Redevelopment in the Postindustrial City', 5.

[75] Ibid., 5.

[76] G. Ritzer, *Enchanting a Disenchanted World: Revolutionizing the Means of Consumption* (Thousand Oaks, CA: Pine Forge Press, 1999), p.xi.

[77] Friedman *et al.*, 'Sport and the Façade of Redevelopment in the Postindustrial City'.

[78] Fanstein and Gladstone, 'Evaluating Urban Tourism'; Harvey, *Spaces of Capital*.

[79] Harvey, *Spaces of Capital*.

[80] Ibid., pp.143–4.

[81] Friedman *et al.*, 'Sport and the Façade of Redevelopment in the Postindustrial City'; Harvey, *Spaces of Capital*.

[82] V. Smith and F. Siegel, 'Can Mayor O'Malley Save Ailing Baltimore', *City Journal*, 2001. Available at: http://www.city-journal.org/html/11_1_can_mayor_omalley.html (accessed 12 Dec. 2003).

[83] D. Donovan, 'Illusions of Occupancy', *Baltimore Sun*, 12 June 2004, 1A.

[84] Harvey, *The Condition of Postmodernity*; Harvey, *Spaces of Capital*; Schimmel *et al.*, 'Professional Team Sport and the American City'.

[85] E. Siegel, 'Time is Running out for Holdout Tenants', *Baltimore Sun*, 7 Aug. 2004, 1A.

[86] Florida, *The Rise of the Creative Class*.

[87] Siegel, 'Time is Running out for Holdout Tenants'.

[88] D. Donovan, 'Boarding Crews Boost Efficiency'. *Baltimore Sun*, 15 Aug 2004, B1.

[89] Whitson and Macintosh, 'The Global Circus'.

[90] See Friedman *et al.*, 'Sport and the Façade of Redevelopment in the Postindustrial City', for a more detailed account.

[91] Harvey, *The Condition of Postmodernity*.

[92] Judd, 'Constructing the Tourist Bubble'; Levine, 'Tourism, Urban Redevelopment, and the "World-Class" City'.

[93] P. Grogan and T. Proscio, *Comeback Cities: A Blueprint for Urban Neighborhood Revival* (Oxford: Westview Press, 2000).

[94] J. Obermark, 'Downtown: Belz Calls on Developers to Invest in Heart of City', *The Commercial Appeal*, 13 Sept. 1995, B4.

[95] J. Leland, 'On a Hunt for Ways to Put Sex in the City', *New York Times*. Available at: http://www.nytimes.com/2003/12/11/garden/11COOL.html?ex = 107264168 and ei = 1 and en = a297cec6cd46cb6c (accessed 16 Dec. 2003).

[96] Jansen-Verbeke, 'Inner Cities and Urban Tourism in the Netherlands'.

[97] Silk, 'A Tale of Two Cities'.

[98] D. Lofton. 99: Year Downtown will Turn Corner. *The Commercial Appeal*, 28 Feb. 1999, J15.

[99] 'Memphis Living', *University of Memphis Tennis: On the Rise.* (Memphis: University of Memphis, 2003); Memphis/Shelby Division of Planning & Development, 'Memphis South Central Business Improvement District' public presentation. http//www.cityofmemphis.org/powerpoint/SouthCBIDOverview.ppt (accessed 2 July 2000).

[100] Chalkey and Essex, 'Urban Development through Hosting International Events'; C. Euchner, *Playing the Field: Why Sports Teams Move and Cities Fight to Keep Them*, (Baltimore: Johns Hopkins University Press, 1993); Silk, 'A Tale of Two Cities'.

[101] 'Peabody Place'. Available at: http://www.belz.com/peabody/ (accessed 12 Aug. 2004).

[102] Silk, 'A Tale of Two Cities'.

[103] V. Ho, 'The Soul of Memphis', *NWA World Traveler*, May 2004, 41.

[104] P. Chatteron and R. Hollands, 'Theorising Urban Playscapes: Producing, Regulating and Consuming Youthful Nightlife City Spaces', *Urban Studies*, 39, 1 (2002), 95–116.

[105] 'Downtown dreams', *Memphis Flyer* (30 March–5 April 2000). Available at www.memphis-flyer.com/backissues/issue580/sport580.htm (accessed 12 Aug. 2004).

[106] The adjacent Peabody-Vance District, for example, is noted by the Metropolitan Inter-Faith Association as being the poorest zip code in Memphis. Available at: http://www.mifa.org (accessed 12 Aug. 2004).

[107] Pyramid Arena. Available at: http://www.pyramidarena.com/overview.html (accessed 30 Oct. 2003).

[108] Cooper, Robertson and Partners, *Memphis Promenade Land Use Plan: Prepared for the Riverfront Development Corporation* (Final Draft, 21 Feb. 2004) (New York: Cooper, Robertson and Partners, Architecture, Urban Design, 2004).

[109] Ibid.

[110] Friends of our Riverfront, *Whose River is it Anyway?* (Memphis: Friends of our Riverfront, 2004).

[111] Memphis 2005, 'The Memphis 2005 Plan'. Available at: http://www.memphis2005.com/plan/index.htm (accessed 27 Feb. 2003).

[112] G. Debord, *Le Societie du Spectacle* (Paris: Editions Buchet Castel, 1967).

[113] Bélanger, 'Sport Venues and the Spectacularization of Urban Spaces in North America'.

[114] Van Ingen, 'Geographies of Gender, Sexuality and Race'.

[115] A. Firat, 'Consumer Culture or Culture Consumed', in J. Costa and G. Bamossy (eds), *Marketing in a Multicultural World* (London and Thousand Oaks: Sage, 1995).

[116] Zukin, *The Culture of Cities*.

[117] Sheller and Urry, 'Mobile Transformations of Public and Private Life'.

[118] Judd and Simpson, 'Reconstructing the Local State'.

[119] Ibid; MacLeod *et al.*, 'Negotiating the Contemporary City'; Smith, 'Guiliani Time'.

[120] J. Hannigan, *Fantasy City: Pleasure and Profit in the Postmodern Metropolis* (London: Routledge, 1998).

[121] G.C. Armas, 'Detroit's losses at top', *Commercial Appeal*, 27 June 2004, A5.

[122] Ibid.

[123] A. Apostolakis, 'The Convergence Process in Heritage Tourism', *Annals of Tourism Research*, 30, 4 (2003), 795–812; D. Chhabra, R. Healey and E. Sills, 'Staged Authenticity and Heritage Tourism', *Annals of Tourism Research*, 30, 3 (2003), 702–19; Y. Poria, R. Butler and D. Airey, 'The Core of Heritage Tourism', *Annals of Tourism Research*, 30, 1 (2003), 238–54; A. Russo, 'The "Vicious Circle" of Tourism Development in Heritage Cities', *Annals of Tourism Research*, 29, 1 (2002), 165–82; N. Wang, 'Rethinking Authenticity in the Tourism Experience', *Annals of Tourism Research*, 26, 2 (1999), 349–70.

[124] Graham, 'Heritage as Knowledge', 1007.

[125] Kearns and Philo, *Selling Places*; G. Waitt, 'Consuming Heritage: Perceived Historical Authenticity', *Annals of Tourism Research*, 27, 4 (2000), 835–62.

[126] Graham, 'Heritage as Knowledge'.

[127] Waitt, 'Consuming Heritage'.

[128] Apostolakis, 'The Convergence Process in Heritage Tourism'; A. McIntosh and R. Prentice, 'Affirming Authenticity: Consuming Cultural Heritage', *Annals of Tourism Research*, 26, 4 (1999), 589–612.

[129] Poria *et al.*, 'The Core of Heritage Tourism'; Wang, 'Rethinking Authenticity in the Tourism Experience'.

[130] F. McLean, 'A Marketing Revolution in Museums?', *Journal of Marketing Management*, 11, 6 (1999), 601–16.

[131] Chhabra *et al.*, 'Staged Authenticity and Heritage Tourism'.

[132] K. Robins, 'What in the World is Going on?', in P. duGay (ed.), *Production of Culture/Cultures of Production* (London: Sage, 1997), pp.11–67.

[133] Graham, 'Heritage as Knowledge'.

[134] Ritzer, *Enchanting a Disenchanted World*.

[135] Ibid. Friedman *et al.*, 'Sport and the Façade of Redevelopment in the Postindustrial City'; Judd, 'Constructing the Tourist Bubble'; Zukin, *The Culture of Cities*.

[136] Harvey, *Spaces of Capital*.

[137] Ibid.

[138] Graham, 'Heritage as Knowledge'.

[139] J. Frow and M. Morris, 'Cultural Studies', in N. Denzin and Y. Lincoln (eds), *Handbook of Qualitative Research* (2nd Edition) (Thousand Oaks, CA: Sage, 2000), pp.315–46.

[140] Van Ingen, 'Geographies of Gender, Sexuality and Race'.

[141] N. Denzin, 'The War on Culture, The War on Truth', *Cultural Studies* ↔ *Critical Methodologies*, 4, 2 (2004), 137–42; H. Giroux, 'War Talk, the Death of the Social, and the Disappearing Children: Remembering the Other War', *Cultural Studies* ↔ *Critical Methodologies*, 4, 2 (2004), 206–11; H. Giroux, 'Cultural Studies as Performative Politics', *Cultural Studies* ↔ *Critical Methodologies*, 1, 1 (2000), 5–23.
[142] Z. Bauman, *In Search of Politics* (Stanford, CA: Stanford University Press, 1999), 4.
[143] Giroux, 'Cultural Studies as Performative Politics'.
[144] Ibid, 11.
[145] E. Said, *Representations of the Intellectual* (New York: Pantheon, 1994), 12–13.

Marketing Sport Tourism: Creating Synergy between Sport and Destination

Tracey Harrison-Hill & Laurence Chalip

Introduction

Marketing is more than advertising and selling. Yet it is common to see sport tourism marketing, particularly for events, described only in terms of the marketing communications and sales roles. Whilst these come under the rubric of the promotion element of marketing, the practice of marketing involves much more. Marketing is essentially about exchanges that create value for customers. The target and, therefore, the basis for marketing strategy is the consumer. To reflect this, rather than considering the consumer in a separate section in this essay, the consumer is considered throughout our examination of the elements of sport tourism marketing.

When examining the role of marketing within sport tourism, it is important to reflect on who is included as a sport tourist. There has been some debate about whether professional sports people should be included, and whether recreational leisure activities constitute sport [1]. Others have focused on active participants in

Tracey Harrison-Hill, Department of Tourism, Leisure, Hotel and Sport Management, Griffith University, Gold Coast Campus, PMB50, GCMC, 9726, Queensland, Australia. Correspondence to: t.hill@griffith.edu.au.

sport rather than spectators of sport [2]. Gibson defined sport tourism as 'leisure based travel that takes individuals temporarily outside of their home communities to participate in physical activities, to watch physical activities or to venerate attractions associated with physical activities' [3]. This definition will be used throughout this essay, and the discussions about marketing to sport tourists will demonstrate why this definition is a particularly useful one for examining sport tourism from a marketing perspective.

Applying the Marketing Concept to Sport Tourism

The marketing concept holds that achieving an organization's goals depends on determining the needs and wants of consumers and delivering the desired satisfactions more effectively and efficiently than do competitors [4]. The primary goals of a marketer are: (1) to attract new customers by providing superior value, and (2) to keep current customers by maintaining their satisfaction in an efficient and effective manner. So, while the most salient element of marketing (particularly to the customer) may be the advertisement or the salesperson, the process of marketing begins before either – via an understanding of consumers, their needs and wants, and the benefits they are consequently seeking from a product or service.

Any product or service should be conceived, designed and delivered with the target market's needs in mind. The famous line from the film *Field of Dreams*, 'If you build it, they will come', is only true if the product or service delivers benefits that consumers desire, and if it does so at a price that consumers are willing to pay to obtain those benefits. From this standpoint, tourism destinations face a unique marketing problem insomuch as each destination has relatively permanent attributes in terms of its natural and built attractions. In other words, the destination and the services it enables cannot be manufactured in the same sense as many other consumer products; rather, the attributes of destinations impose constraints on the design and delivery of products and services they offer. The consequent challenge is to create experiences at attractions that optimally fulfil tourists' needs and wants. Simply providing an opportunity to visit an iconographic sporting location (for example, Wembley Stadium or St Andrews Golf Links) or a sport event (for example, the World Cup or the Olympic Games) may be inadequate because their value to the consumer resides not in the fact that they have been visited, but, rather, in the depth of experiences and consequent quality of meanings they impart [5]. Thus, the marketer needs to understand what benefits consumers might seek to derive from a place, event or activity. Then the marketer should augment the offering to create as meaningful an experience as possible for the consumer. This requires more than simply promoting and selling existing features; it requires the marketer to find means to deepen, sharpen or extend the experience. For example, a more meaningful experience might be created for English football supporters who are 'seeing the arch over Wembley' if their visit to the stadium incorporates such encounters as sitting on the locker room bench where David Beckham changed jerseys, or getting to kick the ball that was used in Euro '96 when England beat the Netherlands 4-0. This augmentation of existing attributes in order to satisfy more fully the target market's desires reflects the difference between a marketing orientation to sport tourism versus simply having sport attractions.

Similarly, when examining the three categories of sport tourism described by Gibson [6], the temptation to focus on the sporting activity itself – the event, the participation or a sporting place – would represent a product (or attraction) focus rather than a marketing orientation. Understanding the benefits that the consumers are seeking from participating, spectating or visiting is vital for the development of memorable experiences and consumer satisfaction. In the debates that have emerged about the boundaries of sport tourism, one argument holds that the development of sport tourism would be better served if sport event tourism, including players [7] and spectators, were the focus. This argument suggests that the inclusion of travel as a recreational sport participant or to visit sites that conjure sporting nostalgia (for example, museums, halls of fame or famous stadiums) would dilute the focus of sport tourism marketing and research [8]. The problem with taxonomic restrictions of this kind is that they reflect a product focus (on events) that fails to contemplate the range of sport tourism experiences the target market may desire. From a destination marketer's perspective, it is reasonable to expect that sport aficionados might be attracted to an array of complementary sporting experiences. For example, the same target market of surfers who come to the Gold Coast of Australia to watch the Quicksilver Pro (a surfing competition) might also be attracted to visit the Gold Coast for a holiday that is based on surfing the famed point breaks [9]. Marketers could therefore utilize the same database, package similar add-on experiences, and use an integrated communications strategy to attract this market – not merely to the event, but to the destination at other times. Similarly, Chalip and McGuirty found that participants in a marathon event could be attracted to remain at the host destination longer if relevant experiences were bundled with the event [10]. The most desirable post-marathon activity for participants was the opportunity to obtain a package that would enable them to participate in recreational sporting activities at the destination. The same logic applies when marketing a facility to tourists. For example Lord's Cricket Ground in London hosts event spectators and also many tourists who come to see the home of cricket and visit the museum. Part of the motivation for spectators to watch a match may be nostalgic rather than to support a team. Understanding this aspect of motivation should assist the marketer to enhance spectators' overall experience [11].

The foregoing examples illustrate the utility of Gibson's contention that sport tourism is appropriately examined with reference to spectating at sport, participating in sport, or visiting a place that invokes sport nostalgia [12]. The conceptual challenge for marketers is not to demarcate or constrain the boundaries of sport tourism; rather, it is to identify the attitudes, interests and activities that characterize tourists whose behaviours demonstrate a need, want or preference for sport. The practical challenge is then to formulate experiences that optimize the depth, quality or array of benefits those tourists obtain while at the destination.

Understanding Sport Tourist Markets

In order for destination marketers to capitalize on sport's contribution to their destination's mix of attractions, they need to determine the roles that sport plays in attracting tourists to the destination, and the ways in which each sport element interacts with other attractions and activities at the destination to formulate the tourist's overall experience. Although it is useful to reflect on sport tourism broadly, it is also necessary to differentiate among sport tourists. The basis for sport interests varies [13]. For example, some American baseball fans will travel to see their favourite team play, but if those fans are merely fans of the team (rather than the sport), then they are unlikely to have any interest in seeing baseball games while they are tourists in Japan or Venezuela. On the other hand, those who are fans of the sport (that is, not merely fans of a team) might enjoy such games. Similarly, a Masters swimmer who trains primarily for competition might have little interest in swimming while on holiday, while a Masters swimmer who swims for the intrinsic pleasure of aquatic exercise might prefer holiday locations at which there are pools suitable for swimming laps.

Since consumers' preferences vary widely, it is necessary for marketers to define the subset of consumers they wish to target. Typically, the target market is identified and described according to segmentation variables such as geographic, demographic, psychographic and behavioural characteristics in order to identify a group of relatively homogenous consumers, which is the 'segment' to be targeted [14]. The goal of the marketer in describing the segment is to formulate a product offering and associated marketing communications that are tailored to the wants and needs of the target, and to do so better than any competitor.

Identification of target market segments helps to pinpoint what particular sport tourists seek from the sport tourism experience. The same activity might meet different needs for different segments. For example, some fans who travel to watch a favourite team may do so in order to express their identification with that team [15], while others do so for the camaraderie of other fans [16]. Conversely, seemingly different behaviours may fulfil a common need. For example, some tourists visit St Andrews Golf links simply to tour the facility; others attend events there; others visit to play golf. Yet tourists emitting any of these three behaviours are commonly 'paying homage to the spiritual home of golf' [17]. From a marketing perspective differences and similarities among consumer benefits are important because they indicate whether marketing communications to different segments should feature similar benefits or different ones. As we shall see, differences and similarities also help to determine how to vary (or not to vary) the nature of experiences that will be provided to sport tourists.

The design of the sport tourism experience and the ways that experience is advertised to the target market are important, particularly if sport plays a pivotal role in their travel choice. Many consumers have an enduring involvement with a particular sport or with sport in general [18]. Similarly, travel decisions are typically high involvement decisions [19]. Thus, the level of information search is likely to be particularly high as sport tourists plan their holiday. Empirical support for this expectation comes from recent work showing that tourists who have been influenced to visit a destination because it is hosting a sport event engage in more information search than do tourists who choose the destination for other reasons [20]. It has also been shown that sport tourists engage in extensive information search even after their trip planning and booking has been finalized [21]. Findings from these studies demonstrate that sport tourists seek information to heighten the emotional anticipation of their forthcoming vacation. Sharing information with others who might also be going to the same event plays a significant role in building the excitement, and also assists in confirming their identification within the sport's subculture [22]. Thus, sport tourists often search aggressively when choosing which sport experience to travel to, and they can be particularly choosey about the attractions and activities that become part of their itinerary.

These characteristics of sport tourists suggest the significant advantages of understanding the benefits sought by target market segments. The ways the sport tourism experience is designed, priced, promoted and delivered will all be affected. These are all aspects of the marketing mix. Each is considered in the following sections of this essay.

Designing Sport Tourism Experiences

Attending a sport event, participating in a sport activity, or visiting a sport museum or a famous stadium are each a form of experience. The precise nature of that experience depends on the design of the experience and the bundle of benefits the tourist seeks. An optimal experience is one in which there is a match between the benefits the experience enables and the benefits sought.

The Product is the Experience

Experience marketing involves adding value for customers through consumer participation and connection [23]. It requires that the consumer be engaged on as many levels as possible – physical, emotional, intellectual and even spiritual. The literature on hedonic consumption provides useful bases for developing an understanding of experience attachment, which is the desired outcome of experience marketing. Pine and Gilmore argue that experiences can be enhanced through two dimensions [24]. The first involves customer participation. Moving consumers from passive observers to active involvement will improve their perception of the experience. The second dimension requires that the consumer be immersed in the experience in order to make it feel more authentic. This is nicely illustrated by the emergence of concept stores, such as Nike Town, that immerse the sportswear consumer in an environment where they can explore the history, technology and folklore of the sports for which the sportswear is produced [25]. Concept stores combine a theme park atmosphere with the retail experience. Stores of this type attract patrons and drive sales. The tools for enhancing participation and creating greater immersion come from the servicescape, the invisible organization and systems, the service providers, and other customers.

The servicescape

The servicescape refers to the physical environment in which the service experience takes place. The physical environment plays a significant role in consumers' perceptions of the experience. In sport tourism, there are two relevant servicescapes. First, there is the environment in which the sport is experienced. Second, there is the destination within which the sport experience is embedded. Both are important because both can affect the sport tourist's experience.

Servicescapes have been shown to affect the expectations and the quality of experience of sport participants and sport spectators. For example, the quality of ski slopes is rated as the most important consideration by skiers planning weekend or vacation trips [26]. Similarly, the perceived value of golf course services predicts the overall satisfaction of golfers, which affects the likelihood that the golfer will return to the course [27]. When studying sport spectators, Wakefield and his colleagues found that stadium parking, stadium cleanliness, food services and crowding correlated significantly with future attendance intentions [28]. Spectators' perceptions of the quality of the physical environment at a stadium have similarly been shown to play a direct role in the quality of spectators' affect [29].

Nevertheless, the effect of the servicescape depends on the sport tourist's choices, expectations and needs. For example, golfers have different servicescape expectations for 9-hole courses, inexpensive 18-hole courses, and high-end 18-hole courses. They consequently evaluate the quality of their experience at those courses differently [30]. Similarly, non-ski services and the overall image of a ski resort play an even greater role in skier satisfaction than do the ski attributes themselves [31]. Hill and Green demonstrated comparable effects when comparing servicescape effects on sport spectators in three different football contexts [32]. They found that the servicescape played a much more significant role when the stadium was famous and the home team was successful, and a lesser role when the facility was not famous or the home team was not successful.

These findings underscore the importance of understanding the sport tourist's motives and expectations. The findings also underscore the value of offering a varied array of sport tourism opportunities, and tailoring each to the motives and expectations of tourists who would be expected to choose each. The degree to which the servicescape will enhance or diminish the overall experience depends on the quality and type of experience the tourist seeks and the ways that the experience is interpreted. Both aspects are, to a degree, under the control of the sport tourism provider.

The sport tourism provider has substantially less control over the destination. Nevertheless, the destination plays a role in the nature and quality of experiences that sport tourists expect to obtain. For example, some runners choose to compete in the Gold Coast Marathon not merely for the enjoyment of the event, but also for the desirability of the Gold Coast as a holiday destination [33]. The challenge for marketers who seek to appeal to sport tourists is to enhance their destination's servicescape in a manner that will optimize the value that sport tourists obtain.

Theming has become a key means by which to embellish the destination's servicescape, particularly when seeking to enhance the quality of the sport tourist's experience. For example, Chalip and Leyns describe the ways in which the shops and restaurants in a precinct near an auto race increased their business during the race by developing themed decorations and entertainments that tied into the auto race [34]. These appealed to tourists who attended the event, thus enhancing their overall experience (and the revenues of local shopkeepers). Similarly, the city of Baltimore made use of theming as a means to attract more tourists to the city's Inner Harbor [35]. The Inner Harbor is a key tourist area for Baltimore, and the Baltimore Orioles (a Major League Baseball team) are a potential attraction for sport tourists. So, Baltimore moved the Orioles from their old stadium to one that is located at the Inner Harbor. In so doing, the city designed a stadium that is themed to fit with the Inner Harbor's overall look and feel. Consequently, the stadium looks substantially different from other baseball stadiums in the United States – a feature that has enhanced its appeal as a tourist destination [36].

The invisible organization and systems

The invisible organization and systems include the infrastructure that assists in the delivery of services and the processes that have been developed to deliver a quality service. Infrastructure often includes technology-based equipment, particularly computer databases. The processes include the planning, methods, recruiting and training of service providers. A useful illustration of the ways that the invisible organization and systems can affect sport tourists' experiences is the use of email groups by tour operators before a tour commences [37]. Consumers who are travelling together on a sport tour are able to converse with each other and the tour guide online before the commencement of the tour to get to know one another. Participants who do so report closer relationships with those on the tour and a consequently enhanced overall experience.

Service providers

Service providers deliver one or more elements of the experience, and therefore also play a role in shaping the experience. This is due to the inseparable nature of service experience delivery. Inseparability refers to the idea that the service provider and the customer need to be involved simultaneously in the production of a service [38]. There is a commonsensical feel to the notion that the quality of interaction with a service provider will affect the quality of the experience. Better service should result in a better experience. Empirical findings from both sport [39] and tourism [40] support this expectation [41].

Nevertheless, sport tourists are by no means homogeneous in their expectations regarding the behaviours expected of service providers or the nature of services that should be provided. In fact, sport tourists can be segmented on the basis of the interactions and services they expect [42]. To a degree, differences are grounded in cultural variations (for which national origin serves as a useful proxy) [43]. Nevertheless, differences in sport tourists' satisfaction with service provision also seem to be grounded in their expectations for services at the site they have chosen for their sport experience [44]. Since many sport tourists undertake a high level of information search when planning their holiday [45], their service expectations are driven significantly by marketing communications. This highlights the need to foster a close link between service design and the marketing communications (for example, advertising, publicity) that describe sport tourism experiences. Since consumers' interpretations and expectations of service systems also vary as a function of national culture, it may be useful to tailor communications to the national origin of sport tourists.

Other customers

In many services, including sport activities and events, the presence of other customers affects the experience, as other customers become a part of the experience. The effect can be either positive or negative. For example, the opportunity to socialize with other aficionados can play a significant role in sport tourists' decision to engage in long haul travel to attend an event [46]. On the other hand, a sense of overcrowding – particularly delays in service delivery – can reduce the sport tourist's enjoyment [47].

The importance of social interaction among sport tourists has been explored in the context of a women's football tournament [48]. The tournament provided a space and an opportunity for players to parade and celebrate their sport identity with likeminded others. It was this sharing of the experience that made it fun and meaningful for the participants and those who accompanied them. The importance of the opportunity to parade and celebrate their identities as football players was underlined by the fact that players felt that year-after-year the event was poorly organized. Yet, their satisfaction with the shared social experience was strong enough to bring them back each year.

This finding usefully illustrates the value of facilitating social interactions among sport tourists. There is more to sport tourism than sport competition or sport participation. By involving sport tourists and providing a connection with the surrounds through the servicescape, the invisible organization and systems, service providers, and their fellow sport tourists, marketers can enable a more satisfying and memorable experience. When done well, this can foster repeat visitation, loyalty and positive word-of-mouth – all hallmarks of an effective marketing orientation.

Cultivating Polysemy

A further means to enhance the experience of tourists to sport events is to provide multiple bases for affective involvement. Drawing on anthropological studies of events, particularly the Olympic Games, Chalip argues that narratives, genres and symbols can be used to enhance the attractiveness of an event [49]. Since these allow an event to cultivate a greater array of emotions and meanings for participants and spectators, he describes these as the elements for creating 'polysemic structures'.

The greater the array of narratives about the event, its participants and its stakeholders, the more stories are available to give the event meaning to its audience and its participants. Similarly, a sport event can enable festivals during which attendees celebrate; it can include one or more spectacles, such as parades or extravagant shows; it can incorporate rituals that mobilize a sense of the sacred. Symbols, like flags, logos and artefacts can be layered throughout an event to render an added sense of significance.

Each of these elements can be fostered by event and destination marketers. Narratives can be promoted via advertising and public relations. Such genres as festival, spectacle and ritual can be designed into events and can be enabled around event spaces. Symbols can be designed, borrowed or appropriated for events. Chalip argues that multiple narratives, embedded genres and layered symbols should be planned and implemented to reinforce one another, thus enhancing their effect. Empirical tests demonstrate that multiple narratives, embedded genres and layered symbols do enhance audience interest [50], and can drive the desire to attend an event [51].

Loyalty to the Experience and Repeat Visitation

As markets mature and competition increases, repeat customers become more important [52]. In tourism, repeat visitors have been described as a key market for destination managers to nurture [53]. Yet, tourism as an industry tends to be distinctive insomuch as many tourists seek a different destination each time they travel [54]. The foremost objective of international travellers is novelty [55]. Indeed, a large segment of tourists perceive uncertainty regarding their trip to be part of the excitement of travel, and would prefer to visit a destination they have not visited previously [56]. This sets travel decisions apart from other consumption decisions, for which novelty seeking is much less common and risk avoidance is more typical.

There are grounds for arguing that sport tourism can be a means to foster repeat visitation. Green and Chalip found that women football players typically planned their holidays around the National Women's Flag Football Tournament in Key West, Florida [57]. Golfers often plan their holidays to visit a favourite golf course [58]. Fairley found that spectators travelled for five days on a bus as an annual journey to a football game, and did so largely for the nostalgia of reliving their group experience [59]. Similarly, fans of the University of Florida Gators have been likened to pilgrims as a consequence of their repeat visits to Gainesville to watch Gator football [60]. Kim and Chalip found that individuals who had previously attended a World Cup soccer event were more likely to attend a future World Cup [61].

This is not to suggest that sport tourists will routinely return to the same destination in order to watch or participate in their sport. Some participants who travel primarily for their sport do travel to new locations [62]. The challenge, then, is to determine which market segments are likely to be repeat visitors. That, in turn, requires some consideration of the bases for repeat visitation by sport tourists.

It is heuristically useful to differentiate between tourism during which sport is incidental, and tourism for which sport is a primary objective [63]. If sport is not the purpose of a trip, then there is little reason to expect that the sport experience will be a sufficient pull back to a particular destination. On the other hand, if the sport experience is key to the trip, then the availability of a previously enjoyed experience might cause a tourist to choose one destination over a comparable destination, but only if the experience is highly desired or unreplicable at alternative destinations.

The marketing tools described above for enhancing the sport tourist's experience provide a basis for fostering repeat visitation. The more distinctive a sport servicescape is, the more difficult it will be to replicate the experience at an alternative destination. The better the infrastructure and the service, the more attractive it will be to return. The more likely the sport tourist is to find opportunities to socialize comfortably with likeminded tourists, the greater the draw. The more effectively that narratives are fostered, genres are embedded, and symbols are layered, the more strongly attached the sport tourist is likely to be.

Places and Prices for Sport Tourism

From a marketing perspective, price is simply what the consumer must pay to obtain the product or service. Consumers' perceptions of value play a significant role in determining price. Value depends on the benefits they obtain from the product or service, not the service itself. When skiers pay for skis, they are buying the exhilaration of sliding down the slopes. The exhilaration is the benefit, not the skis themselves. The price needs to recoup costs of offering the product to consumers (and allow for some profit), but it must do so in a manner that is consistent with the value the consumer places on the benefit to be obtained and the price charged for substitute means to obtain the same benefit.

One means to increase the perception of value and to differentiate one holiday's benefits from those offered by other holidays that include sport is to package together associated products or services at one price. This is known as price bundling. The marketing literature [64] suggests that the advantage of bundling is not just that there may be some price discounting related to buying the bundle; the advantage is also that purchasing the associated products as one package adds the value of convenience for the consumer.

The technique of bundling is well known to tourism marketers, as offering multiple services, multiple attractions and/or multiple destinations in a single package tour has been common for many years [65]. Sport activities have often been bundled with the destination. Sport can be the primary focus, as in a ski holiday package that includes flights, transfers, accommodation at the slopes, lift passes and lessons. At other times, sport activities are bundled as add-ons to a holiday for which sport is not the primary activity – for example, when a New York City tour offers discounted tickets to a sport event at Madison Square Garden – a venue that is famous for the array of sport events it hosts.

Bundling can create opportunities to cross-leverage attractions and activities at the destination, thereby increasing the value of the holiday to the tourist and the value of the tourist to the destination. Chalip and McGuirty demonstrate that a mixed-bundling strategy can be used to appeal to several different segments of sport tourists, even those planning to participate in the same event or activity [66]. The technique requires four steps. First, possible inclusions in bundles are identified. These include augmentations that enable attendees to parade or celebrate their sport's subculture (for example, parties, social events, special entertainments), as well as other attractions and activities at the destination (for example, tours, famous places, things to do). Second, market research is conducted in target markets to determine the relative value of each attraction and activity to potential attendees. Third, the data are cluster analysed to segment the market into relatively homogeneous groups. Fourth, event packages are constructed that offer each segment's valued attractions and activities jointly, while other attractions and activities are made available to each segment as add-ons. Bringing the sport and its host destination together into a bundle adds value by augmenting and intensifying the sport tourist's experience. At the same time, the additional package elements help to lengthen the sport tourist's visit, thereby increasing the overall value of the tourist to the destination.

The bundling technique just described uses destination components to add value to tourists whose primary basis for travel is to obtain a sport experience. Conversely, sport can be bundled with a destination to add value for tourists who may come to the destination for purposes other than sport. Thus, beach destinations may offer surfboard rentals; hotels may offer guests free access to their golf course; or a convention may offer attendees discounted tickets to the game of a local professional team. The basic principle remains the same: the destination and its sport opportunities are cross-leveraged to add value to the tourist's experience.

So far, the techniques described are designed to add value to a holiday. However, sport can also enhance the value of a destination's brand. Conversely, destinations can add value to the brand of a sport. As an example of the former, consider St Albans (in New South Wales, Australia). The town annually hosts the Shahzada – the world's longest endurance horse event. The event is contested over 400 kilometres of trails. The town and its trails are featured in event media and word-of-mouth before, during and after the five-day competition. As a result, recreational riders and fans of the equestrian competition visit the town throughout the year to soak in the atmosphere, and often to rent a horse to ride 'the trail'.

Sometimes destinations have helped to popularize a sport. Beach volleyball, for example, has worked to increase its profile and popularity as a spectator sport by combining events with popular destinations. As recently as the 1980s, the sport was primarily a recreational activity with courts sometimes provided on beaches and at resorts, but without a strong competitive ethos or spectator base. By holding tournaments at popular beach destinations at which the events were initially free to spectators, the sport leveraged itself to its current iconic status, which includes a presence on the Olympic programme.

Bundling and co-branding share the requirement that destinations and the sport they host are marketed jointly. The sport is used to promote the destination, and the destination is leveraged to promote its sport. By capitalizing on the two simultaneously, each adds value to the other. This, in turn, requires that destination marketers and sport marketers form alliances to plan and implement the necessary marketing strategies [67]. Although this does sometimes occur [68], it often does not [69].

Two kinds of alliances are relevant. Horizontal channel alliances are those that increase the scale of similar activities, thereby providing greater incentive for travel and a more integrated array of activities for the tourist. Vertical channel alliances are those that link providers of complementary services in the supply chain, such as travel and accommodation.

The challenge for creating horizontal alliances is that managers sometimes lack the skills required to create and sustain a relationship [70], or they may see themselves as business rivals [71]. Nevertheless, the value of horizontal alliances for sport tourism is aptly illustrated by Queenstown, New Zealand. The destination has changed its image from a ski resort to an adventure sport capital. This was achieved by adding, clustering and growing like-activities until a critical mass was attained, providing a sufficient composite attraction to draw adventure-seeking tourists to the destination even through the off-peak summer season.

Horizontal alliances can also be used by local businesses to leverage a sport attraction. Chalip and Leyns found that most restaurants and retailers on the Gold Coast of Australia did not benefit from the presence of an international auto race [72]. However, when businesses in one precinct formed an alliance to theme their precinct with the race and to create a street festival during the race, participating restaurants and retailers obtained substantial added trade from race patrons.

Vertical alliances do not suffer from the challenge of bringing competitors together, since the businesses typically rely on each other's services and therefore have a stake in what each does. Consequently, alliances among airlines, hotels and car rental agencies are common in tourism services. When sport offers an added attraction, it may also form alliances with travel or accommodation services. For example, it is common for sport event providers to nominate an 'official' airline and/or hotel for their event. In exchange, the airline offers a discounted fare and the hotel provides favourable rates and a commission to the event for each room booked by event attendees.

Alliances of this type are attractive to the partners because they create marketing synergy and consequently add value for each partner. It is therefore somewhat surprising that a stronger alliance between sport marketers and destination marketers has not yet emerged. In part, this may be a result of differences in the contingencies and cultures that pervade the daily work lives of sport and tourism marketers [73]. It may also be a consequence of the relative youth of sport tourism as a field of specialization. Nevertheless, as sport marketers and tourism marketers discover their common aims and purposes, stronger alliances are probable.

Promoting Sport Tourism

Since the benefits a sport tourist can obtain through sport and through its host destination are mutually reinforcing, the promotion of sport tourism is likely to stimulate stronger alliances between sport and tourism marketers. By promoting benefits to be obtained from both sport and the destination, each will benefit. To date, however, the quantity and quality of media that sport and tourism have obtained from one another have not met marketers' expectations, with the result that sport has not lived up to its potential to promote destinations, and destinations have not lived up to their potential to promote sport [74]. This represents a marketing challenge. Recent advances in marketing communications theory and practice amplify that challenge, but also offer new opportunities. Promotion has shifted from a reliance on one-way mass communication to an integrated communications strategy that incorporates more personalized, targeted and synchronous communications [75]. This shift suits sport tourism.

For the sport tourism product to be regarded as a memorable and satisfying experience, the consumer needs to be highly involved within the experience. The experience needs to be an emotive one that captivates the consumer. The promotional challenge is to communicate effectively to consumers the promise of an intangible emotion-laden experience. Zaltman argues that the core requirement is to communicate in a manner that enables the consumer to identify with the story being told [76]. Ideally, the marketer seeks to have the consumer imagine the experience for themselves and, in so doing, desire to be a part of it. For that to occur, the story being told must be relevant to the consumer, and it must make sense given the information the consumer has in memory. For the sport tourism marketer, this requires an understanding of the target market's self-image and the ways the product links to that self-image. Although this will vary among individuals, a shared frame of reference can be obtained by identifying the beliefs, values, rituals and symbols of the sport's subculture [77]. These provide essential raw material for designing advertising, publicity and other promotions intended to communicate the experience to target markets.

There are several means to mediate the resulting message. Mass communication involves the use of mass media, such as television, radio, newspaper and magazines, as well as cinema and outdoor billboards. Embedded advertising within movies, games and television programming is also a form of mass communication (called 'product placement'). If the marketer identifies the media preferences of the sport subculture, advertising media can be chosen for optimal reach and frequency. For instance, to attract spectators to a forthcoming off-road rally car race, such as the Telstra Rally Australia, advertising during the televised coverage of other rally car races would be one means to reach the target market. This could take a number of forms, including an advertisement during a commercial break, being an official sponsor of the telecast, or by obtaining event signage that would be picked up by cameras during the race. It would also be well targeted within magazines for auto-racing aficionados in the form of an ad or advertorials. It might also be advertised using banner ads on rally-based websites. Since the event is ongoing, it would be reasonable to pay for it to be featured in one or more computer games, such as the Sony Playstation World Rally Championship. These various alternatives demonstrate that there is a wide array of targeted promotional opportunities from which a sport tourism marketer can choose.

The primary limitation of the kinds of advertising described so far is that it merely provides exposure for a sport tourism experience; it does not provide a targeted message or a taste of the experience. Although product placement, particularly into a game, may help to enhance the consumer's sense of involvement in the experience, even it does not permit direct one-to-one communication to the consumer. Database marketing does. It permits the marketer to accumulate information on interests, purchases and preferences of consumers and to use that information to create more persuasive one-to-one communications. Consider again the World Rally Championship example. Its website [78] contains a portal called 'My WRC' that enables the user to customize the site to reflect their preferences, subscribe to a newsletter, and access notice boards. The site is also the interface for a database that records consumers' demographic information as well as psychographic information, such as their preferred rally car manufacturer, favourite driver and favoured events. It can track pages that consumers visit at the site, record purchases from the online store, and log input to forums. When they subscribe to the newsletter, consumers are giving permission to receive direct communications from marketers of World Rally Championship events. Given the data that marketers can collect from the website, they are able to create targeted and even personalized messages and offers that are designed and tailored to the consumer's individual interests and preferences. The result is communications that are meaningful to the consumer and that are consistent with their self-identity.

By incorporating synchronous communication media such as online forums and discussion boards, marketers can add further personal meaning to their communications while simultaneously leveraging the social nature of sport consumption. A number of sport subcultures are represented in online communities where members communicate information, share stories and convey their excitement to one another. These communications function as emotive and credible word-of-mouth advertising [79]. They are also a strategic tool via which marketers can foster a sense of community among their customers, obtain feedback about their product and redress perceived service-failures.

The capacity to create a personalized marketing communications environment, and to tailor offers and communications, represents a potentially useful means to synergize sport and marketing more effectively. By identifying the sport experiences that would enhance particular tourists' experience of the destination, destination marketers can better pinpoint and promote the competitive advantages that sport offers. Similarly, by identifying those elements of the destination that enhance sport tourists' experience of the destination, sport marketers can better locate and promote the competitive advantages that their host destination provides.

These potentials again recommend the value of alliances. An alliance between sport marketers and the destination marketing authority would facilitate target-specific promotions because sport and the destination could then be cross-promoted. Indeed, coordination among providers – such as accommodation, attraction, tour and sport organizations – would make it feasible to place information about complementary events, attractions and activities in communications channels tourists use as they plan and take their holidays. The consequent promotional complementarities would provide a distinct competitive advantage.

The Future of Sport Tourism Marketing

There are substantial opportunities to use sport and tourism to cross-leverage one another. Cross-leverage requires the marketer to consider the complementarities of sport and tourism across the entire marketing mix: product, price, place and promotion. It also requires that the marketer discern the complementarities of consumers' different expressions of sport interest – whether as spectation, participation or nostalgic veneration. The psychographics of sport spectators, sport participants and visitors to famous sport sites need to be better understood in order to identify how best to leverage tourists' sport interests and cross-promote sport opportunities. Similarly, complementarities among interests in different sports need to be explored and mapped so that sport tourist segments can be identified and described.

Sport serves as a useful tool for enriching the quality of some tourists' experience at a destination. We need to learn more about the physical, social and psychological characteristics of that experience. We also need to map differences in the role that sport plays when it is the purpose of travel versus when it is an incidental element of travel. In particular, research that elaborates the ways that sport and the destination can complement one another in either instance – when sport is the purpose for travel or when it is an incidental activity – will provide the basis for new tools to differentiate destinations and enhance sport tourists' experiences.

The nature of meanings imparted by sport also needs further exploration. By identifying the processes by which sport narratives, genres and symbols pique a tourist's interest [80] or motivate travel [81], we will be able to intensify the quality of experience that sport tourists obtain. In particular, we need to understand how each of these elements can be used to support the others.

Despite substantial progress in tourism research, there is a great deal to be learned about sport tourists as consumers [82]. Despite continued development of marketing theory, there is a great deal to be learned about the requisite strategies and tactics for leveraging sport tourism [83]. In particular, we need to explore barriers and facilitators of vertical and horizontal alliances for sport tourism, as well as the most effective means for using destination marketing channels to promote sport, and sport marketing channels to promote destinations. The necessary advances will occur via integration of research and theory in tourism, sport, marketing and strategy. The resulting syntheses will advance our understandings of tourists, our models of sport, the formulation of strategy, and the practice of marketing.

Notes

[1] C.M. Hall, *Hallmark Tourist Events* (London: Belhaven Press, 1992).

[2] S.A. Glyptis, 'Sport and Tourism', in C. Cooper (ed.), *Progress in Tourism, Recreation and Hospitality* (New York: Bellhaven, 1991), pp.165–83.

[3] H.J. Gibson, 'Sport Tourism: A Critical Analysis of Research', *Sport Management Review*, 1, 1 (1998), 41.

[4] P. Kotler, A. Stewart, L. Brown and G. Armstrong, *Principles of Marketing* (French's Forest, NSW: Pearson Education, 2001).

[5] L. Chalip, 'The Construction and Use of Polysemic Structures: Olympic Lessons for Sport Marketing', *Journal of Sport Management*, 6, 2 (1992), 87–98. N-S. Kim and L. Chalip, 'Why Travel to the FIFA World Cup: Effects of Motives, Background, Interest, and Constraints', *Tourism Management*, 25, 6 (2004), 695–707. E.E. Snyder, 'Sociology of Nostalgia: Sports Hall of Fame and Museums in America', *Sociology of Sport Journal*, 8 (1991), 228–38.

[6] Gibson, 'Sport Tourism: A Critical Analysis of Research'.

[7] C.M. Hall, 'Adventure, Sport and Health Tourism', in B. Weiler and C.M. Hall (eds), *Special Interest Tourism* (London: Belhaven Press, 1992), pp.45–76.

[8] M. Deery, L. Jago and L. Fredline, 'Sport Tourism or Event Tourism: Are They One and the Same?' *Journal of Sport Tourism*, 9, 3 (2004), 235–45.

[9] S. Dolnicar and M. Fluker, 'Behavioural Market Segments Among Surf Tourists: Investigating Past Destination Choice', *Journal of Sport Tourism*, 8 (2003), 186–96.

[10] L. Chalip and J. McGuirty, 'Bundling Sport Events with the Host Destination', *Journal of Sport Tourism*, 9, 3 (2004), 267–82.

[11] Fairley and Gammon, this volume.

[12] Gibson, 'Sport Tourism: A Critical Analysis of Research'.

[13] B. Stewart, A.C.T. Smith and M. Nicholson, 'Sport Consumer Typologies: A Critical Review', *Sport Marketing Quarterly*, 12, 4 (2003), 206–15. M.R. Weiss and N. Chaumeton, 'Motivational Orientations in Sport', in T.S. Horn (ed.), *Advances in Sport Psychology* (Champaign, IL: Human Kinetics, 1992), pp.61–99.

[14] Gibson, this volume.

[15] V. Dalaks, R. Madrigal and K.L. Anderson, '"We are Number One!" The Phenomenon of Basking-In-Reflected-Glory and its Implications for Sports Marketing', in L.R. Kahle and C. Riley (eds), *Sports Marketing and the Psychology of Marketing Communications* (Mahwah, NJ: Lawrence Erlbaum Associates, 2004), pp.67–79.

[16] S.D. Fairley, 'In Search of Relived Social Experience: Group-based Nostalgia Sport Tourism', *Journal of Sport Management*, 17, 3 (2003), 284–304.

[17] J. Bartlett, 'The Selling of St. Andrews', *Forbes*, summer (1997), 68.

[18] H. Bryan, 'Leisure Value Systems and Recreational Specialization', *Journal of Leisure Research*, 9, 3 (1977), 174–87. N. McGehee, Y. Yoon and D. Cardenas, 'Involvement and Travel for Recreational Runners in North Carolina', *Journal of Sport Management*, 17, 3 (2003), 305–24.

[19] C.J. Clements and B. Josiam, 'Role of Involvement in the Travel Decision', *Journal of Vacation Marketing*, 1, 4 (1995), 337–48.

[20] A. G. Woodside, R. Spurr, R. March and H. Clark, 'The Dynamics of Traveller Destination Awareness and Search for Information Associated with Hosting the Olympic Games', *International Journal of Sports Marketing and Sponsorship*, 4, 2 (2002), 127–50.

[21] T. Harrison-Hill, 'Getting into the Spirit: Using Internet Information Search to Heighten Emotions in Anticipation of the Sport Tourism Experience', in C. Ryan (ed.), *Expanding Tourism Limits*, Vol. 2 (Melbourne: Pergamon, 2004), 165–71.

[22] Green and Jones, this volume.

[23] E.L. O'Sullivan and K.J. Spangler, *Experience Marketing: Strategies for the New Millennium* (State College, PA: Venture Publishing, 1998).

[24] B.J. Pine and J.H. Gilmore, *The Experience Economy: Work is Theatre and Every Business is a Stage* (Boston: Harvard Business School Press, 1999).

[25] J.F. Sherry, 'The Soul of the Company Store: Nike Town Chicago and the Emplaced Brandscape', in J.F. Sherry (ed.), *Servicescapes: The Concept of Place in Contemporary Markets* (Chicago: NTC Business Books, 1998), pp.109–46.

[26] W.A. Leuschner and R.B. Herrington, 'The Skier: His Characteristics and Preferences', in *Forest Recreation Symposium Proceedings* (Upper Darby, PA: United States Department of Agriculture, 1971), pp.135–42.

[27] J.F. Petrick, S.J. Backman and R.D. Bixler, 'An Investigation of Selected Factors' Impact on Golfer Satisfaction and Perceived Value', *Journal of Park and Recreation Administration*, 17, 1 (1999), 40–59.

[28] K.L. Wakefield, J.G. Blodgett and H.J. Sloan, 'Measurement and Management of the Sportscape', *Journal of Sport Management*, 10, 1 (1996), 15–31. K.L. Wakefield and H.J. Sloan, 'The Effects of Team Loyalty and Selected Stadium Factors on Spectator Attendance', *Journal of Sport Management*, 9, 2 (1995), 153–72.

[29] R. Hightower, M.K. Brady and T.L. Baker, 'Investigation the Role of the Physical Environment in Hedonic Service Consumption: An Exploratory Study of Sporting Events', *Journal of Business Research*, 55, 9 (2002), 697–707.

[30] Petrick *et al.*, 'An Investigation of Selected Factors' Impact on Golfer Satisfaction and Perceived Value'.

[31] A. Ferrand and D. Vecchiantini, 'The Effect of Service Performance and Ski Resort Image on Skiers' Satisfaction', *European Journal of Applied Sport Science*, 2, 2 (2002), 1–12.

[32] B. Hill and B.C. Green, 'Repeat Attendance as a Function of Involvement, Loyalty, and the Sportscape Across Three Football Contexts', *Sport Management Review*, 3, 2 (2000), 145–62.

[33] Chalip and McGuirty, 'Bundling Sport Events with the Host Destination'.

[34] L. Chalip and A. Leyns, 'Local Business Leveraging of a Sport Event: Managing an Event for Economic Benefit', *Journal of Sport Management*, 16, 2 (2002), 132–58.

[35] Silk and Amis, this volume.

[36] B.W. Hamilton and P. Kahn, 'Baltimore's Camden Yards Ballparks', in R.G. Noll and A. Zimbalist (eds), *Sports, Jobs and Taxes: The Economic Impact of Sports Teams and Stadiums* (Washington, DC: Brookings Institution Press, 1997), pp.245–81.

[37] Harrison-Hill, 'Getting into the Spirit'.

[38] K.D. Hoffman, *Services Marketing, Marketing Best Practices* (Forth Worth, TX: Dryden, 2000).

[39] Hightower *et al.*, 'Investigation the Role of the Physical Environment in Hedonic Service Consumption'. G. Howat and D. Murray, 'The Role of Critical Incidents to Complement

Service Quality Information for a Sports and Leisure Centre', *European Sport Management Quarterly*, 2, 1 (2002), 23–46.

[40] M. Riley, O. Niininen, E.E. Szivas and T. Willis, 'The Case for Process Approaches in Loyalty Research in Tourism', *International Journal of Tourism Research*, 3, 1 (2001), 23–32. S. Tian-Cole, J.L. Crompton and V.L. Wilson, 'An Empirical Investigation of the Relationships Between Service Quality, Satisfaction and Behavioural Intentions Among Visitors to a Wildlife Refuge', *Journal of Leisure Research*, 25, 1 (2002), 1–24.

[41] Thwaites and Chadwick, this volume.

[42] A.M. Diaz-Martin, V. Iglesias, R. Vazquez and A.V. Ruiz, 'The Use of Quality Expectations to Segment a Service Market', *Journal of Services Marketing*, 14, 2–3 (2000), 132–46. K. Weiermair and M. Fuchs, 'Measuring Tourist Judgement on Service Quality', *Annals of Tourism Research*, 26, 4 (1999), 1004–21.

[43] D.D. Chadee and J. Mattsson, 'An Empirical Assessment of Customer Satisfaction in Tourism', *Services Industries Journal*, 16, 3 (1996), 305–20. J. Wong and R. Law, 'Difference in Shopping Satisfaction Levels: A Study of Tourist in Hong Kong', *Tourism Management*, 24, 4 (2003), 401–10.

[44] M.D. Needham, R.B. Rollins and C.J.B. Wood, 'Site-specific Encounters, Norms and Crowding of Summer Visitors at Alpine Ski Areas', *International Journal of Tourism Research*, 6, 6 (2004), 421–37.

[45] Harrison-Hill, 'Getting into the Spirit'.

[46] Kim and Chalip, 'Why Travel to the FIFA World Cup'.

[47] Needham *et al.*, 'Site-specific Encounters, Norms and Crowding of Summer Visitors at Alpine Ski Areas'.

[48] B.C. Green and L. Chalip, 'Sport Tourism as the Celebration of Subculture', *Annals of Tourism Research*, 25, 2 (1998), 275–91.

[49] Chalip, 'The Construction and Use of Polysemic Structures'.

[50] L. Chalip, B.C. Green and L. Vander Velden, 'Effects of Polysemic Structures on Olympic Viewing', *International Journal of Sports Marketing and Sponsorship*, 2, 1 (2000), 39–57.

[51] Kim and Chalip, 'Why Travel to the FIFA World Cup'.

[52] Kotler *et al.*, *Principles of Marketing*.

[53] P.C. Fakeye and J. Crompton, 'Image Differences Between Prospective First-time, and Repeat Visitors to the Lower Rio Grande Valley', *Journal of Travel Research*, 30, 2 (1991), 10–6. R.J. Gitelson and J.L. Crompton, 'Insight into the Repeat Vacation Phenomenon', *Annals of Tourism Research*, 11, 2 (1984), 199–217. J.F. Petrick and S.J. Backman, 'An Examination of the Determinants of Golf Travellers' Satisfaction', *Journal of Travel Research*, 40, 3 (2002), 252–9.

[54] J.L. Crompton, 'Motivations for Pleasure Vacation', *Annals of Tourism Research*, 6, 4 (1979), 408–24.

[55] S. Yuan and C. McDonald, 'Motivational Determinates of International Pleasure Time', *Journal of Travel Research*, 29, 1 (1990), 42–4.

[56] W.S. Roehl and D.R. Fesenmaier, 'Risk Perceptions and Pleasure Travel: An Exploratory Analysis', *Journal of Travel Research*, 30, 4 (1992), 17–26.

[57] Green and Chalip, 'Sport Tourism as the Celebration of Subculture'.

[58] J.F. Petrick and S.J. Backman, 'An Examination of the Construct of Perceived Value for the Prediction of Golf Travellers' Intentions to Revisit', *Journal of Travel Research*, 41, 1 (2002), 38–46.

[59] Fairley, 'In Search of Relived Social Experience'.

[60] H.J. Gibson, C. Willming and A. Holdnak, 'Small-scale Event Sport Tourism: Fans as Tourists', *Tourism Management*, 24, 2 (2003), 181–90.

[61] Kim and Chalip, 'Why Travel to the FIFA World Cup'.

[62] McGehee *et al.*, 'Involvement and Travel for Recreational Runners in North Carolina'.

[63] L.Chalip, 'Sport and Tourism: Capitalising on the Linkage', in D. Kluka and G. Schilling (eds), *The Business of Sport* (Oxford: Meyer & Meyer Sport, 2001), pp.77–89.

[64] J.P. Guiltinan, 'The Price Bundling of Services: A Normative Framework', *Journal of Marketing*, 51, 2 (1987), 74–85. F.J. Mulhern and R.P. Leone, 'Implicit Price Bundling of Retail Products: A Multi-product Approach to Maximizing Store Profitability', *Journal of Marketing*, 55, 4 (1991), 63–76.

[65] D.C. Bojanic and R.J. Calantone, 'A Contribution Approach to Price Bundling in Tourism', *Annals of Tourism Research*, 17, 4 (1990), 528–40.

[66] Chalip and McGuirty, 'Bundling Sport Events with the Host Destination'.

[67] T. Hill and R.N. Shaw, 'Co-marketing Tourism Internationally: Bases for Strategic Alliances', *Journal of Travel Research*, 34, 1 (1995), 25–32. L. Jago, L. Chalip, G. Brown, T. Mules and S. Ali, 'Building Events into Destination Branding: Insights from Experts', *Event Management*, 8, 1 (2003), 3–14.

[68] C.S. Dev and S. Klein, 'A Market-based Approach for Partner Selection in Marketing Alliances', *Journal of Travel Research*, 35, 1 (1996), 11–7.

[69] Chalip and Leyns, 'Local Business Leveraging of a Sport Event'. M. Weed, 'Why the Two Won't Tango: Explaining the Lack of Integrated Policies for Sport and Tourism in the UK', *Journal of Sport Management*, 17, 3 (2003), 258–83. M. Weed, this volume.

[70] M.J. Kelly, J.L. Schaan and H. Joncas, 'Managing Alliance Relationships', *R&D Management*, 32,1 (2002), 11–22.

[71] O. Harari, 'Stop Trying to Beat your Competitors', *Management Review*, 83, 9 (1994), 53–5.

[72] Chalip and Leyns, 'Local Business Leveraging of a Sport Event'.

[73] Jago *et al.*, 'Building Events into Destination Branding: Insights from Experts'. Weed, 'Why the Two Won't Tango'. M. Weed, this volume.

[74] L. Chalip, 'Marketing, Media, and Place Promotion', in J. Higham (ed.), *Sport Tourism Destinations: Issues, Opportunities and Analysis* (Amsterdam: Elsevier, 2005), pp.162–76.

[75] P. Kitchen and P. de Pelsmacker, *Integrated Marketing Communications* (London: Routledge, 2004).

[76] G. Zaltman, *How Customers Think: Essential Insights into the Mind of the Market* (Boston: Harvard Business School Press, 2003).

[77] Green and Jones, this volume.

[78] International Sportsworld Communicators, World Rally Championships [website], retrieved 7 Oct. 2004, from the World Wide Web: http://www.wrc.com

[79] Harrison-Hill, 'Getting into the Spirit'.

[80] Chalip, 'The Construction and Use of Polysemic Structures'.

[81] Kim and Chalip, 'Why Travel to the FIFA World Cup'.

[82] H.J. Gibson, 'Understanding Sport Tourism Experiences', in J. Higham (ed.), *Sport Tourism Destinations: Issues, Opportunities and Analysis* (Amsterdam: Elsevier, 2005), pp.57–72.

[83] L. Chalip, 'Beyond Impact: A General Model of Sport Event Leverage', in B.W. Ritchie and D. Adair (eds), *Sport Tourism: Interrelationships, Impacts and Issues* (Clevedon: Channel View, 2004), pp.226–52.

Service Quality Perspectives in Sport Tourism

Des Thwaites & Simon Chadwick

Background

Even a cursory glance at the literature surrounding the area of sport and leisure organizations clearly illustrates the changes that have taken place in recent years. For example, on the demand side, the growth in disposable income, coupled with increased leisure time, has contributed to a desire for greater choice in relation to leisure options. Customers are becoming more sophisticated, discerning and more inclined to complain. Additionally, they are less loyal and prepared to seek alternative suppliers when their needs are not met. From a supply side perspective, organizations are faced with a more hostile and turbulent market place exhibiting increasing levels of competition [1], which has been addressed, in part, through an emphasis on service issues. Berrett, Burton and Slack note that in response to this new environment sport and leisure organizations have acknowledged the importance of the customer and placed greater emphasis on marketing activities and the delivery of service quality [2]. A number of studies emphasize that customers are increasingly sensitive to aspects of service and that from a management perspective, quality enhances profitability, improves productivity and underpins successful competitive

Des Thwaites, Leeds University Business School, Leeds, LS2 9JT, UK. Correspondence to: dt@lubs.leeds.ac.uk.
Simon Chadwick, Birbeck College, University of London, Malet St., Bloomsbury, London, WC1E 7HX.

positioning. Service quality is also paramount in terms of customer retention and future levels of economic activity (see Snoj and Mumel for a summary [3]). Consequently, it could be argued that quality is a source of competitive differentiation and subsequent advantage. This stresses the need for organizations to consider not only what they do but also the manner in which they do it.

The aim of this study is to present a range of concepts, models and frameworks, or parts thereof, that heighten appreciation of service quality perspectives in a sport tourism context. The discussion utilizes the literatures relating to services marketing, tourism and service quality, to complement and develop the specific literature covering the delivery of service quality in sport tourism. In a number of cases the discussion has been placed in a sport tourism context by reference to case material drawn from a sport and leisure complex, Club La Santa (CLS), which is situated on the Northern coast of Lanzarote in the Canary Islands. The complex was built in 1972 by La Caja Insular de Ahorros de Canarias, a major banking organization. Although the initial plan was to build a village with accommodation for 6,000 people, this never materialized and a lack of focus and economic problems led to closure. In 1978, the Danish tour operator, Tjaaereborg, acquired the complex and transformed it into a sports and holiday resort. By 1983 La Santa Sport, now renamed Club La Santa opened for business.

The initial decision was to run the complex under the (then) recently developed timeshare concept, although this was not particularly successful. While this facility remains, less than 20 per cent of visitors are involved in the scheme. The complex contains in the region of 400 apartments and accommodates between 1,000 and 1,200 visitors each week. CLS attracts elite athletes and teams from a wide range of sports, as well as accomplished, non-elite performers and those seeking more leisurely sport and recreational activity. Visitors to the complex travel from all over the world, although Denmark, Great Britain and Germany supply the greatest proportion, accounting for approximately 80 per cent of guests.

Whilst it is acknowledged that reference to CLS brings into question the ability to generalize beyond a single case, the issues addressed are common to many sport tourism situations. As such the difficulties faced by CLS will be shared by similar organizations.

Although the focus of the essay is to address the issue of service quality, space constraints limit a comprehensive review of the literature or reference to all the models available. In addition, it is not the intention of this essay to debate the merits of related concepts or constructs, such as experience quality, customer satisfaction or perceived value, irrespective of their relative utility in understanding and measuring the service encounter (for further insights see, for example, Otto and Brent Ritchie [4], Papadimitriou and Karteroliotis [5], and Petrick and Backman [6]).

Sport Tourism

De Knop and Standeven describe sport tourism as travel for non-commercial (holiday) or for commercial (non-holiday/business) reasons to take part in or observe sporting activities [7]. Clearly, this provides a broad canvass and leaves scope for the inclusion of a wide range of activities. Consequently, a number of demand and supply side factors become relevant and serve to differentiate this sector from traditional product markets, with consequent implications for management practice [8]. On the demand side, for example, the service may have elements of high elasticity and seasonality while customer needs, attitudes and preferences may be subject to regular change. There may be little brand loyalty and heterogeneous customer groupings are evident. Supply side factors include the complex nature of the service, representing a mixture of various elements, often multisectoral, such as the transport options and facilities and attractions at the destination. The rigidity and complexity of the main elements on offer may limit speedy response to changing consumer tastes. Supply is likely to be highly fragmented given that many organizations may contribute to the overall experience. In keeping with many services the intangibility, inseparability and perishability of certain aspects of the offer and the high human content of many of the inputs is also relevant.

The Dimensions of Service Quality

At the outset it is important to appreciate that the quality of a service is whatever the customer perceives it to be and, as such, managers must ensure that the customer perspective is incorporated within their definition of service quality. It is generally agreed that customers perceive the quality of a service using two dimensions, usually termed, an outcome dimension and a process dimension. In essence, this relates to *what* the customer receives, which represents the technical quality of the outcome and *how* it is received, which represents the functional quality of the process [9]. A complementary, three dimensional approach is also offered by Lehtinen and Lehtinen [10]. *Physical quality* is discussed in terms of the quality that comes from the physical aspects of the service (for example, food and drink) and the physical support network that facilitates production of the service (swimming pools, equipment et cetera). Wakefield and Blodgett note that the appeal of the facilities' architecture may be the basis for a customer's first impression of the quality of the service provided [11].

The second dimension of the Lehtinen and Lehtinen model [12], *interactive quality* relates to interactions between customers and interactive elements of the service provider. These may be either human or mechanical. Interactions between different groups of customers may also be a significant feature of this dimension, for example, anti-social behaviour by rival fans at a sporting event. This point exemplifies the fact that not all aspects of service quality are under the control of the service provider. The final dimension, *corporate quality* relates to customer perceptions of the organization. Because many aspects of sport tourism are intangible and cannot be tried in advance of purchase, quality assessments can only be made during and following the experience. In these situations, corporate image becomes a useful surrogate measure for the level of quality to be anticipated. Gronroos also notes that a positive image can act as a filter and minimize the negative impact of small failings in either technical (outcome) or functional (process) quality [13].

Servuction System Model

A number of features of the earlier discussion can be highlighted by reference to the servuction system model. Sport tourism is, in many respects, an experience based on a bundle of benefits that may be derived from a variety of sources. The servuction system model illustrates the link between the visible and invisible aspects of a business (see Figure 1) [14]. The visible aspects include both the contact staff and the inanimate physical environment in which the service takes place. The latter is described as the *servicescape* by Bitner [15]. The servicescape is particularly important in a sport tourism situation as customers may spend long periods of time in a particular location, for example, recreation or health clubs, holiday complexes and sporting events. Wakefield and Blodgett indicate that the perceived quality of the servicescape will influence the length of stay and in turn, total expenditure [16]. Gronroos also draws attention to the servicescape suggesting it represents an element of the process (functional) dimension, based on the view that how something is delivered is influenced by where it is delivered [17].

The complexity of securing service quality is clearly illustrated by the servuction process model although it should be appreciated that the model relates to a single supplier. In sport tourism situations the supply may be derived from many independent organizations drawn from the public, private or voluntary sectors. This added degree of complication has led Augustyn to call for a new approach towards quality enhancement in tourism, based on systems theory and involving the development of a Total Quality Tourism Consortium (TQTC) for a particular destination area [19].

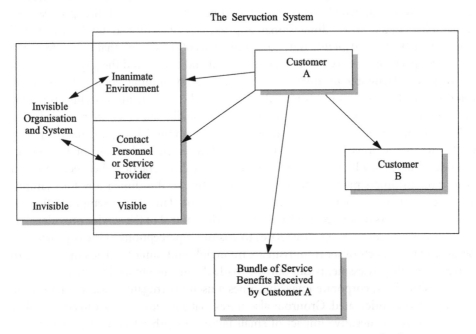

Figure 1 The Servuction System Model. Source: Bateson [18].

Criteria of Good Perceived Service Quality

In attempting to address issues of service quality it is useful for managers to have an indication of the factors that will influence customer perceptions of the service delivered. Based on a review of empirical and conceptual research and practical experience, Gronroos identifies seven important criteria [20]. *Professionalism and Skills* is an output-related criterion which revolves around the organization being able to solve customers' problems in a professional manner. This will involve coordination of both the visible and invisible elements of the organization, as illustrated in the servuction process model. *Reputation and Credibility* is image-based and relates to the customer's belief that the service provider can be trusted, gives value for money and good performance and has values that they can empathize with. The five remaining criteria are all process-related. Through their *attitudes and behaviour* contact staff show concern for the customer and seek to solve problems in a friendly and spontaneous manner. The service provider illustrates *accessibility and flexibility* in the use of its resources, for example, people, systems, locations, opening times, et cetera. *Reliability and trustworthiness* is generated through sticking to promises and ensuring the interests of the customer are central. In the event that things do go wrong the company have effective *service recovery* practices, which can quickly deliver an alternative and satisfactory solution. Finally, the physical surroundings in which the service encounter takes place (*servicescape*) should be supportive and generate positive feelings.

In using the above framework managers should appreciate that this is not comprehensive but represents a general guide that may require tailoring to the specific nature of the organization and the features of the customer segment it seeks to target.

Customer Expectations of Service

There is an argument in the literature that suggests service quality evaluations are influenced by the level of quality we are led to expect, based on factors such as an organization's marketing activity, word of mouth or our previous experience et cetera. Zeithaml and Bitner draw a distinction between factors that influence *desired service* and those that affect *adequate* levels of service [21]. This distinction is developed later in the context of zones of tolerance. The level of service we desire is heavily influenced by personal needs and our philosophies about the service. The former can fall into a variety of categories, including physical, social, psychological and functional needs. The authors cite the case of a fan who attends a game immediately after finishing work. In this situation the availability and range of catering facilities at the stadium will be highly desirable. In contrast, if the fan has eaten before travelling to the game, catering arrangements may be less important. Personal service philosophy represents the underlying attitude to service and what is seen as credible given a person's knowledge of that service. For example, someone who has worked for an airline as cabin crew will have standards based on their experience and training. Consequently, they will be less tolerant of what they perceive to be unnecessary delays or inadequacies if they are travelling as a passenger.

Zeithaml and Bitner suggest that *adequate service expectations* tend to be more short term in nature and tend to fluctuate more than the factors that influence desired expectations [22]. Five factors are identified by the authors:

- Transitory service intensifiers—temporary factors that make the customer more aware of the need for the service, for example, emergency situations.
- Perceived service alternatives—options relating to alternative sources of supply.
- Customers' self- perceived service role—relates to the extent to which customer expectations are influenced by their perception of the quality of their own involvement in the process.
- Situational factors—those factors that customers believe are outside the sphere of influence and control of the service provider.
- Predicted service—an estimate of the anticipated level of performance

Ideally, customer expectations would be fully met, although in practice this is not always the case. The situation is made more complex by the dynamics of expectations [23]. In some situations customers will have difficulty articulating just what they expect from a service provider. They may have a general view of what they require but have difficulty in providing clarification. Unless the service provider can clarify these 'fuzzy' expectations they may prove difficult to satisfy. Ojasalo also distinguishes between explicit expectations and implicit expectations [24]. The former are those that the customer assumes will be met, although in some cases they may be unrealistic. Companies can try to limit this problem by ensuring they are very clear in any communication of the contents of their offer. Implicit expectations are those that appear so obvious that customers may not see a need to articulate them. However, in the event they are not met, dissatisfaction occurs. Managers must attempt to identify implicit expectations and make them explicit.

The Gap Model

One popular model, which focuses on the confirmation of expectations approach, is the gap analysis model, developed by Parasuraman, Zeithaml and Berry [25]. This model aims to facilitate analysis of quality problems and help managers to determine how service quality can be improved (see Figure 2). It should be stressed at this point that despite its popularity, there are criticisms that the model's assumption that customers assess quality by comparing perceptions to expectations is not necessarily valid (see Williams [26] for a summary).

The gap model draws management attention to potential sources of quality problems and suggests areas where remedial attention is necessary. In summary, the model suggests that it is important for management to know what customers want, select appropriate service designs and standards, deliver to these standards and match performance to promises. A range of factors may contribute to deficiencies in these areas [28]. The following section looks at these issues in more detail and provides a context by reference to Club La Santa.

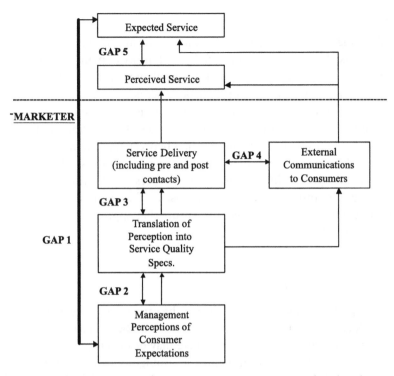

Figure 2 Gap Model of Service Quality. Source: Parasuraman, Zeithmal and Berry [27].

Gap 1 Management Perception Issues

This gap is derived from the fact that management do not really understand their customers. Several causes can be identified, for example, there may be a failure to undertake adequate levels of market research, or to fully utilize research that has been undertaken. Communication issues may also be relevant in the event that there are numerous tiers of authority that limit interaction between management and customers and management and contact staff. Attitudes to factors such as segmentation and the adoption of transactional rather than relational approaches are also relevant.

In the case of Club La Santa (CLS), customers are surveyed during their visit and requested to comment on a range of factors that previous research suggests have an impact on the quality of service provided. Feedback from guests is then used to amend elements of the offer, for example, recent criticism of the standard of the accommodation has led to the provision of 96 premium quality units, while comments about the congested nature of the Olympic-sized swimming pool has led to plans for two further pools to be constructed. Management at CLS has weekly meetings with contact staff in order to identify any potential problems early and individual managers are easily accessible to customers. This approach ensures that they remain in touch with the day-to-day issues that affect the quality of their service.

Gap 2 Quality Specification Issues

Potential failings in this area tend to come from an absence of customer-driven standards, possibly resulting from a failure of process management to focus on customer requirements and the lack of a formal process for setting service quality goals. Inadequate service leadership and poor service design, based on inadequate management commitment, unsystematic new service development processes and a failure to link service design to positioning, may also be contributing factors.

As highlighted earlier, the frequent meetings between management and contact staff and the involvement of customers in the research process allow CLS to build customer-driven quality into their service processes. A willingness to respond positively and substantively to customer feedback rather than merely pay lip service to notions of quality allows management to ensure that appropriate service designs and standards are developed.

Gap 3 Service Delivery Issues

The quality specifications established during the earlier stage (see gap 2) must be met during production and delivery of the service. A number of factors may prevent this and thereby contribute to gap 3. Firstly, there may be deficiencies in human resource policies, such as ineffective recruitment, role ambiguity or conflict, poor employee-technology job fit or inappropriate reward structures. Issues surrounding the empowerment of contact staff, levels of control and teamwork may also be relevant. A second area that contributes to gap 3 is a failure to balance supply and demand, which leads to periods of both over and under capacity. Over reliance of price to smooth out these peaks and troughs in demand may also create quality problems through the attraction of incompatible segments that will invariably lead to some groups having a negative impact on others. This point has been illustrated earlier in relation to the servuction system model. Examples of some of the factors that contribute to gap 3, which has particular relevance to CLS, are discussed in the following section.

In the context of recruitment, management are aware of the critical role that contact staff plays in delivering quality. McColl-Kennedy and White note that the intangibility of aspects of the service makes it difficult for customers to appreciate and evaluate the offer and consequently, the behaviour of front line staff acts as a surrogate for more traditional evaluation methods [29]. In response to this, managers at CLS seek to attract applicants who have already 'lived the experience'. Potential staff may have relatives who are employed at the complex or may have been visitors themselves at some time. As such they will appreciate the ethos of the CLS organization and the importance of delivering a quality service.

Through an understanding of its market, management at CLS is aware that there may be peaks and troughs in demand. For example, elite athletes will tend to train during the winter and compete in the summer. Visits to CLS are therefore more likely in the winter, particularly for Northern European athletes who will need to travel this far south to guarantee the warm weather. In contrast, holidaymakers looking for a family break with access to sports facilities will be likely to visit during the summer months. As elite athletes account for only a small proportion of the winter capacity, CLS management has introduced a number of activities to increase demand at this time. Sports weeks involve internationally-regarded athletes who deliver coaching sessions for large groups of visitors, while a number of internationally-recognized events such as the Volcano Triathlon are also promoted from the complex. This approach attracts many new customers during periods of lower demand, a good proportion of which then return at other times of year for a family holiday.

Through balancing supply and demand, management will avoid the lack of atmosphere that derives from having insufficient people at the complex or the frustration caused by having too many visitors. For example, Sarel and Marmorstein note that dissatisfaction occurs when customers have to queue for lengthy periods before receiving service and as a consequence, this situation has a negative impact on future patronage decisions [30].

Although differential pricing is used by CLS and reflects the added demand during the more popular national holiday periods, price reductions during 'off peak' periods are not excessive and are carried out with a view to ensuring some degree of segment compatibility. Martin and Pranter highlight the notion of compatibility management and stress that organizations should try to attract homogeneous customer groups to avoid one group upsetting another [31]. This takes on great importance given the wealth of evidence supporting the view that retaining existing customers, gaining loyalty and avoiding switching behaviour can aid profitability [32].

The features of the sport tourism environment are representative of those characteristics that encourage the application of compatibility management [33]. For example, customers are in close proximity, engaged in numerous and varied activities, may have to wait for service and are expected to share time, space or service utensils. They may also be drawn from heterogeneous groups. CLS is typical of the above situation and does run the risk of some customers negatively influencing others. The complex attracts a wide mix of visitors and while they may all be similar in their desire to undertake sporting activity, they are dissimilar in other important respects. For example, the mix may contain world-class athletes who focus on the training facility and have little time for the social activities. Families may have children of varying ages, some possibly quite young. Both these groups would value a good night's sleep and a degree of quiet during the late evening. Contrast this with club groups, swim squads et cetera (often older teenagers), who enjoy the bars and night club and tend to 'party' late into the morning. The CLS response to this is to request periods of quiet between midnight and 7 a.m., albeit this relies on customer support, which is not always evident. Some security staff are employed to 'police' the complex, although this is relatively low key. Other initiatives include the relocation of the nightclub to an area away from the accommodation, earlier finishing times for the evening entertainment, and the accommodation of groups of younger visitors in different sections of the complex to family groups.

Gap 4 Communication Deficiency Issues

There are several issues that contribute to this gap, which highlights the need to manage customer expectations through all forms of communication. Organizations should be particularly careful not to 'overpromise' in their marketing communications or through physical evidence cues such as elements of the servicescape. Attention should also be given to the effectiveness of the communication channels between marketing and operations functions. In addition, where an organization provides a service via a number of branches, clear policies and procedures should be in place to ensure a consistent approach is maintained.

CLS has identified some of these issues and has made a deliberate attempt to avoid overpromising in its communications. For example, following negative customer feedback regarding the standard of the apartments, these are now described in the brochure as basic. Accordingly, visitors will have limited expectations and may be pleasantly surprised that the accommodation is not quite as basic as they had expected. The CLS approach to promotion has been to limit mainstream advertising and seek credibility for their message by reference to the leading athletes who use the complex and through positive word of mouth from existing customers. Given that the sport tourism experience cannot be tried in advance of purchase these forms of communication are likely to be seen as more credible than promises made in traditional advertising media. It should however, be noted that these forms of communication are less controllable by management. For example, a visitor may describe the complex in very glowing terms to a friend who will then have exaggerated expectations which will be very difficult for the organization to meet.

The Services Marketing Triangle

Several of the points highlighted in the discussion of the gap model can be reinforced by reference to the services marketing triangle (Figure 3) which suggests that management must address all three sides of the triangle to ensure that service quality can be achieved. *Setting the promise* includes those factors that contribute to generating customer expectations of service standards, for example, the traditional elements of the marketing mix, or aspects of the servicescape. Relating this to the gap model, it is clear that weaknesses in setting the promise will relate to gaps 1 and 4 in particular. *Enabling the promise* will be influenced by management's ability to recruit, train, motivate and reward the right people and provide them with the support mechanisms that are necessary to deliver the promise. These features are more directly related to gap 3, but also have implications for gaps 1 and 4. *Delivering the promise* involves the interactions between contact staff and customers. However, as the earlier discussion of the servuction process model has highlighted, these relationships are subject to the influence of other customers or the inanimate environment (servicescape). The service marketing triangle also serves to illustrate some of the characteristics of services that influence the manner in which they are marketed.

Figure 3 The Services Marketing Triangle. Source: Zeithmal and Bitner [34].

For example, in delivering the promise the service producer and consumer are in contact at the point when the promise is delivered and as such, the process is visible to the customer who will immediately be able to identify any deficiencies (gaps). This illustrates the notion of inseparability and justifies the inclusion of the process dimension in the services marketing mix. Given the specific characteristics of services identified earlier (for example, intangibility, inseparability and perishability), there is general consensus in the literature that the traditional goods-based marketing mix comprising product, place, price and promotion should be extended to include people, process and physical. Coverage of the issues is available in any mainstream marketing text. Factors relating to the delivery of promises have a strong impact on gap 3, but also relates to gaps 1, 2 and 4 to some degree.

Zones of Tolerance

This concept is based on the premise that customers' expectations can be measured at more than one level. Although there will be a *desired* level to which the organization should aim, customers will accept a lower degree of performance, providing it achieves their *adequate* level. The variation between these levels is known as a zone of tolerance and will vary between service attributes and between different customers and may even change for the same customer over time [35]. As an example, a customer may be less concerned about having to queue to enter a sports event if there is plenty of time before the event begins. However, the level of acceptance of this situation will be reduced if there is a likelihood that the delay will lead to entry to the stadium after the event has started.

It is generally agreed that the zone is wider for process elements of the service (functional quality) but narrower for the outcome elements (technical quality). In addition, there is general support for the view that some quality attributes may be more important than others in shaping a customer's assessment of quality. While some attributes may be necessary to generate a good perception of quality, improvements in these attributes will not generate corresponding improvements in the service quality perception. These factors are described as hygiene factors and have the potential to lead to dissatisfaction when they are not present at the required level. In contrast, quality-enhancing factors offer scope for continuous increases in quality perceptions. It is therefore incumbent on managers to be aware of how particular attributes are viewed by customers in their own business context. Zeithaml and Bitner also note that zones of tolerance are likely to be narrower for recovery service than for first time service [36].

Metaphors and Analogies

The use of metaphors and analogies has proved a useful device by which to conceptualise a variety of managerial and business issues and problems. (See for example [37].) As an illustration, Grove, Fisk and Bitner view the service encounter in terms of the actors, audience and the theatre [38]. The performance will be judged in terms of the extent to which these factors are coordinated. Other theatrical concepts such as rehearsals, scripts, routines, uniforms and backstage activities can also be included.

Thwaites adapts this theatrical analogy to the sports context [39]. In the sporting adaptation, actors would be represented by players, the audience by spectators and the setting by a stadium. The author highlights that this approach underlines earlier points emphasized by both the servuction system model and the services marketing triangle. For example, at a sporting event, customer satisfaction may be influenced by the activities of the players who represent the human component, and/or by the stadium factors (servicescape). Other spectators may also influence the outcome. The effect could be either positive or negative depending on factors such as the level of behaviour or overcrowding. The customer interaction issue becomes increasingly relevant when a large number of people are required to share facilities, a feature that typifies a number of sport tourism situations [40]. The sporting analogy also illustrates the invisible components of the performance, similar to backstage activities in the theatrical analogy, for example, masseurs, dieticians, physiotherapists, coaches et cetera. Components of the sporting analogy can also be linked to other models, for example the stadium could be a source of overpromising through physical evidence cues.

SERVQUAL Instrument

Although several methods have been used to measure service quality, such as moments of truth and repertory grids, by far the most popular has been the SERVQUAL instrument and its derivatives. Developed by Parasuraman, Zeithaml and Berry, and subsequently amended in the light of both theoretical and operational concerns, the instrument seeks to measure customer perceptions of the quality of a service based on the extent to which their expectations are met [41]. Notwithstanding its popularity and earlier modifications, it should be borne in mind that criticism remains in relation to both its theoretical underpinning and practical application. (See Buttle [42] and Williams [43] for a summary of the operation of the instrument and a review of the major criticisms.) In the leisure sector there is evidence of its use in a range of settings, for example in tourism [44], in hotels [45], and in racquet and health clubs [46]. Although on occasions the instrument is used in its standard (generic) form, the general view appears to be that it needs to be adapted to the particular context.

Based on a study of six leisure amenities, art gallery, museum, amusement park, theatre, leisure centre and golf course, Williams found support for the view that there were weaknesses in applying the generic model across all sectors and confirmed the need to tailor the instrument to the custom and practice of the target industry [47]. Weiermair and Fuchs' study of Alpine ski resorts [48], and Ekinci, Prokopaki and Cobanoglu's study of Cretan holiday accommodation [49], are examples of cases where adaptations to the generic instrument have improved the quality and specificity of the findings.

To overcome some of the acknowledged deficiencies of the generic SERVQUAL instrument, a range of context-specific derivatives have been developed. For example, McDonald, Sutton and Milne measured service quality in professional team sports (TEAMQUAL) [50], Kim and Kim addressed the service quality of sport centres in Korea (QUESC) [51], O'Neill *et al.* focused on the measurement of service quality and its importance in dive tourism (DIVEPERF) [52], while Papadimitriou and Karteroliotis examined service quality expectations in private sport and fitness centres in Greece (FITSSQ) [53]. The underlying message to managers and researchers, based on the earlier discussions and which draws support from the literature, is that they should recognize the multi-dimensional and multi-perceptual nature of the construct in their development and use of instruments aimed at measuring service quality.

Summary and Implications

This essay has attempted to heighten appreciation of several issues relating to the delivery of service quality in a sport tourism context. In particular, the complex multi-dimensional nature of the construct has been identified by reference to a range of concepts, models and frameworks drawn from the service quality, tourism and sport-based literatures. However, space constraints limit the scope to provide a comprehensive literature review or a detailed critique of the models discussed. These issues are addressed elsewhere as illustrated in the supporting references. The essay is therefore, by definition, selective and offers a flavour of some of the relevant material.

As Thwaites notes, 'service quality represents a customer's subjective interpretation of his or her experience and will be affected by a diverse range of stimuli' [54]. In view of the complexity that results from this situation managers should adopt a customer-orientated approach and seek to recognize the major influences on customer perceptions before, during and after the service encounter. Because sport tourism has the potential to attract heterogeneous groups of customers there is a risk of segment incompatibility, which in turn may lead to one group having a negative impact on another. Interrelationships between customers will certainly influence service quality evaluations, as will relationships with staff and aspects of the servicescape. In the sport tourism context, some elements of the service are invariably produced and consumed at the same point in time which means the manufacture and delivery are visible to the customer. This places a premium on the efficiency of the process. In essence, managers should seek to understand their customers and appreciate the extent to which they prioritise different quality attributes. Systems must then be put in place to ensure that human, physical, technological and financial resources can be configured in a manner that secures effective service delivery.

Although this essay has focused on service quality, there are a number of related constructs that may have utility as measures by which sport tourism evaluations can be made. For example, Otto and Brent Ritchie suggest that service quality measures may be inadequate to develop an understanding of satisfaction in the tourism industry, preferring to utilize the construct of service experience [55]. It is argued that tourism (and consequently sport tourism to an even greater extent), has the potential to bring out strong emotional and experiential reactions as exemplified by Arnauld and Price in a study of white water rafting, that render traditional measures inappropriate [56].

Papadimitriou and Karteroliotis stress that although the two constructs of *service quality* and *service satisfaction* are sometimes used interchangeably, they are in fact different [57]. The latter is seen as related more to the psychological outcomes deriving from a particular service experience. In this respect it is important for managers to be clear about the construct they wish to measure and the purpose of the measurement. For example, Petrick and Backman note the strong support in the literature for perceived value as a major influence on loyalty, repurchase intentions and competitive positioning [58]; nevertheless this measure is often subordinated by managers in favour of service quality and customer satisfaction evaluations.

The wide range of concepts and constructs that are used to evaluate aspects of the service encounter can be highly confusing to the less informed reader. The complex nature of sport tourism merely exacerbates this situation. As part of the agenda for future research it would be valuable to add a comprehensive review of all these concepts and constructs with particular reference to sport tourism. Specific attention could be given to highlighting the interrelationships between them and pinpointing their individual contribution to an appreciation of the service encounter. Discussion of their strengths and weaknesses as objective measures of particular aspects of the service encounter and the validity of any assumptions upon which they are based, would also be useful, as would a continuance of the current work aimed at validating and contextualising the data collection instruments currently available.

Notes

[1] D. Shilbury and H. Westerback, 'Measuring Service Quality. A Study of Victorian-based NBL Teams', *Proceedings of the 2nd Annual Sport Management Association of Australia & New Zealand Conference*, Southern Cross University, Lismore, NSW, Australia, 22–23 Nov. 1996, pp.149–66.

[2] T. Berrett, L.T. Burton and T. Slack, 'Quality Products and Quality Services: Factors Leading to Entrepreneurial Success in the Sport and Leisure Industry'. *Leisure Studies*, 12, 2 (1993), 93–106.

[3] B. Snoj and D. Mumel, 'The Measurement of Perceived Differences in Service Quality— The Case of Health Spas in Slovenia', *Journal of Vacation Marketing*, 8, 4 (2002), 362–79.

[4] J.E. Otto and J.R. Brent Richie, 'The Service Experience in Tourism', *Tourism Management*, 17, 3 (1996), 165–74.

[5] D.A. Papadimitriou and K. Karteroliotis, 'The Service Quality Expectations in Private Sport and Fitness Centres: A Re-examination of the Factor Structure', *Sport Marketing Quarterly*, 9, 3 (2000), 157–64.

[6] J.F. Petrick and S.J. Backman, 'An Examination of the Construct of Perceived Value for the Prediction of Golf Traveller's Intentions to Revisit', *Journal of Travel Research*, 41, 1 (2002), 38–45.

[7] P. De Knop and J. Standeven, 'Sport Tourism: A New Area of Sport Management', *European Journal for Sport Management*, 5, 1 (1998), 30–45.

[8] M. Augustyn, 'Opportunities for Co-operative Sport Tourism Marketing', in C. Pigeassou and R. Ferguson (eds), *The World of Sport Management and Sport Management Throughout the World*. (Montpellier: EASM, 1996), pp.436–54. D. Thwaites, 'Closing the Gaps: Service Quality in Sport Tourism', *Journal of Services Marketing*, 13, 6 (1999), 501–16.

[9] U. Lehtinen and J.R. Lehtinen, 'Two Approaches to Service Quality Dimensions', *Service Industries Journal*, 11, 3 (1991), 287–303. C. Gronroos, *Service Management and Marketing*, 2nd Edn (Chichester: Wiley, 2000), pp.61–96.

[10] Lehtinen and Lehtinen, 'Two Approaches to Service Quality Dimensions'.

[11] K.L. Wakefield and J.G. Blodgett, 'The Effect of Servicescape on Customers' Behavioural Intentions in Leisure Service Settings', *Journal of Services Marketing*, 10, 6 (1996), 45–61.

[12] Lehtinen and Lehtinen, 'Two Approaches to Service Quality Dimensions'.

[13] Gronroos, *Service Management and Marketing*.

[14] J.E.C. Bateson, *Managing Services Marketing*, 3rd Edn (London: Dryden, 1995), p.11.

[15] M.J. Bitner, 'Servicescapes: The Impact of Physical Surroundings on Customers and Employees', *Journal of Marketing*, 56, (April 1992), 57–71.

[16] Wakefield and Blodgett, 'The Effect of Servicescape on Customers' Behavioural Intentions in Leisure Service Settings'.

[17] Gronroos, *Service Management and Marketing*.

[18] Bateson, *Managing Services Marketing*.

[19] M.M. Augustyn, 'The Road to Quality Enhancement in Tourism', *International Journal of Contemporary Hospitality Management*, 10, 4 (1998), 145–58.

[20] Gronroos, *Service Management and Marketing*.

[21] V.A. Zeithaml and M.J. Bitner, *Services Marketing* (New York: McGraw-Hill, 1996), pp.75–99.

[22] Ibid.

[23] D.A. Aaker, *Strategic Market Management* (New York: John Wiley & Sons Inc., 1995).

[24] J. Ojasalo, *Quality Dynamics in Professional Services* (Helsinki/Helsinfors: Swedish School of Economics/CERS, Finland, 1999), p.97.

[25] A. Parasuraman, V.A. Zeithaml and L.L. Berry, 'A Conceptual Model of Service Quality and its Implications for Future Research', *Journal of Marketing*, 49, 4 (1985), 41–50.

[26] C. Williams, 'Is the SERVQUAL Model an Appropriate Management Tool for Measuring Service Delivery in the UK Leisure Industry', *Managing Leisure*, 3 (1998), 98–110.

[27] Parasuraman, Zeithaml and Berry, 'A Conceptual Model of Service Quality and its Implications for Future Research'.

[28] Zeithaml and Bitner, *Services Marketing*.

[29] J.R. McColl-Kennedy and T. White, 'Service Provider Training Programmes at Odds with Customer Requirements in the Five-Star Hotels', *Journal of Services Marketing*, 11, 4 (1997), 249–64.

[30] D. Sarel and H. Marmorstein, 'Managing the Delayed Service Encounter: The Role of Employee Action and Customer Prior Experience', *Journal of Services Marketing*, 12, 3 (1998), 195–208.

[31] C.I. Martin and C.A. Pranter, 'Compatibility Management: Customer-to-Customer Relationships in Service Environments', *Journal of Services Marketing*, 3, 3 (1989), 5–15.

[32] D.A. Aaker, *Strategic Market Management* (New York: John Wiley & Sons Inc., 1995). P.L. Ostrowski, T.V. O'Brien and G.L. Gordon, 'Service Quality and Customer Loyalty in the Commercial Airline Industry', *Journal of Travel Research*, 32, 2 (1993), 16–24. E. Naumann and P. Shannon, 'What is Customer-Driven Marketing?', *Business Horizons*, 35, 6 (1992), 44–52.

[33] Martin and Pranter, 'Compatibility Management: Customer-to-Customer Relationships in Service Environments'. Zeithaml and Bitner, *Services Marketing*.

[34] Zeithaml and M.J. Bitner, *Services Marketing*.

[35] Gronroos, *Service Management and Marketing*.

[36] Zeithaml and Bitner, *Services Marketing*.

[37] S.D. Hunt and A. Menon, 'Metaphors and Competitive Advantage: Evaluating the Use of Metaphors in Theories of Competitive Advantage', *Journal of Business Research*, 33, 2 (1995), 81–90. C. Goodwin, 'Moving the Drama into the Factory: The Contribution of Metaphors to Services Research', *European Journal of Marketing*, 30, 9 (1996), 13–37. S.J. Grove, R.P. Fisk and M.J. Dorsch, 'Assessing the Theatrical Components of the Service Encounter: A Cluster Analysis Examination', *Service Industries Journal*, 18, 3 (1998), 116–34. J. Cornelissen, 'On the "Organisational Identity" Metaphor', *British Journal of Management*, 13, 3 (2002), 259–68.

[38] S.J. Grove, R.P. Fisk and M.J. Bitner, 'Dramatizing the Service Experience: A Managerial Approach', in T.A. Swartz, D.E. Dowen and S.W. Brown (eds), *Advances in Services Marketing and Management*, JAI Press, 1 (1992), 91–122.

[39] Thwaites, 'Closing the Gaps: Service Quality in Sport Tourism'.

[40] Martin and Pranter, 'Compatibility Management: Customer-to-Customer Relationships in Service Environments'.

[41] A. Parasuraman, V.A. Zeithaml and L.L. Berry, 'SERVQUAL: a Multi-item Scale for Measuring Consumer Perceptions of Service Quality', *Journal of Retailing*, 64, 1 (1988), 12–37.

[42] F. Buttle, 'SERVQUAL: Review, Critique, Research Agenda', *European Journal of Marketing*, 30, 1 (1996), 8–32.

[43] Williams, 'Is the SERVQUAL Model an Appropriate Management Tool for Measuring Service Delivery in the UK Leisure Industry'.

[44] G.R. Fick and J.R. Ritchie, 'Measuring Service Quality in the Travel and Tourism Industry', *Journal of Travel Research*, 30, 2 (1991), 2–9. C.A. Vogt and D.R. Fesenmaier, 'Tourists and Retailers' Perceptions of Services', *Annals of Tourism Research*, 22, 4 (1995), 763–80.

[45] McColl-Kennedy and White, 'Service Provider Training Programmes at Odds with Customer Requirements in the Five-Star Hotels'.

[46] J. Clowes, 'An Investigation into the Dimensions of Service Quality to Ascertain the Relative Importance of Individual Dimensions in the Racquet and Health Club Market'. Moving on with Sport Management, *Proceedings of the Sport Management Association of Australia and New Zealand Conference*, Massey University, New Zealand, 28–29 Nov. 1997, pp.3–4.

[47] Williams, 'Is the SERVQUAL Model an Appropriate Management Tool for Measuring Service Delivery in the UK Leisure Industry'.

[48] K. Weiermair and M. Fuchs, 'Measuring Tourist Judgment on Service Quality', *Annals of Tourism Research*, 26, 4 (1999), 1004–21.

[49] Y. Ekinci, P. Prokopaki and C. Cobanoglu, 'Service Quality in Cretan Accommodation: Marketing Strategies for the UK Holiday Market', *International Journal of Hospitality Management*, 22, 1 (2003), 47–66.

[50] M.A. McDonald, W.A. Sutton and G.R. Milne, 'Measuring Service Quality in Professional Team Sports', *Sport Marketing Quarterly*, 4, 2 (1995), 9–15.

[51] D. Kim and S. Kim, 'QUESC: An Instrument for Assessing the Service Quality of Sport Centres in Korea', *Journal of Sport Management*, 9, 2 (1995), 208–20.

[52] M.A. O'Neill, P. Williams, M. MacCarthy and R. Groves, 'Diving into Service Quality—The Dive Tour Operator Perspective', *Managing Service Quality*, 10, 3 (2000), 131–40.

[53] Papadimitriou and Karteroliotis, 'The Service Quality Expectations in Private Sport and Fitness Centres: A Re-examination of the Factor Structure'.

[54] Thwaites, 'Closing the Gaps: Service Quality in Sport Tourism', 514.

[55] Otto and Brent Richie, 'The Service Experience in Tourism'.

[56] E.J. Arnauld and L.L. Price, 'River Magic: Extraordinary Experience and Extended Service Encounter', *Journal of Consumer Research*, 20, 1 (June 1996), 24–45.

[57] Papadimitriou and Karteroliotis, 'The Service Quality Expectations in Private Sport and Fitness Centres: A Re-examination of the Factor Structure'.

[58] Petrick and Backman, 'An Examination of the Construct of Perceived Value for the Prediction of Golf Traveller's Intentions to Revisit'.

Public Sector Support for Sport Tourism Events: The Role of Cost-benefit Analysis

Trevor Mules & Larry Dwyer

Introduction

Economic analysis is important in event impacts assessment. The economic impacts of sporting events include the contribution to employment and income, both nationally and regionally. This study will focus upon four issues relevant to the assessment of sport events. These are: (i) estimating the economic impacts of sport events; (ii) estimating some wider economic effects of sport events; (iii) estimating the 'intangible' (non monetary) impacts of sport events; (iv) cost benefit analysis to determine the extent of public sector support for events. This study will discuss the major concepts associated with economic impact research in sport and sport tourism with a view to suggesting directions for future research in the area.

Many events incur a financial loss to organizers but produce net benefits to the community. For example, Mules and Faulkner [1] show that the Australian Formula One Grand Prix does not generate sufficient revenue through ticket sales, sponsorships, et cetera to cover its operating costs. The main problem facing any government, for any

Trevor Mules, Australian International Hotel School, Canberra, Australia. Correspondence to: trevor.mules@aihs.edu.au, Larry Dwyer, Qantas professor of Travel and Tourism Economics of NSW, Australia, L.Dwyer@unsw.edu.au.

given sporting event is: what degree of support, if any, is warranted? The answer to this question varies according to the perceived benefits and costs associated with the event.

A framework of analysis can be used to help determine which events should be supported, and to what extent, and which should not be supported with public funds. In the absence of accurate data on its economic significance, destinations may under or over-allocate resources to sport tourism, resulting in reduced net economic benefits.

Estimating the Economic Impacts of Sport Events

Despite a substantial literature now existing regarding the appropriate methodology of event assessment [2], 'best practice' does not always characterize the economic evaluation of actual events. Estimation of the economic impacts of a sporting event involves three major steps: first, estimating the expenditure of all inscope event visitors, participants, organizers, associations and sponsors; second, allocating expenditure to particular industries; and third, applying multipliers to the total to estimate the contribution to regional income and Gross Regional Product.

Estimating the Inscope Expenditure of Event Visitors

Only that proportion of expenditure, which represents an injection of 'new money' or 'inscope expenditure' into an area, is relevant to the calculation of the economic impacts [3]. 'In scope' visitors are those spectators and accompanying persons, including media and other personnel, who would not have come to the destination had the event not been held.

There are several major determinants of the inscope expenditure. These include: the number of visitors and their daily expenditure; types of visitors and types of events; trip duration; costs at the event location; and organizer/sponsor expenditure [4]. This expenditure is estimated via surveys of all sources of injected expenditure into the destination.

It needs to be emphasized that organizers and sponsor expenditure must be considered alongside visitor expenditure in estimating the inscope expenditure associated with a special event [5]. Sponsorship from local sources or from within the region is regarded as transferred expenditure unless there are reasons to believe that an additional injection of funds has resulted because of the event sponsorship. If local sponsorship of an event was not forthcoming, it is likely that the funds would have been used to sponsor an alternative event or have been allocated on other expenditure activity. The 1996 Indy car study found that injected expenditure from corporate sponsorship was substantial for a motor car racing event [6]. Unfortunately, many economic impact studies neglect organizer/sponsor expenditure altogether despite the fact that its pattern may be very different from the spending pattern of the typical visitor. Neglect of this category of event-related expenditure can result in a large underestimation of economic impacts.

Complications

The estimation of inscope expenditure must confront certain measurement problems and also requires adjustments to be made to account for the following: 'switched' expenditure, expenditure of 'casuals', 'retained' expenditure, and 'congestion effects'.

Measurement Problems

Sample surveys are used widely in the evaluation of events in order to collect information on expenditure, origins of patrons, participants, et cetera, satisfaction with the event, and other behavioural aspects such as sponsor recall. Sample surveys are necessary because of the impracticality and high cost of intercepting every single relevant person. The two main statistical criteria for sample survey design are that the process be unbiased and efficient. In practice one might add cost effectiveness as a desirable, and often necessary, characteristic [7]. Event evaluation studies need to pay attention to the proper estimation of the number of inscope visitors. This requires good estimates of the total number of people attending the event. For events with multiple performances, such as a multi-day sporting festival, the number of people and the number of attendances are two different things. This is particularly an issue at events where some or all of the performances are free, meaning that ticket sales cannot be used for estimating attendance. While methods exist for 'counting the crowd', such as tag and recapture [8] and aerial photography [9], further research is needed to find cost-effective and practical methods of crowd estimation.

'Switched' Expenditure

While some early studies on the impacts of a major sport event have included all visitor expenditure, most of the later studies include only expenditure by visitors for whom the event was the primary purpose of visit. For the 1996 Transurban Australian Grand Prix, 59 per cent of interstate and 47 per cent of overseas visitors would not have come to the State of Victoria in 1996 in the absence of the event [10]. An amount should be deducted from injected expenditure which reflects expenditure on event-related tourism by persons who would have visited a destination anyway if the event had not been held and whose visit cannot be attributed to the event.

A critical issue in determining if event expenditure is or is not switched is *viewpoint* [11]. If the viewpoint is the State, then the expenditure of residents of the State is being switched from other activities within the State, and the event may result in little or no net change in their demand. This point is also true of expenditure by organizers, media, sponsors et cetera on the event. Any such expenditure that would have occurred elsewhere in the State had the event not been held cannot be counted as new expenditure that is attributable to the event.

In estimating the level of injected expenditure into a destination it is also necessary to allow for 'time switching'. For example, if someone had planned to visit Florida in any case but brought the visit forward to coincide with an event, there is no incremental expenditure resulting from the event. It is assumed that the same amount would have been spent in the state, albeit at a different time. The same exclusion is appropriate for time-switched expenditure by Government, sponsors et cetera. In a study of the America's Cup Defence in Auckland [12], capital expenditure by the Auckland City Council was brought forward from up to five years into the future because of the event. The extent of 'time switching' may be expected to vary according to the tourism attractiveness of a destination. In a study of the Australian Motor Cycle Grand Prix at Phillip Island [13], time switchers were estimated to comprise 15 per cent of interstate visitors and 35 per cent of overseas visitors, with an overall weighted average of 16 per cent. This figure is similar to estimates of time switching associated with the Adelaide Grand Prix in 1985 and 1988 (17 per cent and 13 per cent, respectively) [14]. For sport events held in larger, well-known destinations (New York, Paris, Sydney et cetera) the extent of time switching may be greater. For the 2000 Qantas Australian Grand Prix [15], 44.8 per cent of interstate visitors and 61.5 per cent of overseas visitors would have gone to Victoria in the absence of the Grand Prix.

An additional complication is that some visitors who 'switch' the timing of their visit to a destination to coincide with an event may stay longer and spend more dollars than they otherwise would have. In such cases the incremental expenditure must be regarded as injected expenditure associated with the event. Of course, the opposite effect might result if some potential visitors were to alter their travel plans to avoid altogether the destination holding the event. The extent to which a special event held in a location deters potential visitation from other visitors is difficult to estimate with precision, especially as a proportion of those intending to visit may simply 'switch' their visit to another time.

Expenditure of 'Casuals'

Visitors who are already in a destination, and who were attracted to the destination by features other than the event, may, nonetheless patronize some of the activities associated with the event. These visitors are referred to as 'casuals' [16]. Since the event was not a primary motivation for travel to an area, and does not influence their total injected expenditure, their spending in the area is not attributable to the event and does not count as inscope expenditure.

'Retained' Expenditure

Some researchers and practitioners include, as inscope expenditure, 'retained' expenditure imputed to those event visitors and participants and associations and firms located within a region who would have spent money outside the region had the event been held elsewhere. Retained expenditure equates to the 'import replacement' function of an event held within, rather than outside, a particular region. This effect may not always be very large. For example, it was found that over 60 per cent of the expenditure of local residents who attended the 2000 Qantas Grand Prix in the state of Victoria was financed by diverting expenditure from other in-State activities, while only 0.6 per cent was financed by diverting expenditure from travel outside of the State [17].

Some researchers [18] dispute the legitimacy of including retained expenditure for purposes of economic impact assessment of events on the grounds that it cannot be measured accurately, and, in any case, it does not represent an injection of 'new money' into a destination. Taking this into account, it is perhaps best to include retained earnings only when the event held in some destination resulted from a competitive bidding situation or from a choice out of a particular set of destinations. In such circumstances, the retained expenditure can be estimated on the basis of estimated losses of expenditure by residents who would otherwise have travelled to the successful host destination for the same event.

'Congestion Effects'

Residents may spend less on purchases of goods and services during an event, even if they remain within the destination. For example, they may be less inclined to dine out because of perceived 'crowding' of restaurants or traffic congestion, and visitors may occupy accommodation rooms or airplane seats which otherwise may have been occupied by residents. In addition, the holding of an event may cause some residents of a destination to travel out of the area for all or part of its duration. The event destination thus suffers a loss of sales revenue that would otherwise have accrued to local businesses. For example, international airlines, faced with the prospect of returning from Australia with empty seats during the 2000 Olympics, offered large discounts on outbound travel from Australia. Resident exodus resulted in expenditure of money transferred to outside of the destination. Estimates of resident exodus numbers and duration of absence can be multiplied by average household expenditure data to determine lost revenues to the destination.

Some residents may spend more locally as a result of the holding of an event. Thus, we should include increased economic activity by residents who are not event attendees (for example, bar, restaurant and home consumption expenditures) as long as this expenditure would otherwise have been saved or would have been spent outside of the area and is therefore additional to what they would have spent in the absence of the event.

The extent to which a special event held locally causes residents to spend their money elsewhere or to reduce or increase the amount which they otherwise would have spent, can only be determined from surveys. Since those who do reduce their expenditure by a certain amount during the period of the event may compensate by spending this same amount following the event, only the proportion of the reduced expenditure that goes into additional savings should be counted. Any estimates will be only as accurate as the survey technique allows.

The Multiplier Process

The inscope expenditure of visitors and organizers/sponsors stimulates economic activity, and creates additional business turnover, employment, household income and government revenue in the host community [19]. This ripple effect in an economy is termed a 'multiplier' by economists.

The initial injection of money has *direct, indirect* and *induced* impacts on the local economy. Direct impacts relate to the allocation of the visitor expenditure to different industry sectors. The secondary impacts, which relate to the ripple effect of additional rounds of re-circulating the initial expenditure injection of visitors, are of two types: indirect and induced impacts. Indirect impacts arise when the affected firms purchase inputs from other business operators. These other businesses, in turn, purchase inputs from other firms and so on. Induced impacts arise when employees who reside within the jurisdiction, spend their increased (disposable) wages and salaries on goods and services from businesses within the area.

The multiplier effect is weakened by leakages and interactive effects.

Leakages

There are several forms of leakages that act to reduce the 'ripple effect' taking place. The main forms of leakages are taxes, savings and imports. Matheson [20] documents several types of leakages that reduce the economic impacts of events. He emphasizes that many studies have ignored the issue of whether the money spent at a sporting event stays in the local economy. As Matheson argues, much of the money spent by visitors on hotel rooms, rental cars and restaurants goes to national chains and the profits earned by these businesses do not increase the welfare of citizens in the local economy but, rather, accrue to stockholders outside the area. Similarly, revenue from ticket sales is often paid to the league or the sport's ruling body instead of local organizers. Delpy and Li [21] highlight a form of leakage which they refer to as 'VIP switching'. This refers to the proportion of entertainment dollars distributed to catering and special event companies rather than to local eating and drinking establishments. As the event profile increases, so does the demand for corporate hospitality and entertainment services. These tend to be sourced from larger urban, rather than regional, areas and thus may increase the amount of leakages from regional events. In general, sub-regions of an economy have a higher overall propensity to import than the state as a whole since they tend to be less self-sufficient in producing goods and services for tourist needs. This observation reinforces the importance of selecting carefully the geographical area of the region under analysis.

Interactive Effects

Unless there is significant excess capacity in tourism-related industries, the primary effect of an expansion in tourism is to alter the industrial structure of the economy rather than to generate a large increase in aggregate economic activity. Its effect will thus show up as a change in the *composition* of the economy rather than as a net addition to activity. Many large sporting events are staged in communities that are already popular tourist destinations. If hotels and restaurants in the host city normally tend to be at or near capacity throughout the time period during which the competition takes place, an event may simply supplant rather than supplement the regular tourist economy [22]. Key mechanisms which determine the size of the economic impacts resulting from increased tourism demand include factor supply constraints, real exchange rate appreciation, and current government economic policy [23].

Types of Multipliers

The standard means of deriving multipliers for event impact assessment has involved use of the input-output model [24]. These multipliers can be decomposed into their various effects which are initial, production-induced and consumption-induced effects. Four commonly used multipliers are output, income, value added and employment multipliers. They provide respectively a measure of the effects of an exogenous change in final demand on the output of industries in the economy; income earned by households because of new outputs; value added at factor cost due to the change in output (that is, wages, salaries and supplements earned by households plus gross operating surplus of business); employment generated as a result of increased output.

When using an input-output model as a basis for deriving multipliers, value added multipliers are the preferred measure for the assessment of the contribution of an event to a State economy [25]. Output multipliers exaggerate the impacts, often providing misleading information on the economic contribution of the event to the destination. In contrast, value added multipliers measure only the change in net economic activity at each stage of production. Unlike the use of output multipliers, value added multipliers do not double count changes in economic activity. The authors consider value added multipliers to be preferable because they give a measure that corresponds to Gross Domestic (Regional, State) Product, all of which are more general income measures than household income.

Caution needs to be exercised, also, in the use of employment multipliers. Sport events are not likely to generate lasting employment effects because of their 'one off' or short term nature. Employment multipliers based on input-output tables tend to exaggerate the amount of employment generated. Employment generation models based on input-output tables assume a constant proportional relationship between sales turnover and the level of employment. However, different firms, according to the nature and scale of their business, have different marginal propensities to employ labour in response to increased sales. A major event represents a period of peak demand for firms in the hospitality and tourism industry, and, generally, such firms are used to operating with some unused capacity. The peak in demand would simply use up that capacity. Extra shifts, more rostered hours, and overtime are all likely to be used, rather than new hirings, as firms adjust to the short-term increase in demand. Thus, in some firms, staffing levels may be relatively insensitive to changes in turnover, while other firms may seek better utilization of those currently employed (for example, provision of overtime, weekend work). Further, to the extent that interactive effects lead to reduced activity in some sectors, the net gain in employment from some events may be quite small.

It has been argued recently that input-output modelling is an inappropriate basis to generate the multipliers for event impact assessment [26]. These authors claim that the assumptions of input-output models are unduly restrictive and cannot account for the interactive effects that, they claim, are always present even for small events in regional locations. These critics advocate the use of computable general equilibrium models in event impact assessment. While some would reject this view [27], the issue is likely to dominate economic impact assessment of events in coming years.

Estimating Wider Economic Impacts

There are several other types of economic impacts that are ignored in traditional economic impact assessment of sport events. These are impacts that result from expenditure injections associated with events, but not directly related to the inscope expenditures of visitors, organizers and sponsors. They represent, nonetheless, very real economic effects of events on a destination and need to be recognized in the overall assessment of the economic significance of special events to the host destination.

Positive economic impacts may result from increased tourism flows associated with event-related promotion, induced construction and development expenditure, and additional trade and business development.

Tourism Promotion

The promotion of a destination for holiday travel may be enhanced by hosting a special event. Because an event may enhance the tourism image of an area, there is a 'background' economic benefit attributed to events by future visitors attracted by this enhanced image. This image enhancement can have long-term positive effects on tourism visitation expenditure and tourism investment. For the 1996 Indy car race [28], the value of the event for future tourism was estimated to be A$19.7 million.

The publicity accorded to an event may enhance awareness of the destination and create a favourable image to potential tourists. For example, Sydney, selected as Olympic City 2000, has ranked as a very popular destination to host an international meeting since 1997. This can lead to increased visitation and associated expenditure over the longer term. The event may enable new markets to be tapped. Of course, a poor reputation can be developed if facilities and services come to be regarded as inadequate, for example Seville's unsuccessful hosting of EXPO'92 [29].

Sport events can help to stabilize tourism inflows to a destination. They can provide local tourism operators with useful knowledge of visitor numbers. Relatively long lead times which result in hotel and tour bookings being made years in advance greatly assist in the financial planning of tourism facilities.

Induced Development and Construction Expenditures

Sport events, particularly those scheduled for a dedicated venue, generate additional investment in tourism/recreation infrastructure, thereby increasing the attractions available in an area for use by locals as well as visitors. The Sydney Olympics generated around A$5 billion worth of stadia and sporting infrastructure, as well as investment in road, rail and transport interchange systems, all of which will benefit residents of, and visitors to, Sydney into the future. The main stadium for the Sydney 2000 Olympics has subsequently hosted large crowds at football matches of various codes, including the Rugby World Cup in 2003. Not only did the Olympics have an economic impact, but so too have the subsequent major events staged at the same stadium. Researchers have examined the relationship between building new facilities and economic growth in metropolitan areas [30]. Matheson [31] points out that, in every case, independent work on the economic impact of stadiums and arenas has uniformly found that there is no statistically significant positive correlation between sports facility construction and economic development.

Facility construction associated with events can be a source of economic and urban development. The investment generated by events, privately or publicly sourced, has multiplier effects on income, value added and employment, but so also would alternative forms of investment that it replaces. For purposes of assessing the economic contribution of special events it is only investment that would not have been generated except for the sport event, and which represents the injection of 'new money' into the destination, that is to be counted. The question must be asked: was the money redirected from another project (public capital switching), and, if so, was that project in the impact area or outside? If the state government reallocated funds originally earmarked for roads in one region to build an event facility in another, this switching would be a net gain to the second region and a net loss to the first. The issues here are not straightforward since they involve hypothetical issues of what would have occurred had the particular type of investment not taken place.

In the case of public sector investment, taxation revenue used to fund facilities construction reduces the spending power of residents on other goods and services and thus does not represent a net gain of expenditure within the destination. In any case, it is likely that funding would have been allocated to other infrastructure projects if it had not been allocated to support an event. In this case the expenditure can be regarded as 'switched' from one type of investment to another. An important exception to this is where the investment expenditure is based on a special grant from an external source, for example, a Federal government grant to a State, or an internationally sourced grant to a developing country. In the case of new investment from the private sector, there are two alternatives – no new investment would have been undertaken, or else it would have been investment of another type. Only in the first case will the investment be considered to have economic impacts. For the second case, the issue arises as to the opportunity cost of the investment alternative foregone (see below).

Additional Trade and Business Development

The hosting of sport events can lead to the growth of existing businesses and the establishment of new ones. Successful events can be effective marketing tools for attracting new business and visitors to an area offering companies an effective means of promoting their products and services to a targeted audience. Increased convention business often follows major events and estimates can be based on experiences of other destinations domestic and worldwide. Sport events in Australia have generated business development opportunities for local firms in supplying products and services and have generated export opportunities for some manufactured products [32]. The hosting of sport events can provide valuable international exposure for a host destination among the international business, scientific and educational communities. This is particularly the case where a programme of other activities, for example, theatre, arts, cultural, business et cetera, is developed in association with the event. During the Sydney Olympics a comprehensive programme of artistic and cultural mini events was developed. This can serve to expand visitor spending opportunities, provide residents with an expanded choice of leisure activities, and increase the length of visitor stay. Additionally, the opportunity was seized to develop business to showcase Sydney to the world's major business firms. In this way, a special event became a catalyst for the development of opportunities for access to new technology, exchange of ideas, establishment of valuable business and professional contacts and other socio-cultural impacts.

The hosting of successful events often appears to be associated with increased business confidence. This in turn can induce greater business activity including increased business investment. Special events trigger private and public investment particularly in tourism development such as new hotels, restaurants, shopping centres, and urban renewal to include new roads, improved appearance through streetscape beautification, rehabilitation or creation of green space. Where event tourism brings about increased investor confidence, any induced private investment can be attributed to that source. Only that investment which would not have occurred otherwise is relevant to the economic assessment.

It is important to note that the additional business activity associated with events is already captured in the direct, indirect and induced effects on income and employment. To estimate the *new* business opportunities associated with event tourism, industry surveys are required. These surveys will need to range over both established and new businesses and must estimate the extent of future *injected* expenditure to the destination resulting from events-associated business links.

The benefits of additional trade and business development are often overstated and estimates must be treated with caution. In practice the *ex ante* estimates of economic benefits have far exceeded the *ex post* observed economic development of host communities following mega-events [33]. There are also substantial measurement problems here. Although studies were conducted on the economic impact of the Sydney Olympics [34], these downstream economic benefits were too far into the future at the time to be quantifiable. It would be possible to do *ex post* research on Olympic legacies, and to track their experience in staging events that attract tourists and generate economic impact in subsequent years. This could also be done for public investment in major facilities that have a long life as sporting venues. In doing so, researchers should remember that a dollar in 2004 is not the same as a dollar in 2010. Not only does an adjustment have to be made for inflation, but also for the time preference for money. The latter is achieved by discounting the stream of benefits to a present value.

Negative economic impacts may result from interruption of normal business and under-utilization of infrastructure.

Interruption of Normal Business

Preparation for a sport event may disrupt business operations. Business operators in Sydney complained of loss of business due to Olympics-associated road works for up to three years prior to the 2000 Games.

During the period of the event, residents may spend less than they normally would on purchases of goods and services, even if they remain within the destination. For example, they may be less inclined to dine out because of perceived 'congestion' in restaurants and night clubs, or traffic congestion, and visitors may take accommodation rooms or airplane seats which otherwise may have been occupied by residents.

Interruption of normal business can be determined from estimates of reduced sales revenues to local businesses. A sport event may cause local residents to spend their money elsewhere or to reduce the amount which they otherwise would have spent during that period. Since those who do reduce their expenditure by a certain amount during the period of the event may compensate by spending this same amount following the event, only the proportion of the reduced expenditure that goes into additional savings shall be counted. Any estimates will be only as accurate as the survey technique allows.

The extent to which a special event deters visitation to the destination from non-event visitors is difficult to estimate with precision, especially as a proportion of those intending visitors may simply 'switch' their visit to another time.

Under-utilized Infrastructure

A common legacy of many past sport events worldwide has been a huge debt and much under-utilized infrastructure [35]. Operating losses subsequently incurred by facilities constructed for a specific event, combined with interest repayments on debt, may comprise a continuing burden for local tax and ratepayers and must be regarded as economic costs over the longer run [36]. Indeed, the tax burden has an opportunity cost in terms of other government-provided goods and services foregone or in lower taxes and hence increased consumption activity (with its attendant multiplier effects).

Evaluation of 'Intangibles'

The holding of a sport event may also generate what are called 'intangible' costs and benefits. By their nature, these costs and benefits are not quantifiable as precisely or objectively as are the economic impacts.

Intangibles might include emergent values such as increased community interest in the issues relevant to the event 'theme'. This may lead, for example, to greater future participation by residents, creating obvious community health benefits as well as increased use of sport equipment. Another 'intangible' is the pride felt by locals as a result of their city hosting a special event. Intangibles also include event product extensions such as youth sports clinics, educational training programmes and philanthropic/social causes involving sports scholarships, youth, the elderly, the underprivileged et cetera [37].

Intangibles may also include items such as the disruption to resident lifestyles associated with an event. Examples include: traffic congestion, road accidents, crime, litter, noise, crowds, property damage, environmental damage and pollution, police and fire protection, vandalism. The standard economic method of valuing such impacts is to determine people's willingness to pay to avoid them. Increasing use is being made of hedonic pricing and contingent valuation methods.

There are always particular benefits and costs associated with a special event that are unable to be quantified objectively. Consequently, too often these types of impacts are neglected altogether in economic impact studies of events. In those studies which acknowledge the importance of such 'intangibles' the discussion is qualitative rather then quantitative in content. Intangibles' are best treated within a cost benefit framework [38].

Public Sector Support for Events: The Role of Cost-Benefit Analysis

Economic impact analyses typically consider all factors of production as having zero opportunity costs to a community in terms of what they could produce if invested elsewhere in the economy. There is a need to estimate the real cost to society of devoting resources to event support and to compare the resulting benefits to those which can be obtained from allocating scarce resources to other activities.

Cost-benefit analysis (CBA) of special events is founded on the principles of welfare economics. The benefits of a project outweigh the costs if the consumer's willingness to pay outweighs the value (opportunity cost) of the resources used in the process [39]. A CBA would take into account all of the types of benefits and costs discussed above. The different types of benefits and costs can be measured using opportunity cost or willingness-to-pay valuation techniques. In this exercise, expenditure by governments are costs because they are financed by residents within the host community, who must therefore forego the consumption of other goods and services which they would otherwise have purchased with their incomes.

Burgan and Mules [40] argue that economic impact analysis can be regarded as a special case of CBA, specifically where resources are under-utilized. In contrast to standard economic impact analysis, cost-benefit analysis involves estimating the full value associated with the use of land, labour and capital. When any, or all, of these factors are under-utilized, the use of these resources in event hosting is likely to be greater than in their current use(s). It seems that without financial support from taxpayers, many sporting venues would not be built and many large sporting events would not be held. In other words, if these activities were left entirely to market forces, there would be fewer of them than happens in practice. Economists often represent the 'market forces' outcome as an equilibrium on a demand/supply diagram, such as point E on Figure 1.

Since there is not a defined market for a homogeneous good known as a special event, the demand and supply curves in the diagram could be thought of as referring to sport events. Consumer demand for attending such events is a decreasing function of the admission price and is represented by the demand curve D. (In actual fact the 'price' to consumers includes travel costs, purchase of food and merchandise at the event, et cetera.) The number of such events that would be financially viable, given consumer demand, is the equilibrium quantity Qe.

Such public spending could be justified if the benefits to the host community are greater than the costs. But since the beneficiaries are largely private firms providing hospitality services, the question arises as to why these firms themselves do not fund the event. The answer lies in market failure.

Because individual firms are unable to capture all of the benefits of funding the special event, they are unable or unwilling to do so individually. They might do so collectively, for example by forming a cooperative group to jointly fund the special event. However, individual firms can maximize their profits by opting out of the cooperative, by, for example, allowing others to fund the event while enjoying the extra business that the event generates. This is the 'free rider problem'. If a large enough number of firms choose this strategy, the cooperative will collapse and the benefits of staging the events will be lost to all, both participants and free riders. In other words, there are benefits that accrue to the community beyond the consumers of the event.

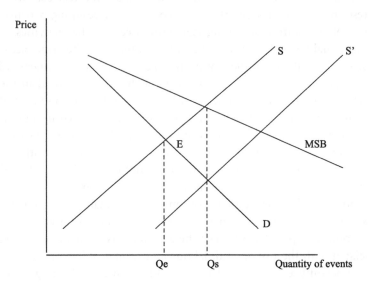

Figure 1 Supply and Demand Conditions for Special Events.

The demand curve shows the price that consumers would be willing to pay for each different quantity of events, and is a reflection of the private benefits that consumers expect to receive from attending such events. However, the existence of an extra layer of benefits gives rise to the marginal social benefits curve (MSB in Figure 1), and the socially optimum level of events would be Qs. This would be the number of events which would maximize social welfare.

Without government funding, special events and facilities for major sporting events would be provided at a level below the optimum or desirable point, if provided at all. The question that arises is whether economic impact is an appropriate measure of the extent to which social/community benefits exceed private benefits.

Burgan and Mules [41] point out that under CBA, the public spending is worth undertaking if the gain to the host community exceeds the cost of subsidizing the special event or sporting facility. Early CBA studies were aimed at cost-reducing public investments in things such as roads, airports, dams, et cetera. Under CBA, the gain from such an investment is usually measured by the resultant increase in consumer surplus. However, since the consumers of tourism services are often non -residents, total consumers' surplus is an inappropriate measure of economic or social gain from the point of view of the host economy: only the consumers' surplus of local residents who attend the event would be relevant, which may be quite a large amount, since locals may outnumber visitors at many events. Also, such a measure does not take account of benefits that accrue to hospitality businesses, which arise from correcting the market failure. This is more correctly measured by the concept of producer surplus.

Since it is residents of the host community whose taxes are being used to fund the public expenditure on the event, only resident consumers matter for the calculation of the consumer surplus part of the net economic benefit, but economic impact is neither consumer surplus nor producer surplus. Burgan and Mules [42] have shown that under certain economic conditions the host economy has sufficient under-utilized resources that the increase in demand caused by the event do not cause costs to rise, in which case it is assumed that the supply curve in the relevant industries is flat, the usual measure of economic impact is equivalent to producer surplus, that is,. the gain to producers of hospitality services which accrue because of the correction of market failure.

It is clearly impractical for public sector managers to make estimates of the consumer surplus and producer surplus attributable to a particular event. Referring again to Figure 1, if the socially optimum quantity of events is Qs, the Government subsidy of events will shift the supply curve from S to S'. The trick is for Governments to provide the level of subsidy such that S' cuts the demand curve D at the same quantity of events as Qs. In other words, welfare is maximized if events are subsidized up to the point where the total number of events which are viable is Qs rather than Qe. In practical terms this amounts to deciding how many events should get Government financial aid, or which events qualify for a subsidy and which events do not. Because Qs is an unknowable quantity, Governments often use as a rule of thumb that an event is worthy of Government financial support if it can demonstrate economic impacts in excess of the amount of the subsidy.

Unfortunately, unless the Burgan and Mules conditions are met, the amount of economic impact is likely to be greater than the amount of producer surplus. At the same time, the amount of producer surplus is less than the net economic benefit, because it ignores the consumer surplus of residents. Thus there is no way of knowing if the rule of thumb using economic impact results in more or less than the right number of events being subsidized.

Note that a CBA involves getting a full list of benefits and costs. As we have discussed above, special events often create 'intangible' costs and benefits which are born by sections of the community other than the organizers and consumers of the event. In principle, these types of benefits and costs can be measured using opportunity cost or willingness-to-pay valuation techniques. The cost of implementing these techniques is often significantly higher than the cost of measuring economic impact, and so they are rarely used. Cambourne, Cegielski and Mules [43] have used willingness-to-pay techniques for a motor sport event in Canberra, but the research was directed at ticket prices rather than the community's willingness to support the event.

In situations where the value of something to the community exceeds its private market value, economists have developed techniques such as contingent valuation [44]. Contingent valuation applied to a sporting event would assess the willingness of taxpayers to pay for the event to be hosted in their region. Thus it would assist the Government in deciding whether the event had benefits to the community over and above the private consumer surplus benefits of those who attend the event. The application of such techniques to the evaluation of major sporting events would be a step forward in assisting policy makers to determine which events are likely to increase the host community's economic welfare.

Conclusion

Despite the limitations of economic impact as a proxy for economic welfare, the concept will most likely continue to be the most popular approach to evaluating the merits of public monies being used to finance events. In most studies the research has involved measuring visitor expenditure by means of a survey, and inputting that expenditure into a model of the host economy in order to calculate multiplier effects. As indicated above, there are two major candidate techniques for generating the multipliers – input-output models and computable general equilibrium modelling. The relative advantages and disadvantages of each technique are likely to be much discussed in the forthcoming research literature on event assessment.

Space limitations preclude discussion of other areas where economic analysis is relevant to sport tourism. Perhaps of most importance is for research emphasis to be directed away from the concept of economic impact, and to place the issue of event evaluation squarely in the framework of CBA. The economic impact analysis then becomes an input into a more comprehensive framework more useful to policy making. The cost of a full CBA study is likely to be prohibitive for small events seeking a small amount of Government support, and so research effort should be directed at finding a cost-effective alternative which would produce a better proxy than economic impact in such cases.

Notes

[1] T. Mules and B. Faulkner, 'An economic perspective on special events', *Tourism Economics*, 2, 2 (1996), 107.

[2] J.P.A. Burns, J.H. Hatch and T.J. Mules, *The Adelaide Grand Prix: the Impact of a Special Event* (Adelaide: The Centre for South Australian Economic Studies, 1986); D. Getz, 'Events Tourism: Evaluating the Impacts', in J.R.B. Ritchie and C.R. Goeldner (eds), *Travel, Tourism and Hospitality Research – a Handbook for Managers and Researchers* (New York: John Wiley and Sons, 1987); B. Burgan and T. Mules, 'Economic Impact of Sporting Events', *Annals of Tourism Research*, 19 (1992), 700–10; J.L. Crompton and S.L. McKay, 'Measuring the Economic Impact of Festivals and Events: Some Myths, Misapplications and Ethical Dilemmas', *Festival Management and Event Tourism*, 2, 1 (1994), 33–43; J.L. Crompton, *Measuring the Economic Impact of Visitors to Sports Tournaments and Special Events* (Ashburn: National Recreation and Park Association, Division of Professional Service, 1999); L. Dwyer, R. Mellor, N. Mistilis and T. Mules, 'A Framework for Assessing "Tangible" and "Intangible" Impacts of Events and Conventions', *Event Management*, 6, 3 (2000a), 75–191.

[3] J.L. Crompton, 'Economic Impact of Sports Facilities and Events: Eleven Sources of Misapplication', *Journal of Sport Management*, 9 (1995), 14–35; L. Delpy and M. Li, 'The Art and Science of Conducting Economic Impact Studies', *Journal of Vacation Marketing*, 4, 3 (1998), 230–54.

[4] Crompton, 'Economic Impact of Sports Facilities and Events', 34; Delpy and Li, 'The Art and Science of Conducting Economic Impact Studies', 239.

[5] Crompton, 'Economic Impact of Sports Facilities and Events', 32; Dwyer *et al.*, 'A Framework for Assessing "Tangible" and "Intangible" Impacts of Events and Conventions', 181; Dwyer L., R. Mellor, N. Mistilis and Mules, 'Forecasting the Economic Impacts of Events and Conventions', *Event Management*, 6, 1 (2000b), 192–204.

[6] KPMG, *Business, Economic and Social Review of the 1996 IndyCar Event – Goldcoast* (Sydney, 1996), p.35.

[7] B. Burgan, B. Mules and T. Mules, 'Reconciling Cost-benefit and Economic Impact Assessment for Event Tourism', *Tourism Economics*, 7, 4 (2001), 321–30; T. Mules 'Globalization and the Economic Impacts of Tourism', in B. Faulkner, G. Moscardo and E. Laws (eds), *Tourism in the 21st Century – Lessons from Experience* (London: Continuum, 2001), Chap. 17.

[8] G. Brothers and V. Brantley, 'Tag and Recapture: Testing an Attendance Estimation Technique for an Open Access Special Event', *Festival Management and Event Tourism*, 1, 4 (1993), 143–6.

[9] M. Raybould, T. Mules, E. Fredline and R. Tomljenovic, 'Counting the Herd: Applications of Aerial Photography to Crowd Estimates at Open Events'. Proceedings of *Delighting the Senses, Ninth Australian Tourism and Hospitality Research Conference*, Bureau of Tourism Research, Canberra, 1999.

[10] National Institute of Economic and Industry Research, *Economic Impact Evaluation of the 1996 Transurban Australian Grand Prix*, A Report for the Department of State Development (Tourism Victoria) (Melbourne, 1996).

[11] Burns *et al.*, *The Adelaide Grand Prix*, p.9.

[12] McDermott Fairgray, *The Economic Impacts of Cruise Ship Visits: 2000/01 Season* (New Zealand: New Zealand Tourism Board and Cruise, 2001), p.25.

[13] National Institute of Economic and Industry Research, *Economic Impact Evaluation of the 1996 Transurban Australian Grand Prix*, p.43.

[14] Price Waterhouse, *Economic Impact Assessment of the 1988 Australian Formula I Grand Prix: A report prepared for the Australian Formula I Grand Prix Board* (Sydney, 1989).

[15] National Institute of Economic and Industry Research, *Economic Impact Evaluation of the 2000 Qantas Australian Grand Prix,* A Report for the Department of State Development (Tourism Victoria) (Melbourne, 2000), p.17.

[16] Crompton, 'Economic Impact of Sports Facilities and Events', 30; Delpy and Li, 'The Art and Science of Conducting Economic Impact Studies', 241.

[17] National Institute of *Economic and Industry Research, Economic Impact Evaluation of the 2000 Qantas Australian Grand Prix,* p.36.

[18] Getz, 'Events Tourism: Evaluating the Impacts', p.106.

[19] Crompton, 'Economic Impact of Sports Facilities and Events', 25.

[20] V. Matheson, 'Upon Further Review: An Examination of Sporting Event Economic Impact Studies', *The Sport Journal,* 5, 1 (2002), 2.

[21] Delpi and Li, 'The Art and Science of Conducting Economic Impact Studies', 235.

[22] Matheson, 'Upon Further Review', 76.

[23] L. Dwyer, P. Forsyth, J. Madden and R. Spurr, ' Economic Impacts of Inbound Tourism under Different Assumptions about the Macroeconomy', *Current Issues in Tourism,* 3, 4 (2000), 325–63; L. Dwyer, P. Forsyth and R. Spurr, 'Evaluating Tourism's Economic Effects: New and Old Approaches', *Tourism Management,* 25 (2004), 307–17.

[24] J. Crompton, S. Lee and T. Shuster, 'A Guide for Undertaking Economic Impact Studies: The Springfest Festival', *Journal of Travel Research,* 40, 1 (Aug. 2001), 79–87; T. Tyrrell and R. Johnson, 'A Framework for Assessing Direct Economic Impacts of Tourist Events: Distinguishing Origins, Destinations and Causes of Expenditures', *Journal of Travel Research,* 40, 1 (Aug. 2001), 94–100.

[25] T. Mules, 'Estimating the Economic Impact of an Event on a Local Government Area, Region, State or Territory', in *Valuing Tourism: Methods and Techniques* (Canberra: Bureau of Tourism Research Occasional Paper Number 28, 1999).

[26] L. Dwyer, P. Forsyth and R. Spurr, 'Economic Evaluation of Special Events', in L. Dwyer and P. Forsyth (eds), *International Handbook of Tourism Economics* (London: Edward Elgar, 2005a forthcoming); L. Dwyer, P. Forsyth and R. Spurr, 'Estimating the Impact of Special Events on an Economy', *Journal of Travel Research,* 43, May (2005b), 351–9.

[27] Mules, 'Estimating the Economic Impact of an Event on a Local Government Area, Region, State or Territory'; C. Hunn and J. Mangan 'Estimating the Economic Impact of tourism at the local, regional and State or territory level, including consideration of the multiplier effect', in C. Corcoran (ed.), *Valuing Tourism: Methods and Techniques* (Canberra: Bureau of Tourism Research Occasional Paper Number 28, 1999).

[28] KPMG, *Business, Economic and Social Review of the 1996 IndyCar Event – Goldcoast,* p.25.

[29] C. Smith and P. Jenner, 'The Impact of Festivals and Special Events on Tourism', *Travel and Tourism Analyst,* 4, 4 (1998), 73–91.

[30] M. Rosentraub, 'Sport and Downtown Development Strategy', *Journal of Urban Affairs,* 16, 3 (1994), 228–39; R.A. Baade, 'Professional Sports as a Catalyst for Metropolitan Economic Development', *Journal of Urban Affairs,* 18, 1 (1996), 1–17; R.A. Baade and V.A. Matheson, 'An Assessment of the Economic Impact of the American Football', *Reflets et Perspectives,* 34, 2–3 (2000), 35–46; V. Matheson, V. and R. Baade, 'Bidding for the Olympics: Fools Gold?', in C. Barros, M. Ibrahim and S. Szymanski (eds), *Transatlantic Sport* (London: Edward Elgar Publishing, 2003); R. Noll and A. Zimbalist, 'The Economic Impact of Sports Teams and Facilities', in R. Noll and A. Zimbalist (eds), *Sports, Jobs and Taxes; The Economic Impact of Sports Teams and Stadiums* (Washington: Brookings Institution, 1997), pp.55–91; D. Coates and B. Humphreys, 'The Growth Effects of Sports Franchises, Stadia, and Arenas', *Journal of Policy Analysis and Management,* 14, 4 (1999), 601–24; J. Siegfried and A. Zimbalist,

'The Economics of Sports Teams and their Communities', *Journal of Economic Perspectives*, 14, 3 (Summer 2000), 95–114; J. Siegfried and A. Zimbalist, 'A Note on the Local Economic Impacts of Sports Expenditures', *Journal of Sports Economics*, 3, 4 (Nov. 2002), 361–6.

[31] Matheson, 'Upon Further Review', 25.

[32] Price Waterhouse, 1992 Formula One Grand Prix: Economic Evaluation (Sydney: Price Waterhouse), p.56.

[33] Matheson, 'Upon Further Review', 21.

[34] Centre for Regional Economic Analysis, *Economic Impact Study of the Sydney 2000 Olympic Games* (Sydney: Arthur Andersen, 1999).

[35] Matheson and Baade, 'Bidding for the Olympics: Fools Gold?', 67.

[36] Smith and Jenner, 'The Impact of Festivals and Special Events on Tourism', 86.

[37] Delpy and Li, 'The Art and Science of Conducting Economic Impact Studies', 237; Dwyer, Mellor, Mistilis and Mules op cit p.182.

[38] A. Dasgupta, and D.W. Pearce, *Cost-Benefit Analysis Theory and Practice* (London: Macmillan, 1978).

[39] B. Burgan, and T. Mules, 'Sampling Frame Issues in Identifying Event-Related Expenditure', *Event Management*, 6, 4 (2001), 223–30.

[40] Ibid., 219.

[41] Ibid., 222.

[42] Burgan and Mules ibid. p.224

[43] B. Cambourne, M. Cegielski and T. Mules, 'Use of Dichotomous Choice Modeling to Fix Event Ticket Prices'. Proceedings of the Events Research Conference, University of Technology, Sydney, 2002.

[44] R.J. Knopp, W. Pommerehne and N. Schwartz (eds), *Determining the Value of Non-market Goods: Economic, Psychological, and Policy Relevant Aspects of Contingent Valuation Methods* (Boston: Kluwer, 1997).

A Grounded Theory of the Policy Process for Sport and Tourism

Mike Weed

Introduction

In discussing the concerns and methods of a range of disciplines within the social sciences, Houlihan describes the types of approaches that tend to be associated with disciplines such as sociology and psychology [4]. He notes that, in comparison to other areas of the social sciences, political science is far less neatly delineated, 'being focused on the sharply contested concept of power and its use in all its myriad forms' [5]. In addition to the lack of any neat delineation, the study of policy, politics and planning takes place at macro, meso and micro levels, with a range of concepts and theories contributing to debates at each of these levels. Furthermore, different aspects of politics, policy-making and the policy process have been studied, such as implementation, bureaucracy and control.

Mike Weed, Institute of Sport and Leisure Policy, School of Sport and Exercise Sciences, Loughborough University, Loughborough, Leicestershire, LE11 3HR, UK. Correspondence to: m.e.weed@lboro.ac.uk

Research and commentary in the general and wide-ranging field of policy studies has focused on: theories of the state [6] such as Marxism, pluralism and corporatism, and 'neo-' versions of these approaches; on aspects of power [7]; on bureaucracy [8]; on the structure of the policy process itself [9]; on organizational theory [10] and on implementation and the role of individuals [11]. However, while policy studies as a field is relatively well developed, there is comparatively little literature on the policy process in leisure, sport and tourism. In the sport sector, much work carried out under the policy and politics banner has tended to be either commentary on political priorities for sport [12] or studies of aspects of sports development [13], whilst tourism academics tend to focus on planning [14], and more specifically on planning for sustainable tourism [15]. Contributions in the broader leisure field have tended to focus on local leisure policies, and the rationale for investment in leisure [16]. Henry's [17] overview *The Politics of Leisure Policy* is now in its second edition and provides perhaps the most substantive coverage of the leisure policy topic in a single volume, albeit in a British context, but tends to focus largely on ideological concerns rather than the dynamics of the policy process itself. Examples of the limited work in this latter area are those by Houlihan [18] on sport and Hall [19] and Hall and Jenkins [20] on tourism. Yet, while the work of these authors is useful in informing an examination of the response by policy makers to the sport-tourism link, they do not extend their analysis beyond sport and tourism respectively, nor do they look in any detail at cross-sectoral liaison. Consequently, the substantive study of policy responses to the sport-tourism link in the UK by Weed [21] and Weed and Bull [22], which was developed into a more generalized formal theory in Weed and Bull [23], utilized a longitudinal grounded theory approach, which drew on much of the general policy studies literature for theoretical sensitivity, rather than the more limited sport, tourism and leisure work. It is the genesis of this work that will be covered in this essay, examining the process of development over an eight year period of a grounded theory of the policy process for sport and tourism.

Before giving a brief introduction to policy for sport and tourism, it is useful to define some terms. It has been suggested by many authors (see elsewhere in this text) that the field encompassing the study of sport and tourism should be referred to as 'sport tourism'. However, the preference here is for the term 'sports tourism' to refer to the 'social, economic and cultural phenomenon arising from the unique interaction of activity, people and place' [24]. In addition to this, a broader concept, 'the sport-tourism link', is used to refer not only to tourism involving some element of sports-related activity, but also to embrace liaison between the sport and tourism areas on issues such as resources and funding, policy and planning, and information and research. This broader term is useful to employ in discussions such as those here on policy, and in any discussion seeking to examine the effects of linking sport and tourism. For those interested, a more detailed discussion of the conceptual reasons for the preference for this terminology can be found in Weed and Bull [25].

An initial scoping study of regional policy for sport and tourism in England showed that many policy initiatives related to sports tourism were implemented unilaterally by agencies from the sport or the tourism sector [26]. Consequently, Weed and Bull concluded that:

> while there exists an increasing level of sport-tourism [policy] activity, this has not been matched by an increase in liaison amongst agencies responsible for sport and tourism policy ... It may be that these bodies are generally reticent to collaborate with any agency outside their area of interest ... as they may feel their interests would be threatened [27].

While this comment was based on UK research, further investigation has shown that similar situations exist in other countries around the world, where there are few examples of agencies responsible for sport and tourism developing links or working together. A number of factors can be identified that contribute to such indifference. In many countries around the world the agencies and structures that exist for developing sport and tourism respectively have been established and have developed entirely separately. This separate development is often compounded by a significantly different 'culture' or 'ethos' in the two sectors. There is often a tradition of public sector support, subsidy and/or intervention in the sports sector (the exception, perhaps, being the USA, where the United States Olympic Committee, although granted a role via legislation, receives no public sector funding), whilst the tourist sector is largely seen as a private sector concern, and agencies are often limited to a marketing or business support role. These factors are further complicated by the different levels at which responsibility for policy development lies. Organizations may exist at national, regional and/or local level, and in countries such as the USA or Australia, which have federal systems of government, the significant role of state governments also needs to be considered. The respective responsibilities of these agencies can mean that in some instances liaison would need to take place not only across sectors, but also between levels. The relative scarcity of such liaison is a testament to the range of problems that exist.

The remainder of this essay will examine the problems associated with policy development for the sport-tourism link. Initially the use of a grounded theory approach is discussed, and a 'map' to organize the discussions of emergent policy issues is described [28]. This map structures discussions around issues at the macro (context), meso (supra-setting, setting and situated activity) and micro (selves) levels. Emerging from these discussions is the identification of a range of tensions in the sport-tourism policy process, and the examination of the factors affecting liaison that underpin them. Finally, and in conclusion, a formal grounded theory model of the policy process for sport and tourism is presented. While the primary purpose of grounded theory is often to explain or understand phenomena, in this case some implications for future research and practice emerge, and these are also highlighted and discussed in the conclusion to the essay.

The Grounded Theory Approach and Layder's Resource Map

Hammersley notes that a key assumption of the grounded theory approach is that the social world must be discovered using an exploratory orientation [29]. Given the nature of the research area under study here, there was little alternative to an exploratory orientation as there had been little or no previous work on the development of sport-tourism policy. The grounded theory approach was developed by Glaser and Strauss in 1967, and they emphasize the importance of 'theory as process', an ever-developing entity which can be extended and modified [30]. As such, initial organizing frameworks are viewed as flexible accompaniments to the incremental collection of data. In this research, ideas associated with policy communities and policy network provided an initial organizing framework [31], but the unfolding nature of the research revealed a range of factors that impact upon sport-tourism policy liaison. Glaser also discusses the importance of 'theoretical sensitivity', which refers to the use of previous literature to 'sensitise' the researcher to the research area, rather than to provide theories and concepts to be tested [32]. The central tenet of a grounded theory approach is that theory emerges from the data rather than constraining it [33].

In 1998, Weed and Bull reviewed a range of theoretical concepts and areas, drawn from the generic policy studies literature, that might be relevant to the study of policy for the sport-tourism link [34]. These concepts/areas included: theories of the state and ideology, state policy development, policy networks/communities, organizational structure, organizational culture, and key staff in the policy process. Such issues provided an initial sensitivity to the area of policy studies, but were not intended to be restrictive or exhaustive. The intention was that other issues would be allowed to emerge as the study of sport-tourism policy development progressed. To allow this emergent approach to take place, the concepts and the ensuing research were organized under the loose framework of a research resource map adapted from Layder [35] (see Figure 1).

Prior to discussing the way in which the research map relates to this area, some brief comments on the elements of the map may be useful. In providing such comments, it should be noted that it is important not to treat the different elements of the map as separate domains of interest which can be pursued independently of each other. Macro phenomena make no sense unless they are related to the individuals who reproduce them over time. Conversely, micro phenomena cannot be fully understood by exclusive reference to their 'internal dynamics': they have to be conditioned by circumstances inherited from the past. In general terms it is best to understand macro and micro features as intermingling with each other through the medium of social activity itself. Perhaps the best way of doing this is to outline the interrelations between the elements of the research map.

In practice, selves cannot easily be separated from the social situations in which they are routinely embedded. For example, various changes in self-conception and perception can often only take place through actively communicating with others on a regular basis (for example, Becker on marijuana use [36]), that is, they can only take place through situated activity. Studies by Roy [37] and Glaser and Strauss [38] draw attention to two aspects of situated activity—firstly that each instance of (even similar) situated activity will bear the unique imprint of the individuals involved, and secondly, the important effect of the nature of the setting. Thus, a concentration on situated activity is always a matter of analytic and methodological emphasis

Concept/Area	Research Element
Ideology *Govt Policy*	**CONTEXT** The general distribution of power and resources in society as a whole that is relevant to the focus of the research. The values and ideologies that influence behaviours. The political, religious and economic situation relevant to the subject of the research.
Policy Community/ Network *Organizational Structure*	**SETTING** The already established forms of organization with which participants interact. The 'ongoing life' that is identifiable apart from specific instances of interaction.
Organizational Culture	**SITUATED ACTIVITY** The dynamics of interaction beyond individual's responses to social situations, the results of which are a function of the interchange of communication between the whole group rather than the behaviours of the constituent individuals viewed singly.
Key Staff *Ideology*	**SELF** The effect on and response of individuals to particular features of their social environment and the typical situations associated with this environment. The conceptions of self and identity, and associated subjective feelings, motivations and experiences, that are connected with particular lines of activity over time.

Figure 1 Research Resource Map. *Source*: adapted from Layder.[39]

rather than an indication of its empirical separation from matters of self, meaning and setting.

There is no rigid dividing line between settings and the wider macro features and processes that provide their context. Settings and contexts are perhaps best thought of as rather different but complementary aspects of social life. They are sustained by social activities in general, but are largely independent of the movements and activities of any individual. As social forms they are reproduced over time because generally people tend to replicate the habits, rules and rituals that sustain these forms in the first place [40], continually breathing new life into the already established character of the social form they enter into. However, the continual movement of people within and in and out of these social forms means that they are continually evolving and thus social production takes place alongside social reproduction. The exact degree to which either one of these predominates in any particular case is a matter for empirical investigation.

Immediate settings of activity are firmly connected to increasingly remote relations of domination and subordination in the wider social fabric. It is impossible to understand the way in which these wider, macro structures are reproduced over time without understanding how the more micro processes feed into them. The organization of occupations and labour markets are good examples of the intermediate social forms that transmit the influences of macro processes and factors into activity and its settings and back again [41]—macro processes feed into activity, while the activity itself has the effect of reproducing these wider social relations.

In returning to Figure 1, the first thing to note is that the central issue—the lack of liaison on policies relating to the sport-tourism link—focuses on the setting. However, here the setting consists of two elements—the organization and the policy community/network. Clearly these two elements exist at manifestly different levels, and so it would appear both useful and sensible to reflect this in the analysis. Therefore, a distinction between two clearly separate levels of setting is needed—the immediate setting of the organization, and the supra-setting of the policy community/network. Furthermore, in as much as the central issue here is the lack of a coherent policy network to deal with the sport-tourism link, the focus is perhaps more accurately described as being at the level of the supra-setting.

Ideas associated with policy communities and networks, which lie at the supra-setting level, are particularly useful as an initial organizing framework because they allow an investigation of the extent to which those factors operating at the other levels of the research map influence the relationships and interactions that take place in the supra-setting. Of these factors, ideology and government policy are seen as providing the context. Government policy sets the legal framework within which the other levels must operate and, whilst its influence on relations in the supra-setting may vary according to the way in which it is perceived and interpreted, it is to a certain extent a given factor because empirical investigation is not required to ascertain what it is. As such, in this sense it differs from the other factors illustrated in Figure 1. Ideology also contributes to the context, although it also appears under self. At the contextual level it refers to those ideologies that are dominant within society or particular sections of society (for example, professions or political parties). The structure of organizations contributes to the immediate setting, and to a certain degree may delineate the extent to which relations may take place within the supra-setting.

At the more micro levels, an analysis of organizational culture may provide useful insights into situated activity—the dynamics of interaction beyond individuals' responses to situations. This is perhaps the most intangible area, but its almost invisible influence on relationships in the supra-setting is of major significance. Finally, key staff and ideology contribute to an understanding of the influences of selves. Because conceptions of self and identity are connected with particular lines of activity over time, it is important to examine the background and experiences of key staff and the extent to which they influence relations in the supra-setting. Ideology has already been mentioned as contributing to the context; however, it also contributes to the self as different individuals have their own personal ideology and set of values through which they interpret the world. The extent to which such personal ideologies coincide or conflict with those ideologies dominant in the society or sections of society within which the supra-setting exists may influence the nature of relations within the supra-setting.

The development of grounded theory requires that issues emerge from data collection and analysis, rather than such collection and analysis being structured by theoretical positions. As such, while the policy concepts outlined in Figure 1, and reviewed in Weed and Bull[42] provided a sensitivity to the area, the development of theory must be emergent. Consequently, the work that developed a substantive theory of the sport-tourism policy process in the UK [43] was organized, not by policy concepts, but by the levels outlined in the research map adapted from Layder [44]. The discussion that follows outlines the key issues at each of these levels [45], and whilst this discussion is now presented at a more general formal level [46], examples are given from the substantive UK work by way of illustration. This more generic formal theory allows a further consideration of the issues highlighted in contexts beyond that of the UK, and as such, as discussed in the conclusion to this essay, it can provide a useful backdrop for future research and policy development.

Issues in the Context

Issues surrounding the sport-tourism link at the context level are affected by a complex relationship between strategic direction and resources. Resources and funds possessed by both sport and tourism agencies are often largely controlled by others, most significantly national or regional/state governments. In the UK, as in many other countries, the national sports agencies (UK Sport and Sport England) are wholly government funded. This resource control allows government to prescribe the sports agencies' policy direction, despite their status as quasi-autonomous. By contrast, because the tourism sector is run along more commercial lines, tourism agencies can often generate funding through commercial activity. However, generating funds through short-term commercial contracts often means that there is little funding to contribute to core strategic functions and consequently such strategic functions are lost. In such circumstances, funding offered by government can be useful, but such funding is often earmarked for particular policy areas. In both sport and tourism sectors, state control of funding inevitably takes precedence over the knowledge and expertise of the specialist agencies in deciding policy. Consequently, as such agencies become implementers rather than developers of policy initiatives, there is an ongoing erosion of their independent strategic capacity.

The willingness of organizations to form relationships outside their policy heartlands—the areas of policy that they consider to be their core concern [47]—is often affected by anticipated or actual change. A key difference is that between evolution and change, with evolution being seen as sustainable and originating from within an organization, whilst change is often externally imposed and is disruptive. Furthermore, organizational stability during periods of change is important. Clearly the effects of disruptive change on organizations' willingness to work outside their policy heartlands means that such periods will not be conducive to developing closer links between sport and tourism [48]. In fact, it appears to be the case that sport and tourism agencies around the world have a very limited conception, if not a misconception, of their respective roles and remits. They certainly are not fully aware of the range of areas where sport and tourism might be linked, although perceptions do vary from country to country, and between regions within countries. This lack of awareness may be a result of a set of dominant ideologies within both the sport and tourism policy communities about the areas they deal with. It may be the case that sports tourism is not seen as a legitimate concern by either the sport or the tourism policy community.

Supra-Setting: Considering Policy Communities

Following Glaser and Strauss's [49] conception of theory as process, the issues in the supra-setting were viewed through a lens sensitized by theories of the policy process, particularly those relating to policy communities and policy networks. The model of the supra-setting that emerged was an adapted combined model, that was developed to be particularly appropriate to a policy sub-sector (the sport-tourism link) that derives from two distinct policy sectors (sport and tourism). This model combines the work of Marsh and Rhodes [50] and Wilks and Wright [51] and proposes a structure comprising a leisure policy universe, within which exist sport and tourism policy communities, and across which may emerge a sport-tourism policy network. There are a number of issues relating to the structure of policy communities for sport and tourism that may affect the emergence of a sport-tourism policy network, and these issues combine to characterize such policy communities as either tightly formed policy circles, or loosely constituted issue zones. This model was developed and discussed in detail by Weed [52] and is illustrated in Figure 2.

POLICY UNIVERSE

POLICY COMMUNITY	
Policy Circle	**Issue Zone**
Stable, restricted membership	Unstable, open membership
Many interdependencies	Few interdependencies
Highly insulated from other policy sectors	Little insulation from other policy sectors
Complex patterns of resource dependencies	Few resource dependencies
Governmental, economic or professional member interests	

POLICY NETWORK

Figure 2 A Model of Cross-Sectoral Policy Development. *Source*: Weed.[53]

Weed and Bull [54] combine the substantive UK work with a review of sport and tourism policy communities around the world, and propose that it is possible to characterize tourism policy communities as showing many of the characteristics of an issue zone. Often membership is unstable and open with no clear leadership and few major interdependencies. Furthermore, there is often virtually no insulation from other policy sectors and member interests are mainly economic, although governments often retain a privileged position as a result of their resource position. By contrast, while sports policy communities are often not strong enough to be labelled so [55], they do show some of the characteristics of a policy circle, certainly in relation to the tourism community. Sports policy communities tend to have a primary core, the membership of which tends to be stable and restricted, although there is a more open secondary community; there are a number of major interdependencies, both in terms of finance and expertise, that dictate the structure of, and relationships in, sports communities; and member interests, particularly in the primary community, are mainly governmental, supplemented by professional connections. The one factor that prevents sports policy communities being characterized as policy circles is their historical lack of insulation from other, more powerful, policy areas such as education and thus, at times, their inability to define their own agenda, something that has been recognized as a significant and important variable [56].

However, whilst neither sport nor tourism communities are able to exclude more powerful policy sectors from impinging on their respective work, they are able to define their agenda within the leisure policy universe. In fact, within the leisure area the communities are able to establish a greater degree of insulation as neither tourism nor sport sectors are seen as more politically important than each other. It is perhaps the case that, due to their greater correspondence with the features of a policy circle, sport policy communities are more able to exclude tourism interests than tourism communities are able to exclude sport. This may have a significant effect on the extent to which such communities can generate a sport-tourism policy network, particularly as they are often more concerned with defining their own agenda within the leisure policy universe rather than seeking connections.

Increasingly, many areas of liaison are dominated by funding mechanisms. This may be both positive and negative for sport-tourism liaison, depending on the nature of the funding mechanism. Funding mechanisms may bring sport and tourism interests together, or they may exclude either sport or tourism interests from partnerships where they should be consulted. While organizations generally recognize the need to be flexible and innovative in tapping into funding sources, there are few examples around the world where this has led to the inclusion of both sport and tourism interests in partnerships where one or the other is initially involved. This is a considerable lost opportunity, as consultation on funding mechanisms and sources would appear to provide a useful stepping-stone for further liaison.

Relationships between sport and tourism policy communities may be dependent on the level of stability within policy communities and, as discussed above, within organizations in those communities. It may be that such stability, and consequently such inter-community relationships, may depend on regionally specific factors that may be geographic, historic, cultural, economic or structural. Furthermore, it may be the case that these regional factors affect definitions of sport, tourism and sports tourism, which will also affect liaison. It is therefore important that national and regional agencies for sport and for tourism work up their own agenda for sport-tourism liaison, in full awareness of each other's aims and objectives and their own boundaries of expertise. As a result of their generally broader remit, and given an established agenda, it appears that tourism agencies may be best placed to take on a catalyst role in suggesting to other agencies areas in which they might work together. However, such an arrangement requires both resources and a reconsideration, by a range of agencies, of organizational territory.

Organizational Issues: Setting and Situated Activity

Setting and situated activity are usefully considered together because, in the minds of many policy makers—and in some of the literature [57]—there is little distinction made between structural and cultural aspects, or indeed any other aspect, of organizational life. In fact, the structures of public sector or quasi-public sector bodies, such as most sport and tourism agencies, are such that cultural and structural factors evolve together; they are inextricably linked. Furthermore, an integrated overview of these levels is consistent with the clear links between them as illustrated in Layder's research map [58].

The work of Mintzberg [59] is useful to sensitize perspectives on the benefits of specialist or professionalized structures as opposed to more generic or holistic structures, and their effects on external relationships. Whilst specialist structures may mean that other agencies know who to contact in an organization and that they know that person is competent, more generic structures allow for greater innovation in developing new relationships. Therefore, because sport-tourism links are likely to be new, it would seem that more generic structures would help to develop such relationships. However, sports agencies, which are often based on professional expertise, tend to be structured along specialist lines as *Professional Bureaucracies* whilst tourist agencies, which have to be responsive to commercial pressures and developments, tend to more holistically structured as *Adhocracies* [60]. These differences may be one of the major barriers to sport-tourism relationships. However, in some cases the influence of individual staff may be such that these barriers can be overcome.

Organizations may allow employees some degree of flexibility and autonomy, although they are not the same thing. Whilst autonomy allows individuals to work unsupervised, it is often the case that such individuals work within an imposed framework that allows little flexibility in moving outside that framework without reference to their superiors. Because it is unlikely that such frameworks will allow for sport-tourism liaison, greater levels of flexibility are often required within organizations if sport-tourism links are to be developed. Evidence suggests that, as a result of their adhocratic structure, staff in tourist agencies have more flexibility than staff working for sports agencies [61].

Strategies and strategy processes serve a function beyond developing the direction of organizations. They are important mechanisms for motivating staff and for developing ownership of strategy. It is therefore important to involve all staff, especially those 'on the ground', in the strategy process. Failure to do this is likely to result in implementation gaps [62] where staff on the ground modify policy in the process of implementation. A failure to include input from a range of staff can also contribute to 'group-think' [63], where options are limited to those that fall within the experience of the group and reinforced as the only options by those within the group. This can narrow the range of options considered and, as with the concept of mobilization of bias [64], where issues are deliberately kept off the agenda for discussion, can work against the development of sport-tourism links because no-one within the group would think of such links as an option. To help guard against this, teams or groups can be regularly changed within organizations, outside groups can be consulted, or a high staff turnover can be relied upon. Of course, each of these solutions brings about its own problems in terms of instability that has already been noted as adversely affecting the development of sport-tourism links.

Selves: Individuals in the Policy Process

The influences of individuals in the sport-tourism policy process appears to be magnified by the respective structures of sports and tourism agencies, each of which tend to give some degree of flexibility or autonomy. However, this notwithstanding, it may still be the case that an individual may clash with the organization and, depending on the structure and culture of the organization, three things may occur. Firstly, in an organization where there is little flexibility or autonomy, clashes between the organization and an individual are likely to result in that individual leaving the organization. Secondly, where there is little flexibility but a reasonable level of autonomy, implementation gaps are likely to occur as the individual works outside the framework laid down. Finally, where flexibility and autonomy exists, it is likely that the work of the individual will change, to some extent, the direction of the organization. Obviously, the influence of individuals is maximized in the third situation, however it is also high, though unseen, in the second situation. In both of these situations, key individuals within organizations have the potential to greatly influence external relationships.

The backgrounds of staff can also influence their ability to work with outside organizations. While, character traits can be important in determining an individual's general ability to work with external agencies, backgrounds can also be important in determining the ability of individuals to work with specific organizations. There is very limited evidence that individuals with a planning background are more likely to be positively disposed towards the development of sport-tourism links [65].

The influence of individuals on organizations' direction has already been discussed. However, the substantive UK research [66] contains examples of three joint sport-tourism initiatives that were carried forward in each case by one key individual who happened to have a planning background. The ability of such staff to take forward these initiatives was influenced by their seniority in their organization, the level of autonomy and flexibility they were granted, and some level of support from senior staff in the other organization. Two of the initiatives were direct liaisons between the regional agencies for sport and tourism, while the third evolved into a wider liaison between a range of leisure interests in the region. Of the two sport-tourism initiatives, the more successful one had fairly modest aims in simply attempting to show areas of working together and to define the way the regional sport and tourism agencies would respond to other agencies working across sport-tourism boundaries. It appeared that, along with the continuing presence of the staff originally involved, this was a major reason for this initiative's success [67].

The above discussions show that there are a number of links across all the levels of analysis. This is particularly relevant at the individual level as many issues that emerged at other levels re-emerged in microcosm in relation to individuals. This clearly demonstrates that any attempt to examine the levels in isolation would be largely superfluous. In fact, perhaps the strength of the Layder research map is that, while it allows the levels in the policy process to be analysed separately, such analysis only serves to highlight the links across the levels [68]. The following discussions will now attempt to link these levels of analysis in developing a grounded theory of the policy process for sport and tourism, focusing particularly on those factors that affect relationships between sport and tourism agencies.

Factors Affecting Relationships Between Sport and Tourism Agencies

The issues outlined in the above discussions resulted from detailed investigations of the development of policy relating to the sport-tourism link in the UK. However, a further review of international policy revealed that many of the issues were also salient in other countries [69]. Again, as noted earlier, this elevates the grounded theory to a more formal level which allows it to guide future research and policy making in the field. Both Weed [70] and Weed and Bull [71] note a number of tensions within and between sport and tourism policy communities that are evident in the above discussions, and these are illustrated in Figure 3.

There are five main tensions listed in Figure 3, along with a number of subsidiary tensions, each of which may affect the extent of liaison between sport and tourism agencies. The first of these is a tension between the need to generate income and the importance of maintaining an independent strategic capacity that emerged as a result of the discussions at the contextual level. Important here is the supremacy of the economic resources possessed by governments as opposed to the specialist knowledge and expertise invested in sport and tourism agencies. As a consequence there is a tension between the development of top-down as opposed to bottom-up policy. The discussions of the setting noted the difference between evolution and change, and the importance of individuals and agencies feeling they have ownership of initiatives. Further tensions,

INCOME GENERATION	**.V.**	**STRATEGIC DIRECTION**
Resources	*.v.*	*Knowledge*
TOP-DOWN POLICY	**.V.**	**BOTTOM-UP POLICY**
National	*.v.*	*Regional*
Imposed Initiatives	*.v.*	*Ownership of Initiatives*
Change	*.v.*	*Evolution*
ORGANIZATION	**.V.**	**INDIVIDUALS**
Professionalization	*.v.*	*Adhocracy*
Framework	*.v.*	*Flexibility*
INTERNAL FOCUS	**.V.**	**EXTERNAL FOCUS**
Organizational Survival	*.v.*	*Future Development*
PROJECT BASED LIAISON	**.V.**	**ONGOING LIAISON**
Initiatives	*.v.*	*Advocacy*

Figure 3 Tensions in the Sport and Tourism Policy Communities.

both within the setting and at the situated activity level are those between organizations and individuals. Organizations may be structured along professionalized lines, where individuals are allowed autonomy to work within an established framework, or in a more adhocratic way, where individuals are allowed a greater degree of flexibility. Within both the setting and the supra-setting there may be an emphasis on either internal or external foci. Both sport and tourism policy communities seem to be more concerned with working within their internal policy heartlands than taking an external view of the leisure sector as a whole. Similarly, individual organizations, particularly those struggling with funding problems, are often internally focused on organizational survival, rather than externally focused on future strategic development. Finally, there is a tension between the need for sport-tourism liaison that is project based and is dependent on particular initiatives, and that which is ongoing and is focused on general positive advocacy for sport-tourism links.

At the root of each of the above tensions are a number of factors. Some of these were initially identified by Weed and Bull [72] and were listed alongside the relevant levels in the research map adapted from Layder [73] (Figure 1). However, in line with a grounded theory approach using 'theory as process' [74], emergent research [75] resulted in modifications and additions to these factors. The generic formal grounded theory of the policy process for sport and tourism [76] identifies seven factors that might affect relationships within and between sport and tourism policy communities, namely: ideology, definitions, government policy, regional contexts, organizational culture and structure, individuals, and the structure of the respective policy communities.

Firstly, ideology causes tensions at all levels of the policy process. At one level ideology can be identified as important in the policy context, contributing to the environment within which policy is made. However, it is also clear that tensions between income generation and strategy, change and evolution, organization and individuals, and organizational survival and future development are caused in some instances by conflicting ideological stances. Such ideologies may be the result of political beliefs, professional frameworks, or they may be more personal ideologies that are not necessarily professional or political.

Linked to ideology in some respects is the influence wielded by individual and organizational definitions and conceptions of sport, tourism and sports tourism. Government definitions of sport and tourism are often imposed on national agencies, causing conflicts related to the tension between resources and knowledge. Definitions and conceptions can also cause tensions between organization and individual and between internal and external foci. A more narrow definition of either sport or tourism leads to a more sharply defined policy heartland and less willingness to work outside this heartland at either the organization or the community level. This is one area that varies considerably around the world. In Australia and Canada, for example, the focus of the national sports agencies is on elite sport, which consequently narrows the focus for collaboration with tourism agencies at national level largely to issues related to major events. However, this is not the case at regional/state level, where examples of sport-tourism collaboration are more common, because the sports agencies have a wider focus that encompasses recreational sport.

Perhaps one of the most significant influences is 'regional contexts'. In this respect, historic, geographic, administrative, economic, structural and a whole range of other factors that vary between regions can cause tensions in different ways in different regions. For example, the extent of the tension between project-based and ongoing liaison is affected by regional contexts such as geographical resources for sports tourism, historical liaison (or non-liaison) between regional bodies, and the strength and structure of the regional economy. To a certain extent individuals may be seen as regional contexts as they can cause specific tensions in their region. However, the influence of individuals is also prevalent at national level and within government and therefore still merits separate consideration. While 'regional contexts' may appear a slightly eclectic label, it is nevertheless a useful one in helping to understand the variations between regional approaches to the sport-tourism link.

Government policy is perhaps the most straightforward cause of tensions within the sport-tourism policy process. As earlier discussions show, government policy, in a range of forms and both intentionally and non-intentionally, causes tensions between income generation and strategy and between top-down and bottom-up policy development in a number of ways. Organizational structure and organizational culture clearly contribute to many of the tensions identified in Figure 3 and it might be expected that they should be considered separately, as originally proposed by Weed and Bull [77]. However, subsequent work has show that it is almost impossible to separate out their influence in practice [78]. In fact, it appears that, in many cases, culture and structure evolved together and are inextricably interlinked. Consequently, it is perhaps more useful to combine these factors and consider them as one.

Individuals have already been mentioned briefly in the discussion of regional contexts. However, initial work on this influence on sport-tourism policy [79] referred to 'key staff' rather than 'individuals'. It is perhaps more useful to use the term 'individuals' as this also allows for the influence of, for example, significant political figures. In this respect the UK research shows that John Major, as British Prime Minister, had a significant influence on sport-tourism relationships because the sports policy statement, 'Sport: Raising the Game' [80], that contained proposals for the English Sports Council to withdraw from the promotion of recreational activities in order to focus more on competitive sport, is widely seen as bearing the personal stamp of the Prime Minister [81]. Consequently, John Major was responsible for a number of tensions related to top-down policy development and organizational change and instability. However, it should perhaps be pointed out that individuals are not always aware of the wider implications and repercussions of their actions. It is unlikely that John Major gave any thought to the effect his proposals would have on sport-tourism relationships and as such the consequences for sport-tourism links were unintended.

These causes of tension within the sport-tourism policy process can now be viewed within the Model of Cross-Sectoral Policy Development illustrated earlier as Figure 2. This model allows for an analysis of the way in which the structure of policy communities at the sectoral level might affect the development of policy networks at the sub-sectoral level. As such, the structure of the communities themselves might be causes of some tensions within the policy process. Generally, sports policy communities can be identified as having a closed primary core but a more open secondary community, whilst tourism policy communities are altogether more open. Although in relation to tourism policy communities, sports policy communities tend to show more of the features of a policy circle, both communities are often unable to insulate themselves from other, more politically important policy areas. Consequently, tensions surrounding the imposition of initiatives and the ability to define strategic direction may be related to the structure of the two policy communities. Specifically, that both policy communities are susceptible to the imposition of initiatives from other, non-leisure, communities.

A Grounded Theory of the Policy Process for Sport and Tourism

This essay has discussed and described the genesis of a grounded theory of the policy process for sport and tourism. In concluding these discussions, an overview and synthesis of the emergent theory can now be illustrated (see Figure 4). The formal grounded theory is achieved by locating the factors that have been identified as the causes of the tensions listed in Figure 3 within the Model of Cross-Sectoral Policy Development (Figure 2) to produce an holistic overview of the policy process. This holistic overview shows a leisure policy universe that contains a sports policy community with a tightly defined primary core, but a more open secondary community (lying towards the policy circle end of the policy community continuum), and a generally open tourism policy community (lying towards

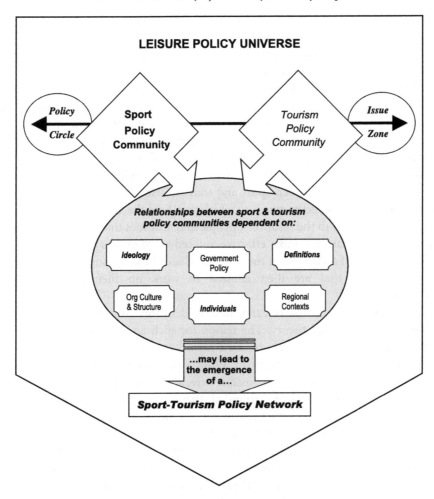

Figure 4 A Grounded Theory of the Policy Process for Sport and Tourism.

the issue zone end of the continuum). Six influences are identified as affecting relationships between these communities and, as per the above discussion, these are:

IDEOLOGIES

DEFINITIONS

REGIONAL CONTEXTS

GOVERNMENT POLICY

ORGANIZATIONAL CULTURE AND STRUCTURE

INDIVIDUALS

The nature and extent of these influences will determine whether any meaningful or sustainable sport-tourism policy network emerges. Some evidence suggests that while sport-tourism policy networks are unlikely to emerge at national levels, there is much greater potential for their development at the regional/state level [82]. This is largely due to the influence that can be attributed to regional contexts and individuals. These influences allow for a considerable variation between regions/states, thus causing problems for national level liaison, but they can also be strong influences on the development of regional/state level liaison. Regional sport-tourism policy networks are more likely to be grounded in the particular needs of the region/state, and are more likely to be amenable to the influence of individuals who believe that mutual benefits are derived from a link between sport and tourism. However, a major factor in the success of such networks is the extent to which they have the ability to determine their own agenda according to the resources, people and attitudes that exist in their region. In this respect, perhaps the most effective antecedent of greater sport-tourism links may be the raising of awareness of the benefits of such links among key policy makers and organizations that are then allowed to work up their own agenda for collaboration.

The approach taken in the research described in this contribution has been the development of grounded theory. The reason for such an approach was the general paucity of any previous research, or even basic knowledge, of the policy processes (or lack of them) for sport and tourism. While a detailed discussion of the nature of the grounded theory method is not possible here, a brief overview of the process of the development of this particular grounded theory is perhaps useful by way of conclusion. This is useful not only to explicitly outline the process, but also to identify the key sources that those interested might turn to for more detailed discussions.

The first stage of the process was an initial 'scoping study' of the extent of policy partnerships in England [83], followed by the development of a 'theoretical sensitivity' to both the general policy process and the issues affecting sport and tourism [84]. Initial data collection took place and some preliminary discussions were possible on the influence of government policy on sport-tourism relations [85]. Developing 'theory as process', these discussions led to further data collection and theoretical development, resulting in the presentation of a model of cross-sectoral policy development by Weed [86]. The development of this model highlighted the need to 'theoretically sample' further data, specifically at the organizational level, which led to an overview of organizational influences on the sport-tourism policy process [87]. At this point, 'theoretical saturation' appeared to have been reached and consequently a 'substantive' grounded theory of the sport-tourism policy process in the UK was developed [88]. Finally, a further review of international policy and initiatives led to the move from 'substantive' to 'formal' theory, and the presentation of a more generic 'formal' grounded theory of the policy process for sport and tourism by Weed and Bull [89].

The development of the grounded theory approach by Glaser and Strauss took place in their 1967 publication 'The Discovery of Grounded Theory'. The various aspects of grounded theory referred to above—scoping studies, theoretical sensitivity, theory as process, theoretical sampling, theoretical saturation, and substantive and formal theory—all have their roots in this publication. However, a more contemporary explication of the grounded theory method can be found in Strauss and Corbin (1990) [90], although aspects of this approach have become contested [91], with some authors arguing for a constructivist revision of grounded theory [92], and it is this latter approach that has been utilized in this research. Certainly, faced with a research area about which there was virtually no previous knowledge, the grounded theory approach proved particularly fruitful.

As noted earlier, grounded theory approaches traditionally seek to explain and understand phenomena, but in this case there are some implications for future research and practice, and it is perhaps useful to include a final word on such implications. The strength of the model described here is its flexibility. It is a multi-dimensional model that can be adapted to the particular policy environment under study. Future studies of sport-tourism policy development in a range of countries might use this model to highlight the extent to which the particular structures of policy communities in such countries might affect and facilitate sport-tourism liaison. For example, if applied in France the model will highlight the much greater influence of governmental interests in the French tourism policy community than in other countries. This in turn will have an effect on the extent to which sport and tourism interests communicate, and government policy, particularly planning policy, will be a more significant influence. As such, the model can set a useful context against which more detailed studies of particular countries' sport-tourism policy development can be conducted.

In terms of practice, it has been noted, both here and elsewhere [93], that the most pressing need in relation to the development of sport-tourism partnerships is to educate policy makers in both the sport and the tourism sectors about the range of benefits that can be realized from collaborative approaches to the sport-tourism link. In this respect, little has changed since Glyptis' pioneering work in 1982, which highlighted the need for:

> A recognition of the tourist potential of sport and the sports development potential of tourism ... [and] the establishment of working partnerships between sport and tourism policy makers and providers at national, regional and local level [94].

While the grounded theory developed here illustrates the factors that influence sport-tourism liaison, it is perhaps useful for practitioners to refer to the initial scoping work for this study that developed a Policy Area Matrix for Sport and Tourism [95]. This matrix sought to illustrate those areas in which policy makers for sport and for tourism might reasonably be expected to collaborate. The matrix shows the benefits of collaboration not only in relation to sports holidays, but also in five other areas that can both facilitate and capitalize on the link between sport and tourism. Within these six areas a total of 21 sub-areas were identified. Obviously space precludes a lengthy discussion of these, but by way of illustration the six main areas were: sports holidays, facility issues, environmental, countryside and water issues, resources and funding, policy and planning, and information and promotion.

A further reference point for policy makers might be the conceptualisation of sports tourism as 'a social, economic and cultural phenomenon arising from the unique interaction of activity, people and place' [96]. Tourism policy has largely tended to focus on the development of place, while much sports policy focuses on facilitating activities. The link between these two areas is a common need to consider people, and the Policy Area Matrix described above can help to highlight areas where sports people and tourists are one and the same. Consequently, the grounded theory discussed in this essay, along with the policy matrix developed by Weed and Bull [97], might encourage policy-makers to consider how policies for activities and places might be developed to maximize the benefits for both the tourist and the sports participant and, more specifically, for the sports tourist. If policy makers can be fully persuaded of the benefits of sport-tourism partnerships, then future research on sport-tourism policy can focus on the more productive area of how policy can be developed to support sports tourists and sports tourism providers, rather than on explaining why effective policy partnerships have not emerged.

Notes

[1] See, for example, M.E. Weed, 'Towards a Model of Cross-Sectoral Policy Development in Leisure: The Case of Sport and Tourism', *Leisure Studies*, 20, 2 (2001), 125–41. M.E. Weed, 'Why the Two Won't Tango: Explaining the Lack of Integrated Policies for Sport and Tourism in the UK', *Journal of Sports Management*, 17, 3 (2003), 258–83. M.E. Weed and C.J. Bull, 'Integrating Sport and Tourism: A Review of Regional Policies in England', *Progress in Tourism and Hospitality Research*, 3, 2 (1997), 129–48. M.E. Weed and C.J. Bull, 'The Search for a Sport-Tourism Policy Network', in M.F. Collins and I.S. Cooper (eds), *Leisure Management: Issues and Applications* (Wallingford: CAB International, 1998).

[2] M.E. Weed and C.J. Bull, *Sports Tourism: Participants, Policy and Providers* (Oxford: Elsevier, 2004).

[3] D. Layder, *New Strategies in Social Research* (Cambridge: Polity Press, 1993).

[4] B. Houlihan, 'Politics, Power, Policy and Sport', in B. Houlihan (ed.), *Sport and Society: A Student Introduction* (London: Sage, 2003).

[5] Ibid., p.28.

[6] See, for example, P. Dunleavy and B. O'Leary, *Theories of the State* (Basingstoke: Macmillan, 1987).

[7] See, for example, S. Lukes, *Power: A Radical View* (London: MacMillan, 1974).

[8] See, for example, P. Dunleavy, *Democracy, Bureaucracy and Public Choice* (Hemel Hempstead: Harvester Wheatsheaf, 1991). G. Tullock, *The Vote Motive* (London: Institute of Economic Affairs, 1976).

[9] See, for example, M. Hill, *The Policy Process in The Modern State* (Hemel Hempstead: Prentice Hall/Harvester Wheatsheaf, 1997). D. Marsh and R.A.W. Rhodes, 'Policy Communities and Issue Networks: Beyond Typology', in D. Marsh and R.A.W. Rhodes (eds), *Policy Networks in British Government* (Oxford: Oxford University Press, 1992). P.A. Sabatier, 'An Advocacy Coalition Framework of Policy Change and the Role of Policy-Oriented Learning Therein', *Policy Sciences*, 21, 2–3 (1998), 129–45.

[10] See, for example, C. Handy, *Understanding Organisations*, 4th edition (London: Penguin Books, 1992). H. Mintzberg, *The Structuring of Organisations: A Synthesis of the Research* (Englewood Cliffs: Prentice-Hall, 1979). G. Morgan, *Images of Organisation*, 2nd edition (London: Sage, 1997).

[11] See, for example, P. Degeling and H.K. Colebatch, 'Structure and Action as Constructs in the Practice of Public Administration', *Australian Journal of Public Administration*, 53 (1984), 320–31. M. Lipsky, *Street Level Bureaucracy* (New York: Russell Sage, 1980).

[12] See, for example, J. Coghlan and I. Webb, *Sport and British Politics since 1960* (London: Falmer Press, 1990).

[13] See, for example, K. Hylton, P. Bramham, D. Jackson and M. Nesti (eds), *Sports Development: Policy, Process and Practice* (London: Routledge, 2001).

[14] See, for example, C.M. Hall, *Tourism Planning: Policies, Processes and Relationships* (Harlow: Prentice-Hall, 2000).

[15] See, for example, E. Inskeep, *Tourism Planning: An Integrated and Sustainable Development Approach* (New York: Van Nostrund Reinhold, 1991).

[16] See, for example, F. Coalter with B. Duffield and J. Long, *The Rationale for Public Sector Investment in Leisure* (London: Sports Council, 1987).

[17] I.P. Henry, *The Politics of Leisure Policy*, 2nd edition (London: Palgrave, 2001).

[18] B. Houlihan, *The Government and the Politics of Sport* (London: Routledge, 1991). B. Houlihan, *Sport and International Politics* (London: Harvester Wheatsheaf, 1994). B. Houlihan, *Sport, Policy and Politics: A Comparative Analysis* (New York: Harvester Wheatsheaf, 1997).

[19] C.M. Hall, *Tourism and Politics: Policy, Power and Place* (London: Belhaven Press, 1994).

[20] C.M. Hall and J.M. Jenkins, *Tourism and Public Policy* (New York: Routledge, 1995).

[21] See, for example, Weed, 'Towards a Model of Cross-Sectoral Policy Development in Leisure'; Weed, 'Why the Two Won't Tango'.

[22] See, for example, Weed and Bull, 'Integrating Sport and Tourism'; Weed and Bull, 'The Search for a Sport-Tourism Policy Network'.

[23] Weed and Bull, *Sports Tourism*.

[24] Ibid., p.37.

[25] Ibid., pp.xiv–xv.

[26] Weed and Bull 'Integrating Sport and Tourism'.

[27] Ibid., 146.

[28] The research map is adapted from Layder, *New Strategies in Social Research*.

[29] M. Hammersley, 'What's Wrong with Ethnography? The Myth of Theoretical Distinction', *Sociology*, 24, 4 (1990), 597–615.

[30] B. Glaser and A. Strauss, *The Discovery of Grounded Theory* (New York: Aldine de Gruyter, 1967).

[31] See Marsh and Rhodes, 'Policy Communities and Issue Networks'; S. Wilks and M. Wright (eds), *Comparative Government-Industry Relations* (Oxford: Clarendon Press, 1987).

[32] B. Glaser, *Theoretical Sensitivity* (Mill Valley, CA: Sociology Press, 1978).

[33] Layder, *New Strategies in Social Research*.

[34] Weed and Bull, 'The Search for a Sport-Tourism Policy Network'.

[35] Layder, *New Strategies in Social Research*.

[36] H. Becker, 'Becoming a Marihuana User', *American Journal of Sociology*, 59 (1953), 235–42.

[37] D. Roy, 'Banana Time: Job Satisfaction and Informal Interaction', in G. Salaman and K. Thompson (eds), *People and Organisations* (London: Longman, 1973).

[38] B. Glaser and A. Strauss, *Awareness of Dying* (Chicago: Aldine, 1965).

[39] Layder, *New Strategies in Social Research*.

[40] Layder, *New Strategies in Social Research*.

[41] Ibid.

[42] Weed and Bull, 'The Search for a Sport-Tourism Policy Network'.

[43] Weed, 'Towards a Model of Cross-Sectoral Policy Development in Leisure'; Weed, 'Why the Two Won't Tango'.

[44] Layder, *New Strategies in Social Research*.

[45] The work described throughout this contribution was derived from an extensive programme of data collection that, as per the grounded theory approach, took place alongside theoretical development. An outline of the programme of data collection can be found in Weed, 'Why the Two Won't Tango'. However, whilst this contribution discusses the genesis of a grounded theory of the policy process, space does not permit the inclusion of empirical data. For those interested, such data is available in Weed and Bull 'Integrating Sport and Tourism'; M.E. Weed and C.J. Bull, 'Influences on Sport-Tourism Relations in Britain: The Effects of Government Policy', *Tourism Recreation Research*, 22, 2 (1997), 5–12; M.E. Weed, 'Organisational Culture and the Leisure Policy Process in Britain: How Structure affects Strategy in Sport-Tourism Policy Development', *Tourism, Culture and Communication*, 3, 3 (2002), 147–64; and in full in M.E. Weed, 'Consensual Policies for Sport and Tourism in the UK: An Analysis of Organisational Behaviour and Problems' (unpublished Ph.D. thesis, University of Kent at Canterbury/Canterbury Christ Church College, 1999).
[46] For more detail see Weed and Bull, *Sports Tourism*.
[47] A.G. Jordan and J.J. Richardson, *British Politics and the Policy Process* (London: Allen and Unwin, 1987).
[48] Weed and Bull, 'Influences on Sport-Tourism Relations in Britain'.
[49] Glaser and Strauss, *The Discovery of Grounded Theory*.
[50] Marsh and Rhodes, 'Policy Communities and Issue Networks'.
[51] Wilks and Wright (eds), *Comparative Government-Industry Relations*.
[52] Weed, 'Towards a Model of Cross-Sectoral Policy Development in Leisure'.
[53] Weed, 'Towards a Model of Cross-Sectoral Policy Development in Leisure'.
[54] Weed and Bull, *Sports Tourism*.
[55] Houlihan, *Sport, Policy and Politics*.
[56] M. Laffin, 'Professional Communities and Policy Communities in Central-Local Relations', in M. Goldsmith (ed.), *New Research in Central-Local Relations* (Aldershot: Gower, 1986).
[57] See, for example, the similar descriptions of the categories of 'culture' and 'structure' described by Handy, *Understanding Organisations*; Minzberg, *The Structuring of Organisations*.
[58] Layder, *New Strategies in Social Research*.
[59] Minzberg, *The Structuring of Organisations*.
[60] For a detailed discussion of the impact of culture and structure on policy responses to the sport-tourism link, see Weed, 'Organisational Culture and the Leisure Policy Process in Britain'.
[61] Weed, 'Organisational Culture and the Leisure Policy Process in Britain'.
[62] Lipsky, *Street Level Bureaucracy*.
[63] I.L. Janis, *Victims of Group Think* (New York: Free Press, 1972).
[64] E.E. Schattschneider, *The Semi-Sovereign People* (New York: Holt, Rinehart and Winston, 1960).
[65] Weed, 'Organisational Culture and the Leisure Policy Process in Britain'.
[66] Weed, 'Why the Two Won't Tango'.
[67] Weed, 'Consensual Policies for Sport and Tourism in the UK'.
[68] Layder, *New Strategies in Social Research*.
[69] Weed and Bull, *Sports Tourism*.
[70] Weed, 'Consensual Policies for Sport and Tourism in the UK'
[71] Weed and Bull, *Sports Tourism*.
[72] Weed and Bull, 'The Search for a Sport-Tourism Policy Network'.
[73] Layder, *New Strategies in Social Research*.
[74] Glaser and Strauss, *The Discovery of Grounded Theory*.
[75] Weed, 'Why the Two Won't Tango'.
[76] Weed and Bull, *Sports Tourism*.
[77] Weed and Bull, 'The Search for a Sport-Tourism Policy Network'.

[78] Weed, 'Consensual Policies for Sport and Tourism in the UK'; Weed, 'Organisational Culture and the Leisure Policy Process in Britain'; Weed, 'Why the Two Won't Tango'.

[79] Weed and Bull, 'The Search for a Sport-Tourism Policy Network'.

[80] Department of National Heritage, *Sport: Raising the Game* (London: DNH, 1995).

[81] M.F. Collins, 'Sights on Sport', *Leisure Management*, 15, 9 (1995), 26–8.

[82] Weed, 'Consensual Policies for Sport and Tourism in the UK'.

[83] Weed and Bull, 'Integrating Sport and Tourism'.

[84] Weed and Bull, 'The Search for a Sport-Tourism Policy Network'.

[85] Weed and Bull, 'Influences on Sport-Tourism Relations in Britain'.

[86] Weed, 'Towards a Model of Cross-Sectoral Policy Development in Leisure'.

[87] Weed, 'Organisational Culture and the Leisure Policy Process in Britain'.

[88] Weed, 'Why the Two Won't Tango'.

[89] Weed and Bull, *Sports Tourism*.

[90] A. Strauss and J. Corbin, *Basics of Qualitative Research: Grounded Theory Procedures and Techniques* (Newbury Park, CA: Sage, 1990).

[91] Glaser wrote a text in 1992 that was an explicit repudiation of the methods outlined by Strauss and Corbin: B. Glaser, *Basics of Grounded Theory Research: Emergence Versus Forcing* (Mill Valley, CA: Sociology Press, 1992).

[92] See, for example, K. Charmaz, 'Grounded Theory: Objectivist and Constructivist Methods', in N.K. Denzin and Y.S. Lincoln (eds), *Handbook of Qualitative Research* 2nd Edition (London: Sage, 2000). K. Charmaz, 'Grounded Theory', in J.A. Smith (ed.), *Qualitative Psychology: A Practical Guide to Research Methods* (London: Sage, 2003). Layder, *New Strategies in Social Research*.

[93] Weed and Bull, *Sports Tourism*; Weed, 'Why the Two Won't Tango'.

[94] S.A. Glyptis, *Sport and Tourism in Western Europe* (London: British Travel Education Trust, 1982), p.70.

[95] Weed and Bull, 'Integrating Sport and Tourism'.

[96] Weed and Bull, *Sports Tourism*, p.37.

[97] Weed and Bull, 'Integrating Sport and Tourism'.

The Management of Sport Tourism

Margaret Deery & Leo Jago

Introduction

Sport tourism makes an important contribution to local and national economies and appears to have substantial potential to further build on this contribution. It is estimated that sports tourism in Australia accounts for approximately $3 billion per annum [1]. Like other domains it is crucial that it is well managed in order that the benefits from sport tourism are truly exploited. It needs to be guided by a strategic plan that identifies the key goals in the area's development and incorporates a series of strategies intended to achieve these goals. The importance of strategic planning and management has been recognized widely in the literature and continues to be refined and debated both in industry and academe [2]. Components of strategic planning include the development of definite time horizons, detailed allocation of resources to the various elements of the plan and the establishment of conduits for

Margaret Deery, Centre for Hospitality and Tourism Research, Victoria University, PO Box 14428, Melbourne City, MC 8001 Australia. Correspondence to: marg.deery@vu.edu.au. Leo Jago, Centre for Hospitality and Tourism Research, Victoria University, Australia.

the communication of the plan. The key element, however, is the coordination of the planning and the implementation of the plan [3].

In fields that comprise many small operators or diverse players such as in the area of sport tourism, a strategic plan is even more critical as there tends not to be a large organization that can set the direction for the sector. The sector comprises many volunteer organizations and government agencies. Indeed, because of this fragmentation, there is seen to be 'market failure' which is why government tends to play a more important role in the sector. A benefit of this is that government is usually good at planning, if not so effective at managing.

A major difficulty with sport tourism, however, is that it is really the amalgamation of two quite separate fields, namely, tourism and sport, and each field is often managed by a separate division of government. This means that no single entity takes overall responsibility for sport tourism and as a consequence, it often advances by default.

In Australia, for example, responsibility for the national tourism industry lies with the Department of Industry, Tourism and Resources whilst responsibility for sport lies with the Department of Communications, Information Technology and the Arts. Whilst both Departments recognize that sport tourism involves a connection between the two of them, neither Department seems to have taken overall responsibility for the area, which inherently results in a lack of development. Government management for sport and tourism are split in a similar manner in most of Australia's states and territories. Likewise, Mike Weed's work in the UK has shown similar patterns. [4]

Although there is clearly a connection between sport and tourism, it is important to recognize that the key drivers of the two fields are quite different. Sport helps promote a healthier lifestyle across the community and provides additional leisure activities for local residents, as well as fostering local, national and international competition. Tourism is to encourage people to travel beyond their home destination and to spend money in the process. The tourism industry tends to regard sport as one of a range of motivators for travel, but there is no obvious connection in the opposite direction.

The problems associated with these 'split responsibilities' in sport tourism were recognized in the lead up to Australia's hosting of the 2000 Summer Olympic Games in Sydney. Sport and tourism were brought together into one government portfolio under a single Federal Minister. This was done to maximize Australia's benefits from hosting this mega event and provided a platform for the development of a national sport tourism strategy. After an extensive consultation progamme, the Federal Minister released a draft sport tourism strategy in 2000. The key elements of the draft sport tourism strategy were industry coordination, education and training, government regulation, infrastructure, the evaluation of economic benefits, and research. The draft strategy document provided background in each area and identified a series of questions for which feedback was sought to underpin the planned final strategy. This draft strategy documented a vision for sport tourism and identified the range of strategies needed to realize this vision. It was a vehicle for bringing together the skills and energy of the many disparate stakeholders within the sport tourism sector. This strategy document, however, did not go beyond draft form.

After the 2000 Summer Olympic Games, there was a government restructure that resulted in sport and tourism being separated again and allocated to two different government departments. As a consequence, impetus for the strategy evaporated as neither Government Minister seemed interested in taking responsibility for a hybrid strategy.

In November 2003, the Federal Government released the Tourism White Paper, which was a medium- to long-term strategy for tourism. Although there was a section within this plan on special events, many of which are sporting, there was no specific mention of sport tourism. Some of the areas identified in the Draft Sports Tourism Strategy have been addressed in the Tourism White Paper, but they have not been discussed as part of a sport tourism component.

Given that the sport tourism sector is a hybrid of two sectors and involves a plethora of public and private agencies, many of which rely on volunteer management, it is critical that national and state governments take a strong leadership role. A fundamental component of this is to have a widely accepted strategic plan that sets the vision and strategies for the sector and is continually reviewed and updated. Failure to do so will prevent the sector from realizing its potential. The benefits from this were shown in relation to the Sydney Olympics where this coming together of government departments helped realize tourism-related benefits from the event not achieved elsewhere.

What is Sport Tourism?

The concept of sport tourism is a complex one. The complexity emanates from the difficulties in defining the concept. Gibson, for example, defined the concept as 'leisure-based travel that takes individuals temporarily outside of their home communities to play, watch physical activities or venerate attractions associated with these activities' [5]. Gibson suggested that sport tourism incorporated three main behaviours: participating, watching and visiting/venerating. In defining sport tourism, most authors refer to definitions of both 'sport' and 'tourism'. 'Sport', for example, has a number of definitions ranging from 'mastery of skills and fitness' [6] to 'a mechanism to overcome social problems such as delinquency' [7]. The definition of 'tourism' in the sport tourism context is neatly defined in the following way: sport attracts people and people as visitors constitute tourism [8].

A number of models or frameworks have been developed for the concept of sport tourism. Research by Gibson, Gammon and Robinson, and Hall, have all contributed to the debate [9]. Of the various models, it is that offered by Gammon and Robinson that has provoked much discussion. Faulkner, Tideswell and Weston [10], for example, argue that the 'tourism sport' (that is, tourism where sport is a secondary motive) category of Gammon and Robinson is too broad – an example is the inclusion of activities such as walking, which is a recreational activity that should not be classified as sport tourism. In quoting the *Dictionary of Sociology*, Torkildsen states that recreation is 'any activity pursued during leisure, either individual or collective, that is free and pleasureful, having its own appeal, not impelled by a delayed reward' [11]. Recreation is differentiated from sport in this definition. Similarly, the Victorian Government's *Strategic Audit of Victorian Industry: The Victorian Sport and Recreation Industry Report,* clearly delineates between sport and recreation, aligning sport with sporting events and recreation with physical recreation, adventure and nature tourism [12].

Faulkner *et al.* argue there are a number of key elements that comprise sport tourism. Essentially they argue that sport tourism is event related and that any definitions should include events as the focus. Their definition includes the following components and this definition is used here.

- Sport tourism is event related
- The focus for sport tourism is competitive sport
- 'Participants' in sport tourism may be attendees, officials or competitors
- The motivation to participate in sport tourism is intentional
- There are specific outcomes from sport tourism that affect:

  ○ The individual

  ○ The community

  ○ The state/nation

In more recent research by Getz, this concept is reinforced through his comment that 'Sport event tourism is internationally recognised as a substantial and highly desirable niche market' [13]. Getz goes on to argue that, from a destination's perspective, sport event tourism revolves around the development and marketing of sport events for economic and community gain. For the consumer, the focus is on participating in or attending a sport event. The author suggests that there are forces such as the media, sponsorship, urban development, facility development and the overall popularity of sport in general.

For many State and National Tourism Officers, event tourism (not just sport events) appears as an important component of their strategic business plans. This helps ensure that events build from a tourism perspective but it does not necessarily take into account the needs of sport per se.

Managing Sport Tourism

Within the *National Sport Tourism Strategy* document [14], it is interesting to note that all the examples provided for sport tourism are events such as the Olympic and Masters Games. In defining the sector, many of the organizations are event related. Those included are major events corporations, facility managers, event organizers and promoters and tour operators. Sport tourism, in this context, is often event related. In attempting to manage sport tourism at the micro-level, therefore, much of the literature concentrates on sporting events. As Getz states, 'Events are a major component of sport tourism, and perhaps the most significant in terms of tourist numbers and economic impact' [15].

Managing sport tourism, therefore, comprises the management of a number of components, each of which requires specific skills and strategies. Much of the literature underpinning this chapter focuses on mainstream management literature with application to the sport tourism and event management contexts. In particular, the literature review will encompass a range of issues such as planning and community fit, project management, risk management including security and crowd control and the leadership style required for sport tourism management. More importantly, however, the literature review examines the type of human resource management needed for what is notionally called a 'pulsating organization' [16] and the staffing needs associated with this. Issues associated with the need for flexibility are also addressed.

Management Literature: Key Themes

There are a number of key themes that relate to the management of sport event tourism at an operational level. These include the types of management style appropriate for managing sporting events. It is suggested by various researchers that the sport event manager requires delegation ability and that there are a number of roles that the manager will undertake [17]. Other generic management concepts that relate to the management of sport event tourism are those of environmental scanning to determine competitive advantage, Porter[18] being the main proponent of this.

Mainstream management theory relating to organizational structure, managing teams, managing change and conflict, communication channels and the functional components of human resource management are all relevant to the management of sport event tourism, although require special application to meet the unique requirements of sport tourism. Take, for example, concepts relating to the management of group dynamics and teamwork. Most sport tourism events would involve teams either as employees or participants. The management of staff teams at a sport event presents some difficulties in that the stages of group development do not necessarily apply as the time span for group development is compressed. The levels of team cohesiveness and performance are therefore necessarily different [19]. Similarly, issues of training and professional development, important components in the delivery of a quality product, require a very focused approach and one that is very organization specific [20].

One of the key issues that differentiates sport tourism from other types of activities is the structure of those organizations that facilitate the events and the workforce that is required to provide both the product and the service. The concept of the pulsating organization [21] and, within that, the framework of the Flexible Firm [22], are presented here to provide the context for the management of sport event tourism. The complexities of sport tourism and, in particular, sport event tourism revolve very much around the need for flexibility. Flexibility and adaptability are important in order that the event can meet the needs of the attendees and participants to deliver a timely and appropriate product and service.

Pulsating Organizations

The structure and management of organizations has received attention from a number of researchers, ranging from the seminal work by Minztberg to more recent studies by Hendry and Pettigrew, Cunningham and Hyman, and Korczynski to name but a few [23]. Little attention, however, has been given to the management of more temporary organizational types such as event organizations. The concept of the pulsating organization is most appropriate for sport tourism. Hanlon and Jago argue that major sport event organizations 'have fluctuating workforce numbers, which is due to the special nature of major sport events' [24]. These authors found that organizations that facilitate major sporting events expand their staffing numbers for an event, then reduce their numbers to the original organizational size within a very short period of time. For example, the Australian Open Tennis Championship expands from approximately 20 to 4,000 staff in a three to four day period. Similarly, the Australian Formula One Grand Prix increases from 40 to approximately 15,000 credentialed employees [25]. Hanlon and Jago describe pulsating events as flexible, flat, highly formalized, decentralized, having teams in functional units, innovative and needing to satisfy personnel [26]. In further defining the concept – and with specific focus on the function of induction – the following definition is offered:

> Pulsating organizations are different from 'generic' organizations. The latter organizations have a relatively stable workforce and hence, established relationships between personnel, and the induction of new personnel is commonly performed on an individual basis. In contrast, induction is more likely to be performed on a group basis at pulsating major sport event organizations, due to the influx of personnel over a limited period of time [27].

The whole management of a sport event, therefore, just as in the case of induction, is necessarily different from management within a generic organization because of the nature of the fluctuating workforce. Issues such as recruitment, retention, induction and staff training are operationalized differently in pulsating organizations. For example, Hanlon and Jago found that, in order to retain staff, innovative strategies are required to retain personnel at different stages of an event cycle. In particular, these authors found that there were two 'vulnerable stages for retaining personnel . . ., the 'tough' stage of an event for full-time personnel, and the 'dead' stage for seasonal personnel' [28].

Research into issues such as the retention of staff [29] and staff selection [30] in organizations, is extremely popular in mainstream management literature. Research into sport event tourism management, however, is far less well developed. The findings from the research on pulsating organizations provide lessons for the management of sport event tourism. In particular, it presents a number of recommendations for the management of staff. These recommendations include improving the clarity of roles of both the seasonal staff and the full time staff – many of those interviewed for the research were keen to work within teams and play a team role. More recent research has also found that event organizations did not have strategies that were tailored for an event cycle or for the type of personnel that was employed [31]. These organizations had difficulty in retaining staff. Sport tourism events, therefore, need to acknowledge the pulsating nature of the organizations facilitating the events and attempt to address the issues surrounding the problems that these can create.

The Flexible Firm

The concept of the Pulsating Organization is the focus for discussion on managing sport event tourism. Within this concept, however, is the Flexible Firm model, which goes some way to explaining the need for and type of flexibility in sport event tourism. Managers of sport events must, necessarily, employ staff on a needs basis – an extreme form of the flexible firm as developed by Atkinson [32]. The Flexible Firm model was originally developed as a model of change among large manufacturing employers, but has been used as the basis for organizational structure in a number of service organizations as well. It is argued that the benefits in using the flexible firm concept are:

- higher productivity from the core workforce;
- lower wage and non-wage costs from the use of peripheral groups;
- the ability to tailor employment levels to demand conditions and, with this, to reduce the costs of carrying 'excess' staff [33].

The key elements to the Flexible Firm model are those of 'core' and 'peripheral' employees. The core workforce is characterized by permanent, highly-skilled employees with internal career paths [34]. As a result, 'core' employees tend to experience a higher degree of job security with resources provided for training in firm-specific skills not readily bought in. This segment of the organization is characterized by functional forms of flexibility [35]. In defining the various types of flexibility, Holland and Deery suggest that 'functional flexibility is a qualitative approach to work, and refers to management's ability to deploy and redeploy particular sections of the workforce on a wide range of tasks in response to market demand as and when required' [36]. In keeping with the concept of the Pulsating Organization, the Flexible Firm Model provides the framework for expanding and contracting the workforce that is so important to facilitating sport event tourism. The core workers, in the case of events, are those full-time employees who have access to training and career development.

By contrast, the peripheral workforce is susceptible to the labour requirements of demand fluctuations and is closely associated with the development of numerical flexibility in organizations. Atkinson argues that the peripheral workforce is associated with the organization's development of numerical flexibility. The key function or strategic aspect of this sector for the organization is the undertaking of day-to-day activities that are important but not vital to the organization. Again, in defining the idea of numerical flexibility, Holland and Deery state that this is 'a quantitative approach to the utilisation of the workforce, and is based on the principle of relating the size of the workforce quickly and easily to the levels of economic activity at short notice' [37]. Casual, part-time and sub-contractors typically provide this form of flexibility [38]. Other forms of flexibility are those of financial, procedural and temporal.

With regard to the management of sport tourism events, the practices of functional and numerical flexibility are pertinent. Sport events require large increases in workforce numbers, making them appropriate for the use of numerical flexibility. These increases occur spasmodically and relate to the pulsating organization notion. Those employees, and volunteers, taken on for the peak activity within the event, become part of the peripheral workforce, a group that Atkinson characterizes as:

> In effect they are offered a job not a career. For example, they might be clerical, supervisory, component assembly and testing occupations. The key point is that their jobs are 'plug-in' ones, not firm specific. As a result the firm looks to the external market to fill these jobs and seeks to achieve numerical flexibility and financial flexibility through the most direct and immediate links to the external labour market than is sought for the core group [39].

Although there are claimed benefits in using flexible workforces such as greater job satisfaction and the ability to combine work with other interests [40], there are also disadvantages associated with the concept. These include the unequal treatment in pay and conditions, the reduced opportunities for training and development, as well as the job insecurity associated with being part of the peripheral group [41]. As part of the peripheral workforce, volunteers not only offer additional personnel, but also specific 'problems' in terms of their management.

Volunteers

In many sporting events, volunteers are the key ingredients that ensure the success of the event. In fact, many sport events would not be viable without the use of volunteers. The management of volunteers, however, varies from the management of paid staff in a number of ways. Tyzack, for example, has examined the issue of the management style used for volunteer and paid staff and argues that the belief that volunteers and paid staff are two different breeds of people has caused considerable stress to individual paid and unpaid workers [42]. She suggests that a lack of communication, appreciation and interest were important sources of stress for volunteers. Another issue that has received an inordinate amount of attention in the research is how volunteers are best rewarded; this issue becomes more vexed when they are working next to paid employees. However, the volunteers have very clear notions of the best ways they can be recognized and rewarded. Some of these revolve around distinguishing the volunteers from the paid staff. Uniforms for volunteers provide a strong means of recognition and make the volunteers feel important. Daniel, Johnson and Miller argue that uniforms serve as an emblem of group membership, a revealer of status and a certificate of legitimacy [43].

Volunteers also value the flexibility of their volunteering activity as a means of reward. Interestingly, in recent research on the impact of the flexible firm on paid staff and volunteers, paid staff valued more highly the opportunity for functional flexibility, while volunteers valued, more highly than paid staff, reduced working hours [44]. Further findings suggest that:

> In terms of gender, females rated more highly the availability of certain temporal practices (flexitime and voluntary reduced hours) than males. Females also rated more highly the value of the numerical practices of job sharing and fixed-term contracts than males [45].

What these findings suggest is that paid staff prefer to have a range of fulfilling tasks, whereas the priority for volunteers is to obtain the appropriate working hours.

Finally, in research undertaken by Deery and Jago on the management of volunteers and their relationship with paid staff, these authors recommended the following:

- Developing clear job descriptions for both paid staff and volunteers;
- Maintaining regular induction programmes;
- Providing clear communication channels between management and staff/volunteers and between the staff and volunteers;
- Managing the balance of power between paid staff and volunteers;
- Training the workforce in understanding the needs of both paid staff and volunteers;
- Training the volunteers in areas such as computing skills and cultural differences [46].

The management of volunteers, as part of a pulsating organization and as the peripheral workforce within the Flexible Firm model, requires special attention. Volunteers are vital to the facilitation and quality of sport event tourism.

Managing Sport Event Tourism and Project Management

This study has discussed the management of sport tourism through the concept of the Pulsating Organization together with the Flexible Firm Model and the role of volunteers within those frameworks. The final element in relation to this discussion is the use of project management principles in managing sport event tourism. Managing sport event tourism is very much like managing a project in that it is goal-oriented, it has a particular set of constraints which are usually time and resources, and the output of the project is measurable [47]. Like the Pulsating Organization concept, there are levels of complexity that impact on the success of any project. Maylor discusses these levels of complexities as a function of having the following features:

- the number of people … involved
- the volume of resources involved such as time, capital and processes and
- the level of innovation involved in the product or the project process [48].

Allen *et al.* confirm the importance of project management in their discussion of the management of special events and argue that managing an event is a matter of controlling the logistics. This includes managing the scheduling, the critical paths and the risk assessment [49].

Conclusion

The strategic and sound operational management of sport tourism is important if this 'industry' is to progress. In the first instance, and at the macro level, it is crucial that government plays a co-ordinating role with regard to sporting events. It is only through government agencies that large events such as the Rugby World Cup and the Olympics can be attracted to specific destinations.

It is at the more operational level, however, that greater attention must be given to the uniqueness of sport event tourism. While many of the mainstream management theories apply to the operation of sport event tourism, the expanding and contracting nature of the workforce for the event creates added pressures and constraints on managers. These pressures can be addressed through the use of a core and periphery workforce and the use of volunteers. In so doing, however, the structure of the 'organization' varies significantly from that of normal organizations.

The implications that arise from an examination of managing sport event tourism can be discussed at the national and at the enterprise levels. At the national level, it is important for greater collaboration and unity to occur between disparate government agencies. Co-ordination and unity between sporting authorities and tourism policy makers at this level will ensure greater understanding at the enterprise level.

At the more micro level, it is important that the implications of expanding and contracting the workforce for sporting events are fully appreciated. Sport tourism staff require training and rewarding in quite different ways from those staff in generic organizations. Many of the people working in sport tourism will be volunteers who will need to be rewarded through providing flexible work hours, balancing the paid and volunteer staff and giving 'rewards' such as uniforms to make them feel special. Finally, organizers of sport tourism need to understand the changes in culture and the work environment that the pulsating organization creates. It requires a sensitivity to the changing workforce and strategies for dealing with these ongoing changes.

Notes

[1] Commonwealth Department of Industry, Science and Resources, *Towards a National Sports Tourism Strategy* (Canberra: Commonwealth of Australia, 2000).
[2] C. White, *Strategic Management* (New York: Palgave Macmillan, 2004), p.5.
[3] Ibid., p.599.
[4] M.Weed, 'Sport and Tourism Policy. The National and Regional Policy Contexts for Sports Tourism Destinations', in J. Higham (ed.), *Sport Tourism Destinations: Issues, Opportunities and Analysis* (Oxford: Butterworth Heinemann).
[5] H. Gibson, 'Sport Tourism: A Critical Analysis of Research', *Sport Management Review*, 1, 1 (1998), 10.

[6] T. Sofield, *Sport Tourism: Concepts and Issues*, Keynote Address, 14th Asian Games Sport Tourism Conference, Busan, Korea, 1 Sept. 2002.

[7] C. Hall, 'Adventure, Sport and Health Tourism', in B. Weiler and C.M. Hall (eds), *Special Interest Tourism* (London: Bellhaven Press, 1992), p.193.

[8] Sofield, *Sport Tourism*, p.5.

[9] Gibson, 'Sport Tourism: A Critical Analysis of Research', 45–76; S. Gammon and T. Robinson, 'Sport and Tourism: A Conceptual Framework', *Journal of Sport Tourism*, 8, 1 (2003), 21–6; C. Hall, 'Adventure, Sport and Health Tourism', in B. Weiler and C.M. Hall (eds), *Special Interest Tourism* (London: Bellhaven Press, 1992), pp.141–58.

[10] B. Faulkner, C. Tideswell and A. Weston, 'Leveraging Tourism Benefits from the Sydney 2000 Olympics'. Keynote presentation, *Sport Management: Opportunities and Change*, Fourth Annual Conference of the Sport Management Association of Australia and New Zealand, Gold Coast, Australia, 26–28 Nov. 1998.

[11] G. Torkildsen, *Leisure and Recreation Management* (London: E. & F.N. Spon, 1996), pp.64–5.

[12] Victorian Government, *Strategic Audit of Victorian Industry: The Victorian Sport and Recreation Industry* (Melbourne: Victorian Government, 2001).

[13] D. Getz, 'Sport Event Tourism: Planning, Development, and Marketing', in Simon Hudson (ed.), *Sport and Adventure Tourism* (New York: Haworth Hospitality Press, 2003), p.49.

[14] Commonwealth Department of Industry, Science and Resources, *Towards a National Sports Tourism Strategy*.

[15] Getz, 'Sport Event Tourism: Planning, Development, and Marketing', p.49.

[16] C. Hanlon and L. Jago, 'Pulsating Sporting Events', in J. Allen, R. Harris, L. Jago and A. Veal, *Events Beyond 2000 – Setting the Agenda* (Sydney: Proceedings of the Conference on Evaluation, Research and Education, 13–14 July, 2000), pp.93–104; C. Hanlon and G. Cuskelly, 'Pulsating Major Sport Event Organizations: A Framework for Inducting Managerial Personnel', *Event Management. An International Journal*, 7, 4 (2002), 231–43; C. Hanlon and L. Jago, 'The Challenge of Retaining Personnel in Major Sport Event Organizations', *Event Management. An International Journal*, 9, 1–2, 39–50.

[17] H. Mintzberg, 'Patterns in Strategy Formation', *Management Science*, 24, 9 (1978), 936; J. Allen, W. O'Toole, I. McDonnell and R. Harris (eds), *Festival and Special Event Management* (Sydney: Wiley & Sons Australia, 2002), p.151.

[18] M. Porter, *Competitive Advantage: Creating and Sustaining Superior Performance* (New York: The Free Press, 1985).

[19] J. Ivancevich and M. Matteson, *Organizational Behaviour and Management* (Boston: McGraw-Hill, 2002), p.329.

[20] Allen et al., *Festival and Special Event Management*, p.142.

[21] Hanlon and Jago, 'Pulsating Sporting Events', p.100.

[22] J. Atkinson, 'The Changing Corporation', in R. Clutterbuck (ed.), *New Patterns of Work* (Aldershot: Gower, 1985), pp.13–34; J. Atkinson, 'Flexibility or Fragmentation? The United Kingdom Labour Market in the Eighties', *Labour and Society*, 12, 1 (1987), 87–105.

[23] Mintzberg, 'Patterns in Strategy Formation'; C. Hendry and A. Pettigrew 'Human Resource Management: An Agenda for the 1990s', *International Journal of Human Resource Management*, 1, 1 (1990), 17–44; I. Cunningham and J. Hyman, 'Transforming the HRM Vision into Reality: The Role of Line Managers and Supervisors in Implementing Change', *Employee Relations*, 17, 8 (1995), 5–20; M. Korczynski, *Human Resource Management in Service Work* (Basingstoke: Palgrave, 2002).

[24] Hanlon and Jago, 'The Challenge of Retaining Personnel in Major Sport Event Organizations', 40.

[25] Hanlon and Jago, 'Pulsating Sporting Events', p.102.

[26] Hanlon and Jago, 'Pulsating Sporting Events', p.103.

[27] Hanlon and Cuskelly, 'Pulsating Major Sport Event Organizations', 232.

[28] Hanlon and Jago, 'The Challenge of Retaining Personnel in Major Sport Event Organizations', 14.

[29] R. Iverson, 'Managing Employee Absenteeism and Turnover for Competitive Advantage', in A. Travaglione and V. Marshall (eds), *Human Resource Strategies: An Applied Approach* (Sydney: McGraw-Hill, 2000), p.231.

[30] R. Gatewood and H. Field, *Human Resource Selection* (Fort Worth: Harcourt College Publishers, 2001), p.24.

[31] Hanlon and Jago, 'The Challenge of Retaining Personnel in Major Sport Event Organizations'.

[32] Atkinson, 'Flexibility or Fragmentation? The United Kingdom Labour Market in the Eighties'.

[33] P. Holland and M. Deery, 'Flexible Patterns of Work', in J. Teicher, P. Holland and L. Nelson (eds), *Employee Relations Management: Australia in a Global Context* (Melbourne: Pearsons Education Australia, 2002), pp.270–92.

[34] S. Procter and M. Rowlinson, 'Flexibility, Politics & Strategy: In Defence of the Model of the Flexible Firm', *Work, Employment & Society*, 8, 2 (1994), 221–42.

[35] L. Jago and M. Deery, 'An Investigation of the Impact of Internal Labour Markets in the Hotel Industry', *The Service Industries Journal*, 24, 2, (2004), 118–29; J. Burgess, 'The Flexible Firm and the Growth of Non-Standard Employment', *Labour & Industry*, 7, 3 (1997), 85–102; S. Woods, *The Transformation of Work: Skill, Flexibility and the Labour Process* (London: Unwin-Hyman, 1989); C. Hakim, 'Trends in Flexible Workforce', *Employment Gazette*, 95 (1987), 549–60.

[36] Holland and Deery, 'Flexible Patterns of Work', 278.

[37] Holland and Deery, 'Flexible Patterns of Work', p.278.

[38] D. Gallie, M. White, Y. Cheng and M. Tomlinson, *Restructuring the Employment Relationship* (Oxford: Clarendon Press, 1998); Burgess, 'The Flexible Firm and the Growth of Non-Standard Employment'.

[39] Atkinson, 'The Changing Corporation', p.20.

[40] M. Emmott and S. Hutchinson, 'Employment flexibility: Threat or promise?', in P. Sparrow and M. Marchington (eds), *Human Resource Management: The New Agenda*, (London: Financial Times/Pitmans, 1998), p.229.

[41] Holland and Deery, 'Flexible Patterns of Work'.

[42] H. Tyzack, 'Volunteering: Laissez faire or managed?', *Australian Journal on Volunteering*, 1, 1 (1996), 23.

[43] K. Daniel, L. Johnson and K. Miller, 'Dimensions of Uniform Perceptions among Service Providers', *The Journal of Services Marketing*, 10, 2 (1996), 42–56.

[44] L. Lockstone, 'Managing the Volunteer: Flexible Structures and Strategies to Integrate Volunteers and Paid Workers' (unpublished Ph.D. thesis, Victoria University, 2004), Ch.9.

[45] Ibid.

[46] M. Deery, and L. Jago, 'Paid Staff or Volunteers? The Dilemma Facing Tourism Organizations', *Capitalising on Research, Proceedings of the Eleventh Australian Tourism and Hospitality and Research Conference*, University of Canberra, Canberra, (2001), 68.

[47] H. Maylor, *Project Management* (London: Pitman Publishing, 1996), p.3.

[48] Ibid., p.7.

[49] Allen *et al.*, *Festival and Special Event Management*, p.344.

Conclusion: Some Thoughts on Where We Are Now and Where We Go Next

In reflecting on the contribution of this book I hope that we have countered in some small way the critics of this domain who have questioned the academic credibility of sport tourism as an area of study. By providing a compendium of theories and examples as to how they might be applied to the study and practice of sport tourism, I feel that this book has taken a first step towards providing some conceptual guidance for the next phases of scholarship in sport tourism research. There has been a time lapse between writing this conclusion and the original compilation of the special issue of *Sport in Society* [1] where these papers were first published. I wanted time to reflect on the contributions of these papers and also to place them in the context of subsequent publications and developments in the world of sport tourism. By taking both a temporal and a conceptual break, I will offer some thoughts on the future of sport tourism and how the papers in the collection might contribute to our never ending quest of moving the body of knowledge further, and improving our practical applications.

I noted with interest some new contributions to the debate on the delineatin of sport tourism in a special issue of the *Journal of Sport Tourism* edited by one of the contributing authors to this book Leo Jago. In particular, two articles (one by Deery, Jago and Fredline, and one by Robinson and Gammon)[2] from this special issue caught my attention and seem to encapsulate some of the ongoing issues in sport tourism scholarship, notably how might sport tourism be defined and what constitutes sport tourism behavior. I might suggest that many of the chapters in this book have much to contribute to this ongoing debate. For example, Deery et al., note that most definition of sport tourism have failed to take into account the outcomes of sport tourism. I would suggest that this is common in most definitions of tourism as the focus is generally on delineating behavior rather than on the impacts of tourism. In fact, we might argue that the lack of attention to the impacts of tourism over the years has facilitated inadvertently many of the negative impacts which are gradually coming to light in many destinations around the world and have fueled the call for sustainable tourism. Indeed, this current concern for sustainable tourism is reflected in the joint declaration by the World Tourism Organization and the International Olympic Committee reaffirming their commitment to sport tourism in the form of 'sustainable economic growth' for countries around the world [3]. I might suggest that the papers in this book address the issue of positive and negative impacts or outcomes of sport tourism from a range of different perspectives including host guest relations (Fredline), economics and the role of public sector monies in funding sport tourism (Mules and Dwyer), urban regeneration (Silk, and Amis), destination branding (Chalip and Costa) and effective management of sport tourism to leverage benefits (Deery and Jago). In reflection, may be an important omission from this book is a chapter focusing on the environmental impacts of sport tourism. Certainly, the environment should be an important focus for both academics and industry, although as yet, few tourism, despite the environmental impact assessments required by the IOC as part of the bid process for any Olympic Games and also the growing awareness of the negative environmental impact assessments required by the IOC as part of the bid process for any Olympic Games and also the growing awareness of the negative environmental impacts of golf and skiing around the world [4].

Another point of debate postulated by Derry et al., is that sport tourism is essentially event (sport) tourism. These authors are not the first by any means to suggest this, however, they are the first to articulate this argument in an academic paper. They argue that the sport in sport tourism refers to sport that is organized and competitive rather than recreational and an incidental part of an individual's trip. They come to the conclusion that for sport to satisfy these two criteria, it (sport) must take place as part of an event. This is an interesting supposition and I share the author's concern over incidental part of an individual's trip. They come to the conclusion that for sport to satisfy these two criteria, it (sport) must take place as part of an event. This is an interesting supposition and I share the author's concern over incidental sport participation being classified as sport tourism, however, I do not agree with the proposition that sport tourism is essentially event sport tourism. Again if we look to examples from this book, we can see that some significant forms of sports tourism exist outside of an event format. For example Thwaites and Chadwick's chapter on service quality in a sport based resort links customer satisfaction to the quality of the sport experience provided. While one might argue that for some participants at such resorts, sport participation may be incidental and lack any semblance of competition, however, for the majority of tourists who choose these types of holidays (as exemplified in Thwaites and Chadwick's studies) the chance to practice their sport using high quality facilities and often with the intent of improving their skills by enlisting the services of an instructor is central to their vacation experience. Likewise, in Hinch et al's chapter on constraints, the topic of winter sports, notably skiing raises the issue again of all sport tourism being event based. For many destinations around the world golf and snow sports based tourism comprise a significant portion of tourism industry both in terms of economic impact and infrastructure. While not all skiers or golfers might be on the highly competitive end of the continuum, studies suggest that competition is part of the experience for many [5] as is the highly organized nature of the environments that are inherent to golf and snow sports destinations in the 21st Century.

We might also point to the small but growing interest in nostalgia sport tourism. While some academics debate the existence of this form of sport tourism [6], others have conducted empirical investigations into varius examples of nostalgia sport tourism including the nostalgia associated with the annual journey of Australian rules football fans to watch their team play and fans taking a tour of Wrigley Field, home of the Chicago Cubs baseball team in the US [7]. While, if we are pedantic we could argue that these examples of nostalgia sport tourism are ultimately associated with an event, in both cases professional sport teams, Fairley and Gammon's chapter with some contributions from Jones and Green's chapter on serious leisure provide some conceptual support to the idea that there is another sport tourism experience that is distinct from spectating or taking part in a sports event. While, we all recognize that work on nostalgia is in its infancy, we hope that these conceptual foundations will guide future studies so that we might establish a true line of knowledge in this area thereby enhancing our understanding of the role of nostalgia and other motivations in sport tourism. Perhaps as Robinson and Gammon [8] (special issue of *Journal of Sport Tourism*) suggest in further developing their 1997 paper on the distinction between sport tourism and tourism sport, that we need to look more closely at the ideas of primary and secondary motivations. Certainly in much of my writing on sport tourism (see the chapter in this book as an example), the issue of push and pull factors, behavioral classification using role theory and the dynamic nature of socio-psychological factors in understanding sport tourism behavior are of utmost importance.

So as the academic debate on the delineation of sport tourism continues, what are some of the issues for the practice of sport tourism? Many of the chapters in this book deal directly with the topic of theory to practice in areas such as marketing (Harison-Hill and Chalip), managing (Deery and Jago), policy (Weed), economics and public sector spending (Mules and Dwyer), service quality (Thwaites and Chadwick), season-ality (Higham) and destination branding (Chalip and Costa). In sport tourism practice I see the overwhelming focus till on event sport tourmsm, in fact this is noted by Deery et al., and used as part of their argument that all sport tourism is event based. In government policy around the world, the quest in particular to host the sport mega event is ever present in their sport tourism strategies (if they have one). Even in France where Bourdeau and his colleagues [9] have focused attention on the importance of active sport tourism, particularly for the alpine regions, France's bid to host the 2012 summer Olympic Games and their annual hosting of the World's largest sporting event the Tour de France, eclipses many of the country's other sport tourism initiatives.

While I would not advocate that academic research should be shaped by government policy and thus the focus of our work should be event based to stay in line with government sport tourism strategies, it does appear however, that we might have a role to play in helping event planners to better leverage the benefits of these large events and incorporate long term planning into the bid documents. An example of this was the work of the Sustainable Tourism Cooperative Research Centre relation to the 2000 Sydney Olympics in Australia [10] In lending our expertise to governments in their quest to host the mega event the issue of legacy is an increasingly important issue. While there is an academic tradition of analyzing the impact of the mega events such as the Olympic Games and World Cup Soccer, a lot of this work has been post hhoc and perhaps what we should be doing is working with the bid teams and the various organizing committees to keep the issue of legacy at the forefront in decisions making. Certainly, the 2010 Winter Games hosted by Vancouver and Whistler, British Columbia have and official committee charged with identifying and putting into practice the legacies of the 2010 games. The word legacy was also forefront in the successful London bid to host the 2012 Olympic games. The charge now is to make sure these legacies come to fruition. In a study on the legacies of the 2004 Athens Olympics that I am currently working on with Sheranne Fairley, we are beginning to understand the complexities of the legacy issue and how certain facts can be portrayed from many different angles. In spending time in Athens visiting the Olympic venues, talking to sport and tourism officials and the citizens of Athens one year after the games there is a mix of responses. There is still a legacy of what Burgan and Mules[11] called psychic income or pride in hosting successful games, despite the worldwide concerns leading up to the games regarding construction delays and concerns leading up to the games regarding construction delays and concerns about security. The sport and tourism officials regard the games as a success in terms of the improved infrastructure for hosting large events, not just sports but concerts, and ice shows that they did not posses before. There is also anecdotal evidence to suggest that traffic congestion has been eased somewhat by the improvements made to public transportation and the roads, although as yet the newly installed tram has not attracted the ridership that planners might have envisioned. As of now it is too early to tell if there has been increased tourism, although Greece did appear to suffer from the displacement effect that plagues Olympic host sites in the years leading up to the games. However, this decrease in international visitation also needs to be contextualized within world tourism flows. During this time period international tourism was negatively impacted by the terrorism events of 9/11, the Bali bombing and the invasion of Iraq, and was further compounded by economic recession in some countries and so tourism throughout the world was in decline in the three years leading up to the 2004 games. In fact, the post event success of the 2000 Sydney games in attracting international tourism to Australia also needs to be framed within these world events, as they too did not experience the predicted increases in tourism between 2001 and 2003.

Thus, as we move forward into the next phase of sport tourism scholarship and practice, we take with us some of the issues from the early days, notably concerns over delineating the domain, however, I also see signs that we are moving beyond this and tackling new issues which have more of a focus on the impacts or outcomes of sport tourism for individuals, communities and countries around the world. It is hoped that the chapters in this book will underpin some of the future work in these areas and frame the next steps in building a conceptually grounded body of knowledge that is directly to practice in various aspects of sport tourism.

References

[1] Special issue Sport tourism: Concepts and Theories of *Sport in Society: Culture, Commerce, Media, Politics*, 8, 2, June 2005. Guest editor, Heather Gibson.

[2] Special issue, Foundations of Sport Tourism of the *Journal of Sport Tourism*, 9, 3, (2004), guest editor Leo Jago. M. Deery, L. Jago, and L. Fredline, 'Sport tourism or event tourism: Are they one and the same? *Journal of Sport Tourism*, 9, 3, (2004), 235–246. T, Robinson and S. Gammon. 'A question of primary and secondary motives: Revisiting and applying the sport tourism framework'. *Journal of Sport Tourism*, 9, 3, (2004), 221–234.

[3] World Tourism Organization. 'Sport and tourism: Living forces for mutual understanding, culture and the development of society' *WTO*, issue 2, 2 ⊃ nd quarter 2004, pp. 1 and 3.

[4] D. Chernushenko, D. 'Sports tourism goes sustainable: The Lillehammer experience.' *Visions in Leisure and Business*, 15, 1 (1996), 65–73f. R. Buckley, C. Pickering, and J. Warnken, J. 'Environmental management for Alpine tourism and resorts in Australia.' In P. Godde, M. Price, & F. Zimmermann (Eds.). *Tourism and Development in Mountain Regions* (2000). (pp.27–45). Wallingford: CAB. A. Flagstad, A., Strategic success in winter sports destinations: A sustainable value creation perspective. *Tourism Management*, 22, 5 (2001), 445–461. S. Hudson. 'The greening of ski resorts: A necessity for sustainable tourism, or a marketing opportunity for skiing communities?' Journal of Vacation Marketing, 2, 2 (1996), 176–185. A. Pleumarom, A. Course and effect: Golf tourism in Thailand. *The Ecologist*, 22, 3 (1992), 104–110. E. Sparvero, S. Trendavilova, and L. Chalip, *An alternative approach to environmental dispute resolution in sport contexts*. Poster presented at the North American Society for Sport Management conference, Regina, Canada, June 1–5, 2005.

[5] S. Hudson, S. The segmentation of potential tourists: constraints differences between men and women. *Journal of Travel Research*, 38, 4 (2000). 363–369. R. Schreiber, 'Sports interest, A travel definition.' *The Travel Research Association 7th Annual Conference Proceedings*, (June 20–23, 1976). 85–87, Boca Raton, Florida.

[6] C. Pigeassou. Contribution to the definition of sport Tourism. Journal of Sport Tourism, 9, 3, (2004), 287–290. M., & Bull, C. (2004). *Sports tourism: Participants, policy and providers*. Oxford, UK: Elesevier Butterworth-Heinemann.

[7] S. Fairley, 'In search of relived social experience: Group-based nostalgia sport tourism.' *Journal of Sport Management*, 17, 3, (2003) 284–304. A. Wilson, 'The relationship between consumer role socialization and nostalgia sport tourism: A symbolic Interactionist perspective.' (2004). Unpublished Master's University of Florida, Gainesville, USA.

[8] Robinson and S. Gammon. 'A question of primary and secondary motives: Revisiting and applying the sport tourism framework'. *Journal of Sport Tourism*, 9, 3, (2004), 221–234. S. Gammon,

and T. Robinson, 'Sport and tourism: A conceptual framework.' *Journal of Sports Tourism*, 4, 3, (1997). 8–24.

[9] P. Bourdeau, J. Corneloup, and P. Mao. 'Adventure sports and tourism In the French mourains: Dynamics of change and challeges for sustainable development.' In B. Ritchie & D. Adair (Eds.). *Sport tourism: Interrelationships, Impacts and Issues*, (2004). (pp. 101–116). Clevedon, UK: Channel View Publications.

[10] Sustainable Tourism Cooperative Research Centre with funding from the Australian Research Council and the Sydney Organising Committee for the Olympic Games. Members of the center who are co-authors in this book are Laurence Chalip, Chris Green and Sheranne Fairley.

[11] B. Burgan and T. Mules, Economic impact of sporting events. *Annals of Tourism Research*, 19, 4 (1992). 700–710.

INDEX

academies 117
accessibility 193
accountability 153, 160
accounting 135
active sport tourism 2, 12, 32–3, 38, 44–6, 54–5, 66, 70, 73, 77, 79
additional trade 215–16
Adelaide Grand Prix 209
Aden, R.C. 52
adequate service 193–4, 199
adhocracies 233–4, 236
Adidas 121–3
adjective elicitation 88
administrators 117
adventure sports 181
advertising 6, 14, 87, 92, 94, 97, 100, 108–9, 121–3, 157, 170–1, 173, 177–8, 182–3, 198
advertorials 183
aerial photography 208
African Americans 77, 157
Air New Zealand 120
airlines 181, 193, 210
Alice Springs Henley-on-Todd Regatta 97
All Blacks 115, 117, 120, 122–3
Allen, J. 254
American Kennel Club 34
American Le Mans Series 95
America's Cup 92, 106, 133, 209
Amis, John 6, 79, 121, 148–69, 259
analogies 200
Andersson, T. 133
anthropology 2, 5, 178
Ap, J. 139, 144
Arctic Winter Games 78
Arnauld, E.J. 202
artefacts 50–1, 54–6, 58, 62, 123, 178
Asia Pacific 71
association networks 90–3, 100–1
Athens Olympics 61, 261
athletes 13, 107, 109–10, 121, 196–8
Atkinson, J. 252

Atkinson, Maureen 86
attainment 45–6
attitudes 193, 195
attraction systems 12–14, 108–9, 126, 171–3
attributes 89–90, 94, 97, 111, 171–2, 199, 202
Auckland City Council 209
Augustyn, M.M. 192
Australia 6–7, 27, 59, 92, 97, 100, 106, 116, 133, 137, 140, 145, 172, 180–1, 183, 206, 208, 210, 215, 226, 237, 246–7, 260
Australian Motor Cycle Grand Prix 209
Australian Rugby Union (ARU) 140
Australian Rules Football 45
authenticity debate 69
auto racing see motor racing
autoregressive integrated moving average (ARIMA) 74

Backman, S.J. 190, 202
badminton 145
Baltimore City Fair 154
Baltimore Convention Center 154–5
Baltimore, Maryland 6, 149, 153–6, 159, 161–2, 176
banking 190
barbershop singing 34
baseball 77, 117, 145, 155, 173, 176
basketball 92, 145, 158
Batty, R. 115, 122
Bauman, Zygman 162
beaches 144, 180–1
Beal, - 41
Beard, J. 73
Becker, H.S. 44, 227
Beckham, David 171
Belk, R.W. 51
Belz Enterprises 157
benchmarks 38
Berlyne, D. 74
Berrett, T. 189
Berry, L.L. 194, 200

Bialeschki, M.D. 16
Birrell, S. 76
Bitner, M.J. 192–4, 200
Blodgett, J.G. 191–2
Blues Highway 158
Bojanic, D. 72
Bonen, A. 16, 77
books 1–9
Bourdieu, P. 41, 44, 260
bowls 145
brands 5, 86–105, 123, 151, 170–88, 191
Brent Ritchie, J.R. 190, 202
Brisbane, Australia 140–1
British Empire 4
British Lions 106, 120
Britton, S. 151
broadcasting 10, 14, 111, 116, 121, 123
Brookings Institution 160–1
budgets 14
Bull, C.J. 33, 54–5, 225–7, 230, 232, 235–7, 242
bundling 179–81
bureaucracy 163, 224–5, 233
Burgan, B. 218–20, 261
Burton, L.T. 189
bushwalking 136
business development 215–16
Butler, R.W. 110, 137
Buttle, F. 200

Caltabiano, M. 74
camaraderie 58, 61, 173
Cambourne, B. 220
Canada 24–6, 57, 78, 237
Canadian Ski Council 24
Canary Islands 6, 190
Canterbury Crusaders 120, 122
capitalism 6, 148–51, 153, 156, 159, 161
career 34–6, 40–1, 43, 45–6, 75, 79
Carisbrook Terrace 122
carnival 59
case studies 133, 137, 140–4, 190, 194–8, 201
Cash, Pat 56
casual expenditure 208–9
casual leisure 34–7, 39, 41–2
catchments 117
Cegielski, M. 220
celebrities 110
Census figures 25
Center on Urban and Metropolitan Policy 160
Centerparcs 115
central business district (CBD) 153–4, 157
Chadwick, Simon 6–7, 189–205, 259–60
Chalip, Laurence 5–6, 54, 58, 60, 86–105, 152, 170–88, 259–60
Chicago Cubs 77

children 72, 197
China 71
Choice Modelling 132
cityscapes 148–69
Civil Rights 161
Clarke, J. 34
class 78
climate 110–11, 126
clothing 111
Club La Santa (CLS) 6, 190, 194–8
cluster analysis 180
co-branding 92–7, 101, 181
coaches 13, 58, 117, 197, 200
Cobanoglu, C. 201
cognition 88–9
Cohen, Erik 69–71
Cole, C. 76
collectors 38
commitment 41–3
commodification 149, 151, 161–2
Commonwealth Games 106
communications 150, 170, 172–3, 177, 182–4, 194–5, 198, 247, 250, 253–4
communitas 59–61
Community Enterprise Board 153
community impact 137–40
compatibility 197
compensatory behaviours 42
Competitions Review 123
competitive advantage 250
complexes 121
computer games 183
concept stores 174–5
congestion 144, 208, 210, 216
constraints 3, 6, 10–28, 35, 41–2, 77, 115, 171, 212
construction expenditure 214
consumption 75, 88–90, 93–4, 99, 148–51, 154–5, 160–1, 171–4, 178–9, 183, 185, 191, 212, 216–20
contact staff 195–6, 198
Contingent Valuation (CV) 132, 220
contracts 93
Cooper Robertson and Partners 159
Corbin, J. 241
core workforce 252, 255
corporate interests 10, 109, 123, 151–3, 191, 207, 211, 225, 249
correspondence analysis 88
cost-benefit analysis (CBA) 7, 139, 206, 217–20
Costa, Carla A. 5, 86–105, 259–60
Courier, Jim 56
Crandall, R. 76
Crawford, D.W. 16–17, 19
credibility 193, 198

Crete 201
cricket 56, 106, 145, 172
Cricket World Cup 106
crime 133, 151, 160, 217
Critcher, C. 34
Crompton, J.L. 74, 144
Crosset, - 41
crowd estimation 12, 208
cruises 57, 66
cultural capital 41
culture 25, 37, 51, 71, 73–4, 76–8, 99–100,
  109–10, 115, 120, 122–3, 132, 138, 148–69,
  177, 215, 226, 233, 236–7, 239, 242, 254–5
Cunningham, I. 251

Daniel, K. 253
Dann, G. 4, 74
database marketing 183
De Knop, P. 190
debt 216
decline 40
Deery, Margaret 7, 246–60
definitions 2, 248–9, 258
deindustrialization 150, 154, 160
DeKnop, P. 32
delegation 250
Dellaert, B. 133
Delpy, L. 211
Delta tour 56
demand continuum 33
democracy 153, 160
Denmark 190
deregulation 150
design 174–9, 196
desired service 193–4, 199
destination brands 5, 86–105, 170–88
Detroit, Michigan 160
discrimination 77–8
disposable income 72
distance decay theory 12
Dogan, H.Z. 144
domains 3, 89, 246
dominant roles 68, 70
Donnelly, P. 52
Doxey, G.V. 137
drifters 71
dropout rates 26
Dwyer, Larry 7, 206–23, 259–60

Echabe, A. 139
economic impact 135–6, 141, 144–5, 207, 210,
  212–16, 250
economics 7, 27, 55, 88–9, 100, 121–2, 132,
  134, 141, 144, 146, 149–50, 152, 154, 159,
  161–2, 190, 206–7, 210–12, 215–16, 233,
  242, 247, 249–50, 259
Edmonton Oilers 57
Egypt 158
Ekinci, Y. 201
elites 10, 110–11, 116, 152, 190, 196, 237
Elkington, John 132
email 176
employment 133, 160, 206, 210, 212–14, 252–3
Empowerment Zone (EZ) 153–4
England 106–7, 111, 113, 171–2, 225, 240
English Sports Council 238
Enterprise Community (EC) 154, 159
entrepreneurship 149, 151
environmental impact 132, 135–6, 141, 144,
  146, 217, 241, 259
Environmental Travel 70
ephemeral roles 68–9, 74, 78
equipment 111
ethos 37–41, 43, 181, 196, 226
Etzel, M. 68, 74
Euro 2004 111, 113
Euro '96 171
Europe 24, 27, 56, 71–2, 111, 115, 123
event hosting 86–105
event sport tourism *see* passive sport tourism
excursionists 55
expectancy-value model 139
expectations 193–4, 198–9, 201
experience 50–1, 54–5, 57–8, 61–2, 174–5
Exploitative Travel 70
exploratory factor analysis 88
EXPO '92 213

FA Cup 107
facility construction 214, 249
Fairley, Sheranne 4, 42, 44, 50–66, 121, 178,
  260–1
familiarity 69–71, 73
family commitments 25
fanship 59, 79, 108, 136, 173, 178, 180
fashion 110
Faulkner, B. 206, 248–9
favouritism 42
feminism 16
Fidgeon, P. 77
FIFA 5
Fiji 126
Fisk, R.P. 200
fitness 13
Flexible Firm model 250, 252, 254
football 56, 58–60, 79, 107, 111, 113, 145, 171,
  175, 177–8, 214
Fordism 150
Formula One 140, 145, 206

Fort Stockton Water Carnival 95
Fox, R. 33
France 90, 113, 241
Fredline, Elizabeth 5, 131–47, 258–9
free riders 218
Friedman, - 155
Fuchs, M. 201
future trends 62, 101, 184, 258–63
fuzzy set analysis 69

Gammon, Sean 4, 32, 42, 44, 50–66, 76, 78, 121, 248, 258, 260
gap model 6, 194–8
gender 76–7
gentrification 6, 151, 153, 155–6, 162
geography 2, 12, 19, 21, 26–7, 126, 149, 173, 211, 233, 237
Gerhardt, U. 67, 76
Germany 71–2, 190
Getz, D. 249–50
Gibson, Heather 1–9, 12, 32–3, 43, 54–5, 66–85, 148–9, 171–2, 248, 258–63
Gilbert, D. 25, 28
Gillespie, D. 39
Gilmore, J.H. 174
Giulianotti, - 59
Glaser, B. 227, 240
globalization 148–50, 153, 159, 161–2
Glyptis, S.A. 241
Godbey, G. 16–17, 19, 43
Goffman, E. 67, 75, 79
Gold Coast 92, 94, 100, 137, 144, 172, 176, 181
golf 12, 35–6, 38, 44, 56–7, 71, 73, 77–8, 108, 111, 115, 171, 173, 175, 178, 180
Gollwittzer, P. 26
Goodale, T.L. 15
Gorman, - 60–1
Gouldner, A. 3
governments 7, 145, 152–3, 156, 206, 209, 211–12, 214, 216–17, 219–20, 226, 229–30, 232, 235–7, 239–41, 247–9, 255, 260
Graburn, N. 59
Grand Prix 140–1, 144–5, 206, 208
Grand Slam 140
grants 154
Gratton, C. 75
Great Barrier Reef 141
Great Britain *see* United Kingdom
Greece 201, 261
Green, B. Christine 3–4, 32–49, 58, 60, 175, 178, 260
Greendorfer, S. 76
Gretzky, Wayne 57
Gronroos, C. 191–3
grounded theory 7, 224–45

group formation 60–2
group-think 234
Grove, S.J. 200
guest-host relations 5–7, 87, 131–47, 211, 219–20
guidebooks 120

Hadlee Stadium 122
haka 122–3
Hall, C.M. 32–3, 71, 133, 225, 248
Hammersley, M. 226
Hanlon, C. 251
Hargreaves, J. 76
Harrison-Hill, Tracey 6, 152, 170–88, 260
Harvey, David 153, 155, 162
Hawaii 137
Henderson, K.A. 16
Hendry, C. 251
Henley Royal Regatta 95
Henry, I.P. 225
heritage 55–6, 161
Heritage Classic Megastars Alumni Game 57
hierarchy 24–6, 109, 113, 126
High Contact Travel 70
Higham, James 5, 78, 106–30, 148, 260
Hill, B. 175
Hinch, Tom 3, 10–31, 42, 78, 108, 115, 117, 148, 259
Hispanic Americans 77
hobbyists 38–9
hockey 57, 145
Holbrook, M.B. 51
Holden, A. 75
holiday-makers 69
Holland, P. 252–3
horizontal channel alliances 181, 185
horse racing 107, 110, 136, 180
host-guest relations 5–7, 87, 131–47, 211, 219–20
Houlihan, B. 224–5
housing 156, 159–60
Hubbard, J. 22, 27
Hudson, Simon 3, 10–31
hygiene factors 199
Hyman, J. 251

Iceland 111
identity 36–7, 39–45, 51–2, 59, 61, 75–6, 79, 152–3, 162, 173, 177, 183
ideology 7, 148, 160, 225, 227, 229, 231, 236–7, 239
image building 87–94, 101, 122–3, 151, 157
immigration 24–5
impact assessment 131–2, 135–6, 141, 144, 146, 206, 210–17, 241, 259

impression management 41
induced development 214
Indy Car Race 92, 94, 100, 107, 144, 207, 213
inertia 110
inflation 216
injected expenditure 215
injury 35
input-output model 212–13
inscope expenditure 207–10
inseparability 176
institutional factors 110–11
intangibles 216–17, 220
interactivity 191, 211–12
interdependence 150
International Athletes 70
International Olympic Committee (IOC)
    258–9
International Rugby Board (IRB) 116
International Swimming Hall of Fame (ISHOF)
    100
interruption 26, 216
investment 144–5, 150–1, 154–7, 159–60,
    213–17, 219
Ireland 71, 106
Irish Lions 106, 120
Irridex 137
Iso-Ahola, S.E. 26, 40
issue zones 231–2

Jackson, Edgar L. 3, 10–31, 42, 122–3
Jackson, G. 16, 21, 33
Jackson, S.J. 115
Jade Stadium 122
Jago, Leo 7, 246–60
Japan 71, 111, 173
Jekubovich, N. 21
Jenkins, J.M. 225
jet-setters 69
Johnson, A. 152
Johnson, L. 253
Johnson, R. 139
Jones, Ian 3–4, 32–49, 58, 260
Journal of Sport Management 148
journals 1–9

Kane, M. 41
Karteroliotis, K. 190, 201–2
Katz, Bruce 160
Kay, T. 16, 21
Kellett, P. 53
Kelly, J. 2
Kentucky Derby 107
Keogh, B. 145
Key West, Florida 178
Keynes, J.M. 150

Kim, D. 201
Kim, N-S. 179
Kim, S. 201
King, Martin Luther 155
Korczynski, M. 251
Korea 71, 201
Kreutzwiser, R. 126

La Caja Insular de Ahorros de Canarias 190
Labour Day 5
landslides 133
Larnach's Castle 122
Las Vegas, Nevada 161
Lattey, C. 77
Law, C.M. 121
Lawson, R. 72
Layder, D. 226–33, 235–6
Le Mans 24 Hours 95
lead times 213
leadership 150, 152–3, 155, 161, 196, 232, 248
leakages 211
Lehtinen, J.R. 191
Lehtinen, U. 191
Leiper, N. 5, 13, 107–8, 110, 126
leisure motivation scale 73
leisure studies 2–3, 10, 13, 15–22, 27–8, 33–4,
    75, 78, 107–8, 121, 156–7, 189, 200–1, 225,
    231, 248
Lepp, A. 71
leverage 101, 154, 180–1, 183–5, 260
Levine, J. 40
Levinson, D. 73
Lewko, J. 76
Leyns, A. 176, 181
Li, M. 211
liberal arts 38
life cycles 19, 21, 26, 67, 71–4, 76, 78
Lightning Ridge Great Goat Race 97
liminoid space 43–5, 58–62
Lindberg, K. 133, 139
Linton, R. 67
logistics 255
logos 41, 87, 90, 92, 178
Lomu, Jonah 122
Lonely Planet 120
long-distance running 34
Lord's Cricket Ground 172
loyalty 178–9, 189, 191, 197, 202

McCabe, J.F. 16, 77
McColl-Kennedy, J.R. 196
McDonald, M.A. 201
McEnroe, John 53, 56
McGehee, N.G. 76–7
McGuire, F.A. 19

McGuirty, J. 172, 180
McKewon, E. 133
Major, John 238
management 5, 7–8, 39, 86, 94, 109–11, 117, 126, 134, 144–5, 148, 154, 158, 191, 193–8, 200, 202, 219, 246–57
Mannell, R. 22, 27
manufacturing 149
Maoris 115, 122–3
mapping 88
marathons 109, 145, 172, 176
marginalization 76
markers 108–10, 121–3
market failure 218–19, 247
marketing 5–6, 14, 53, 66, 79, 86–90, 92, 94–5, 97, 100, 117, 122, 126, 153, 161–2, 170–90, 198–200, 215, 226, 249
Marmorstein, H. 197
Marsh, D. 231
Martin, C.I. 197
Marxism 225
Maryland Science Center 154
Maslow, Abraham 74
mass tourism 69, 71, 73
Massey, Doreen 149
Masters golf championships 108
Matheson, V. 211, 214
Mathieson, A. 132
Mead, G.H. 52
measurement problems 208
media 10, 13–14, 40, 51–2, 92–5, 97, 100, 107–11, 116–17, 120–3, 149, 153–4, 156–8, 160, 180, 182–3, 198, 207, 249
medical staff 117
meetings 195–6
Melbourne, Australia 140–1, 144
Melbourne Cricket Ground (MCG) 45
Melbourne Cup 95
Memphis 2005 159
Memphis Grizzlies 158
Memphis Redbirds 158
Memphis Riverfront Development Corporation 162
Memphis, Tennessee 6, 149, 156–9, 161–2
merchandise 53
metaphors 200
Migrants 70
Mill, J. 68
Miller, K. 253
Milne, G.R. 201
Mintzberg, H. 233, 251
Mississippi River 156, 158–9
Montreal Canadiens 57
Moreland, R. 40
Moscardo, G. 139

motivation 68–9, 73–6, 78–9, 109, 113, 172, 175, 184, 198, 209, 234, 247–8, 260
motor cycle racing 209
motor racing 107, 140, 144–5, 176, 181, 207
mountain biking 136
Mules, Trevor 7, 206–23, 259–61
multidimensional scaling 88
multiplier 210–14, 216–17
Mumel, D. 190
Murdoch, Rupert 116
Murdy, J. 70
Murray, H. 74

National Baseball Hall of Fame 56
National Football League (NFL) 155
National Football Museum 56
National Hockey League (NHL) 57
National Provincial Championship (NPC) 120, 122–3
National Sports Museum 56
National Tennis Centre 140
National Women's Flag Football Tournament 178
natives 151, 155
needs hierarchy 74
negotiation thesis 17–19, 22, 24, 26, 28, 35, 41–2
neo-liberalism 152, 162
netball 145
Netherlands 172
network economy 150, 152, 161
New Haven, Connecticut 152
New York City Marathon 94–5
New York City, NY 180
New Zealand 5, 72, 106, 115–26, 181
New Zealand Maori 115
New Zealand Rugby Institute 121
New Zealand Rugby Union (NZRU) 106, 115, 117, 120, 122–3
News Corporation 116–17, 120, 123
Nike 122, 174
nodes 90–4, 100
noise 133–4, 136, 144, 217
Norbeck, E. 59
North America 3, 15, 24, 27, 56, 71
nostalgia sport tourism 2, 4, 12–13, 42, 50–66, 70, 76, 79, 149, 172, 178, 184, 260
novelty 69–71, 76, 162, 178
nuclear mix 108–9, 121

Ojasalo, J. 194
Olympic Games 5, 7, 12, 53, 57, 61, 71, 92, 133, 171, 178, 181, 210, 213–16, 247–9, 255, 260–1
O'Neill, M.A. 201

online communities 183
Open Tennis Tournament 140
Oppermann, M. 72
organizational theory 225, 233–4
Orioles 6, 155, 176
Otago Highlanders 120, 122
Otto, J.E. 190, 202
Outdoor Recreation Resources Review
  Commission 15
overpromising 198
Overseas Students 69–70

Pacific Islands 123
Papadimitriou, D.A. 190, 201–2
Parasuraman, A. 194, 200
parking 144, 158, 175
participation 15–17, 19, 21, 24–6, 32–3,
  35–46, 53–4, 58–61, 66, 73, 75–9, 134, 146,
  170–2, 174–5, 177–80, 184, 208, 217, 249
passive sport tourism 2, 12, 32, 44–6, 55, 66,
  70, 77
Pearce, P.L. 69–70, 74–5, 139
Pearson, G. 53
peripheral workforce 252–3, 255
perseverance 35, 38
person-role formula 67, 75–6
Petrick, J.F. 190, 202
Pettigrew, A. 251
physical impact *see* environmental impact
physical quality 191
pilgrims 55, 61, 178
Pine, B.J. 174
places 50, 153, 160, 179–82, 184
planning 87–8, 133, 157, 174, 176–7, 180, 208,
  213, 224–5, 234–5, 241, 247
Pleasure First Travel 70
pluralism 225
Policy Area Matrix 241–2
policy process 224–45
politics 148–69, 224
pollution 136, 217
polysemy 178
Porter, M. 250
portfolio of events 99–101
power relations 149, 159, 162, 224, 254
Pranter, C.A. 197
Preakness Celebration 100
preferences 16–17, 22, 42, 51, 68, 70, 73–4, 76,
  160, 172–3, 183, 191, 216
presocialization 40
Price, L.L. 202
prices 12, 179–82, 184, 196–7, 199, 217–20
primary attractions 108, 113, 120, 126, 179–80
private sector 152–3, 156, 158, 160, 214–15,
  218, 226

privatization 150–1
problem-solving 194–5
producer surplus 219–20
product placement 183
production 151
Professional-Amateur-Public (PAP) network 38
professionalism 53, 57, 59, 193, 250
profiles 99
profit 14, 41–2, 54, 153, 189, 197, 211, 218
project management 254–5
Prokopaki, P. 201
promotion 111, 122, 126, 136, 145, 151, 163,
  174, 181–5, 198, 213, 215, 238, 241
prostitution 133, 156
psychographics 183–4
psychology 27, 67, 71, 73–6, 78, 88–9, 95,
  137–8, 184, 193, 202, 224, 260
public sector 7, 206–23, 226
public/private institutions 152–3, 157, 159
publicity 87, 92, 94, 97, 100, 177–8, 182
pulsating organizations 250–5
push/pull factors 74, 77

Qantas Australian Grand Prix 209
quality of service 189–205
QuickSilver Pro 100, 172
Quiroga, I. 60

race 77–8
Raffles Hotel, Singapore 4
rafting 202
Ragheb, M. 73
Raisborough, J. 34
rally car racing 183
Ranfurly Shield 120
recreation 248–9
recruitment 40, 196, 251
Redmond, G. 2, 54, 66
regattas 95, 97, 110
reliability 193
renewal community 159
repeat visits 178–9
repertory grid 88
reputation 193
residents 3, 131–47, 210, 214, 216–17, 219–20
resource map 226–33
retained expenditure 208–10
reversal rite 59
Rhodes, R.A.W. 231
Richards, G. 75
Richter, D.M. 76
Ritchie, J. 135, 190
Ritzer, G. 161
Riverfront Development Corporation 159
road closures 145

Robinson, T. 32, 76, 78, 248, 258, 260
role theory 4, 61, 67–9, 73–4, 76, 78–9
Rose Bowl 95
Ross, G.F. 139
Rovira, D. 139
Roy, D. 227
Rucks, V.C. 21
rugby league 113, 116
Rugby Super 12, 15, 115–17, 120, 122–3, 126
rugby union 106–7, 113, 115–26
rugby war 116
Rugby World Cup (RWC) 106, 116, 140–1, 214, 255
Ryan, C. 70, 73

Sack, A. 152
St Andrews 36, 171, 173
St Jude Children's Research Hospital 158
salaries 116
Samdahl, D. 21
Samoa 126
Sarel, D. 197
Sassen, Saskia 150
scaling analysis 70
Schaefer, William D. 153–4
schema theory 89, 93–4
Scherer, J. 115, 122
Schindler, R.M. 51
Schmidt, C. 61
scholarship 2, 8, 27, 72, 79, 148–50, 162, 258
schools 110, 152, 158, 160–1
Scotland 106, 122
Scott, D. 16–17, 21–2
Scratton, S. 77
Sea Cadets 34
seasonality 5, 106–30, 191, 251–2
secondary attractions 108, 113, 120, 126
Section Eight 156
security 25, 157–8, 197
Seithaml, 200
selves 25, 41, 234–8
Selwood, J. 133
serious leisure 3–4, 32–49, 75, 79, 260
service quality 6–7, 176–7, 189–205
services marketing triangle 198–200
servicescape 175–7, 179, 192–3, 198, 200
SERVQUAL instrument 200–1
servuction system model 192–3, 196, 198, 200
setting 233–4
Seville, Spain 213
Shahzada 180
shamateurism 116
Shamir, B. 39, 42
Shaw, S.M. 16, 77

Sheller, M. 152
Short, J. 151
signifiers 45–6
Silk, Michael 6, 79, 121, 148–69, 259
situated activity 233–4
skateboarding 37
skiing 3, 12, 24–7, 35, 41–3, 72, 75, 77, 111, 133, 175, 179–81, 201
skills 75, 193
Slack, T. 189
sleep 197
Smith, V. 70
Snoj, B. 190
snowboarding 37–8, 43, 75, 111
snowmobiling 111
social experience 50–1, 54–5, 57–8, 61–2
social impact 132–7, 144–5
social psychology 2, 5, 67, 75–6, 78
social theory 4, 32–49, 51–2, 139
social worlds 37–8, 40, 52, 76–8
socialization 17, 40, 44, 51, 60, 76–7
sociology 2, 4–5, 8, 27, 67–8, 76, 78–9, 137–8, 149, 162, 224
Soja, Edward 150
Sony Playstation World Rally Championship 183
South Africa 116
South Africa New Zealand Australia Rugby (SANZAR) 116–17, 120, 123
Spain 90, 213
spatial constraints 25–7
spatial perspective 149–51
special interest groups 115
specialization 75–6
spectators 12–13, 53, 57, 107–9, 113, 117, 120, 126, 141, 171–2, 175, 178, 181, 183–4, 200, 207
Speights beer 122
spiritual travel 70
sponsors 107–10, 117, 120, 122–3, 126, 183, 206–10, 249
Sport England 230
Sport and Entertainment District (SED) 157–9
sportswear 174
spreading activation 90
squash 145
stadia 57, 70, 77, 95, 120–2, 155, 160–1, 171–2, 174–6, 200, 214
stage-based models 137
stakeholders 14, 28, 178, 247
Standeven, J. 32, 190
Statue of Liberty 158
status 41, 43, 45, 59–61, 67–9, 73, 141, 253
Stebbins, R. 34–8, 40, 45, 75, 79
stereotypes 59

Strategic Management Committee 154
strategic planning 7
Strauss, A. 227, 240–1
structural constraints 17–19, 22, 24–5
sub-groups 24, 26
subcultural capital 41, 43, 45–6
subcultures 4, 6, 37, 40–5, 52, 59–61, 78–9, 115, 174, 180, 182–3
subworlds 41
Super Bowl 92
Super League 113
supra-setting 231–3, 236
surfing 37, 42–3, 100, 111, 172, 180
surveys 25, 195, 208, 210, 216, 220
sustainability 131, 144–5, 225, 258
Sustainable Tourism Cooperative Research Centre 260
Sutton, W.A. 201
swimming 100, 173
switched expenditure 208–9
Sydney Olympics 61, 71, 92, 213–16, 247–8, 260–1
symbolic capital 41, 45–6
synergy 170–88
systems theory 192

table tennis 145
tag and recapture 208
Taj Mahal 158
Tajfel, H. 37
target markets 99–100
taxation 133, 150, 154, 158, 160, 211, 214, 216, 218–19
technology 150
teenagers 197
television 10, 14, 59, 120–3, 182–3
Telstra Rally 183
tennis 56, 95, 107, 140, 144–5, 152
terminology 37, 40
tertiary attractions 108, 113, 120, 126
theatrical analogy 6, 200
theming 176, 181, 217
theory generation 2–3
Thornton, S. 41, 45
Thwaites, Des 6–7, 189–205, 259–60
Tideswell, C. 248
time switching 110, 115, 208–9, 216
tinkerers 38
Tjaaereborg 190
tolerance zones 199–200
Tonga 126
Torkildsen, G. 248
Total Quality Tourism Consortium (TQTC) 192
Tour de France 38, 57, 95, 260

tour groups 44
Tourism White Paper 248
Tourist Area Cycle of Evolution 137
tourist attractions 5, 106–30
tourist bubbles 149, 151–3, 155, 158, 160, 162
Tourist Role Preference Scale (TRPS) 70
tourist roles 67–76
Townsville, Australia 140–1
training 39, 53, 57, 117, 176, 196–8, 217, 247, 250–5
Transurban Australian Grand Prix 208
travel 1–9, 11–13, 21, 26, 35–6, 40, 43–6, 54–5, 59–62, 69–77, 79, 107–9, 111, 113, 117, 120–1, 123, 172–4, 177–9, 184, 190, 193, 209–10, 247
travel career ladder (TCL) 75
Travel Industry Association 77
Tri-Nations 116, 123
triangulation 145
triple bottom line 132, 135, 144–5
Triple Crown 100
trolley systems 158–9
trustworthiness 193
Turner, Ralph 67
Turner, V. 59
typologies 4, 12–13, 32–3, 69, 71, 78
Tyzack, H. 253

UK Sport 230
uniforms 253, 255
United Kingdom 7, 27, 56, 71, 73, 113, 190, 225–6, 230, 232, 234, 238, 240, 247
United States 5–6, 56, 72, 76–7, 92, 95, 100, 117, 152, 158, 173, 176, 226
United States Olympic Committee 226
University of Florida Gators 178–9
University of Maryland 155
University of Otago 122
Unruh, D. 37
urban imagineering 151
Urry, J. 152
user conflicts 144–5
USS Constellation 154
utility 88–9

value added multipliers 212
Venezuela 173
vertical channel alliances 181, 185
VIP switching 211
Virden, R.J. 3, 22, 24, 26
vocabularies of motive 68–9
Volcano Triathlon 197
volleyball 181
voluntary sector 14, 34, 38–9, 58, 61–2, 253–5
Volvo International Tennis Tournament 152

Wahlers, R. 68, 74
Waikato Chiefs 122
Waikato Stadium 121
Wakefield, K.L. 175, 191–2
Wales 106
Walker, Gordon 3, 10–31
walking 248
Wall, G. 132
Walt Disney World 71
Warnick, R. 72
weather 110, 126, 197
Weber, Max 3–4
websites 183
Weed, Mike 7, 33, 54–5, 224–45, 247, 260
Weiermair, K. 201
welfare state 150–1, 156
Wembley Stadium 171
Weston, A. 248
Westpac Trust Stadium 121
White, T. 196
Wilks, S. 231
Williams, C. 200–1
Williams, P. 77

Willming, C. 77
Wilson, Jeff 76–7, 122
Wimbledon 95, 107
Witt, P.A. 15
Women's Final Four 92
work commitments 110
World Cup 5, 7, 71, 92, 171, 179, 261
World Rugby Corporation (WRC) 116
World Series 57
World Tourism Organization 258
World Trade Center 154
World War II 154
Wright, M. 231

yacht regattas 110
Yiannakis, Andrew 8, 70, 73
Yinger, M. 40

Zaltman, G. 182
Zeithaml, V.A. 193–4, 200
Zink, R. 41
zones of tolerance 199–200
Zurcher, L. 5, 67–9, 74, 78

#0018 - 150918 - C0 - 244/170/15 - PB - 9780415464185